EXPLORING RUSSIA'S PAST

NARRATIVE, SOURCES, IMAGES

VOLUME 2:

SINCE 1856

David G. Rowley

University of Wisconsin–Platteville

PEARSON

Prentice
Hall

Upper Saddle River, New Jersey 07458

Library of Congress Cataloging-in-Publication Data

Rowley, David G. (date)
  Exploring Russia's past : narrative, sources, images / David G. Rowley.— 1st ed.
    p. cm.
  ISBN 0-13-094702-4
  1. Russia--History. 2. Kievan Rus--History. 3. Soviet Union--History.
  4. Russia (Federation)—History. I. Title.
  DK40.R678 2005
  947--dc22

                                                    2005005036

VP/Editorial Director: Charlyce Jones Owen
Executive Editor: Charles Cavaliere
Editorial Assistant: Shannon Corliss
Marketing Manager: Heather Shelstad
Marketing Assistant: Cherron Gardner
Production Liaison: Marianne Peters-Riordan
Manufacturing Buyer: Ben Smith
Art Director: Jayne Conte
Cover Design: Bruce Kenselaar
Cover Photo: Courtesy of the Library of Congress, Prints and Photographs Division, Prokudin-Gorskii Collection
[reproduction number, LC-P87-7238{P&P}]
Director, Image Resource Center: Melinda Reo
Manager, Rights and Permissions: Zina Arabia
Manager, Visual Research: Beth Brenzel
Manager, Cover Visual Research & Permissions: Karen Sanatar
Image Permission Coordinator: Cynthia Vincenti
Composition/Full-Service Project Management: Mike Remillard/Pine Tree Composition, Inc.

To my students,
past, present, and future

Pearson Education LTD   Pearson Education North Asia Ltd
Pearson Education Singapore, Pte. Ltd   Pearson Educación de Mexico, S.A. de C.V.
Pearson Education, Canada, Ltd.   Pearson Education Malaysia, Pte. Ltd
Pearson Education—Japan   Pearson Education, Upper Saddle River, New Jersey
Pearson Education Australia PTY, Limited

ISBN 0-13-094702-4

CONTENTS

CHAPTER TWELVE

RUSSIA IN THE AGE OF NATION-BUILDING, 1856–1881

CHAPTER THIRTEEN

RUSSIA'S FIRST INDUSTRIAL REVOLUTION, 1881–1900

CHAPTER FOURTEEN

RUSSIA'S CRISIS, 1900–1916

CHAPTER FIFTEEN

REVOLUTION AND CIVIL WAR, 1917–1921

CHAPTER SIXTEEN

THE EXPERIMENTAL DECADE, 1921–1928

CHAPTER SEVENTEEN

RUSSIA'S SECOND INDUSTRIAL REVOLUTION, 1928–1941

CHAPTER EIGHTEEN

THE GREAT FATHERLAND WAR AND ITS AFTERMATH, 1941–1953

CHAPTER NINETEEN

CHAPTER TWENTY

CHAPTER TWENTY-ONE

CHAPTER TWENTY-TWO

PREFACE

Exploring Russia's Past is a comprehensive but concise survey of Russian history written for college and university undergraduates. Each chapter begins with a brief narrative presenting the key developments in political, social, economic, and cultural history. The narrative is followed by a number of primary text documents and primary visual documents that exemplify key themes and provide students the opportunity to make their own analysis of Russian history.

Exploring Russia's Past looks at Russia from three vantage points. First, it considers Russia as a unique nation and civilization. Beginning with the appearance of the Eastern Slavs in the Dnieper River valley and their conversion to Christianity, it follows one branch of the Slavs (that later became known as "Russian") as it took on the characteristics of a nation in the upper reaches of the Volga River and gradually evolved into a major civilization and state. Second, it considers Russia as an empire. The text examines Russia's relation with other peoples of north central Eurasia as it expanded to become a multinational empire and then as it has recently contracted somewhat (after 1991). Third, it considers Russia in the context of world history. Before 1700, Russia's interaction with the nomadic empires of the steppes was typical of the interchange between the nomadic societies of Inner Eurasia and the sedentary civilizations of Outer Eurasia. After 1700, however, the Russian experience was typical of the relationship between the imperialist nations of Europe and the traditional civilizations of Asia.

Exploring Russia's Past considers Russia society in the broadest context; it examines government and politics, foreign affairs, religion and culture, the status and roles of women, social relations, and economic developments. Primary text documents and visual images have been chosen to shed light on many aspects of Russian society and civilization. Most chapters also contain a map that provides relevant information.

Exploring Russia's Past is comprehensive as well in regard to its approach to student learning. As the title suggests, it attempts actively to involve students in understanding Russian history. Each chapter begins with a survey of developments in Eurasia that both situates Russia in the context of world trends and provides key information regarding Russia's neighbors that is essential for understanding Russia's relation with them. The narrative provides essential information with which all students of Russian history must be familiar (and prepares the reader to analyze the primary documents). The documents include several brief readings (generally about eight hundred words each) and pictures or other visual images that come from the time period covered by the chapter. The reader is not told how to read or interpret the readings or images but is asked questions that encourage original and critical thinking. Text and visual documents are chosen to enable students to follow particular themes (art, architecture, social relations, law, role of women, etc.) over the entire course of Russian history.

Chapters have a common structure. An introductory paragraph presents the key theme of the chapter or an important development that sets the stage for the chapter. "Eurasian Context" is a concise summary of world trends and a thumbnail sketch of each of the major civilizations of Eurasia and of the countries on Russia's borders. This is followed by sections on government and foreign affairs, church and culture, roles and status of women, and social and economic trends. The narrative concludes with a consideration of the non-Russian peoples of the empire (or Soviet Union). A brief conclusion summarizes key developments or anticipates the next period in Russian history.

The narrative is followed by (on average) eight primary documents; four text and four visual. These documents are chosen to provide as wide as possible an insight into political, legal, cultural, social, gender, and economic aspects of Russian history. In almost all chapters, at least one text document and one image is directly related to the experience of women, and at least one text document and one image is directly related to a non-Russian region or ethnic group. A hemispheric map showing developments across Eurasia follows the document. A brief list of books recommended for further reading concludes each chapter. A systematic bibliography is impossible in a work of this scope, and the lists are very eclectic, including some classics as well as some of the most recent works, and attempt to represent a wide variety of topics

The text is divided into twenty-two chapters, but more attention is paid to recent events than to early ones. The first two chapters cover several thousand years. Kiev Rus (1000–1240) is covered in Chapter Three. Muscovite Russia is covered by four chapters, which include about a century each. The eighteenth and nineteenth centuries are covered by five chapters, which average fifty years in length. The nine chapters that cover the twentieth century average a little more than one decade each. Continuity is far more usual in history than discontinuity, and beginning and ending points of chapters are chosen more for considerations of length than for any other reason. Chapters begin or end with the death of a tsar or a Soviet leader only when these dates indicate significant breaks or turning points in Russian history.

It is the intention of this text to present the data of Russian history in as straightforward and dispassionate a manner as possible. I follow scholarly consensus where it exists, take note of historical controversy, and try to present the facts in such a way that the reader can make his or her own judgment. It is, of course, impossible to avoid interpretive bias, and the reader should be aware of the following viewpoints that I hold.

First, I absolutely disagree with Winston Churchill's judgment that "Russia is a riddle wrapped in a mystery inside an enigma." The Russians are normal human beings who act in quite understandable ways. Their wealthy elites have been neither more nor less selfish, arrogant, or brutal than other elites in world history, and ordinary Russians have been neither unusually passive nor unusually aggressive in responding to injustice. The behavior of Russians of all classes is completely understandable when considered in its historical context.

Second, I treat Russia as a European civilization, by virtue of its Christian religion, Slavic culture and society, Indo-European language, and, for that matter, its geographical location. Europe has great social and political diversity, and there is no "typical" European nation. Russia is surely no further from the European "norm" (whatever that might be) than are England, Sweden, Spain, or Greece.

Because the Russian (Cyrillic) alphabet is different from the Latin alphabet used in English, transliteration of Russian names and terms creates difficulties for those who write about

Russia in English. It is not that no good system of transliteration exists; the Library of Congress has developed a quite satisfactory system (and one that is used, with minor modifications and many exceptions as described below). The problem is that past attempts at transliteration/translation have produced words that have become standard in English. "Moscow" must be used instead of "Moskva," "Catherine the Great" instead of "Ekaterina," and "Yeltsin" rather than "El'tsin." Any consistent and systematic application of a transliteration system would be confusing and counterproductive. The multi-ethnic character of the Russian empire adds another difficulty: Should terms relevant to Ukraine, Georgia, or Uzbekistan, for example, be transliterated from the national language or from the Russian version of the term?

Since this text is intended for university undergraduates studying Russian history, its first priority is to facilitate further study and research in history, not to provide a consistent guide to Russian orthography. Therefore, all names will appear in the form given in the twenty-sixth edition of the *Library of Congress Subject Headings* (2003). In addition, all geographical terms will be spelled as they appear in primary entry of *The Columbia Gazetteer of the World* (1998). All other names and terms will be transliterated from Russian according to the Library of Congress transliteration system without diacritical marks, the hard sign, and only one capital letter per word (not IAroslav, but Iaroslav). The soft sign will be also omitted, and "-ie" will replace "-'e" where it will help English speakers to pronounce Russian words. Thus *Riazan'* will appear as *Riazan,* and *pomestie* will be used instead of *pomest'e.* Plurals of Russian terms will be formed by simply adding "-s" as in English. The only exceptions are *streltsy* and *Rurikovichi,* which are already familiar in English. Names and terms in the documents will be spelled the same as they appear in the narrative, and in the index names and terms will be followed by their exact Library of Congress transliteration with hard and soft signs (but without diacritical marks).

ACKNOWLEDGMENTS

Charles Cavaliere, Executive Editor at Prentice Hall, deserves the credit for conceiving of this textbook in its current form. The book I originally proposed was quite different, and it was Charles who suggested this format. I took enthusiastic ownership of his concept and have done my best to realize it. I thank Charles, as well, for his help, advice, and patience while I have been at work on this project.

I am indebted a number of reviewers for their invaluable advice, including Eve Levin, University of Kansas; Rex Wade, George Mason University; Donald Raleigh, University of North Carolina; Roshanna Sylvester, DePaul University; Hugh Hudson, Georgia State University; Jonathan Grant, Florida State University; William Benton Whisenhunt, College of DuPage; and one reviewer who wished to remain anonymous. I also thank my former Russian history students at the University of Wisconsin–Platteville whose discussion of many documents (both text and visual) has helped me make the choices for this book. Last, but not least, I owe a huge debt of gratitude to my dear life partner, A. E. Bothwell, for her help in writing this book. Lee read the entire manuscript with great care and gave me excellent advice.

Any deficiencies in this work are due solely to the author's willful refusal to fully implement the ideas and suggestions offered by his editor, reviewers, and partner.

About the Author

David Rowley graduated from the University of Michigan with the individualized major of Sino-Soviet Studies and then earned the M.A. from the University of Chicago and PhD from the University of Michigan in Russian history. As a teacher, David has been a Eurasianist from the beginning of his career; he has taught Chinese, Japanese, Middle Eastern, and World history, as well as the histories of Russia, England, and Europe. He has taught at Northwestern Michigan College, William Penn University, the University of North Dakota, and, since 1999, at the University of Wisconsin–Platteville.

David's dissertation, *Millenarian Bolshevism, 1900–1921,* was published in 1987, and he has published articles on Russian Marxism and Russian nationalism in a number of journals, including the *American Historical Review, Journal of Contemporary History, Kritika,* and *Nations and Nationalism.*

FOREWORD: EURASIA, INNER EURASIA, AND RUSSIA

This book is about the history of Russia in Eurasia, and the story it tells can be summarized as follows: In the tenth century C.E., an East Slavic civilization arose in a state centered on the city of Kiev on the Dnieper River in what is now Ukraine. Their Greek neighbors knew its ruling elite as the Rhos. Following the defeat and occupation of this state by the Mongols in the thirteenth century, Kiev declined and other Slavic cities increased in importance. Moscow, a city to the northeast of Kiev, became the center of a new state which aspired to reunite the East Slavs under its rule and to absorb Mongol territories as well. This state, known at first to western Europeans as Muscovy, ultimately adopted the name Rossiia (the Slavic form of the Greek Rhosia) which is written in English as "Russia." Russia's expansion didn't stop until it had become an empire that, by the nineteenth century, ruled the length and breadth of Northern Eurasia (and, until 1867, part of North America). In the twentieth century the Russian empire, reconstituted as the Union of Soviet Socialist Republics (U.S.S.R.), expanded its influence further into Europe and competed with the United States, its only rival, for world hegemony. At the end of the twentieth century, the U.S.S.R. abruptly collapsed leaving the core Russian state reduced in territory and world influence, but still the largest country in Eurasia (and the world). This text will examine these developments in the context of world history and consider how Russia has been interconnected socially, economically, politically, and culturally with its Eurasian neighbors.

It will also deal with perceptions of Russia's nature and place in the world, both from its own point of view and in the view of outside observers. In fact, that discussion must begin immediately, since three terms—Eurasia, Inner Eurasia, and Russia—have already used that bring with them problematic connotations.

The term "Eurasia" will be used to refer to the largest of the world's continents–that part of the earth that is bordered by the Atlantic, Arctic, Pacific, and Indian Oceans, and the Red and Mediterranean Seas. No geographical features on this continent have served as impermeable barriers to human travel and trade, and, from the beginning of human habitation, Eurasia has been the scene of continual intercultural exchange (and conflict). The perceptual difficulty arises from a tradition that treats Europe as a separate continent from Asia.

Europe is a cultural rather than a geographical continent. It has been treated as a continent in its own right only because a major civilization appeared there that wanted to mark itself off as different from the "Orient," or the East. This civilization, known as Western Civilization because of its location on the western edge of Eurasia, has had the cultural power to make the notion of a European "continent" relatively uncontested. That the notion of Europe is indeed cultural is illustrated by an ongoing argument about where the eastern boundary of Europe lies. Those who look for physical boundaries use the Ural Mountains, but some of those who focus on civilizations would draw an imaginary line from the Baltic to the Black Seas or maybe even further west.

The uncertainty of the dividing line between Europe and Asia directly depends on definitions of Russia's essential nature. Is Russia European or Asian? Those who define Western civilization in terms that exclude Russia try to draw the boundary further to the west. Those who see Russia as fundamentally European accept the Urals as the eastern boundary of Europe and speak of "European Russia" and "Russia in Asia." In order to avoid any definitions that carry unnecessary preconceptions, Russia will be considered to have arisen in the middle of one continent: Eurasia.

The term Eurasia has been loaded with a set of preconceptions of its own. A school of thought known as Eurasianism, that was especially popular among Russian emigres after the Revolution of 1917, defines Eurasia as a specific ecological unit: a more or less uninterrupted, unforested plain extending from the Carpathian Mountains to the Pacific Ocean. The Eurasianists called this the "steppe system," and they argued that it naturally predisposes those who live in it (if they can marshal the power) to build an empire and rule it in its entirety. This was precisely the territory that the Russian empire encompassed at its greatest extent, and the Eurasianists held that Russia is neither European nor Asia but "Eurasian" a synthesis of the geopolitical vision of Genghis Khan with the spiritual worldview of Eastern Christianity.

As used in this book, however, the term Eurasia is intended to refer to the entire continent and should not be taken as implying adherence to the tenets of the "Eurasian school." I do not believe that the Eurasian steppe infects its inhabitants with dreams of empire. To describe the part of Eurasia that the Russian empire expanded to fill this text will borrow the more inclusive term "Inner Eurasia" from the Russian and world historian David Christian.[1] In his usage, Inner Eurasia refers to the subregion of northern Eurasia bounded in the west by the Carpathian Mountains and the Pripet Marshes and bounded in the south by the Black Sea, the Caucasus Mountains, the Caspian Sea, and the series of complex mountain ranges that extend eastward to the Pacific Ocean. That Russia expanded only to those borders and no farther is explained more by the relation of the Russian state to its neighbors than by geography. The mountains that marked the boundaries of Russia's expansion were not, after all, barriers to Genghis Khan.

Finally, what is "Russian Civilization," and when did it originate? These questions, too, are controversial. Three current nations—Belarus, Russia, and Ukraine—can claim to have descended from the East Slavic civilization that originated in the Dnieper River valley in the late first millennium C.E. To call that original civilization "Russian" would suggest that Russia was its natural and direct descendant, and Belarus and Ukraine are lesser variants. This book will not ignore Belarus or Ukraine, and it does not wish to imply that Russia was the only authentic descendent of the original state of Rhosia. Nevertheless, its primary focus will be Russia, the state that grew to be a world political and cultural power, and a descendent of that first East Slavic state and civilization.

[1]David Christian, *A History of Russia, Central Asia and Mongolia, Volume I, Inner Eurasia from Prehistory to the Mongol Empire* (Oxford: Blackwell, 1998).

INTRODUCTION TO VOLUME TWO: PREHISTORY TO 1856

THE RUSSIAN EMPIRE

By 1856, the year in which this volume begins, Russia was the largest country in the world. It was a European "Great Power," and therefore a world power as well. England controlled the largest maritime empire, but Russia possessed the largest contiguous land empire in the world. From west to east, it extended from the Vistula River across the breadth of Inner Eurasia and over the Bering Strait into the North American continent. From north to south, it extended from the Arctic Sea to the borders of Outer Eurasia. Nor had those in charge of Russia's foreign policy reached the end of their ambitions, Russia competed with England and France for hegemony over Turkey, Iran, and China.

POLITICAL AND SOCIAL STRUCTURE

Russia was an absolute monarchy. The monarch, known as tsar or emperor (both terms deriving from the Roman imperial tradition), claimed to rule by divine right unlimited by any earthly authority. Similar aspirations had been shared by western monarchs, such as James I of England and Louis XIV of France, but their descendants were gradually forced to accept the rule of law and the sovereignty of parliaments, while Russian monarchs were not. In Russia, there was no written (or unwritten) law which was superior to the will (or the whim) of the monarch, nor was there a functioning national representative assembly. Assemblies of

Turn to page 28 for a map showing key geographic locations and features for this time period.

the Land (singular, *zemskii sobor*) had been summoned by Russian tsars in the sixteenth and seventeenth centuries, but none had met since.

The Russian emperor was the source of law, but the making of law was beyond the capacity of a single person, and Alexander I (1801–1825) created a Council of State to review, refine, and publish legislation under his direction. In 1826, Nicholas I (1825–1855) ordered the first review of the law in two centuries, and a complete collection of Russian laws was published in 1835. It was not, however, a real codification, since it did not lay down general legal principles, standards, and norms (aside from affirming the absolute sovereignty of the Tsar). Instead, the compilers sorted through existing Russian law and resolved contradictions by choosing the most recently promulgated law.

Alexander I had organized the bureaucracy into ministries (including foreign affairs, war, navy, finance, commerce, education, interior, and justice), and established a Council of Ministers. These ministers did not make up a "government" or cabinet that deliberated policy; instead, they were individually responsible to the Tsar who served as his own prime minister and made his own decisions. Nicholas I, fearing that the professional civil service diluted the authority of the emperor, preferred to rule though personal agents rather than the official bureaucracy. He relied heavily on secret ad hoc committees for developing policy, and he expanded His Majesty's Own Chancery, an institution originally intended to manage the Tsar's household, into his personal agency for implementing policy. The Chancery was divided into six departments, the most notorious of which was the "Third Section," which supervised censorship and investigated subversion.

The empire was divided into fifty provinces, each administered by a governor under the authority of the Minister of the Interior. Each province was divided into ten counties (singular: *uezd*). These counties and the towns and cities of the province were administered by executive boards which were elected by the property-owning classes; they were also under the supervision of the Ministry of the Interior.

The difference between the political systems of Russia and those of western Europe in the early nineteenth century was not what the rulers aspired to, but what the wealthy elites permitted to them. In England, in 1688, the landed aristocracy had asserted the sovereignty of parliament, and in the nineteenth century the rising middle class struggled to reduce the amount of wealth that qualified a man to vote (women were not allowed to vote until the twentieth century). In France, in 1789, it was the demand of the aristocracy for the summoning of the Estates General (which, as in the case of Russia's zemskii sobor, had not met for two centuries) that permitted the middle class to begin the French Revolution. Across Europe, the middle classes led the Revolutions of 1830 and 1848.

In Russia, however, the aristocracy tied its fortunes with those of the monarch. The growth of the insignificant Principality of Moscow into a multinational empire (from the fourteenth through the sixteenth centuries) had been achieved by a close alliance between the Grand Prince (later called "Tsar") and the boiars (the top rank of the aristocracy). A brief period of anarchy had occurred during the Time of Troubles (1598–1613), when the Tsar died without an heir and boiars began to fight among themselves for the title of Tsar. As a result, the central government was weakened, allowing lower-class rebellion and encouraging foreign invasion, and the Russian state was nearly destroyed. To bring the anarchy to end, the landed elite called a zemskii sobor in 1613 which elected a new tsar, Michael Romanov.

Learning from the Time of Troubles, the aristocracy allowed Michael (1613–1645) and his son, Aleksei (1645–1676), to rebuild a strong monarchy. Aleksei's son, Peter I (the Great, 1689–1725) regimented the aristocracy, creating a single noble class by eliminating distinctions among the various traditional categories and instituting a Table of Ranks, which defined noble status in terms of service to the state. The Table of Ranks provided a way for commoners to achieve noble status, but the principal consequence of his policies was to preserve the aristocratic nature of the Russian government and to reinforce the tie of self-interest between monarchy and aristocracy.

Aristocratic guards regiments participated in numerous palace insurrections in the eighteenth century, but they never challenged the principle of monarchy and (except in the case of Catherine II) always placed a member of the Romanov dynasty on the throne. Catherine II (the Great, 1762–1796), though not a Romanov, had been married to Peter III (a grandson of Peter the Great) and was made Empress by the guards. The last successful interference of aristocrats in a Romanov succession occurred in 1801 when Paul (1796–1801) was deposed and murdered and replaced by his son, Alexander I (1801–1825). Noble army officers in 1825 staged an abortive revolution, but they should be considered as radical intellectuals rather nobles pursuing self interest against the monarchy.

In fact, in the first half of the nineteenth century, the nobility was more supportive of the monarchy than ever, and they enjoyed a privileged position in Russian society. Catherine II had issued a Charter of the Nobility that clarified the rights and privileges of the nobility and attempted to give it a collective identity. The charter confirmed the rights of the nobility: freedom from the obligation to serve, exemption from the poll tax or obligation to quarter troops in their homes, and exemption from corporal punishment. Nobles were recognized as full owners of their estates, including mineral and timber rights, and their exclusive right to own serfs was confirmed. Finally, nobles could not be deprived of wealth, rank, or estate without trial by a jury of their peers. The Charter also provided for an elected Marshall of the Nobility and noble assemblies at both the Provincial and District levels. In 1859, the nobility made up only 1.7 percent of the population.

Perhaps the greatest difference between Russian and western European societies was in its urban populations. The non-noble, property-owning urban population of France and England had a relatively strong sense of community interest, while in Russia the urban population was stratified and divided. The Law Code of 1649 recognized a merchant elite, who were exempt from taxes, were permitted to travel abroad, and were used by the Tsar to supervise trade and to collect customs duty and sales taxes. The remainder of the urban, tax-paying community was divided into three categories based on wealth and status. Peter planned self-governing town institutions, but they were never fully implemented. Catherine the Great issued a Town Charter based on her Charter to the Nobility which granted self-government to towns and cities. An assembly of all citizens elected a town duma of six members, which was given authority to enforce law and order, promote trade, provide for social welfare, and manage public building. Catherine retained the former status distinctions from the past. The Charter recognized six categories of towndwellers based on wealth and status, and it limited the right to vote and to serve: All registered citizens could attend the assembly which elected the duma, but only those with an income of over fifty rubles a year or property worth more than one thousand rubles were allowed to vote and be elected. No middle-class solidarity developed: The wealthiest merchants aspired to noble status and felt no common interests with the lower orders. In 1859, Russia's free, non-noble groups made up about 18 percent of the population. This included clerics and soldiers (active and retired).

The vast majority—slightly more than 80 percent—of Russia's population were farmers who were permanently tied to the land. Historically, rent-paying agricultural tenants had been the principal source of income for the nobility, and nobles had, since the fifteenth century, pressed the Tsar to issue decrees restricting the peasants' ability to move. They got their way in 1649 when Tsar Aleksei's *Ulozhenie* (Law Code) forbade peasants to move without permission of the authorities and rescinded the statute of limitations on the return of runaway peasants. Farmers who lived on land owned by the government were called "State peasants;" they lived in self-governing communities and could not move without permission of community leaders. "Serfs," farmers who lived on land owned by a member of the nobility, were subject to their lord. Serfs made up a little less than half of the peasant population of Russia.

The *mir* (peasant community, sometimes called the "commune") had practiced self-government from time immemorial. The *skhod* (the mir assembly), composed of heads of households (typically men, but occasionally women), planned and coordinated farm work and governed the community. It applied customary law to crimes or complaints between peasants (when the outside world was involved, the tsarist legal system intervened), and it acted as the agent of the government in collecting taxes and raising recruits. The skhod also chose mir officials. All mirs needed at least a headman, clerk, and tax collectors, and larger mirs chose elders, foremen, constables, and other officials. The mir was stratified by wealth, and large, wealthy families usually chose the head officials and made sure their sons were not sent into the army. Despite some internal friction, however, the mir consistently presented a united front against the outside world of government officials and merchants.

One of the remarkable features of the Russian mir was its practice of periodically redistributing land. Every ten to twenty years, the skhod reevaluated household size and reallocated the cultivated land based on the number of able-bodied workers in each household. This created another source of dissatisfaction for peasants. It was in the interests of the heads of households to maintain multigenerational families, in which sons and their wives remained in their parents' household. Households could not be broken up without permission by the skhod, and the skhod was made up of heads of households. In Russia in the nineteenth century, only 10 percent of peasants in their thirties were the heads of households.

There was widespread discontent among the peasantry and particularly among the serfs. Nicholas I attempted to regulate what lords could demand of their serfs, but the power of the landlord was still virtually unlimited. One of the most onerous burdens that could be imposed on serfs was to be made a household servant. There was no limit on what sorts of occupations a lord could impose upon his household serfs. Many were maids, cooks, butlers, carriage drivers, gardeners, kitchen staff, and other domestic servants. In addition, in extremely wealthy noble households serfs could be required to become tailors, teachers, singers, and musicians.

Work as a household serf was the most demeaning and demoralizing kind of labor. Such serfs had no time for themselves, their work was extremely boring, and they lived in complete poverty. It is true they were fed and clothed by their lord, but they had no opportunity to earn an income of their own. Household serfs constituted a burden on the peasant commune as well, since they remained on the tax rolls, and therefore their share of the taxes were paid by the members of the commune who engaged in agriculture. The problem got worse as the century wore on. In the 1830s, approximately 4 percent of all serfs were household serfs; the proportion had risen to almost 7 percent by 1858. The Russian nobility had three to five times more servants than the nobles in Europe as a whole.

THE RUSSIAN ORTHODOX CHURCH

The conversion of the Eastern Slavs to Christianity began in the tenth century, and Christianity had become universal among them by the fourteenth century. The Eastern Slavs were initially converted by missionaries from Constantinople, and the Russian church therefore follows the Eastern Orthodox tradition, which was at that time diverging from the Roman Catholic Church. The Emperor Justinian (527–565) elaborated a theory of "symphony" between state and church, in which the secular government provided for the material needs of the population and the church provided for their spiritual needs. He created a church hierarchy that paralleled the imperial hierarchy at every level, except the very highest. He raised five bishops (Constantinople, Rome, Antioch, Jerusalem, and Alexandria) to the status of Patriarch, and he apportioned the ecclesiastical administration of the provinces among them. There was no head of the church to parallel the position of emperor, since Justinian considered the Roman Emperor to be the head of both state and church.

The eastern Patriarchs accepted this arrangement, but the bishops of Rome, who were beyond the control of the Eastern Roman Emperors, did not. They argued that the bishop of Rome, called the Pope, was the successor of St. Peter, who had been chosen by Jesus Christ to lead the Church. They considered that their office had supremacy over the whole Christian church in matters of both faith and government. The Eastern and Western Churches broke with one another in 1054 over doctrinal issues, but the division became even more bitter in 1204 when the armies of the Fourth Crusade conquered and sacked Constantinople and installed an Emperor and Patriarch appointed by the Pope. This occupation lasted until 1261, but the split in the Church had become permanent.

The Eastern Orthodox Church emphasizes ceremony and ritual in its liturgy, and it venerates icons, religious paintings, as sacramental objects. It recognizes two categories of clergy. The black clergy are celibate and include monks and prelates in the church administrative hierarchy (bishops, archbishops, etc.). Parish priests, called the white clergy, must be married. From the beginning, the Russian Church was headed by a metropolitan (whose capital was Kiev and then moved to Moscow in the fourteenth century). At first, the Metropolitan of Rus was appointed by the Patriarch of Constantinople, but in 1443 the Russian Church asserted its independence and began to choose its own metropolitan. In 1589, the patriarchs of the Eastern Church accepted the Russian Church as an independent, national church and recognized its head as a patriarch.

The Orthodox Church played a key role in the development of the Muscovite state, keeping alive the idea of the unity of the Eastern Slavs and tying its fortunes with those of the Grand Prince of Moscow. The Byzantine tradition of symphony between church and state was adopted by Muscovite rulers, beginning with Ivan III who adopted some of the symbols and ceremonies of the Byzantine Empire. However, whereas Ivan III and Ivan IV, in the fifteenth and sixteenth centuries, deemed it their religious responsibility to aid the Church, Aleksei, in the seventeenth century, seemed more interested in how the Church could serve his political goals. Wanting to prepare Russia to expand its influence into the Balkan Peninsula, Aleksei called for the liturgy of the Russian Church to be brought into conformity with current Greek usage. (Originally the same, both Greek and Russian liturgy had changed over time.) Opponents of change called the Old Ritualists (also known as the Old Believers) refused to accept the reforms (which included changing the spelling of Jesus and making the sign of the cross with three fingers instead of two). In the resulting schism, the Russian church lost many of its most passionate believers, depriving it of the strength to resist subordination to the state.

At the beginning of the eighteenth century, Peter I secularized the state and further subordinated the Church to it. He abolished the patriarchate and created a bureaucratic body, the Holy Synod, to administer the church. At the end of the century, Catherine the Great secularized church land. (The church had been the single largest landowner in Russia.) In Catherine's reign, the number of monasteries and convents declined by two-thirds, and the number of monks and nuns by more than one half. The numbers of parish priests increased, but not in proportion to the general population. Nicholas I revived Orthodoxy as one of the legitimizing principles of the Russian state, and he increased Church funding and the role of religion in education, but the state continued to dictate the terms of the "symphony."

EDUCATION

Before the seventeenth century, the Church had a monopoly on education. Priests taught their sons and local boys to read and write; seminaries trained candidates for the priesthood and for government service. In the seventeenth century, secular education began to appear. The Kiev Academy, modeled on the western European grammar school and teaching Greek and Latin, had been founded in 1632, and after Kiev was annexed by Russia in 1654, it became a model for schools in Moscow. In the late-seventeenth century, a number of Russian boiars owned libraries with books in Latin and Western European languages.

After 1700, Peter the Great established entirely secular schools in mathematics, navigation, and technology. In 1755, Elizabeth founded the University of Moscow and two high schools to prepare students for it. Catherine the Great established a Commission for Popular Schools in 1782, a teachers' college in 1783, and in 1786 (the year the first class of teachers graduated), a nationwide network of schools, with a major school in the capital of each province, and minor schools in the principal towns of each uezd. Minor schools provided the first two years and major schools last two years of elementary education. The curriculum included religion, foreign languages, philosophy, natural science, mathematics, history, and geography. These schools were publicly funded; teachers were hired by the state, books were provided free of charge, and tuition was free and open to children of all classes, girls as well as boys.

Alexander I expanded Catherine's system in 1802 when he created a Ministry of Education. He instituted a four-tier system by adding primary schools at the parish level, expanding the curriculum of the district and provincial schools, and creating a university system at the top. Universities already existed in Moscow, Dorpat, and Vilna; Alexander established new ones in Kharkov, Kazan, and St. Petersburg. At the lower levels, education continued to be provided at no charge, and at the university level, scholarships were given to needy students. In addition, private schools flourished, and parochial schools and seminaries continued to supply professionals as well as priests. Most doctors and lawyers, as well as a large number of civil servants, graduated from seminaries.

Nicholas I continued to expand the school system. There had been 62,000 students in public schools by end of eighteenth century, by the 1830s there were about 250,000, and by mid-century there were more than 400,000. Admiral Shishkov, Minister of Education in the 1820s believed that education should be limited to the propertied classes, and that it was harmful for ordinary people to be educated. He need not have worried, for in the reign of Nicholas I, only one out of every 142 people in the empire actually received an education. Nicholas would have preferred to restrict high school and university education to the nobility, but such a policy could not be implemented; Russia's need for educated professionals and civil servants was too great. However, in 1827 Nicholas did decree that serfs could not attend high schools or universities. He also closely monitored the faculty and curricula of schools and universities, expecting schools to propagate Orthodoxy and Slavic nationalism. Nicholas raised the printing budget of the Holy Synod from 2,000 rubles in 1825 to 500,000 by 1850.

LITERATURE

As noted above, the Eastern Orthodox Church uses the vernacular language in the liturgy, and Greek missionaries who wanted to spread their faith to the Slavs created an alphabet for the Slavic language. Conversion to Christianity, therefore, meant that Kiev Rus automatically acquired a written language, and a Slavic literature quickly developed, which included not only the Bible, sermons, saints' lives, and other religious writings but secular works as well. These included historical chronicles and an epic poem about wars with steppe nomads, *The Lay of Igor's Campaign*. The Autobiography of Avvakum, a leading Old Ritualist, written in 1670, though a confession of religious faith, was written in a vigorous, vernacular style. Secular poetry also began to appear in the seventeenth century.

Peter the Great created a publishing industry to spread western European knowledge and ideas—not only scientific and technical works, but history, western mythology, and etiquette. Peter's successors continued Peter's project of translating and publishing western books, but Catherine the Great took it to a new level. By the end of her reign, almost nine thousand books from the Western tradition were published, including Greek and Latin classics, French Enlightenment authors (including Voltaire's complete works), and English literature. In 1783, to further encourage publishing, Catherine allowed private individuals from any social estate to own printing presses. Paradoxically, this entailed the institution of censorship, which had been unnecessary as long as all books to be published were chosen by the state. Catherine put local police chiefs in charge of reviewing privately published books to ensure that they were not offensive to the monarch, the orthodox church, or public morals.

In the middle of the eighteenth century, Vasilii Trediakovskii and Mikhail Lomonosov helped created a literary language (in both theory and practice) and later in the century Nikolai Karamzin, poet, short story writer, and historian, wrote a fluent (if ornate) Russian prose that prepared the way for the standard literary Russian of the nineteenth century. Aleksandr Pushkin is generally recognized as the greatest of all Russian poets, and his appearance in the early 1820s began the Golden Age of Russian poetry. His poetry is the standard by which all others are measured, and his descriptions of Russian society prepared the way for the Russian realistic novel later in the century. Nikolai Gogol, second in importance only to Pushkin, wrote prose—plays, short stories, and a novel—all of which combined realistic descriptions of Russian life with social satire and elements of surrealism. Mikhail Lermontov continued Pushkin's poetic tradition. He also criticized Russian society from a liberal perspective, and, also like Pushkin, Lermontov died in a duel.

THE INTELLIGENTSIA

Russian society was notable for a social category known as the "intelligentsia," which was made up of that part of Russia's highly educated elite that thought independently (and critically!) of official Russian political and religious orthodoxies. In the first half of the nineteenth century, the intelligentsia was made up of members of the gentry who obtained university educations (or the equivalent) but chose not to enter government service and devoted their lives to social criticism. The pioneer in this development was Aleksandr Radishchev, a nobleman who had been educated at the St. Petersburg Corps of Pages and the University of Leipzig in Germany. After rising through the civil service, Radishchev retired to his estate where he wrote *A Journey from St. Petersburg to Moscow*, a celebration of Enlightenment values and a biting criticism of social injustice, serfdom, government corruption, and autocracy. After gaining approval from the police by submitting an innocuous manuscript, Radishchev published his book on his own press in 1790. He was arrested, found guilty of disrespect to the Empress and sedition against government. His death sentence was commuted to exile to Siberia, and he was subsequently pardoned by the emperor Paul in 1796.

A generation later, Radishchev's ideals were taken up by a number of military officers who dreamed of ending serfdom and of introducing the rule of law and civil liberties in Russian political life. Some proposed a constitutional monarchy, others a republic on the model of the United States. They are known as the Decembrists, because, when Alexander I died in December 1825, they staged a rather inept insurrection. Nicholas I, Alexander's successor, resolutely suppressed the rebellion and did his best to suppress critical thought for the duration of his reign.

Between 1825 and 1855, the intelligentsia did not advocate (or work toward) changes in the Russian monarchy, but they continued to think independently and to criticize shortcomings in Russian society. Between 1801 and 1854, almost four hundred journals of literature and literary criticism were founded. Most were of very short duration, but in any given year, at least fifty such journals were in operation. In these years, the direction of Russian literature and intellectual life was largely shaped by a literary critic, Vissarion Belinskii, son of a doctor from Penza province. Belinskii attended the University of Moscow but was expelled, a common occurrence for critical thinkers. He then earned his living by writing criticism for literary journals. Belinskii began his career reflecting the romantic idealism and nationalism of the time, but by the 1840s, he had become a realist and an advocate of increased westernization in the spirit of Peter the Great.

Belinskii was influential in many ways. He recognized and celebrated the genius of Pushkin, Gogol, Lermontov, Fyodor Dostoyevsky, and Ivan Turgenev, and helped create their literary reputations. He believed that literature should be evaluated by its social as well as by its artistic significance and that Russian literature should objectively describe Russian society. He also showed how criticism of literary works could obliquely criticize Russian society and avoid censorship.

The rise of the romantic movement in Europe after the French Revolution posed a serious intellectual challenge for Russian thinkers. In the age of the Enlightenment, with its cosmopolitan view of a common human nature and its confidence in reason and science, it was natural to think that Russia, through education and institutional reform, would naturally share in western progress. This was not self-evident to the Romantics, however; they conceived of nations as unique, organic entities, each with its own genius and special destiny. Aleksei Khomiakov, who founded the Slavophile movement, thought he had found the Russian soul in pre-Petrine Muscovy, and he decided that the Russian nation was congruent with the Russian Orthodox Church. He opposed the secularism, individualism, and materialism of the West (and of Peter the Great), and celebrated what he called the *sobornost* or "organic community" of Muscovite Russia, in which people had been united by faith and love, valued things of the spirit, and cooperated rather than competed with one another. Khomiakov, in typical romantic fashion, idealized the peasantry, considering them to embody the Christian virtues of humility and brotherhood.

The term "westernizers" was applied to another group among the Russian intelligentsia who applauded Peter's reforms and wanted Russia to continue the Enlightenment project of education, institutional reform, individual freedom, and constitutional government. Vissarion Belinskii was considered a westernizer, as was Aleksandr Herzen. As a youth, Herzen had idolized the Decembrists for their heroic self-sacrifice, and the severe punishments imposed on them permanently alienated Herzen from the government of Nicholas I. In 1829, he enrolled at the University of Moscow where he joined a circle that studied Saint-Simon's program of socialism, radical democracy, and brotherly love. The study circle was arrested in 1834, and after a year in prison, Herzen was exiled to the provinces, where he was employed as a civil servant. The Tsar pardoned him in 1839, but in 1840 he was exiled once again for criticizing the local police chief in a private letter (opened by the authorities). In 1842, Herzen again returned to Moscow, where he debated with the Slavophiles, defending Peter the Great's project and advocating radical democracy and atheism. Herzen was also the first Russian feminist, following the writings of George Sand. Realizing that he could not freely express his ideas in Russia, Herzen emigrated to France in 1847.

ROLES AND STATUS OF WOMEN

East Slavic, Orthodox Christian society was patriarchal, and women occupied a subordinate position. The Church taught that the ideal wife should be humble, silent, and submissive. It became a practice for the groom to send his fiance a chest with needles and pins, signifying that making cloth and sewing clothing was her duty, and a small whip, symbolizing her subordination to him. Parents chose their children's spouses and the bride's family paid a dowry to the family of the groom. The Church taught that celibacy was the ideal life and that sex was basically sinful, although acceptable as long as it was intended to produce children. Conjugal sex was considered an unclean act, and sexual relations were forbidden on holy days or fast days. In addition, after giving birth, a woman was considered unclean for forty days, during which time she was forbidden to prepare meals, attend church, or go out in public. Only elderly women could bake the sacramental bread for the mass.

Divorce was permitted by the Orthodox Church, and men most frequently availed themselves of it, using divorce to rid themselves of an older wife while retaining her dowry (which would otherwise have belonged to the woman). There was a double standard in divorce, since women could be divorced for sins that men were immune from: adultery, the attempted murder of a husband, and relations outside the home which "ruined her honor." Women could divorce their husbands for desertion, impotence, and incurable disease. On the other hand, Russian women had greater property rights than was typical in western Europe. A woman's movable property and land remained hers after marriage, and a wife could buy property with her own money and sell, mortgage, or bequeath her property without the permission of her husband.

Catherine the Great established schools especially for girls, and in principle all primary education sponsored by the government was open to girls, although a smaller proportion of girls than boys attended. Universities were closed to women. Nevertheless, from the reign of Catherine the Great, women became active participants in the literary and intellectual trends of the day. Poetry and prose by women writers was published regularly in Russian literary journals. However, typical of patriarchal societies, there was a strong prejudice against women as serious artists, and their works were for the most part not valued by literary critics.

The idea of the equality of men and women had only begun to be entertained among a few progressive members of the intelligentsia by the middle of the nineteenth century. It did not exist at all in other spheres of Russian society. When Russian law was codified in 1836, it had this to say about women: "The woman must obey her husband, reside with him in love, respect, and unlimited obedience, and offer him every pleasantness and affection as the ruler of the household."

THE ECONOMY

Throughout its history, by far the greatest proportion of Russian labor-power was devoted to self-sufficient, subsistence agriculture. Russians lived primarily on what they called "black bread" made with rye flour. They also grew barley, oats, and buckwheat. Wheat was grown on the southern steppe. Russians grew hardy vegetables such as onions, cabbage, cucumbers, and beets, and they grew apple orchards. Their livestock included horses, cattle, sheep, pigs, and chickens. They grew hemp and flax for fibers to spin into yarn and weave into cloth.

Trade of fur pelts for silver coins from the Middle East had first attracted the Rus to the land of the Eastern Slavs, and export of luxury fur continued to play a significant role in the Russian economy for centuries. From earliest times, Russians also traded grain and wool cloth with steppe nomads in exchange for hides and cattle. *From the sixteenth century, trade with western Europe began to increase, Russia exporting furs, pitch, cordage, and masts and importing military equipment, wine, and everyday supplies, such as dyes, paper, pins and needles, and sugar.* In the seventeenth century, Russia exported increasing amounts of grain, and it also began to produce its own iron. A native armaments industry had been established in Tula by 1630.

Peter the Great sponsored a huge increase in manufacturing by building state-owned factories and also by supporting private entrepreneurship, which he did by paying subsidies, imposing protective tariffs, and excusing all merchants who owned factories from the obligation to quarter soldiers in their homes. In Peter's reign 180 large-scale enterprises were established, including 40 ironworks, 15 other metal foundries, 24 textile mills, and numerous leather, glass, and gunpowder works. In 1700, Russia imported most of its iron, by 1725, it was exporting iron to Europe, and, by 1800, Russia led the world in the production of pig iron. In the eighteenth century, the textile industry expanded and diversified, and the production of rope and shipbuilding products more than doubled. Catherine the Great's conquest of the Black Sea steppe greatly expanded the economy. In the last two decades of eighteenth century, grain production almost doubled, and wheat shipped from the newly built port of Odessa on the Crimean Peninsula helped feed the rapidly growing cities of western Europe. Russia's exports were twice as large as its imports.

The Russian economy stagnated somewhat after 1815. Russian production techniques did not keep pace with those of England. Handicraft production changed little. Exports of Russian pig iron declined in the face of competition from English wrought iron and steel. Russian transportation developed slowly. Hard-surface road construction had begun in France and England in the eighteenth century, whereas the first hard-surfaced road in Russia, connecting Moscow and St. Petersburg was only begun in 1817 and was not completed until 1834. By 1840, England had fifteen hundred miles of railroad track, while Russia had less than twenty miles. The first railroad, the railroad connecting Moscow and St. Petersburg, was not completed until 1851.

On the other hand, Russian wheat exports to Western Europe continued to increase. By 1850, thirty-six million bushels were exported, approximately 3.5 percent of the total grain crop. The textile industry continued to thrive, and for the first time, Russian textile mills began to process cotton. In 1802, the first sugar beet processing plant was built in Russia, and sugar production quickly became a major industry. Because of Russia's great size and lack of roads, transportation was a major obstacle to the distribution of goods. Most consumer goods were produced locally; cities were able to support factories while the provincial towns and villages were supplied by artisans in small workshops.

Part of the reason for the lack of railroads was Nicholas I's belief that railroads would bring revolution to Russia. Despite an underlying fear of the social changes brought by the Industrial Revolution, Egor Kankrin, Minister of Finance (1823–1844), nevertheless fostered Russian industry by imposing protective tariffs. The Ministry of Finance also built schools for commerce, engineering and forestry. By 1850, more than 40 percent of the cities in European Russia were industrial, up from 4 percent only a century earlier.

Historians have tended to overemphasize Russia's comparative backwardness in relation to Western Europe, and it has been common to blame this on serfdom. While it is true that Russia had lagged behind Europe in terms of prosperity since the Mongol era, the explanation is best found in Russia's cold climate, relatively poor soil, and low population density. It is also the case that Russia did not experience the agricultural revolution (use of nitrogen-fixing cover crops, mechanization, scientific livestock breeding, and production of cash crops for the market) that was an essential prerequisite to the Industrial Revolution. It must be remembered, however, that one of the ways the Agricultural Revolution prepared for the

Industrial Revolution was by creating a class of impoverished landless wage laborers (available to work in the new factories) through the process of enclosure and dispossession of small farmers.

In the southern black-earth districts, some nobles did organize their estates to produce wheat for the market, and there were a number of "improving" landlords who attempted to organize production efficiently and to use labor-saving equipment (which their peasants frequently sabotaged). Overall, however, the peasant commune controlled production, and the commune was most interested in self-sufficient, subsistence agriculture, not production for the market. In addition, community farming made it impossible for individual farmers to experiment with new techniques. Periodic land redistribution prevented the appearance of a landless rural working class.

The fact that an agricultural revolution did not occur in Russia may have meant slower industrial growth, but it meant less misery for the agricultural population in Russia than in Britain, for example. Western observers noted that Russian peasants were much better off than Scottish or Irish peasants, and their living conditions were certainly better than the dispossessed agriculturalists living in industrial cities. Historian Jerome Blum reports that in the Kaluga district in the first half of the nineteenth century the wealthiest peasants tilled an average of fifty-two acres and owned an average of eight horses, four cows, nineteen sheep, and four pigs. In the same region, the poorest peasant households owned almost six acres of land, two horses, two cows, seven sheep, and two pigs.[1] By contrast, in Ireland before the great famine of the 1840s, it was not unusual for a family to subsist on potatoes grown on a quarter-acre of land.

Furthermore, there is no evidence that the institution of serfdom stood in the way of industrialization. Though peasants and serfs were bound to their commune or landlord, they were, in fact, a mobile workforce whenever it suited those who controlled them. In the central and northern regions of Russia, where soil and climate were relatively unfavorable for agriculture, many landlords charged *obrok* (cash rent) rather than *barshchina* (labor services) and allowed their peasants freedom to travel to work elsewhere to earn the money. In the 1840s, 25 to 30 percent of male serfs lived permanently away from their commune and simply sent in their obrok payments. Many more engaged in seasonal labor. These serfs worked in Russia's factories and mines, served as laborers and cab drivers in the cities. Sometimes the males of a commune would work together as an economic unit (known as an *artel*), typically in construction and carpentry. In addition, 300,000 migrant laborers traveled south every year to help harvest the wheat crop.

PEOPLES OF THE EMPIRE

The origins of the Russian Empire can be traced back to the expansive policies of the principality of Moscow beginning soon after the Mongol conquest of western Inner Eurasia in the thirteenth century. In the two centuries following the Mongol invasion, Moscow princes steadily added to their territory by purchasing, inheriting, or forcibly annexing territory from their neighbors. Grand Princes Ivan III (1462–1505), Vasilii III (1505–1533) and Ivan IV (1533–1584) finished the process of uniting all of the Eastern Slavs who had been part of the Mongol empire and creating a single state with a uniform administration and military force. Ivan IV ("the Terrible") transformed Muscovy (as the new state began to be known in western Europe) into an empire by annexing Kazan and Astrakhan, two territories occupied by Muslim Tatars. Ivan IV also expanded westward at the expense of Lithuania, the state which ruled those Eastern Slavs who had not been incorporated into the Mongol Empire.

Expansion of the empire continued (although at a slower rate) during Time of Troubles and the reign of Michael Romanov, and it quickened under Tsar Aleksei in whose reign Russia expanded eastward across Siberia, southward toward China and the nomads of the Central Asian steppes, and westward toward Kiev. Peter I gained access to the Baltic Sea, while Catherine II annexed the Ukrainian, Belarusian, and Lithuanian territories of Poland, and seized the northern Black Sea coast (including the Crimean Peninsula occupied by the Crimean Tatars). Catherine further contributed to ethnic diversity of the empire by inviting German colonists to settle on the steppe. Alexander I annexed the Grand Duchy of Poland, Finland, Bessarabia, Azerbaijan, Georgia, and Armenia.

Russia even expanded into North America. The Russian-American Company was founded in 1799 and claimed the coast and islands of what is now Alaska. Russians then moved south, building Fort Ross near San Francisco in 1812. In 1815 to 1817, Russia established contact with Hawaii and built a Russian Orthodox Church there. The young United States of America, which also had interests in the Pacific Coast of North America, opposed Russian expansion, and in 1824, Alexander I agreed to limit Russian claims to Alaska. In 1841, Nicholas I sold Fort Ross to the United States.

Catherine and Alexander, in the spirit of Enlightened cosmopolitanism, fostered the vision of Russia as a tolerant, multiethnic empire. Catherine, in particular, deemphasized Orthodox Christianity and represented the Russian Empire as engaged in a broad project of spreading Enlightened civilization. Russia's rulers generally favored education in the Russian language and the building of Orthodox churches, but neither was an absolute requirement. As long as a people accepted subordination to the Emperor, the language they spoke and the religion they professed was negotiable. Catherine ended the practice of forced conversion of the nomads. In fact, she thought that Islam could be used as a "civilizing" force in Central Asia, and she encouraged the construction of Mosques and missionary activity by pro-Russian Muslim clerics. When a non-Russian nation was incorporated into the empire, its noble elite were granted the rights and privileges of membership in the Russian nobility. The only exception was that non-Christian nobles were not allowed to own Christian serfs (but were free to own serfs of other religions). Jews were also discriminated against by a "Pale of Settlement" that restricted Jews to Belarus, Ukraine, New Russia, and the western borderlands annexed from Poland and Turkey.

Nicholas I expanded imperial rule in Central Asia by subordinating the nomadic Kazakh federation, and by 1848, Russia controlled Central Asia as far south as the Syr Darya River, and Russian settlers began to move into the region. Nicholas was unable, however, to complete the conquest of Inner Eurasia. In Central Asia, the Khanates of Khiva, Bukhara, and Kokand successfully repelled Russian invaders, and in the Northern Caucasus, Chechens and Circassians preserved their independence.

In the south and east, Nicholas continued the tradition of toleration for the religions and traditions of the indigenous peoples. In the west, however, Nicholas I aggressively promoted the Russification of the population. After the Polish rebellion of 1830 to 1831, Nicholas dissolved the Grand Duchy of Poland, abrogated its constitution, abolished its *sejm* (parliament), disbanded the Polish Army, and closed the University of Warsaw. The Polish provinces were absorbed into the administrative system of the Russian Empire.

At about the same time, Ukrainian intellectuals, under the influence of romantic nationalism, began to study the language, history, and folklore of the peasantry of Ukraine. Nicholas I, however, refused to accept any ethnic distinctions in his western provinces. He made Russian the language of local administration and of higher education, and he required that history textbooks treat Ukraine, Belarus, and Lithuania as historically a part of Russia. He suppressed the Kirillo-Methodian Society, an organization for the study of history and folklore, and arrested its leaders. Nicholas also attempted to assimilate the Jewish population, whom the law code of 1835 referred to as "aliens." He abolished their local organs of self-government, pressured them to send their children to state schools, and conscripted Jewish boys at the age of twelve (instead of the standard age of twenty). Jews, however, resisted assimilation, as did the other peoples of the empire.

CONCLUSION: THE CRIMEAN WAR, 1854–1856

Russia had not only added significantly to its territory since the reign of Peter I, it had also steadily risen in stature as a European and world power. From the death of Peter I until the very end of Nicholas I's reign, Russia had never lost a war. In the eighteenth century, Russia had established itself as the hegemonic power in eastern Europe. Between 1812 and 1814, Russia repelled Napoleon's invasion and then drove his armies back to France, liberating Europe from Napoleon's empire. In 1814, Alexander I led a Russian army into Paris, and he shared in redrawing the map of Europe at the Congress of Vienna in 1815.

A preponderance of power, and the arbitrary exercise of it, inevitably leads to an opposing alliance, and this soon occurred when France and England, previously historic enemies, joined forces against Russia. If Russia was the largest land empire in the world, England was the world's largest maritime empire, and both wanted hegemony over Outer Eurasia. England encroached upon China from the south, while Russia pressed it from the north. England had secured control over India, but England and Russia contested dominance in Central Asia, Afghanistan, and Iran. Both Russia and Britain had propped up the Ottoman Empire in order to keep Russia out of the Balkans and the Middle East, and France aimed at exerting its financial and commercial hegemony over the Ottoman Empire.

Nicholas I gave England and France the opportunity to combine against Russia in 1854 when he sent an army into Moldavia and Wallachia, asserting his right to intervene on behalf of Orthodox Christians in the Ottoman Empire. The Ottoman Sultan, joined by England and France, declared war. The Russian navy defeated the Turkish fleet, but Nicholas I was not anxious for war. He did not advance on Constantinople, and he withdrew Russian troops from Moldavia and Wallachia, offering to negotiate. Britain and France, however, *did* want war. In 1854, their combined forces destroyed the Russian Black Sea fleet and landed troops on the Crimean Peninsula. Anglo-French forces won three major battles and laid siege to Sevastopol. In 1855, while this siege was underway, Nicholas I died of pneumonia. It was left to his son, Alexander II, who succeeded him, to resolve the crisis.

NOTE

1. Jerome Blum, *Lord and Peasant in Russia: From the Ninth to the Nineteenth Century* (Princeton, N.J.: Princeton University Press, 1961), 272.

_____ TEXT DOCUMENTS _____

Haxthausen on the Commune and the Tsar

August von Haxthausen was a German expert in agriculture who traveled in Russia during the reign of Nicholas I to study Russian rural life. In 1847, he published a record of his journey, Studies in the Interior of Russia, *which profoundly influenced the way educated Russians thought about the peasantry.*

- What parts of this description are realistic? What parts appear to be fantasy?
- How does this work as a justification of autocracy?
- What might socialists find attractive in this?

Throughout Russia proper there . . . has developed . . . a rural organization in which the principle of communal property [of the ancient Slavs] has been fully retained. The forests and pasture land always remain undivided; the plowlands and meadows are apportioned to the various families in the commune, who, however, do not own the land but have only the right to use it temporarily. Formerly the lots may have been redistributed annually among the married couples of the community, each receiving a share equal to all the others in terms of quality. Today, however, in order to avoid expenses and great inconveniences the land is reapportioned after a certain number of years. If, for example, a father should die and leave six sons who are not of age, the widow generally continues to manage the farm until her sons marry. Then, however, they do not divide among themselves the plot which their father had cultivated; instead this land reverts to the commune, and all six sons receive a share equal to that held by the other members of the community. All together they might hold five to six times the amount of land which their father had held. If the six sons should marry when their father is still alive, then he claims for each one of them an equal allotment of the communal land. Since the sons continue to live in the same household with their father, he does not have to worry about establishing them. On the contrary, a marriage is fortunate for the family. Even if she has no dowry, the arrival of a daughter-in-law means an additional share of the communal property. The marriage and establishment of his daughters is thus the least of a Russian peasant's worries. . . .

The mother's command over the daughters is just as absolute as the father's authority over all his children. The same respect and obedience are shown to the communal authorities, the *starets* and the white heads and above all to their common father, the tsar. A Russian has one and the same word for addressing his natural father, the *starets*, his master, the emperor, and finally, God, namely, "father. . . . little father" (*batushka*). Similarly he calls every fellow Russian "brother" (*brat*), whether he knows him or not!

The common Russian (*muzhik*) knows absolutely no servile fear, but only a childlike fear or awe in the presence of his tsar, whom he loves with a devoted tenderness. He enters the

_____
Source: August von Haxthausen, *Studies on the Interior of Russia,* edited and with an introduction by S. Frederick Starr, translated by Eleanore L. M. Schmidt (Chicago: University of Chicago Press, 1972), 278–284. © University of Chicago Press. Reprinted with permission.

military reluctantly, but once a soldier he harbors no resentment or ill will, serving the tsar with the greatest loyalty and devotion. The famous Russian word *prikazano* (it is ordered) has a magical effect on him. It goes without saying that whatever the tsar commands must be done. The Russian would never resist or defy the tsar's order; indeed, the impossibility of its execution would never occur to him. Even in the case of mere police proscriptions, the Russian does not say "it is forbidden" *(zapreshcheno)* but rather "it is not ordered" *(ni prikazano or nevoleno).* The profound reverence shown the tsar is evidenced above all in the Russian's attitude toward everything regarded as belonging to the monarch. He has the greatest respect for the *kazennye,* the state lands or the tsar's property. A Russian proverb says: "The *kazennye* do not die are not consumed by fire and do not drown in water."

There is almost no case of persons responsible for collecting taxes ever having been attacked or robbed, even though they travel long distances alone and often carry considerable sums of money. In northern Russia, in the province of Vologda, where the customs are untainted and the inhabitants very honest, the tax collector, upon arriving in a village, knocks on every window and cries "kassa." Everyone brings him his tax for the year and drops it into a sack. Knowing he will never be cheated, the collector does not bother to check the amount. When night falls, he enters the first good house and places the sack of money under the icon of the saint. He then looks for lodging and sleeps without a care, confident that the next morning he will find everything just as he had left it!

. . . The patriarchal ruler, the tsar, appears to be absolutely essential to the existence and perpetuation of the nation. Consequently, we never find popular insurrections which challenge the authority of the government or the tsar as such. Rather, uprisings are directed against individuals and usually for so-called legitimate reasons: for and against the false Dmitrii, for Pugachev, who posed as the banished Peter III, and lastly in 1825 for a similar reason. The people always obeyed the government which ruled over them, even the Mongols. To be sure, they frequently complain about alleged injustices, but, after verbally expressing their grievances, they cease complaining and everyone is content.

The Autobiography of Aleksandra Kobiakova

Aleksandra Kobiakova (1823–1892) was a novelist who was born into the merchant class. She published her first novel in 1858 and her second in 1860, and in the same year the leading liberal journal of the day published her autobiography. The events related in this selection occurred during the reign of Nicholas I.

- What does this reveal about gender relations in early nineteenth-century Russia?
- How do betrothal practices appear to be changing?
- What does it reveal about the merchant class?

All the members of my family lived under one roof and belonged to the third merchants' guild. We lived in a two-storied stone house; there was a candle factory on the premises, and next to the store belonging to my grandfather's brother was a wine cellar. We had no shop assistants. The old men clung to the old ways. They had beards and wore Russian kaftans, drank neither wine nor tea, and loved to read the Scriptures. They considered coarse language and swearing sinful. Around town they had a reputation for honesty but were not considered wealthy. They never quarreled, but neither did they show much affection for each other, probably because of their upbringing rather than lack of love or mutual understanding.

My grandmother was typical of women raised in that harsh environment, which gives them a strong will and erases their soft feminine traits. Grandmother was naturally intelligent and, in different conditions and under different circumstances, she would have become a remarkable person, but all her strength was spent in vain or was pitifully misdirected.

Many people found her difficult, the more so since at home her despotic will was obeyed absolutely by everyone, even by grandfather himself. She led a simple and most austere life. She saw sin lurking everywhere and in everything–in short haircuts, rouge, singing–all were sins and crimes. My mother was a cheerful woman by nature who enjoyed life's pleasures and had been pampered by her father like an aristocratic young lady. Her temperament clashed with my grandmother's in particular. Grandmother's older daughter-in-law was much more to her liking, and Grandmother loved her best.

My mother found no joy, diversion, or sympathy within her family and ascribed all her afflictions to the mores of the merchant class. She believed that no woman could find happiness in that estate and that is why she wanted to see me marry a government official, someone she thought would be a more educated person.

I was fifteen years old when I started seeing a young man from a local townsman's family. He intended to study medicine after graduating from the Gymnasium. Because of my sheltered home life I felt predisposed to like the future doctor at our very first meeting. He seemed to me the only ideal a fifteen-year-old girl, whose imagination was aroused by reading romantic novels, could dream about.

Source: Toby W. Clyman and Judith Vowles, *Russia Through Women's Eyes: Autobiographies from Tsarist Russia* (New Haven, CT: Yale University Press, 1996), 60-74. © Yale University Press. Reprinted with permission.

The young man did not hide his interest in me and tried to please me in every way. He brought me books, and I was by no means indifferent to his generosity. Mother came to love him like a son and he, unconstrained by our social conventions, flatly declared that he hoped to become her son-in-law when he graduated. I returned his feelings and considered him my betrothed. He was four years older than I. My attachment to him was far from passionate, nevertheless it was strong and deep, and it was strengthened by the persecution to which my family subjected me because of our friendship. And it would probably have been short-lived had their opposition not aroused my defiant nature, which saw a challenge in every obstacle. Daily quarrels at home added fuel to my budding emotions, and I proudly endured them for the sake of my beloved dream. My mother was so simple and naive that she really believed that K. might someday be her son-in-law. My father disliked him and avoided his company, although he never said anything to me about it. Kos—tsyn left for Moscow to study at the Medical Surgical Academy; we wrote often. A year later he came back to Kostroma for the summer vacation and was as affectionate and attentive as before. All kinds of rumors were circulating about us in town. My relatives were in an uproar, but we remained true to our vows and comforted each other with dreams of our beautiful future together. His love for me was beyond reproach, and I felt it deserved to be fully reciprocated. . . .

I turned seventeen. One of the garrison officers, a worthy man, proposed to me. All my relatives hounded me with their advice, practically forcing me to marry him. I spent the next few weeks in that inner struggle that torments the heart when one of life's fateful questions rises before you and your answer is dictated by another's mind and will. Filled with doubt and indecision, I wrote to Kos—tsyn. He responded with a letter to my father in which he swore that he would shoot himself if they forced me to marry someone else. Father summoned me and we both spoke our minds. I told him that I thought it despicable to go back on my word. He said that he didn't want to impose his will upon me any longer and that I could decide my own fate.

From that time on I was entirely free to reject any suitor; my family left me in peace. But then the vacation came and, with it, the man for whom I had endured so many scenes, family arguments, and sleepless nights. And, just imagine! Not even the shadow of my former friend remained. He blatantly ridiculed my family's simple ways and argued with my mother. He quarreled with me and went out of his way to contradict me as rudely as possible. His outbursts were wild and senseless. For example, he would say that if he became an army doctor he would lock up his wife to prevent other officers from looking at her, and if she made the slightest attempt to gain her freedom, he would send her back to her parents. In short, he showed me the kind of husband he would be–a tyrant who preached passive obedience to his wife and denied her any will of her own or even a semblance of female dignity. At first his attitude enraged me, but then I became frightened. Inwardly I cried, but outwardly I argued and fought with him. I showed him the short pieces I'd written in his absence and listened to his moralizing: "Woman is created not for the pen but for the needle and oven prongs." I read him some verses I had jotted down and was reprimanded for passing off someone else's work as my own. I could bear it no longer. . . . I was amazed at the change in his character, once so gentle and kind, but now rude and captious. A woman outraged has only one recourse–revenge and contempt. So I, in turn, started tormenting him with my feminine whims and contrariness.

[She ultimately broke off the engagement with him.]

Muraviev on East Asia

In 1847, Count Nikolai Muraviev was appointed governor-general of Eastern Siberia. He wrote the following memorandum, "The Views of Count Nikolai N. Muravev Regarding the Necessity for Russia to control the Amur River," in 1849–1850.

- What does this reveal about the mentality of imperialism?
- Who was Russia's greatest rival? What was the nature of their competition?

Russia must occupy the mouth of the Amur River and that part of Sakhalin Island which lies opposite, as well as the left bank of the Amur River, for the following reasons:

I. Concern for the eastern frontier of the empire.

Rumors have for quite some time circulated through Siberia concerning the intentions of the English to occupy the mouth of the Amur River and Sakhalin Island. God forbid they should become entrenched there before we do! In order to establish more thorough and complete control over trade with China, the English undoubtedly need to control both the mouth of the Amur and the navigation on that river. If the Amur were not the only river flowing from Siberia to the Pacific Ocean, we might not have any objection to their intentions, but navigation via the Amur is the only suitable route to the east. This is a century-old dream of Siberians of all classes; it may be instinctive, but it is no less well grounded.

Upon review of all circumstances known to me, I can state that whoever controls the mouth of the Amur will also control Siberia, at least as far as Baikal, and that control will be firm. It is enough to control the mouth of this river and navigation on it for Siberia, which is increasing in population and flourishing in agriculture and industry, to remain an unalterable tributary and subject of the power which holds the key to it.

II. Strengthening and securing possession of the Kamchatka Peninsula.

Only when we have the left bank of the Amur and the navigation rights on it can we establish communication with Kamchatka, and thus be in a position to establish Russia's firm control over this peninsula. The reason is that the route via Yakutsk and Okhotsk or Aian offers no means of supplying Kamchatka with sufficient military capacity, nor to provide it with proper population, which in and of itself, under the protection of fortresses, would comprise the strength of this distant oblast and furnish local land and naval forces with their necessary provisions. With the establishment of steam navigation on the Amur, Kamchatka could be provisioned from Nerchinsk with people and all necessities in no more than two weeks. The Amur River flows from our frontiers to the island of Sakhalin for more than 2,000 versts, and according to all available information, is navigable for its entire length.

Source: Reprinted from Basil Dmytryshyn, E. A. P. Crownhart-Vaughan, Thomas Vaughan, eds. and trans., *The Russian American Colonies* (Portland, OR: Oregon Historical Society Press, 1989), 482–484. © 1989, The Oregon Historical Society. Reprinted with permission.

III. Support for our trade with China.

The decrease in the Kiakhta trade already indicates that the intentions of the English in China cannot be beneficial to us. During the first years after their war [Opium War, 1839-42], we did not realize this, because the Chinese, motivated by their enmity toward the English, preferred to turn to us as their reliable and gracious neighbors. But time and material benefits mitigate the outburst of animosity and moderate a flame of friendship which does not represent substantial benefits. I believe that the only way to promote our trade with China is to change it from local to widespread, so that by sailing on the Amur we could supply the products of our manufacture to all the northeastern provinces of China, which are more distant from present activities of the English, and consequently, from their competition which is dangerous to our trade.

IV. Maintaining our influence in China.

The English war and peace in China have laid the foundation for the transformation of that populous empire under the influence of the English. But during the lifetime of the late Chinese Emperor, we still hoped he would personally announce that since he had been insulted by them, he could not be favorably disposed toward them and consequently would not allow the spread of English influence in his empire.

Now, with the ascension of his 18-year-old son, one can be certain that the English will hasten to turn this event to their advantage with their usual natural entrepreneurial spirit, speed and persistence, so as to gain control not only of trade, but also of China's politics. I cannot judge whether we can prevent this, when five of China's ports have been not only accessible to the English, but have actually almost become English cities.

I believe it would be prudent for us to have better security along the frontiers with China, to the extent of our domestic needs, so the English will not gain full control there, and thus we must control the Amur. I also think that we must capitalize on current developments in China so we can reveal our plans to them, based on the general benefits to both empires; to wit, that no one but Russia and China should control navigation on the Amur, and that the mouth of that river should be protected, and of course, not by the Chinese.

Radishchev, *A Journey from St. Petersburg to Moscow*

In 1790, a nobleman, Aleksandr Nikolaevich Radishchev, published A Journey from St. Petersburg to Moscow *on his privately owned printing press. The copy he had submitted for approval by the censors did not contain, among other things, the following excerpt. When its true contents were discovered, Radishchev was arrested and exiled to Siberia.*

- To what intellectual traditions does Radishchev appeal?
- What is Radishchev's purpose in this selection? How does he make his case?

Having brought our beloved fatherland step by step to the flourishing condition in which it now finds itself, we see that science, art, and manufacturing have been brought to the highest degree of perfection that humans are capable of, in our land we see human reason freely spreading its wings and unerringly ascending everywhere to greatness and that it has now become the trustworthy guarantor of public law. Under [reason's] sovereign protection, our hearts are free to rise up in prayers to the almighty creator. We can say with inexpressible joy that our fatherland is an abode that is pleasing to the divine being, since its construction is not based on prejudice and superstition, but on our inner feelings of the mercy of the father of all. We do not know the enmities that have so often separated people because of their beliefs, we also do not know the compulsion to believe. Having been born in this freedom, we truly respect one another as brothers that belong to one family and have one father, God.

The torch of science, hovering over our legislation, now distinguishes it from the legislation of many other countries. The balance of powers and the equality of property destroy the root of civil discord. Moderation in punishment creates respect for the laws of the supreme power which are respected like the commands of tender parents to their offspring and prevents even guileless evildoing. Clarity in the laws pertaining to the acquisition and protection of property prevents family quarrels from arising. The boundary that separates one citizen and his property from another is deep, clear to everyone, and respected as sacred by everyone. Private injuries are rare among us and are amicably reconciled. Public education is concerned with making us gentle, making us peace-loving citizens, but above all, making us human beings.

Enjoying domestic tranquility, have no foreign enemies, having brought society to the highest bliss of accord, is it possible that we could be so alien from humanitarian feeling, so alien from the impulse of pity, so alien from the tenderness of noble hearts, so alien from brotherly love, that we can allow in our sight a never-ending reproach to us, a disgrace to our furthest posterity, that a whole third of our fellows, our equal fellow citizens, our beloved brothers in nature, are in the heavy bonds of slavery and bondage? . . .

Oh, our beloved fellow citizens! Oh, true sons of the fatherland! Look about and understand your delusions. Servants of the eternal divinity, pursuing the benefit of society and the

Source: A. N. Radishchev, *Puteshestvie iz Peterburga v Moskvu. Polnoe sobranie sochinenii*, (Moscow-Leningrad: Izdatel'stvo Akademii Nauk SSSR, 1938), 311–312, 313, 314–315, 320–321. Translated by the author.

happiness of humanity, of one mind with us, have explained to you in their teachings in the name of the most merciful God in whom they believe, how contrary it is to his wisdom and love to rule capriciously over your neighbor. They have tried with arguments taken from nature and from our hearts to prove to you your cruelty, injustice, and sinfulness. Even now their voice, solemn in the temples of the living god, cries loudly, "Think about your errors, soften your hard-heartedness, break the fetters of your brothers, open the prison of servitude, and let those who are just like you taste the sweetness of community life, for which they have been destined by the All-Merciful just as you have. . . ."

In school, when you were young, they taught you the foundations of natural law and civil law. Natural law showed you that human beings, hypothetically outside of society, were given the same constitution by nature, and therefore had the same rights, and were consequently equal to one another, and no one should rule another. Civil law showed you people who had exchanged unlimited freedom for the peaceful enjoyment of that freedom. But if you all have set limits on your freedom, and obey the law, since all are equal from birth in natural law, they must also be equally limited. . . . All this is familiar to you, you have imbibed these laws with your mother's milk. It is only the prejudice of the moment, only greed (please don't be offended by my words), only greed blinds us and makes us become like madmen in darkness.

But who among us wears the fetters, who feels the weight of slavery? The farmer! The person who feeds our leanness and satisfies our hunger, the one who gives us our health and prolongs our life, all the while himself not having the right to dispose of what he makes or what he produces. But who has the best right to a field if not the one who tills it? . . . At the beginning of social life, he who was able to cultivate a field had the right to possess it, and, having cultivated it had the exclusive right to its fruits. But how far we have diverged from the original social constitution regarding property! With us, the one who has that very natural right is not only completely denied it, but while working in someone else's field, he sees that his own subsistence is dependant on the power of another. . . .

Do you not know, beloved fellow citizens, what ruin is in store for us and in what danger we find ourselves? All the callous feelings of the slaves, that are not softened by a nod toward the blessing of freedom, will get stronger and will intensify their inner feelings. A stream that is stopped in its flow, becomes stronger as the obstruction to it becomes stronger. Having burst through the dam, nothing can stop its outpouring. It is the same with our brothers who we are keeping in chains. They are awaiting for the right opportunity. The bell rings. And all the destruction of bestial atrocity pours out instantly. Around us we will see sword and poison. Death and fire will be our due for our harshness and inhumanity. And the longer it takes us and the more stubborn we are about releasing their bonds, the more implacable they will be in their revenge. . . .

This is what stands before us, this is what we must expect. Ruin and grief are steadily approaching, danger is hovering over our heads. Time has already raised its scythe, it waits for an hour of opportunity, and the first flatterer or lover of humanity who arises to awaken the unfortunates will hasten the scythe's stroke. Beware!

ART

Consider the images that appear below.

- What do these works of art reveal about Russian culture?
- Can you make any generalizations about changes in Russian society?

Figure I-1 Mother of God of Vladimir
This is the most revered of all Russian icons. It was painted in Constantinople and brought to Kiev in 1131. In 1155, it was removed to the city of Vladimir, and in 1395, the icon was taken to Moscow where it has remained ever since.
Source: Tretiakov Gallery, Moscow.

Figure I-2 "The Crucifixion"
This icon was painted in 1500 by Dionisii, a student of Russia's greatest icon painter, Andrei Rublev.
Source: Tretiakov Gallery, Moscow.

Figure I-3 Christ Carrying the Cross
   This icon was painted toward the end of the seventeenth century.
Source: Tretiakov Gallery, Moscow.

Figure I-4 "Harvesting: Summer"
This was painted by Aleksei Gavrilovich Venetsianov (1780–1847).
Source: Tretiakov Gallery, Moscow.

ARCHITECTURE

Consider the two photographs below.

- What do these buildings reveal about Russian culture?
- Can you make any generalizations about changes in Russian society?

Figure I-5 Cathedral of the Dormition
This Cathedral was commissioned by Ivan III and built in 1479. It is the centerpiece of the Kremlin.
Source: Getty Images, Inc. Photodisc.

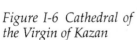

Figure I-6 Cathedral of the Virgin of Kazan
The Kazan Cathedral in St. Petersburg was completed in 1811 in the reign of Alexander I.
Source: Dorling Kindersley Media Library.

COINS

Below are a number of coins representing some of Russia's rulers.

- How do they change over time?
- What do the changes suggest about the evolution of Russian politics and society?

Figure I-7 Vladimir (978–1015)
Source: de Chaudoir, *Obozrenie Russkikh deneg.* Part 1, plate 1, drawing 6.

Figure I-8 Ivan III (1462–1533)
Source: de Chaudoir, *Obozrenie Russkikh deneg.* Part 2, plate 4, drawing 5.

Figure I-9 Aleksei (1645–1676)
Source: de Chaudoir, *Obozrenie Russkikh deneg.* Part 2, plate 8, drawing 1.

Figure I-10 Coin: Peter I (1689–1725)
Source: de Chaudoir, *Obozrenie Russkikh deneg.* Part 2, plate 11, drawing 2.

Figure I-11 Coin: Catherine II (1762–1796)
Source: de Chaudoir, *Obozrenie Russkikh deneg.* Part 2, plate 38, drawing 4.

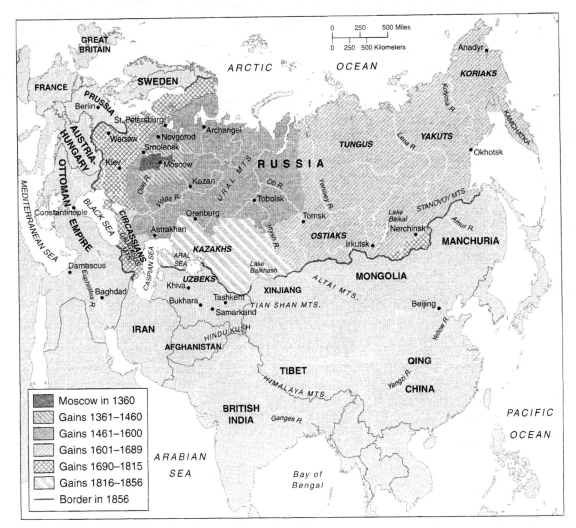

Figure I-12 The Expansion of Russia from 1300–1856

The city of Moscow became a principality in the late thirteenth century when Grand Prince Alexander made his son, Daniil, its prince. At first, Daniil's successors undertook the national project of gathering the lands of Rus, but they then began to conquer and absorb non-Russian neighbors. There was no apparent limit to the expansiveness of the Russian state, and, by 1856, Russia was a multi-national empire that included almost all of Inner Eurasia and part of North America, as well.

CHAPTER TWELVE

RUSSIA IN THE AGE
OF NATION-BUILDING, 1856–1881

Nicholas I's reign ended disastrously. Repression of independent thought after 1848 had further alienated Russian society from the government, and defeat by England and France in the Crimean War humiliated the army and isolated Russia from Europe. In response, Nicholas's son, Alexander II, began a series of fundamental reforms, beginning with the emancipation of the serfs, intended to restore Russia's greatness and heal the rift between government and society. The crucial question facing Nicholas's successors was whether the Russian monarchy could manage to maintain its political legitimacy without accepting the principle of popular sovereignty and allowing the citizenry a national forum in which to express its aspirations.

THE EURASIAN CONTEXT

The Revolutions of 1848 across Europe resulted in the victory of the propertied classes: the capitalists and financiers in the west and the aristocracy in the east. As the century progressed, however, the middle- and working-classes grew, and they increasingly demanded popular participation in government. No government could ignore the idea of popular sovereignty, if only as a self-serving political tool. In France, Napoleon III used the trappings of democracy, including universal manhood suffrage and national referenda, to make himself Emperor of France. Camillo di Cavour and Otto von Bismarck used the nationalist impulses of the Italian and German people, respectively, to create large and powerful nation-states.

Turn to page 53 for a map showing key geographic locations and features for this time period.

Austria made major concessions to Hungarian nationalists in order to create a partnership for maintaining control over its empire's Slavic peoples.

The middle of the nineteenth century marked the beginning of the "Age of Materialism" in Europe. Materialism as a popular mood was epitomized by the Industrial Revolution which promised to solve the basic economic problem of scarcity. In a more abstract sense, materialism was manifested in a confidence that science (the study of matter behaving according to laws of nature) was the ultimate source of truth. This was the age of Darwin, whose *Origin of Species* (1859) depicted humans as animals who had evolved by means of a selfish and violent competition to survive, and of Karl Marx, whose *Das Kapital* (1867) proved "scientifically" that capitalism would be replaced by communism not through the efforts of self-sacrificing utopian dreamers but because of the inexorable operation of natural laws.

Materialism in politics was epitomized in Otto von Bismarck's assertion that the great issues of the day would not be solved by speeches and ideals but by "blood and iron." Bismarck (chancellor of Prussia, 1862–1890) used the military to collect taxes against the will of the elected parliament, but regained the support of German liberals by winning quick victories in wars with Denmark (1864), Austria (1866), and France (1870), that united the formerly fragmented German Confederation into a single German state. The new state, the Empire of Germany, replaced France as the dominant power on the continent.

Europe's military and industrial power, combined with the notion that species progress through violent competition, contributed to the rise of a new imperialism. Europeans began to believe that their ability to conquer other peoples proved their superiority and imposed on them the duty of "civilizing" subject populations. After a major rebellion in India in 1857, which the British brutally suppressed, Great Britain began to rule the colony with a new sense of aloofness and superiority. In the 1870s, Belgium, France, Germany, and Great Britain began a scramble to colonize Africa; by 1914, 90 percent of the continent was in European hands.

The rise of European wealth and power was relatively heightened by the concurrent decline of the Eurasian empires. In the middle of the nineteenth century, China was shaken by social unrest. In the 1850s, three popular rebellions broke out which took more than a decade to suppress. At the same time, England and France defeated Qing forces in the Arrow War (1856–1858) and the Second Opium War (1860). New treaties were imposed which opened new ports, allowed foreigners to travel to the interior of China, lowered taxes on trade, and provided for diplomatic representation in the capital, Beijing. The European powers encouraged Qing emperors to accept huge loans for modernization projects and imposed conditions of repayment that further eroded Chinese sovereignty.

In 1853, the United States sent a naval force to Japan to force the Shogun to open Japanese ports to western trade, and by 1856, the United States had obtained the sort of "unequal treaty" that England had imposed on China in 1842. In 1868, a group of young Samurai warriors took advantage of the Shogun's capitulation to foreigners to overthrow the feudal system. Under the pretext of "restoring" the Emperor to power, they established themselves as a ruling oligarchy and began a successful program of rapid industrialization and economic, social, and military transformation on the European model. Japan imitated European imperialism, as well. In 1876, Japan forced Korea to open two ports to Japanese trade.

In the middle of the nineteenth century, Ottoman rulers initiated a series of reforms known as Tanzimat (reorganization). They instituted free and compulsory primary education and a system of secondary and higher education. The government also began to replace Muslim and customary law with commercial, maritime, penal, and civil codes on the French model. State courts replaced traditional Islamic judges. One goal of adopting western law was to repeal the Capitulations, but Ottoman subordination to the West actually increased. As in China, the European powers pressured the government to accept huge loans, then used its leverage to take control of Ottoman finances and investment policy.

In Iran, Nasir al Din Shah (1848–1896) also followed a program of continued westernization. He reformed the tax system, centralized the bureaucracy, subordinated the provinces to central control, encouraged trade and industry, and reduced the political power of the Muslim clergy. In 1871, he established a European-style cabinet and a legislative council of senior princes and officials. Nevertheless, Nasir al Din was as unsuccessful as any other Eurasian ruler at escaping subordination by the West. England forced him to abandon all claims to Afghanistan, and Russia forced him to give up claims in Central Asia.

Afghanistan continued to play a key role in British-Russian imperial rivalry in southern Eurasia. England was extending its control of the Indian subcontinent northward to Punjab and Kashmir at the same time that Russia was consolidating its rule over the Caucasus and Central Asia. Afghanistan was caught in the middle. In 1878, when Afghan rulers accepted a diplomatic mission from Russia but not from Britain, British forces invaded. The British defeated the Afghan army, mollified the emir with an annual subsidy, and began to dictate Afghan foreign policy.

POLITICAL DEVELOPMENTS AND FOREIGN AFFAIRS

Alexander II (1855–1881) succeeded his father in the middle of the Crimean War, with Sevastopol falling to the invaders soon after he became Tsar. The Russian army was far from defeated, but there was strong opposition to war in the Russian public (which thought the war pointless) and in the government (which thought it too expensive). Moreover, Austria, which had sent its own army into Wallachia and Moldavia after Russia had withdrawn, began to indicate that it might join the alliance against Russia. In consequence, Alexander decided to end the war. In March 1856, he signed the Treaty of Paris in which Russia lost all its gains from its victory over the Turks in 1829: territory on the mouth of the Danube, the exclusive right to represent Christians in the Ottoman Empire, and the right to keep a fleet on the Black Sea. Russia was even forced to dismantle its fortified ports. Russia was militarily humiliated and diplomatically isolated.

Domestically, Alexander immediately reversed many of his father's most repressive acts, and began to plan fundamental reforms. The most overdue reform in Russian society was the emancipation of the serfs, and in late 1856, Alexander took up the peasant question, as his father had, by establishing a secret committee. The first public announcement came in 1857: The government officially declared that although the nobility were rightful owners of their land they would be required to sell some of it to their former serfs when emancipation came. Gentry commissions that began to meet in 1858 resisted the idea of emancipation, especially one that granted land to the peasantry, but the public press emphasized the need for freed serfs to be given land of their own.

Even after Alexander II forbade the press to discuss emancipation, the question remained in the public mind thanks to Aleksandr Herzen. Herzen had begun to publish the *Bell* (*Kolokol*), a journal of independent opinion by the editors and news sent by Russian correspondents. Though outlawed in Russia, the *Bell* was smuggled into the country and was avidly read as the only source of uncensored news. The Tsar himself was rumored to read it, and even some of his own officials wrote anonymous letters criticizing government policy. In the *Bell*, Herzen strenuously promoted a landed emancipation.

Planning for emancipation continued in the Ministry of Interior, and, when it was publicly announced in March, 1861, it did, indeed, provide the peasants with land. The terms of the reform, however, favored the nobility in every way. First, the transition would be gradual. For two years, peasants would continue as before, under the authority of their landlord and owing the same labor and cash obligations. Second, the law recognized that all land was legally owned by the noble landlords, and former serfs would have to pay the full value of any land that they acquired. Third, the nobility determined (within some broad guidelines) both the price of the land and how it would be divided.

Emancipation of the serfs was followed by a fundamental reform of the army. In 1861, the standard term of military service was set at fifteen years, and a system of reserves implemented, significantly reducing the size (and cost) of the standing army. Military education was enhanced at all levels, and all inductees were given a primary education. The command structure of the army was decentralized; field officers were allowed more initiative, and regiments were divided into smaller, more mobile tactical units.

In 1863, Alexander II supervised a major reorganization of local government that allowed for greater public participation than ever before. Elective bodies (singular, *zemstvo*) were established at both the county and provincial level and were given the responsibility for general economic development and social welfare. Zemstvo boards maintained roads and bridges, built prisons, hospitals, and schools, and promoted industry, commerce, and agriculture. At the county level, a zemstvo assembly was elected by landowners, wealthy towndwellers, and peasants. The assembly, which met only once a year, elected an executive board that administered the county on a daily basis. The provincial zemstvo assemblies were indirectly elected by the county assemblies, and each chose a provincial executive board. In 1870, city government was reorganized according to the same principles.

Although they represented a significant step forward, the zemstvo reforms left much to be desired from the perspective of popular sovereignty and self-government. Zemstvos had no executive powers and limited funds. The Ministry of the Interior still controlled the police and administered the law, and the Minister had wide latitude to intervene in zemstvo affairs, including final approval of zemstvo chairpersons. Furthermore, zemstvo institutions were dominated by the nobility; 42 percent of county zemstvo members and 74 percent of provincial zemstvo members were nobles. Significantly, no provision was made for a national zemstvo assembly which could have cultivated a closer bond between the government and civil society.

In 1864, the judicial system was completely restructured. Formerly, justice had been an administrative function. Petitions, documents, or police reports were submitted to the local office of the Ministry of Justice, and suits were decided and guilt or innocence determined by ministry officials in complete secrecy. The judicial reform of 1864 opened the system to popular involvement. At the local level, the county zemstvo appointed a justice of the peace to deal with minor crimes. For more serious cases, courts were established at the county, regional, and provincial levels, with the Imperial Senate as the court of last appeal. Judges at all levels were chosen by the Minister of Justice, but they were professional jurists appointed for life, and hence less subject to political interference. Trials were open to the public, parties in civil disputes and defendants in criminal trials were able to speak in court and to hire lawyers to represent them. Juries, drawn from the general population, heard all criminal cases except those involving political crimes.

Following the Crimean War, Russia was diplomatically isolated. France and the Ottoman Empire were traditional enemies of Russia, England had become Russia's principal competitor for influence in Eurasia, Austria had declared its enmity during the Crimean War, and Prussia had been alienated by Nicholas I when he had supported Austria in 1850. Relations with Europe worsened when, in 1863, Russian forces invaded Poland to put down a nationalist uprising. The Polish rebels won sympathy across Europe, especially in France and England. Only Prussia was supportive of Russia's actions. Although Bismarck was concerned about nationalism spreading to Polish regions in Prussia, he had other motives for cultivating a friendship with Russia. Bismarck wanted to unify the German Confederation into a single German state, and he remembered Russia's role in blocking such a development in 1850. His support paid off; this time Russia stood aside while Bismarck created the German Empire. Bismarck also supported Alexander's announcement in the late 1860s that he intended to abrogate the Treaty of Paris and rebuild a Russian navy on the Black Sea.

Nationalist impulses in the Balkans drew Russia into yet another war with Turkey. In 1875, Herzegovina, Bosnia, and Bulgaria revolted against Turkish rule, and the semi-autonomous nations of Serbia and Montenegro went to war in their support. The following year Ottoman forces suppressed the Bulgarian rebellion and defeated Serbia. At this point, conservative elements in Russian society began vociferously to advocate Panslavism, the idea that all the Slavic peoples should be liberated and united under Russian leadership. Alexander II was as leery of Panslavism as his father had been of Slavophilism, but he felt it necessary to respond to Turkish aggression, and he declared war on Turkey in 1877. Russian forces won a decisive victory in Bulgaria and then marched on Constantinople, forcing the sultan to sue for peace. The Treaty of San Stefano (1878) ceded to Russia southern Bessarabia and additional territory in the Caucasus. Serbia, Montenegro, and Romania gained full independence. Herzegovina, Bosnia, and Bulgaria were made autonomous provinces. Bulgaria was to be occupied and protected by Russia for two years.

This outcome was entirely unacceptable to Austria, and the other great powers were none too pleased at Russia's gains. A Congress of the great powers was held in Berlin in 1878, and it severely revised the Treaty of San Stefano. Serbia and Montenegro were reduced in size. Austria was given the right to occupy Bosnia and Herzegovina. Bulgaria was divided into three parts, and only a much-reduced Bulgaria north of the Balkan mountains was made autonomous. Alexander's reign ended where it had begun, with Russia still isolated from Europe.

Russian foreign policy was far more successful in the east than in the west. In the northern Caucasus, Russia's superior numbers, resources, and weapons finally took their toll on the native resistance movements. In 1859, the charismatic Chechen leader, Shamil, was defeated and captured, and the region was fully subordinated. In Central Asia, Russia subordinated the Khanates of Bukhara, Kokand, and Khiva. The city of Tashkent was taken in 1865, and it was made the capital of a new province, Turkestan, and a base of operations from which to annex the entire region. In 1868, Russian forces defeated the Emir of Bukhara and annexed a large part of his territory, including Samarkand. A much smaller Emirate retained its independence under Russian "protection." In 1873, Russia treated the Khanate of Khiva in the same way, while in 1876, the Khan of Kokand was deposed and his territory entirely absorbed into Russian Turkestan. In 1881, Russia annexed the territory between the Aral and Caspian Seas. Russia had now expanded to the borders of outer Eurasia: Iran, Afghanistan, and China.

During the Arrow War and Second Opium War, Russia's ambassador, Count Nikolai Ignatiev, presented himself as a friendly neighbor anxious to mediate between China and the invading British and French. While helping to negotiate the Treaty of Aigun (1858), Ignatiev arranged for China to cede to Russia the territory north of the Amur and east of the Ussuri Rivers, more than 300,000 square miles of territory. Besides being rich in natural resources, the Amur region was strategically significant: Russia gained a border with Korea and secured better access to the Pacific Ocean. Khabarovsk was founded in 1858 and Vladivostok in 1860. Then, in the Treaty of Beijing (1860), Russia was granted the same commercial, travel, and diplomatic concessions that Britain and France had secured.

The only region from which Russia withdrew was North America. Russian officials had decided that the North American continent was too distant and too expensive to colonize, and that future conflict with the United States would result from any further attempts to expand. In 1867, Alexander sold Alaska to the United States for seven million dollars.

RELIGION AND CULTURE

Public education continued to be a high priority for the government. In 1862, Alexander promulgated a law requiring the establishment of school boards in all localities for the purpose of providing primary education, and teacher training schools were set up to provide teachers for them. The results were impressive. In 1856, there had been eight thousand primary schools with a half a million students; in 1878 there were almost twenty-five thousand schools and more than one million students. The government, concerned by the possibility that education could produce subversion, however, strictly regulated the curriculum. In 1862, the government, fearing subversion, brought an end to the Sunday School movement, a voluntary effort in which educated Russians taught basic literacy to peasants. State-organized primary schools imparted only a basic knowledge of reading, writing, and arithmetic. Fees were charged, attendance was voluntary, and the law required that religion, taught by priests, be included in the curriculum.

A similar conservative attitude prevailed in secondary and higher education. In an attempt to restrict university enrollment to the nobility and the wealthy, the Ministry of Education made a gymnasium education a requirement for admission. Gymnasia, which emphasized Greek and Latin, were the preserve of the nobility and were thought to foster conservative values. Realschules (high schools on the German model), which taught modern science, math, and technical subjects, were favored by the more practical non-noble classes, and were suspected of fostering liberal ideas.

Literacy grew rapidly among all segments of the population. Between 1864 and 1875, the number of booksellers grew from 63 to 611. Russians with primary educations read luboks, which evolved over the century from one-page broadsides with more illustrations than text to inexpensive books that were mostly text. Luboks presented folktales, religious stories, and tales of adventure in exotic lands. Russia's educated elite continued to subscribe to "thick journals," which published literary and social criticism as well as poetry, short stories, and novels in serial form.

In 1858, Alexander announced a policy of freedom of speech, but he had no real intention of relaxing government control of social thought. In 1865, "temporary rules" for censorship were announced, which remained in effect until 1905. Publishers were allowed to print material without prior approval, but there was a catch. Under the old system of preliminary censorship there was no penalty for submitting a book to the censors that they found unacceptable; it simply was disapproved. Under the new system, publishers of inappropriate material were criminally liable to fines and imprisonment if they broke the "temporary rules." Editors and publishers, therefore, had to censor themselves.

Consistent with the new hard-edged attitudes of the "age of materialism," Russian social thought became more aggressive. Slavophilism became politicized. Ivan Aksakov and Iurii Samarin continued to idealize the peasantry and to celebrate the communal ethos of the Russian Orthodox Church, but they also sharply criticized all kinds of imitation of the West, strongly supported the tsarist monarchy, and promoted Orthodoxy as the state religion. Their only criticism of the existing system was directed against the bureaucracy, which they felt to be too rationalistic and westernized.

Nikolai Danilevskii went even further. In *Russia and Europe* (1869), he applied the biological concepts of scientific racism to Slavophilism. Danilevskii argued that world history was the story of the rise and fall of civilizations based upon the lifecycle of the races who made them. The European race, he argued, was growing old and decrepit, while the Slavs were a young people now rising to greatness. Slavs, he said, would be the next race to dominate the world. Danilevskii's ideas were adopted by the Panslavs who used the notion of Slavic racial unity to justify their demand that Russia should liberate the Southern Slavs from Ottoman rule.

The "westernizing" trend in Russian society also changed with the times, adopting the positivism, materialism, and atheism of the West. Radical social critics tended to study the natural sciences while at the university. Liberal politics and economics—the ideology of the European middle class—had little appeal for Russian intellectuals. Instead, they embraced the most current and idealistic western doctrines, including anarchism, socialism, feminism, and radical democracy.

Perhaps the greatest influence on the westernizers was Aleksandr Herzen, who had left Russia an advocate of liberal westernization. Once in Europe however, he was appalled by the condition of the working classes, repelled by the philistine smugness of the middle class, and dismayed by the repression of the Revolution of 1848. Herzen created an alternative to the western model by making the Slavophile vision of the communal and cooperative peasant mir the basis of a revolutionary ideology. Herzen argued that if the Russian autocracy were eliminated, and the peasant mir allowed to flourish, Russia would be transformed directly into a socialist society without having to experience the evils of capitalism.

Just as Herzen had played a key role in promoting the emancipation of the serfs, so also was he a leader in criticizing the form in which it finally came. In June 1861, only months after the emancipation, Herzen argued that the reforms had not gone far enough. Peasants, he said, needed "land and freedom." They should have been given all the land, and they should not have been forced to pay for it. In November, Herzen called on progressive Russians to "go to the people" to educate them and to help them struggle against the oppressive regime.

Within Russia, the most influential progressive was Nikolai Chernyshevskii, son of a parish priest from Saratov. After earning a master's degree from St. Petersburg University, Chernyshevskii became the literary criticism editor of the *Contemporary*, the leading liberal thick journal. An atheist, a materialist, and a positivist, Chernyshevskii fervently promoted the utilitarian approach to literature. He argued that art should portray the world realistically, criticize political and social injustice, and offer progressive solutions to contemporary problems. While in prison in 1862 to 1863 for his ideas, Chernyshevskii practiced what he preached. He wrote a novel, *What is to be Done,* which advocated socialism, sexual equality, service to society, and the scientific outlook. He portrayed the lives of young people who rose above prejudice and convention and sacrificed themselves in pursuit of their ideals.

In high literature, the period from 1848 to 1881 was the age of the novel. Russian novelists, particularly Turgenev, Dostoyevsky, and Tolstoy, acquired a wide European readership. Many critics believed that the Russians had become Europe's leading masters of the realistic novel. Ivan Turgenev, the first of the triumvirate, came from a gentry family from central Russia. He achieved fame for *Sportsman's Sketches* (1851), a collection of essays remarkable for their descriptions of nature and sympathetic portrayal of serfs. In 1852, he was arrested for a "subversive" essay on Gogol. After spending five years confined to his estate, Turgenev emigrated to Germany and later to France. Literary critics emphasize Turgenev's mastery of form and his approach to the novel as a work of art. The general public appreciated the topicality of his works, especially *Fathers and Sons* (1862), which contrasted the romantic idealism of the older generation with the scientific nihilism of the generation of the 1860s.

Fyodor Dostoyevsky experienced a religious conversion while in prison, which transformed him from a liberal westernizer into a Russian nationalist and critic of modernity.

Though considered a realistic writer, Dostoyevsky's works are filled with fantasies and allegories, and he used his novels as vehicles for philosophical and religious discourse. His novels, most notably *Crime and Punishment* (1866) and *The Brothers Karamazov* (1879 to 1880), criticized modern rationalism and imparted a strong Christian message.

Leo Tolstoy, a titled aristocrat, studied at the University of Kazan and served in the army in the Caucasus and in the Crimean War. His novels *War and Peace* (1869) and *Anna Karenina* (1876) are unequaled masterpieces of realistic prose—in their descriptions both of the world and of the psychology of the characters. Tolstoy underwent a conversion experience soon after publishing *Anna Karenina,* and he developed his own form of Christianity. He thought that civilization was corrupting and states were evil; he advocated pacifism, anarchism, and a simple life based on manual labor.

Tolstoy and Dostoyevsky make an interesting contrast. Both could be described as "conservative Russian nationalists, fervent Christians, and masters of psychology," yet they arrived at these attitudes from two quite different points of view. Tolstoy criticized modern society from the Enlightenment standpoint that civilization is corrupting and nature is good; Dostoyevsky criticized modernity for its atheism and nihilism. Tolstoy celebrated the natural goodness of the Russian people and depicted Russian society as essentially healthy; Dostoyevsky glorified the beauty and tragedy of the Russian soul. Tolstoy thought of Jesus as a model human being and sought to put into practice the social ethics of the Gospels; Dostoyevsky was preoccupied with Jesus as the redeemer of sinful humanity. Tolstoy was interested in his characters' consciousness; Dostoyevsky was interested in their subconscious. Tolstoy argued that art should serve the people; Dostoyevsky believed in art for art's sake.

ROLES AND STATUS OF WOMEN

The Great Reforms did nothing to change the basic relationship between husband and wife, father and daughter. A married woman was allowed to travel only on her husband's passport, and therefore only with his permission. Women could not work or study outside the house without their husbands' explicit approval. Men chose the place of residence; a woman who left without her husband's consent could be legally forced to return, while a man could not be so constrained by his wife. Only the father's rank was passed to children; children of noble women who married non-nobles did not inherit their mother's title.

The "woman question," that is, the reevaluation of traditional attitudes regarding the role and status of women, came to Russia in the 1830s and 1840s via the novels of George Sand, and was first raised in the Russian press after the Crimean War. During the war, female nurses had served at the front (against strong opposition from conservatives). At the end of the war, the doctor who had supervised the Crimean War nurses published an article suggesting that women could serve socially useful functions besides those of wife and mother. His view was supported by an economist Maria Vernadskaia who thought women's labor was essential for economic progress. M. L. Mikhailov, the first to deal with the question systematically, argued that women were the intellectual equals of men, that physical differences made women neither inferior nor incompetent, that women should be allowed careers outside the home, and that they needed the same kind of liberal education as men. In the late 1850s, Maria Trubnikova, Nadezhda Stasova, and Anna Filosofova established a women's publishing cooperative that promoted the liberation of women from traditional restraints. They also set up courses for women, and Sunday schools to teach peasants to read and write.

The government responded quickly to the idea of women's education. In 1858, a system of secondary schools for women of all classes was established. The government did not adhere to the notion of women's liberation—they explicitly announced that Russian women were to be educated to be good mothers—but the curriculum did include the liberal arts. By 1881, 45 percent of secondary school students were women.

Women had never been allowed to enroll in universities in Russia, but soon after his accession to the throne, Alexander II gave permission to the general public to attend university lectures, and women began to avail themselves of this opportunity. The university reforms of 1863 continued to forbid women to enroll in degree programs, but in the 1860s, medical institutes began to train women as midwives. It was not until 1878 that women were allowed to take university courses for credit, but only three years later, women made up 20 percent of all university students.

In 1871, women were allowed by law to be teachers and to work in telegraph, railroad, post, and business offices. By the end of Alexander II's reign, it was no longer a novelty for middle-class women to be employed in offices and shops, but the female proportion of the workforce was still minuscule. The participation of working-class women in factory and workshop production was more significant. By the end of the century, 13 to 17 percent of the manufacturing workforce was female. In all fields of work, women were paid less than men for the same work, and they were the first to be fired when business slowed.

As in the previous period, there were many women writers, some of whom wrote best-sellers, but they were largely ignored by highbrow literary critics. Evgeniia Turnemir, a noblewoman who wrote under the surname of Tur, wrote short stories, essays, and books for children. Nadezhda Sokhanskaia, whose pen-name was Kokhanovskaia, wrote plays and stories about the provincial gentry of which she was a part. Maria Vilinskaia-Markovich, who wrote under the name Marko Vovchok, gained fame for collecting and publishing a volume of Ukrainian folk-tales, which Ivan Turgenev thought important enough to translate into Russian. She then wrote a series of stories of provincial lives that idealized the peasantry and vilified the landowning gentry. Nadezhda Khvoschinskaia, who published prose under the name V. Krestovskii, wrote fiction mainly about the "new woman" trying to escape from the oppression of traditional patriarchal society. Avdotia Panaeva-Golovachova, who worked on the staff of the *Contemporary* for most of its existence, published novels and stories whose titles speak for themselves: "A Monster of a Husband," and "Domestic Hell."

In Russia's largest cities, a small but much-noticed subculture arose in which women and men attempted to put feminist ideals into practice. Instead of wearing dresses made of bright colored satin or crinolines with hoop skirts, corsets, and tightly gathered waists, young feminists wore formless, dark woolen dresses. Instead of elaborate hair styles, they cut their hair short. Young women often formed collectives and shared living quarters, supporting themselves as teachers and office workers. To escape the control of fathers who attempted to regulate their lives, women made "fictitious marriages" with sympathetic men. Such marriages were legally made but were not observed. Intended solely to free a woman from the legal authority of her father, there was no subsequent relationship between the couple.

SOCIAL AND ECONOMIC DEVELOPMENTS

One of the goals of the Great Reforms had been to dissolve the boundaries between Russia's social estates, and the reform of the judicial system was a big step forward in that regard. The corporate system established by Catherine II, in which nobles and towndwellers were judged in courts of their peers, was replaced by a system in which all citizens of the empire were equal before the law. This was reinforced in 1874 when Alexander decreed that all males over the age of twenty-one were subject to conscription. Soldiers were drawn not only from the peasantry and poll-tax-paying residents of towns, but from the nobility, the propertied middle class, and formerly exempt ethnic groups.

The emancipation and the great reforms began a relative decline in the status and power of the nobility. The very act of emancipation showed that the interests of the nobility were no longer sacrosanct, and the principle of equality of all citizens eroded nobles' sense of pre-eminence. Nevertheless, the nobility continued as Russia's elite class. They still provided the highest levels of the civil service and the officer corps, and they were vastly overrepresented in zemstvo assemblies and executive boards.

Even though the nobility lost land and labor power, they were allowed to manage the emancipation in their own interests. The prices nobles set on the land were not based on its real economic value (that is, the value of crops that could be produced from it) but on the amount of rents and fees they had been able to extract in the past (which were often subsidized by peasant income from manufacturing or trade). Within government-mandated maximums and minimums, landlords had wide latitude to arrange things in their own interest. In the southern black earth regions, nobles kept as much land as possible. In the north where land was less productive, landlords sold as much as they could. Overall, peasants lost 20 percent of the land they formerly cultivated. In the end, 30,000 landlords ended up with 256,000,000 acres of land, while 20,000,000 serfs retained 313,000,000 acres. Landlords naturally chose to keep the best land for themselves.

The Great Reforms accelerated the rise of a civil society whose emergence had been underway at least since the reign of Catherine the Great. The numbers of professionals—teachers, lawyers, doctors, agronomists—rose dramatically. Equally important, the new professions were increasingly independent of the government. Lawyers were no longer employees of the Ministry of Justice. Teachers, doctors, and agronomists were hired by the zemstvos.

A new social stratum, known as the *raznochintsy* also emerged as a significant social force. Meaning "people of various ranks," the term had been in use for almost two centuries to refer to people who did not fit into the officially recognized categories of Russian society. In the reign of Peter I, the term referred mostly to retired soldiers and lower-ranking officials who had not advanced far enough in the Table of Ranks to have earned noble status. After 1818, raznochintsy also referred to the children of those who had achieved personal noble status. By the middle of the century, it was used to refer to anyone who had gained an education and earned a living through mental labor but was not of noble blood. In the second half of the nineteenth century, the intelligentsia was no longer the exclusive preserve of the nobility, but was increasingly dominated by raznochintsy.

Under the influence of the Great Reforms, the merchant estate began to lose its caste-like character. In addition to becoming subject to the same legal system and the same conscription obligations as other citizens, merchants also lost the exclusive right to trade (that is, among town dwellers; nobles and peasants had always had that right). In addition, reorganization of local government deprived the merchantry of their past monopoly on political power and forced them to compete with other social groups to be elected to city assemblies.

The principle of equality of all citizens was not applied to the peasantry. Serfs were given the same rights as state peasants—the right to marry, to engage in trade, to own property, to sign contracts, and to sue and be sued. Nevertheless, all peasants continued to pay the poll tax and they were subject to their own system of courts. Moreover, the government retained the communal principles of the traditional mir. Land was not purchased by the individual peasant household, but by the mir. The skhod, therefore, continued to apportion taxes, organize farm labor, and redistribute the land. Peasants were still tied to the land; they could not leave the mir without the skhod's permission. On the other hand, the volost, a new unit of local government, was created to administer the newly freed serfs. Volost officials were elected by the peasants, subject to Ministry of Interior approval. The volost was an extension of the government, not of the peasant community, and it had jurisdiction over all the mirs within its territory. Volost courts judged peasants according to customary law.

The cost of land imposed a huge burden on former serfs. Overall, Russian peasants were required to pay 680 million rubles for land that had an economic value of only 460 million. Of this amount, 20 percent was paid directly by the peasants to the lord; the remaining 80 percent was given to the landlord in the form of a government bond. The peasants then made redemption payments to pay off their debt to the government. Because the productive capacity of the land was so much less than the price charged, it was impossible to pay the debt. Redemption payments were chronically in arrears, and peasants were continually discontented.

The Russian autocracy was fully aware of the dangers of rapid social and economic change. Alexander was, of course, interested in the long-run prosperity of his empire, but he wanted to avoid the corrosive effects that an unregulated Industrial Revolution had produced in western Europe: a politically and socially presumptuous middle class, an impoverished and radical working class, and a general loss of respect for traditional values. In pursuit of a uniquely Russian path to industrial development, Alexander instituted policies that postponed an economic take-off for a generation.

The economy, however, was not stagnant. Between 1865 and 1880, the population grew by 22 percent from 75 to 98 million. The length of railroad track grew by 83 percent, coal production by 33 percent, and production of cotton goods by 72 percent. However, grain production increased by only 14 percent, and the balance of payments surplus (45 million rubles in 1865) had turned into a deficit (124 million rubles in 1880).

Nor was the Russian working class as passive as Alexander II no doubt wished. Between 1861 and 1865, there were 85 strikes or other work disruptions. In May 1870, 800 textile workers went on strike in St. Petersburg, and between 1870 and 1875, there were 175 strikes across the empire. In 1878, 50 strikes occurred, and the next year, 60. The most strike-prone industries were textile production, metal-working, and the railroads.

PEOPLES OF THE EMPIRE

The Russification policies of Nicholas I were intensified in the reign of Alexander II. After the Polish rebellion of 1863, the government began an all-out attack on Polish national culture. Many nobles were arrested and exiled, and Polish peasants, when emancipated, were given a greater proportion of the land than in the rest of Russia. The Catholic Church was forced to sever its connections with Rome, and many Uniate Church communities were forcibly converted to Orthodoxy. Almost all Polish officials were fired and replaced with Russians, and Russian was made the official language both in the administration and in the educational system. Even primary schools were supposed to use Russian, although the law could not be systematically enforced. Ukraine suffered as well. In 1863, the Ukrainian language was forbidden in any publication other than literature and folklore. In 1876, Ukrainian books could no longer be imported, and Ukrainian could not be used in theaters.

The government was more tolerant of the non-Slavic nations of the empire. The Finnish Diet met regularly after 1863. It extended its educational system, fostered the Finnish language, provided for freedom of religion, and even established its own army. In the Caucasus, there was little interference with the development of Georgian and Armenian national cultures. In Central Asia, the Russian government did not attempt to Russify education or local administration and tolerated Islamic religion and law. The peoples of Central Asia presented no *nationalist* challenge to the empire; their identities were built on tribe and religion, not on nation.

Alexander II began his reign by signaling a new toleration toward Jews. In 1859, Jewish parents were allowed to withdraw their children from religious instruction in the public schools. In 1861, Jewish children younger than fourteen could not be converted to Ortho-doxy without their parents' consent. Jews were allowed to live in some cities within the Pale of Settlement (such as Kiev) from which they had been excluded. Jews were allowed greater access to education. In 1853, little more than 1 percent of secondary school enrollment was Jewish, but by 1873 this had increased to 13 percent. On the other hand, the Pale remained in place, and Jews continued to be considered aliens. Furthermore, with the rise of Panslavism and scientific racism hostility toward Jews increased in the general population. In 1871, the police did not intervene to stop a three-day riot (pogrom) against the Jewish community, which the local city leaders blamed on "Jewish exploitation." Worse was to come.

RADICALS AND REBELS

During the reign of Nicholas I, opponents of the autocracy had written poems, essays, and treatises to be read by other members of the intelligentsia. In the reign of Alexander II, some critics of the regime began to call for revolution; not only did they attempt to spread their ideas among ordinary people, they also made plans to take direct action against the regime. The new attitude was first revealed in the fall of 1861, following the disillusionment of the intelligentsia with the terms of emancipation, when anonymous flyers and pamphlets were secretly posted and scattered around the streets of the capital. One titled "To the Young Gen-eration" denounced the autocracy and explained that a revolution might be necessary to overthrow it. Another, "Young Russia," called upon Russians to kill the Tsar and his govern-ment. At the same time, the universities were swept with demonstrations and riots.

The government turned to repression. In 1862, Nikolai Chernyshevskii was imprisoned. Universities were brought under tighter control. In 1863, women were excluded from at-tending lectures in universities, and hundreds of young Russian women traveled to Switzer-land to study. The conflict escalated, and in 1864 a circle of students, led by Nikolai Ishutin began to talk about killing the Tsar and forcing the government to summon a zemskii sobor (such as had elected Michael Romanov as tsar in 1613.) They talked of joining forces with the peasantry to eliminate the monarchy and build a decentralized, socialist society. Ishutin's group included his cousin, Dmitrii Karakozov, who, without the group's knowledge, man-aged to fire a pistol at the Tsar in 1866. Scores of their associates were arrested, including thirty-nine women.

Soon after, Sergei Nechaev, the son of a housepainter from Ivanovo, created plans for a vast underground network of secret revolutionary cells which aimed at instigating a mas-sive peasant rebellion. Most of the conspiracy was a figment of Nechaev's imagination, but his charismatic personality attracted a loyal following who believed that such an organiza-tion existed. Nechaev's downfall came when he arranged the murder of a disloyal associate, attracting the attention of the police. While the police arrested and tried seventy-nine people (including thirty women) for membership in his circles, Nechaev escaped to Europe, where he managed to convince Mikhail Bakunin that his organization was real. In 1872, Nechaev was extradited from Switzerland, and he spent the rest of his life in prison.

By the early 1870s, opposition to the autocracy began to assume the character of a mass movement. Universities had long been breeding grounds for counter-cultural ideas, and mass expulsions had vastly increased the numbers of unemployed young idealists with no career opportunities ahead of them. Then, in 1873, the Tsar recalled Russian students who had been studying abroad, and among those who returned were the many young Russian women who had been radicalized by their experience in Switzerland. There was a sense among this mass of alienated young people that drastic measures had to be taken. Women's liberation had progressed with painful slowness, and society was becoming more repressive. Moreover, under the influence of Herzen's idea that the Russian peasant commune was the building block of a future socialist society, they began to be alarmed at the intrusion of capitalism and market values in the countryside. All in all, they came to the conclusion that they had to act immediately if they were to save Russia and put their native land at the forefront of European progress. Ten years earlier, Herzen had called upon the intelligentsia to "go to the people"; in 1873, they were ready to do just that.

"Russian populism" (*narodnichestvo*), was not a unified or organized movement. Two circles (one organized by Nikolai Chaikovskii, one by Aleksandr Dolgushin) promoted the idea that progressives should go out among the people and catalyze a mass movement against the tsarist regime, but they were neither the organizers nor the cause of the "Movement to the People." Hundreds and perhaps thousands of young people spontaneously decided to travel to the countryside in the summers of 1873 and 1874. Some, under the influence of Petr Lavrov, a former political exile who had emigrated to the west, believed that the people must make the revolution on their own initiative, and the role of the intelligentsia was to share their knowledge with the masses. Others were convinced by Mikhail Bakunin that the people were ready to rise up, and all they needed was the spark that the radical intelligentsia could provide. Some young people went to teach literacy and primary education, some went to teach socialism, and some went to incite immediate insurrection.

They failed. The peasants were distrustful of the intelligentsia, whom they perceived as intrusive outsiders. In some cases, peasants took advantage of the educational efforts of the populists, but they were not attracted to the populists' idea of socialism. When the populists did manage to incite a revolt, the results were disastrous. In the Chigirin district, one populist called on the peasants to rise up against the landlords, showing them a (forged) proclamation from the Tsar which declared that all the land belonged to the peasantry. This led to the most widespread peasant uprising of Alexander's reign and to executions, mass punishments, and repression.

Mass arrests in the summers of 1873 and 1874 effectively brought the "Movement to the People" to an end. More than eight hundred people were arrested, and two major trials were held. After sentences were handed down, the Tsar, making a mockery of his own legal reforms, personally intervened. He revised many of the penalties upward and re-arrested and deported many of those who had been acquitted. Five women were condemned to hard labor, the first time in Russian history that women had been so punished. In the aftermath, the radical intelligentsia became more politically focused. An underground political party, Zemlia i Volia ("Land and Freedom"), was created to coordinate revolutionary activities more effectively.

Many wanted to continue to make appeals to workers and peasants, but some proposed a direct attack upon the government through the assassination of leading officials. In 1878, Vera Zasulich, to avenge the brutal treatment of a political prisoner, shot and seriously wounded the St. Petersburg Chief of Police. Although there was no doubt of her guilt, a jury acquitted her of all charges (revealing the profound alienation of civil society from the monarchy). The crowd protected her from re-arrest, and Zasulich managed to escape abroad. The following year, Sergei Kravchinskii assassinated the head of the Third Department and fled abroad before he could be arrested.

Later in 1879 the Zemlia i Volia party split into two factions. The Chernyi Peredel ("Black Repartition") chose to work for popular revolution and advocated continued organizational work among the laboring masses. Narodnaia Volia (the "People's Will"), however, was determined to use assassination to punish the government and frighten it into reform. The executive committee of Narodnaia Volia began to plan the assassination of Alexander II. After many failed attempts and close calls, Alexander was killed by a bomb in 1881.

CONCLUSION

In the last decade of his reign, Alexander II continued to tinker with administrative reforms and had implemented polices aimed at fostering civil society. Yet he also refused to countenance the creation of a constitution or a representative assembly that might infringe on his personal rule. The alienation of Russia's incipient civil society from the tsar, as shown by the sympathy given to revolutionaries like Vera Zasulich, led Alexander's interior minister, Mikhail Loris-Melikov, to suggest a compromise. In 1880, just after his appointment, Loris-Melikov proposed the creation of two legislative commissions which would review plans for administrative and economic reform. These commissions would include hand-picked representatives of civil society as well as government officials. Alexander II approved the plan on March 1, 1881, the very day of his assassination. His heir and successor, Alexander III, soon vetoed it.

Some historians have thought it ironic that the revolutionaries, by assassinating Alexander II, prevented the realization of just the sort of constitutional reform they had been hoping to force. This was not the case, however. The so-called "Loris-Melikov Constitution" would not have established a fundamental law, a representative assembly, or an independent legislature. Even if Narodnaia Volia had not succeeded that day, and the reforms had been implemented, the revolutionary movement would have surely have continued, and Russian civil society would have continued to sympathize with it.

_____ TEXT DOCUMENTS _____

Vernadskaia, "Destiny of Women"

Maria Vernadskaia (1831–1860), the first Russian woman to make a career as a professional economist, was also a pioneer Russian feminist. She wrote this article in the late 1850s.

- What does Vernadskaia suggest are proper roles for women?
- How does she make her argument? What assumptions does she challenge?
- How does she conceive of the relation between the individual and society?

What is a man? A human being. What is a women? A strange question—she, of course, is also a human being. If that is so, if we decide to recognize woman as a human being, then all that is human in nature must be accessible to her, and it must be accessible in reality. A woman can feel, can think, can crave education, can understand the desire to become useful in some way. Finally, a woman can work and toil for her own benefit as well as for the benefit of the public. . . . If woman is the same sort of being as is man, then the principles of honor and morality should be the same for both.

No vices are exclusively man's or exclusively woman's. All people, whichever gender they are, are excited by the same passions. Therefore, all people are subject to the same vices when they yield to their passions, and they have the same virtues when they gain a victory over their passions. To be concerned with arranging a woman's life, with determining her social status, and with the fulfillment of special obligations invented for her by society means not to recognize her as fully human, however strange this may sound. . . .

The responsibilities of women, properly understood, are not so very complex and difficult. First of all, there is no such thing as purely womanly responsibilities; there are only human responsibilities. Every person, regardless of gender, has a duty to be useful, but to be useful is not easy: for this purpose it is necessary for people to work on themselves. Not only must they enrich their minds with knowledge, but they must also struggle constantly with their passions and bad inclinations, which exist to some degree in every person. One must study oneself and, according to one's tastes and capabilities, choose an occupation for oneself that would be useful for both family and society. Only when a person is truly useful, only when her work brings actual benefit to society—only then can she claim social rights and hope for freedom and independence, for only then would she be worthy of them. Useless members of society, regardless of their sex, will always be more or less subordinate, and to tell the truth, this is rightfully so. . . .

Take two children, a girl and a boy, from nearly any family. What beliefs are instilled in them? The boy is constantly told that he is a man, that it is a disgrace for him to cry or be afraid, and that he must exhibit the strength of his will because he is a man. As for the girl,

Source: Robin Bishna, Jehanne M Gheith, Christine Holden, and William G. Wagner, Eds. *Russian Women, 1698–1917. Experience and Expression, An Anthology of Sources* (Bloomington, IN: Indiana University Press, 2002), 35, 40, 41, 42. Reprinted with permission of Indiana University Press.

she always is commended for her sensitivity, until finally she begins to regard sensitivity as a virtue. Hence, she becomes maudlin, always with a gushing heart, and ultimately drives herself to some kind of nervous sentimentality. What is at fault here—nature or education? The same things can happen with the imagination. Because of some peculiar preconceived notion, educators focus on developing a girl's imagination. But if you raise the girl in the same way as the boy, teach her the necessity of having a strong will, and develop both her imagination and intellect, these instilled shortcomings will disappear on their own.

"Fine," say many, "that's all wonderful. But who will watch the household and cherish the children if women begin to occupy themselves with other pursuits?" The answer is: those women who have the ability and the inclination to do so will rear children and manage their households. What would then happen to the households and children whose mothers are unfit for those tasks? This question may be answered by posing another: are there not, at the present time, just as many households which are poorly managed and where children are brought up in a haphazard manner? Think about it, and immediately several examples will come to mind. What do these households and children stand to lose if they no longer are subjected to inept supervision? I think that they will lose nothing, on the contrary, they will gain something. In the meantime, bad housewives and bad mothers can become wonderful actresses, doctors, merchants, or scholars and, instead of being a burden, can be a real asset to society.

Nearly all of men's professions are accessible to women, and women cannot use their physical weakness as an excuse because, as civilization progresses, the advantages and even the necessity of physical strength are becoming less and less important. Even a very weak woman, if she has a revolver in her hands, can overcome the strongest of savages armed only with a tomahawk. A woman who sits in a quiet and comfortable train carriage will reach her destination faster than the strongest man on horseback.

With time, the value of brute strength will lessen even more; as for moral strength, women even now are equal to men. If society would only realize that women must be useful, that they must work, that they are created not just for pleasure but also for serious activity–then women would take an equal place to men in society and would have equal rights, for anyone who works for the benefit of others is entitled to having a place in society commensurate with his or her contribution to it.

Emancipation of the Serfs

The following excerpt includes some of the provisions of the 1861 law that emancipated the Russian serfs.

- How will peasant life be organized and administered?
- How will the new order in the countryside be different from the past? In what ways will it be similar?
- What might be the social and economic consequences of this reform?

46. The administration of the village community is composed of: (a) The village assembly, (b) The village elder [starosta]. In addition, those communities that deem it necessary may have: special tax-gatherers; overseers of the granaries, schools, and infirmaries; forest and field wardens; village clerks, and so forth.

47. The "village assembly" is composed of the peasant-householders belonging to the village community and, in addition, all elected village officials.

51. Under the jurisdiction of the village assembly are: (a) The election of village officials and the appointment of delegates to the volost assembly. (b) Decisions concerning the expulsion of harmful and pernicious members from the community; the temporary removal of peasants from participation in the assemblies, for not more than three years. (c) The release of members from the community and the acceptance of new ones. (d) The appointment of guardians and trustees; the verification of their actions. (e) The settlement of family divisions [of property]. (f) Matters relating to communal utilization of land belonging to the commune, that is: the redistribution of land, the imposition and removal of tiaglo, the final distribution of communal land into permanent plots and so forth. (g) Where the land is under plot or household (hereditary) utilization, the disposition of plots of communal land that for any reason remain idle or are not under household utilization. (h) Consultations and petitions concerning community needs, the organization of public services, care for the poor, and instruction in reading and writing. (i) The transmission to the appropriate office of complaints and requests dealing with community affairs, through special delegates. (j) The fixing of levies for communal expenses. (k) The apportionment of all fiscal taxes, land, and communal monetary levies, and likewise the land and communal obligations in kind imposed upon peasants; and the systematic keeping of accounts for the aforesaid taxes and levies. (l) The checking of the accounts of officials elected by the village community, and the fixing of a salary or other recompense for their services. (m) Matters dealing with the discharge of recruit obligations, to the extent that they concern the village community. (n) The apportionment of obrok and obligatory labor services by tiaglo [here meaning a household taxpaying unit], by souls, or in any other customary manner, wherever the obligations to the estate owner are discharged through the joint responsibility of the entire community. (o) The taking of measures for the prevention and recovery of arrears. (p) The allocation of loans from the village reserve storehouses and of sundry kinds of assistance. (q) The bestowal of power of attorney for representing the community in legal matters.

Source: George Vernadsky, *A Source Book for Russian History from Early Times to 1917, Vol. 3, Alexander II to the February Revolution* (New Haven, CT: Yale University Press, 1972), 600–602. © Yale University Press. Reprinted with permission.

54.   For deciding the following matters, the consent of not less than two-thirds of all peasants having a vote in the [village] assembly is required: (a) Replacing communal utilization of land by plot or household (hereditary) utilization. (b) Distributing communal land into permanent hereditary plots. (c) Redistributing communal land. (d) Establishing communal voluntary associations and using communal capital. (e) Expelling pernicious peasants from the community and placing them at the disposal of the government

130.   For the release of peasants from the village communities the following general conditions must be observed: (a) A peasant who wishes to receive his release from the community, after renouncing forever his share in the communal allotment must give up the plot of land he was using. . . . (c) The family of the person released must not be in arrears in the payment of fiscal, land, or communal taxes, and in addition his own taxes must be paid up to January 1 of the following year. (d) There must not be, upon the person released, any uncontested private proceedings or liabilities which have been presented before the volost administration. (e) The person released must not be under trial or investigation. (f) The parents of the person released must consent to his release. (g) Those in the family of the released peasant who are underage or otherwise incapable of working, and who remain in the community, must be guaranteed a means of support. (h) The person wishing to obtain his release must present a certificate of acceptance from that community to which he is transferring.

169.   The apportionment of fiscal and land obligations, in money and in kind, among the peasants in the village community is done by the commune.

187.   Each village community, whether its land is utilized by the communal method or by the plot or household (hereditary) method, is jointly responsible for the strict discharge of fiscal, land, and communal obligations by each of its members.

The Gorchakov Circular

Prince Aleksandr Gorchakov (1798–1883) was a distinguished diplomat who became Russian Foreign Minister in 1856. He wrote this policy statement on Russia's mission in Central Asia for the Foreign Ministry in 1864.

- How does Gorchakov explain and justify the need for Russian expansion?
- How does this compare with earlier Russian attitudes toward the peoples of the steppe?
- What does this reveal regarding changes in Russian society?

The position of Russia in Central Asia is that of all civilized states which are brought into contact with half-savage nomad populations possessing no fixed social organization. In such cases, the more civilized state is forced in the interest of the security of its frontier and its commercial relations, to exercise a certain ascendancy over their turbulent and undesirable neighbors. Raids and acts of pillage must be put down. To do this, the tribes on the frontier must be reduced to a state of submission. This result once attained, these tribes take to more peaceful habits, but are in turn exposed to the attacks of the more distant tribes against whom the State is bound to protect them. Hence the necessity of distant, costly, and periodically recurring expeditions against an enemy whom his social organization makes it impossible to seize. If, the robbers once punished, the expedition is withdrawn, the lesson is soon forgotten; its withdrawal is put down to weakness. It is a peculiarity of Asiatics to respect nothing but visible and palpable force. The moral force of reasoning has no hold on them.

In order to put a stop to this state of permanent disorder, fortified posts are established in the midst of these hostile tribes, and an influence is brought to bear upon them which reduces them by degrees to a state of submission. But other more distant tribes beyond this outer line come in turn to threaten the same dangers, and necessitate the same measures of repression. The State is thus forced to choose between two alternatives—either to give up this endless labor, and to abandon its frontier to perpetual disturbance, or to plunge deeper and deeper into barbarous countries, when the difficulties and expenses increase with every step in advance.

Such has been the fate of every country which has found itself in a similar position. The United States in America, France in Algeria, Holland in her Colonies, England in India; all have been forced by imperious necessity into this onward march, where the greatest difficulty is to know where to stop.

Such have been the reasons which have led the Imperial Government to take up, first, a position resting, on one side, on the Syr Darya, on the other, the Lake of Issik Kul, and to strengthen these lines by advanced forts.

It has been judged indispensable that our two fortified lines, one extending from China to the Lake of Issik Kul the other from the Sea of Aral, along the Syr Darya, should be united by fortified points, so that all posts should be in a position of mutual support leaving no gap through which nomad tribes might make their inroads and depredations with impunity.

Source: Alexis Krausse, *Russia in Asia: A Record and a Study, 1558–1899* (New York: Henry Holt and Co., 1899), 224–225.

Our original frontier line along the Syr Darya to Fort Perovskii, on the one side, and on the other, to Lake Issik Kul had the drawback of being almost on the verge of the desert. It was broken by a wide gap between the two extreme points; it did not offer sufficient resources to our troops, and left unsettled tribes over the back with which any settled arrangement became impossible.

In spite of our unwillingness to extend our frontier, these motives had been powerful enough to induce the Imperial Government to establish this line between Issik Kul and the Sir Darya by fortifying the town of Chemkend, lately occupied by us. This line gives us a fertile country, partly inhabited by Kirghiz tribes, which have already accepted our rule, and it therefore offers favorable conditions for colonization, and the supply of provisions to our garrisons. In the second place, it puts us in the neighborhood of the agricultural and commercial population of Kokand.

Such are the interests which inspire the policy of our August master in Central Asia.

It is needless for me to lay stress on the interest which Russia evidently has not to increase her territory, and, above all, to avoid raising complications on her frontiers which can but delay and paralyze her domestic development. Very frequently of late years the civilization of these countries, which are her neighbors on the Continent of Asia, has been assigned to Russia as her special mission.

Breshkovskaia on the "Movement to the People"

Ekaterina Breshko-Breshkovskaia (1844–1934), one of the first generation of revolutionary populists, continued her political activism in the revolutionary movements of the early-twentieth century when she became known as "the grandmother of the Russian revolution." She emigrated from Russia in 1921.

- What does this reveal about the characteristics of the revolutionary intelligentsia in the 1870s?
- What does it reveal about their attitudes toward the peasantry?

Our home [an apartment she shared with other young women] had a reputation for hospitality and freedom, and the youth of Kiev liked it and often brought us new comrades and acquaintances.

As yet we had carried on no actual work of conspiracy in the house, though continually there were talks on revolutionary and social subjects. Once I found Axelrod dining with an

Source: Excerpts from Catherine Breshkovskaia, *Hidden Springs of the Russian Revolution*, edited by Lincoln Hutchinson. Copyright © 1931 by the Board of Trustees of the Leland Stanford Junior University. Used with the permission of Stanford: Stanford University Press, www.sug.org.

unknown gentleman. After everybody had left, Axelrod, who was at that time a member of the Chaikovskii circle in Kiev, told me mysteriously, and even timidly, that he invited me on his own authority to a conference . . . [that] would be held in strictest secrecy. It was, he said, to consist exclusively of members of the Chaikovskii organizations and it had cost him some trouble to get permission to take me. . . . I myself should not have accepted the invitation had not Axelrod earnestly wished me to do so. In the first place, I did not think that the deliberations would cover anything that would demand especial boldness, and therefore the enforced secrecy did not appeal to me. In the second place, I was not attracted by the prospect of a long walk at night after my day of hard work. But Axelrod was waiting for me, and we went together along the dark streets into the unknown. Axelrod had warned me that the meeting would be held in an unfurnished and uninhabited building.

After a long walk we stopped at a house surrounded by scaffolding. We stepped over planks and logs of wood and entered a corner room which was nearly finished. Probably the workers lived in it, for a table made of planks and some benches were in the room. We were met by Emme, Rashevskii, Dalinskii, and a tall, rosy, black-haired young man with large, lively, even gay eyes. This was Andrei Zheliabov. He was the youngest among us and maintained a somewhat respectful attitude. At that time he was just beginning his revolutionary career, and obviously considered himself inexperienced, wishing merely to take part in the movement, not to decide what direction it should take.

Our deliberations were to be based on a questionnaire which had been brought from abroad by Dalinskii. I have forgotten most of the questions and how many of them there were. However, one has remained very vividly in my mind because we discussed it in detail. The organization abroad asked its Russian comrades if they considered it necessary to undertake, in addition to revolutionary propaganda, educational work as well, and if they thought that the opening of schools in villages and towns should be a compulsory part of their program.

Emme and Dalinskii felt that revolutionaries ought not to do purely educational work, because teaching in children's schools would use up much strength and yield little return on account of the general ignorance of the population. But I, who have always been in close contact with the masses, knew how eagerly they aspired to even the most elementary knowledge. I maintained that even if we revolutionaries were not able to open schools for peasant children we ought at least to educate all the capable older children as far as our means would allow. I alleged that it would be very difficult to inculcate, among illiterate people, our socialistic views and our resolve to do away with the monarchy. Axelrod, who often shared my views, supported me, and the question was answered in the affirmative. It was declared desirable that we should teach the older children.

The meeting was long. The speeches were slow and hesitating, and two fiery heads, my own and Axelrod's, grew tired and gradually sank. Finally we went so soundly to sleep that the comrades did not waken us until dawn. We were very much ashamed of ourselves, especially when we found that our comrades had passed a good many resolutions on various questions. These they read to us, among them one saying that schools for older children were desirable for all the Chaikovskii groups.

Before our shameful collapse Axelrod had told us with delight of Zheliabov's origin. He was the son of a serf on the estate of a rich southern landlord and had passed his childhood among the household serfs as a servant. He was now a student at the University of Odessa. At that time such a thing was very unusual, and it aroused not only attention but also astonishment and delight among the friends of the people. A serf boy in the position of a university student was undeniable proof that our people were worthy of the efforts and sacrifices made in order to enhance their intellectual and spiritual capacities. This was forty-five years ago, but I can still see Andrei's vigorous figure and beautiful face, radiant with happiness. He was probably a bit astonished at our delight, but he was obviously pleased to see the sincere joy with which the "intelligentsia" welcomed and accepted as a comrade one who had risen from the people.

[Zheliabov later became a leader of Narodnaia Volia and helped plan the assassination of Alexander II.]

Figure 12-1 Keppen, "Battle of Kinburne"

This painting, "Grenadier Stepan Novikov saves A. V. Suvorov in the Battle of Kinburne," by K. I. Keppen, was completed in 1855. The battle it referred to took place in 1887 during Catherine the Great's Second Turkish War.
- What was the relevance of this in 1855?
- What nationalist and what imperialist themes does it represent?

Source: Suvorov Museum, St. Petersburg.

Figure 12-2 Peasant Dress

This is a photo of a nineteenth-century dress made to be worn while making hay.
- What does it reveal about peasant life, society, and material culture.

Source: Museums on Line.

Figure 12-3 Peasants
This is a late-nineteenth-century photograph of peasants preparing to go to work in the fields.
- What does this reveal about the impact of the emancipation on the mir?
- What does it reveal regarding technology and the social organization of labor.
Source: Musée de l'Homme, Paris.

Figure 12-4 Emir of Bukhara and His Ministers
In 1868, Russia defeated the Emir of Bukhara and annexed a large part of his territory. The Emir was permitted to rule a greatly diminished region under Russian "protection."
- What can you infer about the nature of Bukharan society and politics from this photograph?
- What does this reveal about the Russian conception of empire?
Source: The Victoria and Albert Museum, London.

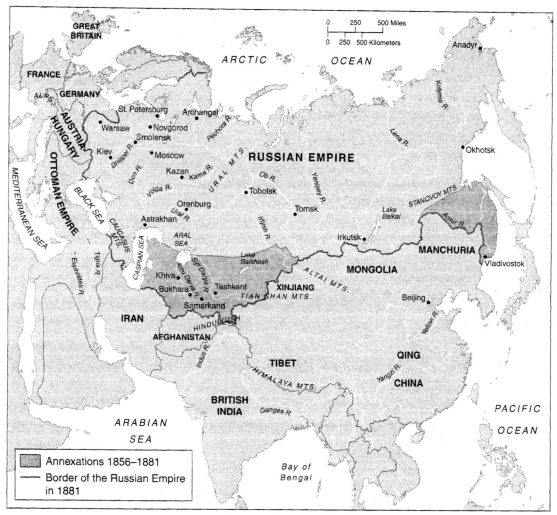

Figure 12-5 Russia in 1881

In the reign of Alexander II, the Russian Empire expanded to the borders of Iran, Afghanistan, and China in Central Asia and to the territory north of the Amur River and east of the Ussuri River in Manchuria.

_____ FOR FURTHER READING _____

(In addition to the books by Engel, Kahan, Moon, and Saunders from the previous chapter.)

Eklof, Ben, John Bushnell, and Larissa Zakharova, Eds. *Russia's Great Reforms, 1855–1881.* Bloomington, IN.: Indiana University Press, 1994.

Eklof, Ben and Stephen Frank, Eds. *The World of the Russian Peasant: Post-Emancipation Culture and Society.* Boston: Unwin Hyman, 1990.

Engel, Barbara Alpern. *Between the Fields and the City: Women, Work, and Family in Russia, 1861–1914.* New York: Cambridge University Press, 1994.

Hillyar, Anna. *Revolutionary Women in Russia, 1870–1917: A Study in Collective Biography.* New York: St. Martin's Press, 2000.

Lincoln, W. Bruce. *The Great Reforms: Autocracy, Bureaucracy, and the Politics of Change in Imperial Russia.* DeKalb, IL: Northern Illinois University Press, 1990.

Mosse, W. E. *Alexander II and the Modernization of Russia.* New York: I. B. Tauris, 1992.

Stites, Richard. *The Women's Liberation Movement in Russia: Feminism, Nihilism, and Bolshevism, 1860–1930.* Princeton, NJ: Princeton University Press, 1978.

Venturi, Franco. *Roots of Revolution: A History of the Populist and Socialist Movements in Nineteenth Century Russia.* New York: Knopf, 1960.

Wortman, Richard S. *Scenarios of Power: Myth and Ceremony in Russian Monarchy, vol 2, From Alexander II to the Abdication of Nicholas II.* Princeton, NJ: Princeton University Press, 1995.

CHAPTER THIRTEEN

RUSSIA'S FIRST INDUSTRIAL REVOLUTION, 1881–1900

In the last two decades of the twentieth century, the gap between Russia and western Europe narrowed considerably. Russia experienced an Industrial Revolution; manufacturing and railroad construction increased dramatically, and cities mushroomed. The economy grew faster than that of any other European nation. Russian intellectual life was fully integrated with that of Europe, and Russian poetry, prose, and drama had become essential reading for cultured Europeans. The Russian state, however, was a glaring anachronism; it was the only major state in Europe to have no written constitution and no elected representative assembly. Sovereignty was vested in the person of a hereditary monarch who was above the law. By 1900, the contradiction between autocracy and popular sovereignty was producing a political crisis.

EURASIAN CONTEXT

In the second half of the nineteenth century, European ruling elites realized the need to accommodate the demand for political participation by their increasingly well-educated populations. France had allowed universal male suffrage in 1848, Spain 1890, Belgium 1893, and England in 1918. Although lip service was paid to the ideals of popular sovereignty and democracy, elites preserved their power by dictating party programs, manipulating nominations, and turning elections into advertising campaigns. Public attention was diverted from social problems by lurid newspaper reporting, professional sports, and organized leisure. The movement for women's rights was effectively ignored. Across Europe, women were given more property rights and greater access to employment (always with substantially lower pay than men), but European women continued to be denied the right to participate in politics.

Political and economic institutions became more complex and bureaucratic. Governments took responsibility for public health, order, and education to an unprecedented extent. Industries became concentrated in the hands of trusts and cartels and were no longer operated by entrepreneurs but by professional management hierarchies. Small craft unions were replaced by industry-wide unions with thousands of members and professional management.

A mood of satisfaction and optimism dominated most segments of European society. Workers were winning high wages, better working conditions, and shorter workdays. Consumer goods were abundant and affordable, and department stores became the symbol and focus of modern society. Europeans also read newspaper accounts of the great achievements their nations were making in gaining colonies abroad and spreading "civilization" among "savage" peoples. However, among the intellectual and artistic elite, disenchantment with the dominant positivist and materialist outlook was growing. The discovery of radioactivity undermined the idea that the universe was predictable, and the new science of psychology suggested that human beings were not even in control of themselves but were subject to irrational and subconscious drives. Artists abandoned realism and sought either to express their own mental state or to affect the imagination, rather than the rational faculty, of their audience. Friedrich Nietzsche called into doubt the possibility of objective truths (either scientific or moral), and his pronouncement "God is dead" became emblematic of the age.

In the last two decades of the nineteenth century, continued industrialization went hand-in-hand with the advance of imperialism. Between 1880 and 1900, virtually all of Africa and Southeast Asia was colonized, and China and the Ottoman Empire were economically subordinated to European powers. Across Eurasia, no society had found a way to match the growth of European military power. China was permitted to retain its territorial integrity, but its sovereignty continued to erode, as European powers also began to establish "spheres of influence," regions within China in which the imperialist power was given a monopoly on resource extraction and railroad and industrial development. In the treaty ports of Shanghai, Nanjing, Canton, and Tienjin, European entrepreneurs built arsenals, dockyards, factories, and schools. New industries created both a native working class and a native professional/managerial class among whom anti-western Chinese nationalism emerged. In 1895, Sun Yat-sen made his first attempt to mobilize Chinese nationalism against the Qing dynasty, and in 1900, conservative elements used Chinese nationalism in the Boxer Rebellion against Chinese Christians and foreigners. Neither was successful.

As Japan became more similar to Europe politically, socially, and economically, its leaders also decided to adopt the European practice of imperialism. The Japanese first cast their eye on their nearest neighbor, Korea, and began to promote a pro-Japanese faction in the Korean court in Seoul. China resented this intrusion into the political life of its tributary. In 1895, war broke out, and Japan easily defeated Chinese forces on land and sea. In the Treaty of Shimonoseki (1895), Japan obtained the Kwantung Peninsula, Taiwan, and some Pacific islands, and China recognized Korea's independence. Europe, however, was unwilling to allow Japan to have a foothold on the Asian mainland. Germany, France, and Russia combined to force Japan to withdraw from the Kwantung Peninsula and give it back to China.

In the last two decades of Nasir al Din Shah's rule in Iran, he faced increasing opposition from regional leaders and from the Muslim clergy. England and Russia supplied him with money to bribe political leaders and to hire troops to intimidate the population. In return, the Shah promised not to interfere in Afghanistan and Central Asia, and he signed a "Treaty of Capitulations" that gave the two countries access to Iranian markets. Tsar Alexander II sent military officers to organize a "Cossack Brigade," which became Iran's most effective fighting force; its Russian officers also promoted Russian interests. Russia took northern Iran as its sphere of influence and obtained concessions for insurance companies and banks. In 1888, English entrepreneurs, with the backing of the British government, obtained a monopoly on banking, mining, and industrial development in the south, but Russian influence in the Shah's court caused it to be canceled. In 1890, a British venture, "The Imperial Tobacco Corporation" obtained a monopoly on the sale of tobacco in Iran. This led to a boycott, massive demonstrations, and even rumors that a holy war would be declared against the agents of the West. The Shah cancelled the concession (agreeing, however, to compensate the shareholders for their losses). In 1896, Nasir al Din was assassinated by an Iranian nationalist cleric.

Afghanistan remained a buffer zone between Russian Turkestan and British India. Its ruler, Abdul Rahman Khan (1880–1901), followed a neutral foreign policy and accepted British direction (and money) in modernizing and unifying the country. He replaced tribal organization with provincial governors, built a centralized bureaucracy, and created a national assembly of princes and religious leaders.

The modernizing elements in the administration of the Ottoman Empire realized some major goals in 1876 when they influenced the new sultan, Abdülhamid II (1876–1909), to approve a constitution that provided for a bicameral legislature, a cabinet, and freedom of the press, and turned Islam from a state to a private religion. Unfortunately for liberal government, the new sultan soon fell out with the reformers. He allowed the parliament to meet twice, but the distraction of the Russo-Turkish war of 1877 allowed him to dismiss the parliament and suspend the constitution.

Abdülhamid managed to preserve the territorial integrity of his empire (with the minor exception of East Rumelia, which was lost to Bulgaria), but not its economic sovereignty. When the government was unable to repay its debts, an Ottoman Public Debt administration, staffed by Europeans, took over tax collection on behalf of the Sultan and supervised railroad construction (with special consideration for European investors). Liberal and nationalist opposition to Abdülhamid's despotism and subservience to the West grew, and in 1889 a group of students at the Imperial Military Medical college formed the Committee of Progress and Union, better known in the West as "the Young Turks." They called for democratic reform and an end to Westernization, and promoted Turkish nationalism over Ottoman imperialism. Many of them wanted to form a federation with Turkic peoples in the Caucasus and Central Asia.

POLITICAL DEVELOPMENTS AND FOREIGN AFFAIRS

Alexander III (1881–1894) came to the throne determined to preserve the powers and prerogatives of the autocracy after the assassination of his father. He intended to resist any notion of popular sovereignty and to restrict the public involvement in government that had been granted by the Great Reforms. The young tsar was prompted in this direction by his tutor and adviser, Konstantin Pobedonostsev. Pobedonostsev had begun his career as a liberal jurist who helped to reform the judiciary in 1864. As he had risen in the administration, however, Pobedonostsev had become more and more conservative. In 1880, Alexander II had appointed him the head of the Holy Synod, and in 1881 Alexander III turned to him for counsel and advice.

His first action was to deal with Loris-Melikov's proposed legislative commissions which had been held in abeyance until the new tsar could consider them. For more than a month Alexander wavered, but in the end, allowed himself to be bullied by his former tutor into abandoning the idea of reform. He published a manifesto, over his name but written by Pobedonostsev, that affirmed unlimited autocracy. Under further pressure from Pobedonostsev, Alexander forced Loris-Melikov and his associates into retirement and then began a series of counter-reforms.

Alexander first subverted the judicial reforms by enacting the so-called "Temporary Regulations," which gave the government the power to declare a state of emergency in any region of the empire. When such an emergency was declared, officials were authorized to bypass the court system and carry out searches, make arrests, and impose terms of exile. They also provided for secret military tribunals instead of open civilian courts. In addition, in 1885 the Ministry of the Interior was given the power to interfere with judges, to hold secret trials whenever "the dignity of state power" was threatened, and to deny jury trials to those who assaulted government officials.

Then Alexander began to rescind his father's local government reforms. In 1888, the volost government, elected by peasants since 1861, was put under the supervision of a land captain (*zemskii nachalnik*), an official appointed by the Minister of the Interior from among the local nobility, who was given the power to suspend volost officials or prevent them from assuming office. The land captain took over the duties of the justice of the peace (formerly elected) and was given the authority to arrest, fine, and imprison without trial.

In 1890, the zemstvo system was restructured to favor the nobility. Election of zemstvo assemblies was by classes voting separately and disproportionately. Nobles elected more than half of the zemstvo members, peasants more than a quarter, and other property owners less than one-sixth. (People without property had no representation at all.) Furthermore, peasant voting was no longer direct; instead, peasants elected a slate of candidates from which the land captain made the official appointments. In additional, all members of zemstvo executive boards (elected by the zemstvo assemblies) were subject to review by the governor of the province and the Minister of the Interior. In 1892, similar changes were imposed on city government. Property qualifications for voters were increased in such a way as to reduce the electorate by roughly two-thirds. In St. Petersburg, a city of 1,200,000, only 8,000 residents were qualified to vote, and in Moscow, with a population of 1,000,000, only 7,000 people could vote.

In international affairs, the reign of Alexander III was a time of peace. The Panslavs continued to promote their dream of Russian leadership of an independent Balkan peninsula, but Alexander followed an extremely cautious foreign policy. He joined a revived "Three Emperors' League" among Austria-Hungary, Germany, and Russia in 1881 and renewed it in 1884, but he kept it secret in order not to offend the Panslavs. In 1887, the Three Emperors' League was not renewed (Austria and Russia were at odds, and Germany chose to ally with Austria), but Bismarck secretly managed to maintain neutrality with Russia for three more years. In 1890, however, the new German emperor, Wilhelm II, forced Bismarck into retirement and rescinded the treaty of neutrality with Russia, believing it to be incompatible with his relationship with Austria and Italy.

Russia's only expansion in the reign of Alexander III was in Central Asia, where its army seized the region of Merv, on the border of Iran and Afghanistan, in 1884. This led to war with Afghanstan, in 1885, over the boundary line between the two countries. This incursion, so close to India, alarmed Britain. War between the two imperialist powers was avoided when Britain accepted the boundary proposed by Russia, and Russia accepted Britain's supervision of Afghanistan's foreign policy.

In the last years of Alexander III's reign, he accepted France's bid for closer ties with Russia. Ever since its defeat in the Franco-Prussian War in 1870, France had dreamed of revenge, and Russia was an ideal ally. Russia was a major power, French and Russian imperial interests did not conflict, and, in the event of war, Germany would have to fight on two fronts. Russia would benefit from such an alliance because it would end its diplomatic isolation and would gain access to French capital. The French government began buying Russian government bonds and encouraged French capitalists to invest in Russian enterprises. In 1894, France and Russia signed an agreement of mutual aid should either be attacked by Germany or by another country supported by Germany.

Alexander III died unexpectedly of nephritis in 1894 at the age of forty-eight. He was succeeded by his twenty-six-year-old son, Nicholas II, who had been taught by his father and his tutor, Konstantin Pobedonostsev, that it was his sacred duty to defend his prerogatives as Tsar. A few months before his father's death, Nicholas had married Alix, Princess of Hesse-Darmstadt, born in Germany but raised in London by her grandmother Queen Victoria. Under the tutelage of Pobedonostev, Alix became a fervent believer in the Orthodox Church (taking the name Alexandra when baptized in her new faith), in the Russian autocracy, and in the sacred union of Tsar and people. Unfortunately for the Romanov dynasty, her enthusiasm reinforced Nicholas's own convictions.

Nicholas began his reign by revealing an utter lack of sensitivity to public opinion. In an address to zemstvo delegates in early 1895, Nicholas reaffirmed his commitment to unlimited autocracy and announced that creation of a national zemstvo advisory council was a "senseless dream." Soon after, at festivities connected with his coronation, twelve hundred people were trampled to death due to lack of proper crowd control. That same evening the Tsar and Tsaritsa attended a ball as if nothing had happened.

In his first years on the throne, Nicholas II made no change in his father's foreign relations: France and Russia remained close, and Russia and England continued to negotiate their spheres of influence in Central Asia. In 1896, without consulting Afghanistan, the two imperialist powers extended Afghanistan's eastern border all the way to China by creating a narrow territory to separate Russian Turkestan from India (what is now northern Pakistan), thus creating a buffer zone between their colonial possessions.

In East Asia, Nicholas infuriated the Japanese. In 1895, Japan had been forced to withdraw from the Kwantung Peninsula at the insistence of Russia, France, and Germany, on the pretext of maintaining China's territorial integrity. Only two years later, however, Russia secured a twenty-five-year lease for precisely the same territory, which it then began to treat as a permanent acquisition. Major construction projects were begun, including a Russian Orthodox Church in Port Arthur. In addition, Russia built the China Eastern Railway (connecting Chita with Vladivostok) and the South China Railway (connecting the China Eastern Railway with Port Arthur).

In 1899, Nicholas initiated the first International Peace Conference at the Hague. It was attended by twenty-six countries, including all the Great Powers. The Conference established an International Court of Justice, and approved some laws of war but did not achieve consensus regarding disarmament or the use of binding arbitration to resolve international disputes.

RELIGION AND CULTURE

Alexander III's cultural policies paralleled his reactionary counter-reforms in law and administration. In 1882, he decreed that preliminary censorship could be applied to any newspaper or journal that had been given three warnings. He also established a committee of ministers with the power to suspend permanently the publication of a newspaper or journal and to ban subversive editors and publishers from future employment in publishing. In 1884, a new law ended university autonomy. Appointment of administrators and faculty was taken from independent university councils and given to the Ministry of Education. Students were forbidden to form clubs or organizations even of a nonpolitical kind. Tuition and fees were raised on the assumption that students from richer families were less rebellious.

Under Pobedonostev's influence, Alexander III blamed social discontent on too little attention to religious education and too much education for the lower orders of society. Pobedonostsev's plan to transfer the entire public school system to the jurisdiction of the Russian Orthodox Church was never realized, but the government pressured zemstvos to finance more church schools, and the number of church schools jumped from fewer than six thousand at the beginning of Alexander's reign to more than thirty-two thousand at the end.

Alexander pursued a clear class policy in public education. In order to limit gymnazia to the wealthy elite, he raised tuition sharply and called for admission policies that took social status into account. Similarly, he discouraged the expansion of secondary education, in the hope that ordinary workers and peasants would attain only basic literacy and numeracy. He saw no reason for their education to extend beyond the ability to read the simplistic religious propaganda that Pobedonostsev's Holy Synod published in bulk.

Pobedonostsev aggressively promoted the Russian Orthodox Church. He opened thousands of new churches, and allowed no other religions to seek converts. Children of mixed marriages were required by law to be raised in the Orthodox Church. On the other hand, Pobedonostsev feared sophisticated theological thought. He preferred that the education of priests end with graduation from undergraduate seminary, and he therefore imposed difficult entrance exams for admission to graduate theological academies. He eliminated many liberal arts courses from the seminary curriculum in order to isolate the clergy from secular culture, and he also opposed theological discussion among the laity. A "Society of Lovers of Spiritual Enlightenment" had met regularly, offered public lectures, and published a journal since 1863, but soon after he took charge of the Holy Synod, Pobedonostsev disbanded the organization and suspended its journal.

Ironically, Konstantin Pobedonostsev, for all his apparent desire to take Russia back to the Muscovite era, was a leader in European conservatism. His argument against constitutions and elected parliaments was no old-fashioned revival of "divine right of tsars," but a shrewd critique of how wealthy elites in western Europe subverted constitutional government and parliamentary rule. He argued that the liberal contract theory of government, based on the principle of individual interest, fostered selfishness and ignored the public good. He pointed out that elections favored the wealthy (who bought votes and influence) and demagogues (who appealed to base interests). Pobedonostsev argued that the public welfare was best defended by the rule of an individual so elevated in power and prestige that he could not be swayed by self-interest and hence would act only in the interests of all his subjects.

Russians were intellectual and cultural leaders in many other respects. Fyodor Dostoyevsky had been among the first in Europe to cast doubt on liberal confidence in progress and to warn that positivism and materialism would only produce atheism and despair. Some (including the philosopher Lev Shestov) argued that Dostoyevsky had anticipated Nietzsche's existentialist critique of rationality and objectivity. Dostoyevsky differed from Nietzsche, however, in his solution to Europe's intellectual crisis, that is, Christian faith.

The religious message of the Slavophiles and Dostoyevsky was taken up by Vladimir Solovyov, son of one of Russia's most famous historians. Solovyov earned advanced degrees in philosophy and also attended the Moscow Theological Academy. In 1881, while a professor at the University of Moscow, Solovyov suggested that Alexander III, as a Christian, should pardon his father's murderers. He was forced to resign. Solovyov shared with Dostoyevsky the faith that Russian society could be saved by a revolution of the spirit in which people lived the communal ideas of the Slavophiles. Nevertheless, Solovyov was also a westernizing liberal opposed to extreme Russian nationalism. He was an ecuminist and called for a reunification of the Christian churches.

Solovyov's mystical poetry and his descriptions of his religious visions exerted a powerful influence on Russia's symbolist poets. The symbolists rejected the realism and social utilitarianism of the previous generation and adopted the Neoplatonism. They believed that there is a higher level of reality from the visible world, that there are correspondences between the two worlds, and that intuitive knowledge is superior to empirical knowledge. Their art was carefully crafted, full of allusion, and was written for the intellectual elite, not the masses. Symbolists Zinaida Gippius, Valerii Briusov, and Konstintin Balmont were the most important poets of the 1890s.

Leo Tolstoy had a profound religious experience in 1877, but it led him in a quite different direction. Tolstoy took Jesus' "Sermon on the Mount" to be the essence of Christianity and the ultimate expression of ethical values. On this basis, he rejected the established church and its dogmas, government in all its forms, and modern civilization in general. He preached pacifism and anarchism in their purest forms. Tolstoy believed that art should be of universal appeal, intelligible to people of all classes, and that its purpose was to inspire people to do good and to oppose evil. Besides nonfiction, in which he applied his religious principles to current social problems, Tolstoy wrote short stories, plays, and the novel *Resurrection*, a biting critique of Russian society and legal system. Tolstoy gained a wide following in Russia and around the world, influencing, among others, Mohandas Gandhi.

The realistic novel, dealing with the great questions of social life, became a thing of the past. Anton Chekhov turned away from big issues and complex plots to nearly plotless "slice of life" stories. Chekhov, grandson of a serf and son of a merchant from Taganrog, had earned a degree in medicine, but chose to earn his living by writing. In the 1870s, he began writing humorous stories for satirical journals, and in 1884, he published his first collection of serious short stories. In his work, Chekhov laid bare the misery of the poor, the heartlessness of the rich, and the generally futile search for love and happiness. His stories revealed the emptiness of modern society without proposing solutions or alternatives. His plays, which revolutionized the stage in Russia and around the world, had, like his stories, little plot (in the usual sense of the term) and usually ended inconclusively.

Maksim Gorky, pseudonym of Aleksei Peshkov (1868–1936), was a poet, novelist, and dramatist more remarkable for his biography and subject matter than for his art. Gorky was born into a poor urban family in Nizhnii Novgorod. He went to work at the age of eleven, engaged in many different kinds of manual labor and spent time as a tramp. Gorky was a voracious reader and was entirely self-educated. His realistic stories and plays about the lower orders of Russian society—tramps, thieves, prostitutes, and outcasts—were published in major journals in the middle of the 1890s, and, in 1898, the publication of his collected stories brought him instant fame and acquaintance with Chekhov and Tolstoy.

ROLES AND STATUS OF WOMEN

The last decades of the twentieth century saw a conservative backlash against the movement for women's equality. Those dissatisfied with trends in modern society frequently blamed them on women for leaving their "natural" sphere of home life to work in offices and factories. Leo Tolstoy, for example, was quite reactionary in his attitude toward women, whom he believed to be morally inferior and necessarily subordinate to men. The natural function of women, in his opinion, was to bear children, cook, and wash their husbands' shirts. Not surprisingly, Alexander III's and Pobedonostsev's reactionary ideology extended to women, too. In 1882, they closed the St. Petersburg medical school for women, and they discontinued the admission of women into the Universities of Moscow, Kazan, and Kiev. Only the University of St. Petersburg retained the right to enroll women.

The arguments for the liberation of women had been a part of the general positivist and progressive outlook of the sixties and seventies, and they had become passé in the eighties and nineties. Vladimir Solovyov celebrated "Sofia," the principle of divine reason, but did not advance the cause of women's liberation. Zinaida Gippius's poetry dealt with love, freedom, and tragedy, but she was unconcerned with women's legal disabilities.

In the mid-1890s, however, a women's movement again appeared. Anna Shabanova had been associated with the populists and had been arrested for political activity, but after spending time in prison she returned to society willing to pursue reform through peaceful change. She became a doctor (studying in Helsinki), and she joined Anna Filosofova, now getting on in years, in founding the Mutual Philanthropic Society in 1895. This marked a transition from the old feminism (that focused on legal equality and the emancipation of wives from rule by their husbands) to a new women's movement (that demanded political participation and the right to vote). Since the government would not permit the existence of an organization that might have an agenda of social change, the official purpose of the Mutual Philanthropic Society was to provide charity, and it was active in establishing nurseries, shelters, dormitories, and cafeterias for poor women.

These middle-class feminists soon found themselves in competition with socialists for popular support. In 1879, the German Social-Democratic party leader August Bebel published *Women and Socialism,* which advocated the equality of women in the socialist movement and argued that women could not achieve equality in the current system. Clara Zetkin, a German who married a radical Russian emigre, further elaborated on Bebel's themes and argued that a women's rights movement could not liberate women by itself, because it did not address the fundamental cause: capitalism. She summoned women to join the socialist party and achieve liberation through revolution.

In Russia the first Marxist discussion of the women's question was written by Nadezhda Krupskaya, the wife of V. I. Lenin, one of the rising stars of the Marxist movement in Russia in the 1890s. While sharing her husband's exile in Siberia for illegal political activity, Krupskaya wrote *Women Worker,* in which she described the misery and poverty of peasant women and factory women. Women, she said, must be allowed to join the working class movement to work for the liberation of themselves and all workers. Krupskaya convinced Lenin to add the demand for the full equality of men and women to the program of the Russian Social Democratic Labor Party, which he was then helping to write.

SOCIAL AND ECONOMIC DEVELOPMENTS

In the late eighteenth century, European thinkers developed the notion of "civil society" to refer to the community of opinion among the educated classes as reflected in newspapers, journals, and other publications independent of government control. It was thought that this civil society was the expression of the true mood of the nation, and that it created a climate of opinion that limited the options open to the government. It was (and is) understood that a civil society is an essential protection against autocratic or dictatorial rule.

One of the reasons frequently given for the fact that autocratic government lasted longer in Russia than in any other European country is that its "civil society" was never powerful enough to induce the Tsar to promulgate a constitution or create a parliament. There is some truth to this, although (as we have seen) public opinion did in fact influence the emancipation of the serfs, the Great Reforms, and Russia's war with Turkey in 1877 to 1878. It is also the case that Alexander II's reforms did much to promote civil society by making all citizens equal before the law and subject to the same social obligations and taxes.

Nevertheless, the Tsar could not recognize a civil society as a community of independent social opinion that spoke for the nation. Speaking for the nation was a right the Tsar arrogated only to himself. Nor did the Tsar want Russia's social estates to speak for themselves; instead, the Ministry of War spoke for the military, the Ministry of Interior represented the interests of the gentry and of the peasantry, the Holy Synod spoke for the clergy, and the Ministry of Finance for merchants and industrialists.

Alexander III increased the role of the nobility in local government, believing in the traditional unity of interests between the monarch and the aristocracy. Alexander established a Gentry Bank in 1885 to save nobles from bankruptcy and thus preserve their estates and prevent the land from being transferred to merchants and peasants. Alexander misjudged the situation, however. The nobility was no longer a self-conscious estate; it was already in the process of pursuing its professional and economic interests rather than its noble status. Those nobles who remained in the countryside and engaged in agriculture began to identify with other wealthy agricultural entrepreneurs. Those who sold their land and invested the proceeds in industry began to identify with industrialists. Those nobles who entered the professions identified with urban professionals, and it turned out that nobles who served on zemstvo and town boards were among the most progressive liberal reformers.

Unlike the western European situation, in which merchants, professionals, entrepreneurs, and white-collar workers formed a "middle class" which shared a common set of values, Russia had no unified middle-class consciousness. Professionals and white-collar workers considered themselves to be members of the intelligentsia, and they had more sympathy for revolutionary parties than for the government. Merchants and industrialists, on the other hand, were very conservative and religious; many of them were Old Believers or came from Old Believer families. As the century wore on, the merchant class became more secular, but it adopted the values of Russian imperialism and Panslavism. The Great Reforms had taken away most of the special privileges of the highest urban guilds, but they remained a close-knit community separate from the majority of city dwellers and from the intelligentsia as well.

Perhaps the greatest obstacle to the rise of a civil society was the gulf between the wealthy and the educated, on one hand, and peasants and workers on the other. The attitude of government was paternalistic; it wanted to correct any problems that might lead to popular discontent but had no desire to give ordinary people control over their lives. For the peasantry, the greatest problem was the redemption payments for the land they had been allotted in the emancipation. These payments were more than the productive capacity of the land could supply, and the government knew it. First, in 1881, the payments were scaled down. Then, in 1892, when 70 percent of redemption payments were past due, they were reamortized to postpone the final due date and decrease annual payments. This was done a third time in 1896, when the repayment schedule was set to end in the 1950s.

The government continued to cling to the idea that the stability of the state was tied to the preservation of the mir. In 1885, the poll tax was eliminated and along with it the principle of joint responsibility for taxes. Even though this removed the historic justification for tying peasants to the mir or for periodic redistribution of the land, both of these practices were continued. Peasant households were still forbidden to leave the commune without permission of the skhod. The right of a peasant family to request that its land be separated from the mir and turned into an individual farm (which the emancipation had given to any household that had made all its redemption payments) was revoked. The government even interfered in the right of adult children to move out of their parents' household. Believing that the breakup of the multigeneration household caused poverty (and hence unrest), the government decreed in 1886 that peasant households could not be broken up without a two-thirds vote of the skhod.

The autocracy took a similarly paternalistic attitude toward workers. Factory legislation in 1882 outlawed night work in textile mills for women and children, forbade the employment of children under twelve, limited to eight hours the workday of children between the ages of twelve and fifteen, and required youths' work schedule to be arranged to allow school attendance. In addition, the powers of employers to arbitrarily fine or otherwise discipline workers was limited. In 1886 the government required that wages should be paid twice a month, and that wages must be paid in cash and not in kind. At the same time, the government imposed stiffer penalties for going on strike, and made it illegal to miss work.

Russian workers identified more with the countryside than the city. Only 20 percent of Russia's workers lived in Moscow and St. Petersburg; most, in fact, lived in villages. Some factories closed in the summer so their employees could work the land, and 10 percent of all factories closed during the harvest. Even in factory cities, the typical worker had been born in a village and returned there after retirement. As late as 1908, one-half of all single workers and one-third of married workers in St. Petersburg maintained their entitlements to land in their home mir. Most workers had relatives, if not immediate family members, who remained in agriculture.

Strikes were illegal in Tsarist Russia, but they occurred frequently. The first major strike after the accession of Alexander III occurred in 1885 in the Morozov textile mills, in which approximately eleven thousand workers participated. According to official data (probably underestimated), strikes steadily increased in participation from seventeen thousand workers in 1894 to ninety-seven thousand in 1899, occurring most frequently in the textile and metalworking industries. They were generally not political in nature; the most frequently expressed demands were for shorter working days, higher pay, fair treatment, and respect.

In the last two decades of the nineteenth century, Russia underwent an industrial revolution. Between 1880 and 1900, the production of sugar more than doubled (205,000 to 795,000 tons), cotton nearly tripled (93,000 to 260,000 tons), coal more than quadrupled (3,300,000 to 16,000,000), and the production of oil rose by a factor of twenty-nine (350,000 to 10,300,000 tons). In the same years, the length of railroad track was increased 13,700 to 32,000 miles. Freight volume increased by 50 percent, and the length of telegraph lines almost doubled. Exports increased from 499 million to 716 million rubles, and Russia's balance of trade was transformed from a deficit of 124 million rubles in 1880 to a surplus of 90 million in 1900. Overall the Russian economy grew at a rate of 4.7 percent in the 1890s, faster than any other European nation.

The capital that funded the Russian industrial revolution came partly from foreign investment, but mostly from the export of wheat, at the expense of the peasantry. The government extracted the maximum production of wheat at the minimum price by requiring taxes to be paid in cash in the fall. The flood of grain to the market at harvest time drove prices to the lowest possible level, allowing it to be exported at competitive prices. As Ivan Vyshnegradsky, Minister of Finance from 1887 to 1892, famously said, "We will go hungry, but we will export." "We" did not, of course, refer to Vyshnegradskii's family or other members of the ruling elite; it was the peasants who did not have enough to eat.

The Ministry of Finance had been fostering Russian industry by raising import tariffs in the 1880s, but Sergei Witte, made Minister of Finance in 1892, is given much of the credit for Russia's industrial expansion. Witte believed in railroad building as the key to economic growth. It was he who began the construction of the Transiberian Railroad which was intended not only to stimulate the iron, coal, and manufacturing industries, but to expand agriculture in Siberia and to serve as a strategic link with East Asia. Witte also put Russian currency on the gold standard to attract foreign investment, which probably doubled over the 1890s.

Peoples of the Empire

Russia's Jews were the first to suffer the effects of Alexander III's reactionary and Russian-chauvinist outlook. (Pobedonostsev, is reported to have said that the "Jewish question" would be solved only if one-third emigrated, one-third became Christian, and one-third died.) In 1881, a wave of pogroms (race riots in which Jewish businesses and homes were destroyed and Jews beaten or killed) spread across Ukraine. Not only did Russian police and soldiers do nothing to stop these outbursts, they often participated. The following year Alexander promulgated anti-Jewish laws: Jews were no longer permitted to move to the countryside, even within the Pale of Settlement, and Jewish merchants were forbidden to open their businesses on Sundays or Christian holidays. In 1887, the government set quotas for Jews in both secondary higher education. Within the Pale, 10 percent of the student body could be Jewish, in the provinces 5 percent, and in Moscow and St. Petersburg only 3 percent. (In the reign of Nicholas II, these figures were reduced further.) In 1889, Jews were denied the right to practice law without special permission from the Minister of Interior. In 1890 to 1892, Jews also lost the right to vote everywhere except in cities within the Pale of Settlement. In 1892, twenty thousand Jewish artisans were evicted from Moscow, and in 1893, a law was passed forbidding Jews to be given Christian names. Pogroms continued to rage sporadically, and thousands of Jews emigrated every year to Palestine and the United States.

Russia imposed on its eastern peoples neither the same discrimination it practiced against Jews nor the consistent Russification it forced on Poles and Ukrainians. Nevertheless, there was increasing pressure on the non-Russian peoples of the empire to learn Russian and to carry on official government business in Russian. In addition, there was large-scale emigration of Russians to the provinces, where they were given preferential treatment. The most fertile land in the Caucasus and Central Asia was made available to Russian peasants, depriving nomadic herders of pasture. Russians who migrated to the cities and industrial regions of the provinces were favored in employment: Educated Russians were employed as administrators and business professionals, while working-class Russians were hired as laborers. A good example of this is the Caspian port of Baku in Azerbaijan. In the 1860s, before oil was an industrial commodity, it was a city of about 13,000; by 1897, when Baku was producing more than half the world's supply of petroleum, it had grown to 112,000. More than one-third of Baku's population were Russians—managers and workers in the oil industry—who lived in a separate enclave from the Azerbaijani and Armenian communities.

Central Asia was treated like a colony in the classic sense, being used as a supplier of raw materials and a market for exported goods. Russian policies fostered cotton production at the expense of food crops, which made the region dependent on the import of wheat from Russia. In the cities, the native population was outnumbered by Russian immigrants who were employed in the civil service, transportation and communications, industry, education, and who took over commerce as well.

Central Asian Muslims were categorized as *inorodtsy* or aliens, the term that had been used to refer to nomadic peoples since the Muscovite period. They were not considered citizens, were not subject to the draft, and were not expected to integrate into Russian society. They frequently rebelled against Russian economic policies, which only reinforced the Russian belief that Central Asians were backward and benighted. The nomadic peoples of Central Asia had a weak sense of ethnic identity and were usually mobilized by Muslim leaders. During a cholera epidemic in Tashkent in 1892, riots broke out because men did not want their women to be examined by male doctors and because the authorities insisted on immediate burial of victims. Russian attempts at flood control and locust control were opposed as interfering with God's plan. In 1898, a Holy War was declared in Fergana that required an army of two thousand to suppress.

In the Caucasus, modern secular nationalism became more pervasive. Georgians resented Russian administrators and felt that Armenian merchants were unduly favored. Several nationalist parties arose in the 1890s, and a Georgian Social-Democratic party was founded in 1893. Armenian nationalism was directed against both the Ottoman Empire and the Russian Empire, each of which ruled approximately half of historic Armenia. The Sultan responded to demands for reforms with massacres. Alexander III and Nicholas II closed hundreds of Armenian schools, libraries, and newspaper offices.

THE RISING TIDE OF REVOLUTION

The turn to political assassination by Narodnaia Volia in the late 1870s had been a sign of failure. The peasantry, the object of the narodniks' revolutionary ardor, was unresponsive, and the decision to murder the Tsar was more a self-destructive gesture than a hopeful project for change. The decline of the revolutionary movement after 1881, therefore, had less to do with the government's repressive measures, than with the pointlessness of continued self-sacrifice. The generation of the seventies made its compromise with the world, and the new generation, for the most part, looked on passively. The only revolutionary activity was a conspiracy among fifteen university students to assassinate the Tsar on March 1, 1887. Their plot failed, and they were all arrested. Five of them, including a young man named Aleksandr Ulianov, were hanged.

Social activism did not revive until after 1891, when a major famine, accompanied by a cholera epidemic, hit the Volga region. The government did virtually nothing, and what famine relief occurred was undertaken by private citizens, including Leo Tolstoy. Populists interpreted the famine as the consequence of the rise of government-sponsored capitalism, and they began, once again, to form local circles and networks.

In the 1890s, those who shared the old populist outlook began to call themselves "Socialist Revolutionaries," and they revived the dream of overthrowing the autocracy. They took an interest in the working-class movement, but they still believed that the preservation of the mir was the key to socialism and progress. There was a wide variety of opinion regarding tactics: Some wanted to rely only on agitation among the people, some revived the idea that assassination of government officials could serve the revolution. In the late 1890s, several attempts were made to create a national Socialist-Revolutionary Party, but they were prevented by lack of consensus over tactics and police repression.

In the meantime, a new trend in the revolutionary movement was begun by Georgii Plekhanov and his fellow members of the Chernyi Peredel. (They had split with Narodnaia Volia over the issue of political assassination and had emigrated to Switzerland in 1880.) They discovered in Marxism a solution to the dilemmas of populism. If Marx was correct, and socialism would not be made by farmers but by the industrial working class, then the rise of capitalism was not something to resist but to celebrate. The rising strike movement in Russian industry between 1885 and 1900 suggested that the working class really was the revolutionary force of the future.

While Plekhanov led the Russian Marxists-in-exile, a new generation of Marxist revolutionaries appeared in the 1890s. Most notable was Vladimir Ilich Ulianov (who took the pseudonym of Lenin when he became a revolutionary). Vladimir was born in 1870, the son of a school administrator who had been promoted to hereditary noble status. While Vladimir was in the gymnasium, his older brother was arrested and executed for his role in the 1887 plot to kill the Tsar. Vladimir read all his brother's books, including Chernyshevskii's *What is to be Done*, and became a revolutionary himself.

Vladimir attended the University of Kazan, from which he was almost immediately expelled for political activity; in the end, he earned his law degree by correspondence from the University of St. Petersburg. By the early 1890s, Vladimir had become a Marxist, and in 1895, he and L. Martov founded the Union for the Struggle to Liberate the Working Class. Their goal was to turn the Marxist movement from a debating society into an active organizer of the working class. In what had become a revolutionary's rite of passage, Vladimir was arrested and exiled to Siberia where he remained until 1900.

CONCLUSION

As the century closed, the Russian empire appeared stable and prosperous. It was at peace, its hold over its empire was secure, and its industrial revolution proceeded apace. The revolutionary movement was small and disorganized, and most of its leaders were in Europe or in Siberian exile. In February 1899, however, a troubling omen appeared. In response to yet another arbitrary and restrictive university edict, students at the University of St. Petersburg held a rowdy protest and were dispersed by the police. A student mass meeting declared a strike against the university, which immediately spread to Russia's other universities. Within a month, nearly all the high schools in Russia were shut down by student strikes and riots, as well. The government made a few minor concessions, but it also reduced university enrollment, expelled thousands of students, and then drafted them into the army for the duration of their expulsion. In February 1901, one of these expelled students assassinated the Minister of Education, N. P. Bogolepov.

These student protests were only the first symptoms of massive popular dissatisfaction with the tsarist regime. A revolution was brewing.

TEXT DOCUMENTS

Letter to Alexander III

Immediately after the assassination of Alexander II, the Executive Committee of Narodnaia Volia sent a letter to the new Tsar, from which the following excerpt is taken.

- How do the members of Narodnaia Volia justify their actions?
- What kind of a society do they want?

In the course of ten years we have seen how, notwithstanding the most severe persecutions, notwithstanding the fact that the government of the late Emperor sacrificed everything, freedom, the interests of all classes, the interests of industry and even its own dignity, everything, unconditionally, in its attempt to suppress the revolutionary movement, that movement has nevertheless tenaciously grown and spread, attracting to itself the best elements of the nation, the most energetic and self-denying people of Russia, and for three years now has engaged in desperate, partisan warfare with the government. . . . They have hanged our followers, both guilty and innocent; they have filled the prisons and distant provinces with exiles. Whole dozens of our leaders have been seized and hanged. They have died with the courage and calmness of martyrs, but the movement has not been suppressed, it has grown and gained strength. . . .

Casting a dispassionate glance over the depressing decade through which we have lived, we can accurately foretell the future progress of the movement if the political tactics of the government do not change. The movement must go on growing, gaining strength; terroristic acts will be repeated in ever more alarming and intensified forms. A more perfect, stronger revolutionary organization will take the place of the groups that are wiped out. . . .

Whatever may have been the intentions of the Sovereign, the acts of the government have had nothing in common with the popular welfare and desires. The Imperial Government has subjugated the people to the state of bondage, it has delivered the masses into the power of the nobility; and now it is openly creating a pernicious class of speculators and profiteers. All its reforms lead to but one result, that the people have sunk into ever greater slavery, into a state of more complete exploitation. . . .

We turn to you, casting aside all prejudices, stifling that distrust, which the age-long activity of the government has created. We forget that you are the representative of that power which has so deceived the people, and done them so much harm. We address you as a citizen and an honorable man. We hope that the feeling of personal bitterness will not suppress in you the recognition of your duties, and the desire to know the truth. We too might be embittered. You have lost your father. We have lost not only our fathers, but also our brothers, our wives, our children, our best friends. But we are ready to suppress our personal feelings if the good of Russia demands it. And we expect the same from you also.

Source: Vera Figner, *Memoirs of a Revolutionist* (New York: International Publishers Co., Inc., 1968), 309–312 (excerpted). Reprinted with permission of International Publishers Co., Inc., New York City.

We do not lay conditions upon you. Do not be shocked by our proposition. The conditions which are indispensable in order that the revolutionary movement shall be transformed into peaceful activity, have been created, not by us, but by history. We do not impose them, we only recall them to your mind. In our opinion there are two such conditions:

1. A general amnesty for all political crimes committed in the past, inasmuch as these were not crimes, but the fulfilment of a civic duty.
2. The convocation of an assembly of representatives of all the Russian people, for the purpose of examining the existing forms of our state and society, and revising them in accord with the desires of the people.

We consider it necessary to mention, however, that in order that the legality of the Supreme Authority may be confirmed by popular representation, the process of selecting delegates must be absolutely unrestricted. Therefore the elections must be held under the following conditions:

1. The deputies must be sent from all ranks and classes alike, and in numbers proportionate to the population.
2. There must be no restrictions imposed upon either the electors or the deputies.
3. Electioneering, and the elections themselves, must be carried out in complete freedom, and therefore the government must grant as a temporary measure, prior to the decision of the popular assembly, (a) complete freedom of the press, (b) complete freedom of speech, (c) complete freedom of assembly, (d) complete freedom of electoral programs.

This is the only way in which Russia can be restored to a course of normal and peaceful development. We solemnly declare before our native land and all the world, that our party will submit unconditionally to the decision of a Popular Assembly which shall have been chosen in accord with the above-mentioned conditions; and in the future we shall offer no armed resistance whatever to a government that has been sanctioned by the Popular Assembly.

And so, your Majesty, decide. Before you are two courses. On you depends the choice; we can only ask Fate that your reason and conscience dictate to you a decision which will conform only to the good of Russia, to your own dignity, and to your duty to your native land.

Manifesto of Alexander III

This manifesto, issued by Alexander III upon his accession to the throne, was written by Alexander's tutor and closest adviser, Konstantin Pobedonostsev, who was also the head of the Holy Synod.

- According to Pobedonostsev what is the source of the Tsar's authority to rule?
- Compare his outlook with that of Narodnaia Volia. What does this bode for the future?

It has pleased God, in His inscrutable judgment, to bring a martyr's end to the glorious reign of Our beloved father and to lay upon us the sacred duty of autocratic power.

Acknowledging the will of Providence and the law of Imperial succession, We accepted this burden in a terrible hour of public grief and horror, before Almighty God, trusting that, foreordained as it was that We should assume power at such a dangerous and difficult time, He would not refrain from granting Us His assistance. We trust also that the fervent prayers of Our devoted people, known throughout through the whole world for their love of and devotion to their sovereigns, will draw God's blessing upon Us and the labor of government to which We have been appointed.

Our father, deceased in God, having received the autocratic power from God for the good of the people entrusted to him, remained faithful to his sworn duty unto death, and sealed his great service with his blood. Not so much by the strict commands of authority, as by beneficence and gentleness, did he accomplish the great work of his reign: the emancipation of the bonded peasants [serfs], having secured the cooperation of the landed nobility, ever receptive to the voice of goodness and honor; he established justice in the realm and made all his subjects forever free, calling them to share in local government and the country's economy. May his memory be blessed for all time!

The base and wicked murder of the Russian sovereign in the midst of his loyal people, prepared to lay down their lives for him, by worthless scum, is a terrible, shameful, unheard of thing in Russia, and has darkened the whole land with grief and horror.

In the midst of Our great grief, the voice of God commands us to rise courageously to the business of government, with hope in Divine Providence and faith in the strength and truth of autocratic power, which We have been called upon to affirm and protect for the people's good against any encroachment upon it.

So also let courage animate the troubled and horrified hearts of Our Faithful subjects, of all who love the Fatherland and have been devoted from generation unto generation to the hereditary royal power. Under its shield, and in unbroken union with it, our Land has more than once survived great troubles, and with faith in God has risen in power and glory from grievous trials and tribulations.

Consecrating Ourselves to Our great service, We call upon all Our Faithful subjects to serve Us and the state in fidelity and truth, for the eradication of the vile sedition disgracing

---

the Russian land, for the strengthening of faith and morality, for the proper upbringing of children, for the extermination of falsehood and theft, and for the introduction of truth and good order in the operations of the institutions given to Russia by her benefactor, Our beloved father.

Protests by Peasant Women

Peasant dissatisfaction with social and economic relations in Russia was an ongoing reality which the emancipation of the serfs did not change. The police were kept busy preserving order. The following documents are police reports from the reign of Alexander III.

- What are the peasants upset about? What does this reveal about the impact of the Emancipation?
- What role do women play? How do you explain it?
- What is the attitude of the authorities toward the peasants?

REPORT OF THE VICE-GOVERNOR OF VORONEZH

The Korotoiaskii district police chief reports that the carrying out by the bailiff of the decision of the Korotoiaskii Council of peace mediators regarding the restoration of the landowners Bondarevs' property, infringed upon by the peasants of the hamlet of Zubovskoe and local village leadership, was subject to resistance.

In regard to this the police chief's assistant was ordered to provide the bailiff assistance; having arrived on the spot on the 25th of this past July, he summoned the peasants of the hamlet of Zubovskoe. Upon reading the council's decision to the peasants, it was suggested that they take down the fencing around their gardens that should be returned to the Bondarevs, but the peasants refused to carry out that demand on that occasion as well.

Then the police chief's assistant and bailiff began to remove the fencing, but once again met resistance on the part of the women who expressed themselves as follows: at the sign of one of the women who was standing near, a whole crowd of them, armed with sticks, rakes, pokers, etc., flung themselves toward the fencing with shouts: "Don't approach—we won't give them over!"

Source: Robin Bishna, Jehanne M. Gheith, Christine Holden, and William G. Wagner, Eds., *Russian Women, 1698–1917. Experience and Expression, An Anthology of Sources* (Bloomington, IN: Indiana University Press, 2002), 341–343. Reprinted with permission of Indiana University Press.

Despite all exhortations [to the contrary], the women refused to hand over the fencing, while the bearers of responsibility—their husbands, stood off to the side, apparently, not taking any part, convinced that they [the authorities] would not touch their wives, and only rarely did a few run out of the crowd, inciting the leader of the police, summoned there to help the bailiff, to commit insubordination.

After this, almost all of the policemen, summoned from neighboring settlements, with few exceptions, flatly refused to tear down the fencing.

When the police official and three guards and a few policemen began to get close to the people, the women attacked them and knocked down one of the guards, as a result of which one woman was injured; seeing her with a bloody face, the men also began to beat the officials and police.

When the crowd quieted down, they began to exhort them again to let them carry out the judicial decision, but the peasants firmly refused to submit to this.

At the present time I think it helpful to billet a company of soldiers in the hamlet of Zubovskoe as a punitive measure for two to three weeks. The peasants must comprehend that governmental power exists not only in the guise of policemen upon whom they send armed . . . [peasant women]. With the presence of military force the decision of the court would obviously be carried out.

REPORT BY THE GOVERNOR OF VIATKA PROVINCE

The peasants of the village of Archangeloe . . . owed arrears of two thousand rubles on state and land taxes, which out of obstinacy they had not wanted to pay for the duration of four years.

On the 22nd of last November the police officer of . . . Urzhumskii district, having a commission to declare to the above-mentioned peasants the provincial decree on peasant matters regarding the business of abandoning without benefit of a petition their postponement of payment of the aforesaid arrears, arrived in the village . . . together with the *starshina* [elder], two constables, and eighty policemen of lower ranks. Having gathered the peasants in the assembly hut, the police officer informed them about the provincial office's decision concerning their plea and suggested that they give him a signed statement to that effect, but all of the peasants in the hut (about two hundred persons) announced that they would not give the requested statement until they received the additional allotment of land. Being in an agitated state, the peasants answered the officer's demand for payment of the arrears with an absolute refusal. Seeing this and the unsuccessful nature of persuasion, the officer, in the presence of the above-mentioned officials, read out to the peasants the appropriate articles of the Criminal Code, warning what punishment awaited those guilty of disobeying the authorities. After that, the officer intended to draw up a list of the property of the more obstinate tax delinquents and set off for the homes of the elder Danil Rezvykh and peasant Aleksandr Rezvykh for that purpose, but there a crowd of almost all the residents of both sexes of the village of Archangeloe met him with an expression of open resistance to his instruction to inventory the movable property of those tax delinquents. Moreover, several inhabitants took the liberty of taking insolent actions against both the officer and the officers with him. Thus, by the way, the peasant woman Varvara Stepanova threw a clump of mud at the officer's face, while she threatened a police officer with a stick, a second peasant woman—Stepanida Totmeninova—hit a police officer with a stick, the peasant woman Irina Kozhevnikova tore a scarf from the neck of one of the officials, the peasant women Evdokiia Rezvykh and Efrosiniia Evstigneeva shoved another official in the chest. Besides that, the entire crowd shouted, branding the district police chief, officials, and policemen as thieves, robbers, and brigands. Such unruly behavior of the peasants forced the officer to discontinue his attempts to recover the arrears and return to his apartment, where the peasants gathered, locked the gate, and yelled that they would not let either the officer or officials out; but after some time, learning about the officer's dispatching a courier to an Urzhumskii official with a report about what had happened, the peasants dispersed to their homes. Upon the arrival on the spot of the requested police chief's assistant, the peasants, persuaded after various explanations and reprimands of the correctness of the demands for their arrears, acknowledged their guilt and began unquestioningly to hand over money owed to the tax collector. From the evidence provided thereafter by the police chief, it is clear that the said peasants voluntarily paid twelve hundred rubles on 22–24 November and that the payments are continuing.

Reports of Factory Inspectors in the 1880s

In its paternalistic style, the Russian government passed laws regulating factory conditions and industrial relations, but, because of its sympathy with the interests of the factory owners, it seldom enforced them. The following excepts come from inspectors sent by the Ministry of Finance to see if worker protection laws were being carried out.

- What does this reveal about working conditions in Russian factories?
- What does this reveal about relations between workers and managers?
- What does it suggest about trends in Russian society?

In the majority of factories there are no special quarters for the workers. This applies to workers in paper, wool, and silk finishing. Skilled hand craftsmen like brocade weavers can earn good wages, and yet most of them sleep on or under their looms, for lack of anything else. Only in a few weaving factories are there special sleeping quarters, and these are provided not for the weavers, but for other workers—the winders and dyers, etc. Likewise, the velveteen cutters almost always sleep on the tables where they work. This habit is particularly unhealthy, since the work areas are always musty and the air is saturated with dye fumes—sometimes poisonous ones. Carpenters also generally sleep on their workbenches. In bast-matting factories, workers of both sexes and all ages sleep together on pieces and mats of bast which are often damp. Only the sick workers in these bast factories are allowed to sleep on the single stove. In silk factory No. 61, the young female workers sleep side by side on the floor of their workroom. . . . Conditions are similar in dye works No. 82: workers

Source: Thomas Riha, Ed. *Readings in Russian Civilization, Vol 2, Imperial Russia, 1700–1917*, 2nd ed., revised, (Chicago: University of Chicago Press, 1969), 411–413. © University of Chicago Press. Reprinted by permission.

sleep all over the plant, even in the washing room and the bleach room, in the midst of harmful fumes. . . . There are no special sleeping quarters, either, in tarpaulin factory No. 83. The female canvas makers sleep together with their children on the benches where they sew, in rooms filled with the sharp odor of fresh tarpaulins. . . .

. . . Sanitary conditions in factories everywhere are as a rule completely unsatisfactory. . . . Here are some examples from my notes: In candy factory No. 11, "the shop buildings are extremely dark and dirty. Most of the chocolate department is in the basement, which is poorly lit and damp. The workers continually track in mud from the courtyard which is saturated with excrements and slops." In cloth factory No. 48 which was typical of such establishments, "the air in the dye-house was so saturated with steam when I inspected it that it was impossible to see anything. I groped my way about the dyeing room as if blindfolded—evidently, there was no ventilation at all. The machines were very crowded together, and belts crisscrossed in all directions. Moving around the machines is extremely hazardous, and accidents could easily happen to the soberest and most careful workers."

In chemical factory No. 144 "musty gases in rooms where tinned salt is prepared are so strong that someone unaccustomed to them could remain there only a few minutes. In the department where mercury is prepared, the only precautions against the deadly fumes are the cloths which the workers tie over their mouths. Not only are there no more reliable safety measures than this, but the family of one of the workers actually lives in an adjoining room." . . .

In plant No. 115 "in some departments, especially in the spinning room and the old weaving building, the machines are very crowded together. The lack of ventilation causes terribly thick cotton dust to accumulate in the combing and scotching rooms. Devices to evacuate the dust are inadequate. Much of the machinery, particularly in the scotching room, is uncovered and dangerous. There is no ventilation in the singe and burn room, and the smoke there is so thick and heavy that I was unable to remain there more than two or three minutes. . . ."

Because of this lack of ventilation and protective covering, I invariably saw such dust in carding shops of the spinning mills I visited that I would become completely covered with it, like flour, in just a few minutes. This dust was especially heavy in those spinning mills where the poorer grades of flax are processed. There the dust literally drifts in thick clouds, so that it becomes difficult not only to breathe, but also to see anything in the grayish fog. However undemanding our workers generally are, as I saw for myself, even they consider it necessary to take precautions against this awful dust. These workers have improvised a "respirator": they take a long bundle of flax, put it over their mouths, and tie the ends around in back of the head, and thus try to save their lungs.

According to my observations of 131 industrial establishments, only 71 pay their workers regularly. But even this figure, I suppose, is much higher than it should be, since factory owners and directors quite naturally would say yes when I asked if wages were paid regularly, and I myself did not always have an opportunity to check up on the truth of their statements. . . . [In a significant majority of the factories] wages are not fixed and depend completely on the will and the financial position of the owner or manager. The number of "accountings" per year is relatively fixed, but that is all. When an accounting is made, the mutual liabilities of employer and employee are summed up, but there is not necessarily any concurrent payment for wages. . . . . Should a man's monthly wages just cover his fines he will be so notified by a slip in his box. . . .

. . . Fines are as varied as the factories themselves. The factory administration is free to determine the grounds for fines and the amounts payable. . . . In many industrial establishments the grounds for fines and the sizes of fines are not fixed in advance. The factory rules may contain only one phrase like the following: "Those found violating company rules will be fined *at the discretion of the manager.*"

The degree of arbitrariness in the determination of the worker's wages, was unbelievably extreme in some factories. . . . Moreover, fines are levied for so many causes that falling under a severe fine is a constant possibility for each worker. For instance, workers who for any reason came into the office in a group, instead of singly, would be fined one ruble. After a second offense, the transgressors would be dismissed—leaving behind, of course, the ten-ruble fine for breach of contract.

Figure 13-1 "Calvary"

Nikolai Ge (1831–1894), one of the Itinerants, was strongly influenced by Leo Tolstoy's social and religious doctrines, and among his most famous paintings are a series of scenes from Jesus' life. This one was painted in 1893.

- Compare this with previous representations of Christ.
- What does this reveal about trends in Russian society?

Source: Tretiakov Gallery, Moscow.

Figure 13-2 Haying at the Leushinskii Monastery

This photograph was taken at the turn of the century by Sergei Prokudin-Gorskii, official photographer of the tsar.

- What does it suggest about trends in agriculture and Russian society?

Source: Prokudin-Gorskii Collection of the Library of Congress.

Figure 13-3 Bashkir Switchman

This is another of Prokudin-Gorskii's photographs. Although it was taken after the turn of the century, it is of the Trans-Siberian Railroad, most of which was constructed in the 1890s.

- What does the railroad signify for Russia?
- Why do you think this Bashkir is working on the railroad? What does this reveal about trends in Russian society?

Source: Prokudin-Gorskii Collection of the Library of Congress.

Figure 13-4 Schoolboys in Samarkand

This is yet another photograph taken by Prokudin-Gorskii.

- What generalizations can you make about the nature of this school?
- What does this suggest about Central Asian society?

Source: Prokudin-Gorskii Collection of the Library of Congress.

_____ FOR FURTHER READING _____

(In addition to the books by Engel, Kahan, Hillyar, Moon, Stites, and Wortman from the previous chapter.)

Byrnes, Robert F. *Pobedonostsev: His Life and Thought.* Bloomington, IN: Indiana University Press, 1968.

McDermid, Jane and Anna Hillyar. *Women and Work in Russia, 1880–1930: A Study in Continuity Through Change.* London: Longman, 1998.

Menning, Bruce W. *Bayonets Before Bullets: The Imperial Russian Army, 1861–1914.* Bloomington, IN: Indiana University Press, 1992.

Nathans, Benjamin. *Beyond the Pale: The Jewish Encounter with Late Imperial Russia.* Berkeley and Los Angeles: University of California Press, 2002.

Rieber, Alfred J. *Merchants and Entrepreneurs in Imperial Russia.* Chapel Hill, NC: University of North Carolina Press, 1982.

Rogger, Hans. *Russia in the Age of Modernization and Revolution, 1881–1917.* London: Longman, 1983.

Von Laue, Theodore. *Sergei Witte and the Industrialization of Russia.* New York: Columbia University Press, 1963.

Weeks, Theodore R. *Nation and State in Late Imperial Russia: Nationalism and Russification on the Western Frontier, 1863–1914.* DeKalb, IL: Northern Illinois University Press, 1996.

CHAPTER FOURTEEN

RUSSIA'S CRISIS, 1900–1916

In the industrial age, the only ideology that has been used successfully by ruling elites to justify their authority has been popular sovereignty, the idea that the population composes a single and united community whose interests the government serves. This notion was utterly alien to Tsar Nicholas II and his advisers, who labored under three fatal illusions: that the peasantry venerated the Tsar and were the bedrock on which the regime rested, that educated society could be controlled if only the nobility was fostered as the leading class, and that the peoples of the empire felt pride at being the subjects of an ancient and glorious dynasty. The government was wrong on every count. The peasantry had never thought that social relations in Russia were just, and had always believed that the land rightfully belonged to those who tilled it. The Russian nobility was not a monolithic entity and in fact contributed some of the most active supporters of constitutional, representative government. The peoples of the empire were increasingly resentful of Russian occupation and exploitation.

As a consequence, Russia experienced a series of rebellions in the first decade of the twentieth century, the most dangerous of which arose in 1905 in the major cities of the empire. The government made concessions sufficient to halt the unrest and then proceeded gradually to rescind them. Petr Stolypin (Prime Minister, 1906–1911) developed a progressive reform program, which might have saved the system. His assassination in 1911, however, left the government in the hands of reactionary and incompetent officials and a Tsar who was utterly out of touch with reality.

EURASIAN CONTEXT

In the first two decades of the twentieth century, industrialization, urbanization, and consumerism continued to grow in Europe, and the imperialist powers consolidated their rule over their recently seized possessions in Africa and Southeast Asia. Middle-class complacency was shaken, however, by a number of disturbing trends. Women (who in most countries could not own property, vote, or attend political meetings) began actively to demand equal political rights. Many socialists (disillusioned by the lack of progress achieved by workers' parties in European parliaments) proposed direct action: taking over factories or organizing general strikes to bring the system to its knees. Anarchists used terror to induce change; between 1897 and 1912, two Prime Ministers of Spain, the Empress of Austria, the King of Italy, and the President of the United States were assassinated. Nationalists in the Balkans were becoming increasingly militant and violent.

European scientists and intellectuals were also introducing disturbing ideas. The new physics questioned the material basis of reality and the predictability of natural events. The science of psychology argued that people were not rational beings but were driven by subconscious urges. Declining birthrates among the wealthy, ethnically dominant segment of society and increasing birthrate among poor immigrants and minorities led to anxieties over decadence and racial degeneration. Cubists and abstract artists created works that many people found ugly and disturbing.

Nothing, however, was more devastating to European confidence than the First World War (1914–1918). The war, which pitted Germany, Austria-Hungary, and Turkey against Russia, France, and England, began in August 1914 in a holiday atmosphere. Most Europeans thought it would be an ennobling and regenerating experience, and the public in every belligerent country was confident the war would be won in months or even weeks. They were wrong. The two sides were so evenly matched in both military forces and stubborn determination, that the "holiday" turned into a nightmarish four-year war of attrition in which more than fourteen million people died.

War and revolution in Europe had been preceded by war and revolution in Asia. In Turkey at the beginning of the twentieth century, the countryside experienced crop failures, the cities suffered from inflation, and the government was unable to pay its troops. In 1906, Turkey was swept by rebellions, riots, and mutinies. In 1908, the Committee for Union and Progress (CUP), known in Europe as the Young Turks, led a military revolt that forced Sultan Abdülhamid to restore the constitution of 1877; when he blocked further reform, it forced the him to abdicate. CUP subordinated the religious establishment to secular control, improved the rights of women, and westernized the educational system. When faced with popular unrest in 1913, the CUP installed a dictatorship which allied with Germany and Austria in 1915.

The Shah of Iran was assassinated in 1896 by a Shiite nationalist. The new Shah obtained large loans from Russia, and, in exchange, reduced import tariffs. This allowed Russia to flood Iran with cotton cloth from Turkestan, bankrupting most Iranian textile producers and fueling nationalist anger. In 1905, merchants and clerics went on strike across Iran, and the following year the dying Shah granted a constitution and an elected parliament. In 1907, however, his successor revoked the constitution, and the rebellion resumed. This provided a justification for Russian and English forces to intervene. Russia occupied the north and exploited its economy, while England occupied the south and took possession of Iran's oil fields.

In China, the Boxer Rebellion of 1900, a xenophobic popular attack on Chinese Christians and foreign diplomats, provided the pretext for yet another invasion by European armies. In 1905, the Chinese government began a series of modernizing and westernizing reforms and promised an eventual constitution and parliament, but it was too late to save the Qing dynasty. In the cities, nationalists demanded a republic, and in the countryside, gentry with regional loyalties sought more power. In 1911, the two forces combined to overthrow the Emperor. Sun Yat-sen, the leader of the nationalists, stepped aside to allow general Yuan Shi-kai to become President of the new Republic, believing him to be the only person with the power to preserve a united China. When Yuan declared himself emperor, however, the rebellion resumed. The central government collapsed, and China was divided and ruled by regional warlords.

Early in the century Japan gained world-power status by fighting Russia to a standstill in a major war in Manchuria. In 1900, Russia had helped suppress the Boxer Rebellion, but left its troops in Manchuria afterward. Japan was willing to concede a Russian sphere of influence in Manchuria, but not Korea. Japanese rulers wanted Korea to be recognized as part of its own sphere of influence, and it wanted Russian troops out of the region. This Russia refused, since it wanted to connect Vladivostok to the South China Railway in Manchuria, and it needed to build a railroad across Korea to do so. After four years of Russian intransigence, Japan declared war. Early in 1904, Japan defeated the Russian navy and laid siege to Port Arthur, which fell in December. In February 1905, Japan defeated the Russian army at Mukden. The Russian Baltic Fleet had been dispatched to Asia, and, after sailing around the world, it arrived at the Strait of Tsushima in May 1905 only to be annihilated by the Japanese.

Russia was humiliated, but not defeated. The land war was more costly than Japan had anticipated, and Russia, with three times the population and many times the natural resources of Japan, would win a war of attrition. Although Japanese public opinion was in favor of continuing, economic conditions forced the Japanese government to negotiate an end to the war. Russia, though materially able to continue, had no support from its public. U.S. President Theodore Roosevelt, who wanted to maintain a balance of power in East Asia, offered to mediate, and both Russia and Japan accepted. In the Treaty of Portsmouth (September 1905), both countries agreed to withdraw from Manchuria. Russia recognized Japan's sphere of influence in Korea and ceded to Japan its lease on the Liaodong Peninsula and Port Arthur, its coal mines, the South Manchurian Railroad, and the southern half of Sakhalin Island. However, Russia refused to admit that it had been defeated and, therefore, did not pay an indemnity.

Japan asserted its new status as world power by securing equal trade treaties with the European powers and by annexing Korea in 1910. When World War I broke out, Japan entered on the side of England, France, and Russia, and took over Germany's sphere of influence in the Shandong peninsula in China as well as Germany's island possessions in Oceania. Japanese soldiers did not fight in Europe, but Japanese ships patrolled the Mediterranean on behalf of the allies.

REVOLUTION, COUNTER-REVOLUTION, WAR

As the twentieth century began, Russian society was profoundly discontented. Crop failures and localized famines caused peasant rebellion in central Russia in 1901 and in Ukraine in 1902. An economic recession from 1899 to 1903 led to wage cuts, which workers resisted. There were twenty-nine thousand strikes in 1900, thirty-two thousand in 1901, and eighty-seven thousand in 1903. Unions in Rostov organized a general strike in 1902.

Encouraged by popular unrest, Russia's revolutionary parties were revitalized. In 1900, representatives of a number of populist groups announced the creation of the Socialist Revolutionary (SR) Party with the goal of mobilizing the peasantry to overthrow the old regime and to build socialism on the basis of the peasant commune. The following year, a secret organization was formed within the SR Party to carry out political assassinations. Its victims included the Minister of Education in 1901, the Minister of the Interior in 1902, the Governor of Ufa province in 1903, and the new Minister of the Interior in 1904. They failed, however, in an attempt on the life of Konstantin Pobedonostsev, Procurator of the Holy Synod and principal ideologist of autocracy.

The Russian Social-Democratic Labor Party (RSDRP) had attempted to hold a national organizing conference in 1898, but it was broken up by the police. In 1900, V. I. Lenin emigrated to Switzerland where he joined with L. Martov and G. Plekhanov to publish a journal, *Iskra*, which they hoped would serve as the organizational center for Russian Social-Democrats. *Iskra* organized the Second Congress of the RSDRP, held in Brussels and London in 1903, which adopted both a minimum program (a parliament, democratic elections, an eight-hour workday, and the transfer of all land to the peasantry) and a maximum program (socialist revolution and the dictatorship of the proletariat). Two factions emerged at the Congress, Mensheviks led by Martov and the more militant and disciplined Bolsheviks led by Lenin. Neither faction condoned terror, but the Bolsheviks were willing to accept money from "expropriators" who robbed banks and donated the proceeds to support revolution.

Government repression turned liberals into revolutionaries. The Minister of the Interior regularly interfered in zemstvo affairs, often refusing to permit elected zemstvo officials to take office and preventing zemstvo leaders from holding national meetings. Professional organizations were either banned or closely monitored by the government. Pavel Miliukov and Petr Struve (a former Marxist) began, in 1902, to publish an illegal journal, *Osvobozhdenie* (Liberation), that called for a constitutional monarchy, civil liberties, and an elected parliament. In 1903, liberal zemstvo officials and professionals founded an underground organization, the Union of Liberation, with a nationwide network of local cells.

The government attempted to suppress unrest in a number of ways. It continued to break up revolutionary organizations and to imprison and exile their members. Police agents infiltrated revolutionary parties; in fact, one of the leaders of the SR's terrorist organization was a police double-agent. The regime briefly attempted to convince workers that the Tsar was their friend by organizing "police unions" to press for higher wages and better working conditions. They were quickly disbanded, however, because the demonstrations were too large (the Tsar feared all mass movements, even of loyalists), and the unions tended to demand too much.

The government also began to use anti-Semitism to divert lower-class dissatisfaction away from itself. Soon after 1900, officials within the Ministry of the Interior produced a document, *The Protocols of the Elders of Zion,* which purported to be a record of Jewish plans to seize control of Russia and then to rule the world. In 1903, in Ukraine, the police disseminated anti-Jewish propaganda claiming that Jews killed Christian children and used their blood to make Passover matzos. In April 1903, a pogrom erupted in Kishinev in which forty-five Jews were killed, almost six hundred injured, and fifteen hundred homes and shops looted or destroyed. The police intervened only at the end of the second day.

The outbreak of the Russo-Japanese War in February 1904 caused an upsurge in patriotism and temporarily quieted demands for radical change, but the government soon alienated public opinion. Interior Minister Pleve repeatedly interfered in zemstvo activities and obstructed the work of a zemstvo organization to help wounded soldiers and to aid the families of those killed in action. When an informal meeting of zemstvo leaders in St. Petersburg called for civil rights, elected local government, and a national legislative assembly in early November, Nicholas II declared them enemies of Russia. Then, when Port Arthur was captured by the Japanese on December 19, 1904, the Russian public was shocked and blamed the disaster on government incompetence.

In January 1905, a more outrageous tragedy occurred. An Orthodox priest, G. A. Gapon, had organized a patriotic, Christian working-class movement. He encouraged workers to draw up a petition asking the Tsar for an eight-hour workday, progressive income tax, free universal education, and an elected constituent assembly. On Sunday January 9, 1905, the workers and their children, dressed in their Sunday best, many carrying icons, gathered to deliver the petition to the Tsar. The procession was intercepted by soldiers who fired on the crowd, killing more than 150 and wounding more than 1,000. The next day the government banned all workers' assemblies.

"Bloody Sunday," as the massacre was known, galvanized public opinion. Workers demonstrated in cities across Russia, and protests in St. Petersburg were so large that martial law was declared. University students across Russia were so disruptive that all universities were closed in March. In May, professional unions united into a single "Union of Unions," and an All-Russian Peasants' Union met (with one hundred delegates from twenty-two provinces). In May and June, the workers of Ivanovo-Voznesensk organized a general strike that shut down all the factories in the city. The military began to be hit by mutinies, the most spectacular of which was that of the battleship *Potemkin* in June 1905. Sailors seized control of the ship in the Odessa harbor and sailed it to Romania.

In August, the Tsar directed Minister of the Interior Aleksandr Bulygin to summon a national consultative assembly, in which elected representatives could give their advice on legislation. Elections would be indirect and only property owners would be allowed to vote. This minor reform was too little, too late. The liberal and socialist parties all refused to participate in the elections, and social unrest continued. The revolution peaked in October with a general strike that affected nearly all of Russia. It began when the railway union, which included telegraph and telephone workers, stopped work. Mass public demonstrations spontaneously arose in most cities. In the capital, nearly everyone stopped working: banks, courts, businesses, schools, offices, and hospitals closed, no newspapers were published, and electricity and gas was shut off. On October 13, the unions of the city elected delegates, almost six hundred in all, formed a St. Petersburg Soviet (council) of Workers' Deputies to coordinate the working class movement.

At this point, the Tsar and his advisers concluded that they had to choose between real concessions or military dictatorship. Since Nicholas could find no one willing to serve as dictator, he turned to Sergei Witte to propose constitutional reform. Witte drafted a manifesto, signed by Nicholas II on October 17, which granted freedom of speech and assembly, equality before the law, and an elective Duma (parliament) that would approve laws and supervise the bureaucracy. This was the turning point of the revolution. Although mistrustful of the government, the liberals and the middle classes were reluctant to deepen the revolution. They withdrew from the streets leaving the working class to fight by itself. The Social Democrats called for continued struggle, and the Bolsheviks even led an armed insurrection in Moscow. However, the Russian army was able to suppress the insurrection, and it began to restore order across Russia.

The forces of reaction were aided by a new patriotic party, the Union of the Russian People, popularly known as the Black Hundreds, predominantly of lower-middle-class origin. Aided and abetted by the police, they attacked socialist demonstrations and carried out pogroms against Jews. A wave of pogroms in the fall of 1905 left at least one thousand dead and forty thousand families bankrupt. The Tsar lightened the sentences of those convicted of violence against Jews, and he accepted honorary membership in the Union of the Russian People for himself and his son.

The resistance of the Tsar to real reform was also revealed in the Fundamental Laws, which were announced in April 1906. The Tsar retained the title of "autocrat," and he remained the sovereign ruler and the commander of the armed forces. He had the power to initiate laws and to make emergency decrees when the Duma was not in session. He was the source of the constitution, and he alone could amend it. The military and court budgets were beyond the purview of the Duma. The Duma's intended function was to consider laws that the administration submitted to it. It could only with great difficulty propose legislation, and any laws it passed could be vetoed by the Tsar or the upper house, the Council of State (half of which was appointed by the Tsar, and half of which was elected by the church, the nobility, and other conservative institutions). The Duma could ask questions of ministers, but it could not insist on answers, and it could not remove ministers from office.

Elections to the Duma, when they were held in the winter of 1906, discriminated according to sex, wealth, and social estate. Women, soldiers, servants, workers in small workshops, and landless peasants were not allowed to vote. The voting power of one landlord was equal to 3.5 townsmen, 15 peasants, and 45 workers. Despite this, of the 497 members of the First Duma, only 45 belonged to parties of the right. The liberal Constitutional Democrats (Kadets) had the most deputies, 184, and leftist parties had 124. The Duma came into immediate conflict with the Tsar, calling for universal suffrage, guarantees of civil liberties, an end to martial law, subordination of the Council of Ministers to the Duma, and the transfer of all state, crown, and noble land to the peasantry. After only 76 days, the Tsar dissolved the Duma.

In the meantime, the peasantry continued to rebel against the old order. Across central Russia, peasants stopped paying rent and taxes, seized nobles' land, and looted and burned manor houses. In June, after dismissing the First Duma, the Tsar fired Sergei Witte as Prime Minister and appointed Petr Stolypin in his place. Stolypin had gained fame in 1902 to 1903 when, as a provincial governor, he had ruthlessly suppressed peasant unrest, and Nicholas II expected him to use the same methods to bring order to all of Russia. In August, Stolypin set up military tribunals in the countryside. Those charged with anti-government activity were denied legal counsel and were tried in secrecy by army officers; if convicted, they were executed without the opportunity to appeal. Over the next two years, thousands of peasants were executed and tens of thousands were exiled to Siberia.

Stolypin believed that the mir, far from being a bastion of stability, was dominated by "the lazy and the drunken" who fomented discontent and prevented progress. In what he called a "wager on the strong," Stolypin proposed to break up the commune by permitting households to withdraw their land from the commune and to create individual family farms. Stolypin believed that this would speed up the modernization of agriculture and would create a class of prosperous farmers who would be a force for stability in the countryside.

In the cities, Stolypin shut down more than two hundred newspapers and arrested their editors and publishers. He also interfered in the elections to the Second Duma, hoping to produce a more conservative body. Instead, the Second Duma, elected in the Winter of 1907, was even more radical than the first, and it was dissolved by the Tsar after less than three months. Stolypin, violating the Fundamental Laws, changed voter qualifications to give the gentry even greater voting power and to favor Russians over non-Russians. In the elections for the Third Duma, 200,000 noble voters (approximately 1 percent of the population) elected 50 percent of the duma deputies. Peasants, workers, Poles, and the peoples of the Caucasus all lost electoral power, while Central Asians were denied the vote entirely.

The Third Duma, elected in 1907, was much more conservative, and was allowed to serve until the end of its five-year term in 1912. The Fourth Duma, elected in 1912, was equally conservative. Nevertheless, until the very end of his reign, Nicholas II continued to despise Duma leaders and to entertain plans to turn the Duma into an advisory body or to eliminate it completely. The Tsar also began to hate Stolypin for his arrogance and for his criticism of Grigorii Rasputin's interference in state affairs. Rasputin, an itinerant peasant holy man, had become influential at the court, since Tsaritsa Alexandra believed that he had been sent by God to save their son and heir to the throne, Aleksei. Aleksei suffered from hemophilia (a genetic disorder in which the blood does not clot), and Rasputin seemed miraculously able to stop Aleksei's bleeding.

In September 1911, Stolypin, the last reformer of the tsarist era, was assassinated. After his death, Nicholas's administration lacked any forward-looking vision and was increasingly out of touch with reality. The celebrations of the tricentennial of the Romanov dynasty in 1913 drew small crowds and generated little popular enthusiasm.

After the turn of the century, the Russian-French and German-Austrian alliances hardened. Russia and Austria continued to oppose one another in the Balkans, and France's desire for revenge against Germany was undiminished. England, locked in an arms race with Germany, began to cultivate ties with both France and Russia. In 1906, Britain loaned money to Russia for the first time since the Crimean War, and in 1907, the two countries recognized one another's spheres of influence in Iran, Afghanistan, and Tibet. Russia also overcame its hostility to Japan, which was allied with Britain. In 1907, Russia and Japan signed a commercial treaty which recognized a Japanese sphere of influence in southern Manchuria and inner Mongolia and a Russian sphere in northern Manchuria and outer Mongolia. In 1910, Russia and Japan signed a military alliance.

Hostility between Austria and Russia was intensified by a Balkan crisis in 1908. Russia believed that Austria had agreed to work with it to convince the Great Powers of Russia's right of naval access to the Turkish Straits and Austria's right to annex the Ottoman provinces of Bosnia and Herzegovina. Instead, Austria unilaterally invaded Bosnia and Herzegovina and annexed them to its empire. Serbia, which itself had wanted to absorb the two provinces to create a larger nation of southern Slavs (Yugoslavia), protested vehemently, but Austria, backed by Germany, ordered a partial mobilization of its army, and Serbia backed down. Russia was angry and humiliated.

Russia then encouraged Bulgaria and Serbia to expand southward at the expense of the Ottoman Empire. In 1912, the two Balkan nations declared war on Turkey and drove its forces from the peninsula. In the following year, Bulgaria, dissatisfied at the division of the newly won territory, attacked Serbia. In the end, Bulgaria and Serbia both gained territory at the expense of Turkey, but Serbia was again thwarted by Austria which forced the creation of Albania, thereby cutting Serbia off from the Adriatic Sea.

On June 28, 1914, Franz Ferdinand, heir to the throne of Austria-Hungary was assassinated in Belgrade by a Bosnian student with ties to officers in the Serbian army. Austria decided to invade Serbia and suppress Slavic nationalism. After presenting an ultimatum which it knew Serbia would reject, Austria declared war. Further Austrian expansion into the Balkans was unacceptable to Russia, and it began to mobilize its army; France, bound by treaty obligations to Russia, did the same. Germany felt threatened by the mobilization of troops on its eastern and western borders and informed Russia and France that it considered mobilization to be an act of war. Neither desisted, and Germany declared war against Russia on August 1 and against France on August 3. Britain, though not bound by treaty, declared war on Germany on August 4, and Japan joined the allies on August 23.

Germany's war plan was based on the assumption that Russia would mobilize more slowly than France. It therefore planned a massive attack on—and quick victory over—France, after which it would turn its attention to Russia. This plan was foiled by Russia's speedy invasion of East Prussia. Even though Russian armies suffered costly defeats and were driven from German soil, Germany was forced to divert two divisions from the French to the Russian front. As a result, France was able to halt the German invasion, and Germany was forced to fight an exhausting war on two fronts.

Although Russia fought successfully against Austria, it could not withstand the relentless German invasion. In the summer of 1915, Germany occupied Poland, and by the end of the year it had seized western Ukraine and Belarus. By the end of 1916, the German front extended from the Gulf of Riga to the Dniester River. The Russian army was plagued by shortages of rifles and ammunition, by problems in transportation and communication, and by generally incompetent leadership. The political situation in Petrograd (the capital's German-sounding name had been replaced with a Russian one) deteriorated in 1915 when, on Rasputin's advice, Nicholas II went to the front to raise the morale of the troops. He left the government in the hands of ministers whose principal qualification for office was their ability to ingratiate themselves with Rasputin, the Empress' confidant and adviser.

RELIGION AND CULTURE

The government was aware that education, in a land that rejected the concept of popular sovereignty, was dangerous. The State Council vetoed laws passed by the Duma that would have made education of all children compulsory and free and that would have permitted education to be provided in the national languages. Education remained tied to social status. Even though Greek and Latin was deemphasized in the gymnasia, and gymnasium and realschule curricula had become similar, realschule graduates were still denied entrance into universities.

Despite lack of government enthusiasm for education, school attendance continued to increase. In 1914, 51 percent of all children between the ages of eight and eleven attended school, and university enrollments rose from under 30,000 in the mid-1890s to 120,000 in 1914. The intelligentsia organized a variety of Sunday schools and evening courses to teach workers and peasants to read and write. Between 1894 and 1913, the literacy rate in Russia doubled from 20 to 40 percent. Seventy-five percent of Russia's 900 towns had libraries and reading rooms, all provincial capitals had museums and theaters, and there was a wide variety of locally published newspapers, journals, and books.

The Revolution of 1905 had profound implications for the Russian Orthodox Church. When the Tsar announced a policy of religious freedom in December 1904, he did not mention the Orthodox Church, since it did not occur to him that Russia's official church was not free. The Metropolitan of St. Petersburg, however, immediately pointed out that the Orthodox Church was in fact under state control and that it should be allowed autonomy like any other of Russia's religions. To Pobedonostsev's surprise and horror, the Holy Synod agreed. (Whereupon Pobedonostev resigned as Procurator.) The Holy Synod continued to recognize the Tsar as its "supreme patron" and "guardian," but it also wanted to summon a Sobor, a Church council, that could reorganize the church and elect a Patriarch. The Tsar refused. A number of radical priests began to call for the overthrow of the regime.

At the same time, religion had assumed new importance in secular culture. Vladimir Solovyov had brought theology into educated discourse and had influenced the Symbolists. After 1900, two leading Symbolists, Dmitrii Merezhkovskii and Zinaida Gippius, formed the Religious-Philosophical Society to discuss the meaning of Christianity for Russian culture, beginning a movement known as "Godseekers." Solovyov had pointed out that Marx's scientific materialism denied ethnical truth and provided no moral ground for valuing socialism over capitalism. Under Solovyov's influence Nikolai Berdiaev, Sergei Bulgakov, and Petr Struve turned from Marxism toward Christianity and liberalism, and in 1909, they published a collection of essays, titled *Vekhi* (Signposts), which renounced the populist revolutionary tradition. They criticized the intelligentsia for its paternalistic attitude toward the peasantry, and they argued that the intelligentsia should serve its own interests and promote law, ethics, and religion. On the other hand, a small group of left Bolsheviks (which included Maksim Gorky and Anatoly Lunacharsky), calling themselves "Godbuilders," insisted that Marxism was "the highest religion" because it promised to realize on earth the paradise that other religions only imagined in an afterlife.

Leo Tolstoy lived until 1910, and while his literary output slowed, his moral opposition to government, capitalism, and the established church continued to appeal to many Russians. Maksim Gorky wrote some of his best works between 1900 and 1916. His novel *Mother* (1906) celebrated the idealism and self-sacrifice of Russian revolutionaries, and his *Confession* (1907), which identified the proletariat with God, was the foremost literary expression of Godbuilding. Gorky collaborated with Bolshevik publishing ventures, and he donated money to their cause.

The Symbolist movement in literature was continued by Aleksandr Blok, whose romantic, lyric poetry was infused with mysticism. Andrei Belyi also wrote symbolist poetry but is best known for his novel, *Petersburg*, in which he introduced modernism into Russian literature. The Acmeists, a new school of poets which included Anna Akhmatova, Nikolai Gumilev, and Osip Mandelshtam, was interested in the world in itself and not as a symbol of a higher reality, but, like the Symbolists, they employed classical allusions and themes and attempted to convey philosophical truths. The Futurists, led by Vladimir Mayakovsky and Velimir Khlebnikov, rejected both estheticism and realism, celebrated contemporary urban culture, used free verse and nonsense words, and reveled in offending middle-class taste.

Between 1906 and 1914, the glorification of decadence came into vogue. The epitome of the decadent novel was Mikhail Artsybashev's *Sanin* (1907), in which the hero rebelled against convention, advocated sexual freedom, and confessed incestuous desire for his sister. Though tame by contemporary standards, it was shocking in its day. Urban culture imitated art; pornography proliferated, and sex clubs were formed in which members indulged in uninhibited and unconventional sexual activity.

ROLES AND STATUS OF WOMEN

There was considerable prejudice against women in the unions and the revolutionary movement. Union men were reluctant to accept women in leadership roles, and it was commonly thought (because women were paid less than men) that their presence in the workforce kept wages down. Many revolutionaries accepted the stereotype that women were more conservative and traditional then male workers and peasants. Nevertheless, women were involved in all aspects of the revolution, and unions that were predominantly female, such as textile workers, joined the general strikes.

Middle-class and professional women also participated in the revolution. Soon after Bloody Sunday, liberal women formed the "Imperial Union for Women's Equality" to coordinate the activities of local organizations across Russia. They held a congress in May, which demanded a constitutional convention, universal suffrage, and national autonomy within the empire. They also called for equal rights for peasant women in the land reforms, equal access to education, reform of the laws regulating prostitution (to subject male customers as well as female sex workers to periodic medical examinations), and labor laws protecting women. In July, the Union of Women's Equality was accepted into the Union of Unions.

In December 1905, a more moderate Women's Progressive Party was formed. It called for a constitutional monarchy, but it advocated peaceful and gradual change, not revolution.

The Women's Progressive party did not admit men and did not ally with male political parties, and pursued a woman-centered agenda with particular emphasis on family law and divorce law. The Mutual Philanthropic society was even more conservative. It did not participate in public politics but limited its activities to sending petitions to the State Council and other government officials asking them to include women in their deliberations and to grant women the right to vote in Duma and zemstvo elections. An Imperial Women's Congress met in 1908; it included middle-class feminists, women from the revolutionary parties, and working-class and peasant women, but it was the last major feminist gathering for almost a decade. The general reactionary atmosphere of the Stolypin years had a chilling effect on the women's movement just as it did other progressive and revolutionary movements.

When Duma elections were announced in 1905, women were denied the franchise. The right-wing parties were, of course, passionately opposed to women's suffrage. The Octobrists ignored the question, in effect opposing it. The other liberal and left-wing parties ultimately came out in favor of the franchise for women; the Social Democratic party had advocated the political equality of women since 1903.

The Social Democrats were opposed to feminism, however. They argued that capitalism was the root cause of the subordination of women, and that socialist revolution would solve the woman question without the need for a separate women's movement. The leading Bolshevik advocate on women's issues was Aleksandra Kollontai (1872–1952), daughter of an army officer. She began to read Marxist literature in 1891, and in 1898, she left her husband to become a revolutionary. Kollontai attended the Union for Women's Equality conference in 1905, but was repelled at its middle-class lack of concern for working women. She joined the Union of Textile Workers in 1907 and organized a "Mutual Aid Society for Women Workers" to serve as a front for revolutionary activity. After attending the first sessions of the Imperial Women's Congress in 1908, Kollontai had to flee the country to avoid arrest.

Women did make some gains in the early twentieth century. In 1900, women's university courses were begun in Moscow; by 1905, all the universities offered special degree programs for women. In 1914, women were finally admitted into universities and allowed into the same courses and degree programs as men. Women also entered the professions in greater numbers (although they typically had to be overqualified to be chosen over male candidates, and they were paid far less). After 1897, women were allowed to become doctors, but their employment was still largely restricted to obstetrics, gynecology, and pediatrics. After 1905, women were allowed to teach in women's courses at the university level, and in 1907, women were allowed to earn masters' and doctors' degrees. Women were allowed to become lawyers, but they could not argue in court.

Women also made progress in the struggle for reproductive rights. In 1912, women were granted, by law, a two-week paid leave for giving birth and four weeks at one-quarter pay after delivery. (This leave policy was not automatic; it had to be requested, and many employers did not publicize it.) Women also began to demand the right to contraception and to end unwanted pregnancies. Abortion was not legalized, but, as is usual in industrial societies, it became more frequent. In Moscow, the number of abortions doubled between 1909 and 1914; in St. Petersburg in increased ten times between 1897 and 1912.

The one profession which Russian women were actively encouraged to enter was prostitution. Prostitution had been legal in Russia since the 1840s and was regulated by the police. They did nothing to prevent child prostitution, or to protect prostitutes from abuse; they merely made sure that prostitutes had regular medical exams, in order to protect their customers from disease. It was estimated that 70 percent of Russian men visited prostitutes, and in St. Petersburg at the turn of the century there were 30,000 to 50,000 prostitutes in a population of 1,400,000. Agents for brothels waited at railroad stations, and recruited young peasant women arriving from the country. Servants and laborers typically earned less than twenty rubles a month, while prostitutes earned at least forty and sometimes many times that. Prostitution was on the agenda of many of the feminist organizations; some wanted to regulate it in the interests of public health; others wanted to outlaw it entirely.

Social and Economic Trends

Russia's population continued to grow. Between 1861 and 1912, rural population doubled and the urban population tripled, most of the increase occurring in the largest cities. Moscow grew from 900,000 in 1890 to 1,500,000 in 1912; during the same period St. Petersburg more than doubled to 2,200,000. The urban population was dominated by young adult workers who were born elsewhere, moved to the city to earn a living, and then returned home in middle age. In Moscow in 1897, for example, 67 percent of the population was between the ages of sixteen and fifty. The population was also primarily working class; manual laborers and factory workers made up 75 percent of Moscow's population in 1902.

The nobility retained its social status and high profile in the government and military, but its economic basis and relation to the land was changing. As always, the noble class was extremely stratified: in the early twentieth century, only 1 percent of the nobility owned more than 20 square miles of land, while 75 percent owned less than one square mile. In 1877, nobles had owned 35 percent of all arable land, but by 1905, this figure had declined to 22 percent. In fact, by 1905 half of all nobles owned no land at all. As a result, the nobility had to work for a living, and they engaged in business, the professions, and government service. Nobles made up 30 percent of government officials, 50 percent of the officer corps, and 70 percent of university graduates.

The merchant estate (which included industrialists) clung to its privileged status and was the least revolutionary segment of the population. For the most part, merchants accepted the autocratic system and were content to work within it. Their major contribution to Russian society was to take responsibility for public service projects, such as water and sewage, roads, schools, and hospitals, and to patronize the arts. Merchants did not make up a cohesive social class; they were divided by regional loyalty (Moscow vs. St. Petersburg), industry (heavy vs. light), and wealth.

After the Revolution of 1905, unions were legalized, and pay and working conditions improved. Strikes were still against the law, however, and the union movement was repressed during the Stolypin reaction. More than half of the unions formed in 1905 had been dissolved by 1909, and employers rescinded many of the concessions they had made. The workday was lengthened, the power to levy fines for violation of factory rules was reintroduced, and worker grievance committees were disbanded.

The workers' movement became more active after the Lena Goldfields massacre of April 1912, in which soldiers fired on a crowd of demonstrating miners, killing 172. In 1911, there had been only five hundred strikes, in 1912 there were two thousand, and in 1914 (in the eight months before the war began) there were four thousand. The strike movement subsided after the outbreak of the war, but it was not unusual for workers to hold one-day strikes on May Day and on the anniversaries of such events as the Emancipation, Bloody Sunday, and the Lena Goldfields Massacre.

The agricultural economy declined after the turn of the century. There were poor harvests in 1901 and 1902 and again from 1905 to 1908. Even though redemption payments were canceled in 1905, rents and taxes went up and so did the poverty rate. In 1906, free internal migration was legalized, and the government provided financial assistance to all peasants who wanted to move to Siberia. Between 1904 and 1913, five million farmers migrated. They had more land and livestock and a higher standard of living that farmers in European Russia, though less access to education and health care.

Stolypin's plan to encourage the break-up of the commune into separate family farms was revolutionary in its intention: the mir was no longer seen as the bedrock on which the regime rested. Reverence for the mir had turned into contempt. Though he wanted to foster individual initiative, however, Stolypin opposed the rise of capitalism in the countryside. Peasant land could not be sold to another social estate, and it could not be mortgaged (and hence could not be lost through foreclosure). Furthermore, in an attempt to prevent stratification in the peasant community, land settlement commissions arranged the division of land so that one family did not receive more land than it could farm itself.

Though revolutionary in principle, the Stolypin reform made little change in practice. Only 10 percent of peasant families consolidated their lands. Furthermore, when land was divided, it was usually only consolidated into single fields within the framework of the old commune. Only 1 percent of peasant households actually separated their farms from the commune, and those who did so were generally disliked by their neighbors.

According to many economic indicators, Russia in the first decades of the twentieth century lagged behind other industrialized countries. Slightly more than 75 percent of the Russian population were agricultural workers, while in western Europe that figure was less than 50 percent. Russia contributed 5 percent of world industrial output compared with 14 percent for Great Britain and 16 percent for Germany. Only 21 percent of the Russian population could read and write, while in Great Britain the figure was nearly 100 percent. To foreign observers, Russia continued to appear rural. In 1900, two-thirds of the buildings were made of wood. Most streets were unpaved, and water and sewage was not piped. Most towns had no factories or railroad stations.

On the other hand, Russia's great size and population made it an economic powerhouse. In 1913, Russia's population was 170,900,000, three times larger than Germany and four times larger than Britain or France. Russia produced more textiles than Germany, more total manufactured goods than Austria, and more grain than any other country in Europe. Russia's growth rate of 3.25 percent was surpassed in Europe only by Sweden (3.75 percent) and in the world only by Japan (3.4 percent) and the United States (3.5 percent). Between 1900 and 1916, Russia's railroad system and its production of coal, pig iron, sugar, and cotton approximately doubled. In agriculture, the output of grain increased from 48 million tons in 1900 to 69.4 million in 1913, and livestock production increased proportionately. In 1913, Russia had a trade surplus of 146,000,000 rubles.

PEOPLES OF THE EMPIRE

Official anti-Semitism continued until the very end of the Romanov dynasty. In 1906, the Council of Ministers suggested an end to discrimination against Jews, but Nicholas II vetoed the idea. In 1913, Mendel Beilis, a Jew, was accused of ritual murder, and the government prosecutor brought in "experts" who testified that Jews habitually murdered Christian children. Fortunately, Russian citizens were not as ignorant as their Tsar and his officials; a jury acquitted Beilis. In the First World War, 600,000 Jews served in the army, a greater proportion than any other group, yet Jews were accused of avoiding service. Jews living in the borderlands were suspected of sympathy with Austria, and many were deported to the interior of Russia.

Finnish autonomy was relentlessly eroded by the Russian government. In 1898, Finns were drafted into the Russian army; in 1902, the Russian governor began to replace Finnish officials and judges with Russians; and in 1903, the "Temporary Regulations" were applied to Finland. As a result, the Finns, inspired by the Revolution of 1905, organized a general strike and won the right to restore a native government. In 1906, a new Finnish parliament was elected by universal suffrage, and Finland became the first nation in Europe to give women the right to vote. The victory was short lived; the Finnish parliament was repeatedly dissolved by the Tsar, and in 1910, he gave the Russian Duma the authority to legislate for Finland.

Both the Revolution of 1905 and World War I brought change to the Caucasus. In Azerbaijan, the Muslim Azeri population lived in segregated ghettoes and held the most menial jobs. In 1905, poor Azeris rioted against the privileged foreigners and the Azeri intelligentsia promoted pan-Turkism, technological but not cultural modernization, and Islam. In Georgia in 1905, a widespread peasant revolt occurred in the west and general strikes were organized in industrial cities. Mensheviks and Bolsheviks both won considerable support from the Georgian working class, although only Menshevik delegates were elected to the first two Dumas. For Armenians, the war was a catastrophe. The Turkish government feared that Armenians living in Turkey would aid the Russians, and in 1915, it decided to deport the entire population of 1,750,000 Armenians to Syria and Mesopotamia. The death toll (resulting from starvation during the forced migration and from outright massacres) may have reached 1,500,000 making this the first genocide of the twentieth century and proportionally one of the worst in history.

Central Asia was also in turmoil in the years of revolution and war. More than one million Russian peasants had emigrated to Turkestan in the 1890s, resulting in continual conflict between peasant and nomads. Furthermore, in 1916, Kazakhs rose in a national rebellion when the tsarist government began to conscript non-Russians to work as laborers at the front. Many Russian colonists were killed by the rebels and many more Kazakhs and Kirgiz were killed by the army.

In the Khanates of Central Asia, several rebellious movements appeared. A majority of laborers on the railroad and in the mines and factories were Russian, and they were organized by the Russian revolutionary parties. At the same time, bands of poor natives who had lost their land roamed the countryside, plundering Russian settlements. In addition, Uzbek intellectuals (educated in Russian and Turkish universities), known as Jadidists, attempted to combine modern learning with Muslim faith and dreamed of national independence. They organized demonstrations against the regime in 1905, and they were considered dangerous not only by Russian officials but also by the rulers of Bukhara and Khiva. Most Jadidists fled into exile after 1907. Finally, the residents of many of the cities of Central Asia rebelled against conscription in 1916.

CONCLUSION: DECEMBER 1916

The social strains that caused the Revolution of 1905 were repressed but not resolved, and they reemerged as World War I dragged on. Fifteen million Russian men were conscripted, and women took up the burden of working longer hours in both farm and factory. In the cities, the length of the working day increased, working conditions deteriorated, and wages failed to keep up with inflation. In the countryside, agricultural production was maintained, but a shortage of consumer goods reduced the incentive to deliver crops to the market. In addition, the army used so great a proportion of Russian railroad stock for the war effort that there was reduced capacity for shipping grain; as a result the cities faced food shortages. By late 1916, Petrograd received only one-third the usual amount of food.

The property-owning and professional classes, inspired by patriotism and visions of imperial glory, were also increasingly dissatisfied with the government. They blamed Russia's poor military performance on the autocracy. Liberals called for a ministry responsible to the Duma. Monarchists blamed the German Empress Alexandra and her dissolute and corrupt confidant, Rasputin. In November, the leading Kadet, Pavel Miliukov, speaking in the Duma, declared the government guilty of either stupidity or treason, and in December, Rasputin was murdered by a cousin of the Tsar. The Romanov dynasty was facing its last crisis.

--------------- TEXT DOCUMENTS ---------------

Petitions to the First State Duma

After the Duma began to meet, constituencies across Russia sent it petitions and reso-lutions advocating laws or policies they wanted the Duma to enact. Three such state-ments appear below. These three documents appeared, chronologically, after Document 4 (below), the law that established the Duma. Nevertheless, they express attitudes that had been a part of the revolutionary movement that had forced the tsar to create the Duma, and so they appear first.

- What demands reflect traditional peasant concerns, and what demands are new?
- What does this reveal about trends in Russian society?

I. A RESOLUTION BY PEASANTS

We, the undersigned peasants . . . gathered in a village assembly on 24 June 1906 with a total of 147 household heads in the presence of our village elder, Ilia Morozov. After discussing current events, we resolved to request the State Duma as soon as possible to demand the fol-lowing from the government:

1. Free all those innocent people being held in prisons.
2. Replace the present ministers with [new ones] chosen from the State Duma, who should be respon-sible to the people.
3. Abolish the State Council.
4. Make all social estates equal in rights.
5. Transfer all noble, crown, monastery and other [private] lands to the entire working people.
6. Introduce universal, mandatory elementary education in the country; in addition, make access to secondary and higher education open and tuition-free for all.
7. Abolish the office of land captain and replace it with someone elected by the people.
8. Eliminate the emergency security measures in our province and, in general, such extraordinary measures are not to be taken in this country.
9. Abolish the shameful death penalty.
10. Replace the onerous indirect taxes with a progressive income tax.
11. Do not prosecute the brewing of koumiss [fermented mare's milk], since it is brewed not for the sake of drunkenness, but for preserving our health in difficult moments of peasant life (because government liquor is too expensive and not always available).
12. Ask the Sovereign Emperor to pay heed to the pleas and petitions of the entire Russian people and to liberate it from the yoke and arbitrariness of the officials who surround it.

This came from peasants in Seltinsk Township, Viatka Province, June 24, 1906.
Source: From *Supplication to Revolution: A Documentary Social History of Imperial Russia* by Gregory L. Freeze, copyright 1988 by Oxford University Press, Inc.. Used by permission of Oxford University Press, Inc.

These requests to their deputy to the Duma came from Ekaterinoslav Metalworkers in June 1906.

- What does this reveal about the interests and goals of unions in Russia?
- What similarities does this share with peasant demands?

II. INSTRUCTION FROM WORKERS

1. Introduction of legal protection of labor in the state.
2. Immediate introduction, through legislation, of an eight-hour working day (with preservation of current wages).
3. Abolition of obligatory decrees for overtime work.
4. Establishment of local mediation offices for the employment of workers in all branches of production, with the participation of representatives from worker organizations in its administration.
5. Amnesty for all political [prisoners] and abolition of capital punishment.
6. Unlimited freedom of conscience, speech, press, assembly, strike and union.
7. Establishment of reconciliation offices with an equal number of representatives from labor and capital to normalize all relations of employment and final wage settlements and to settle disputes and disagreements that arise between the workers and employers.
8. Abolition of the practice of hiring labor through contractors.
9. Abolition of fines and suspensions.
10. State insurance for illness, accidents, and professionally-related disease; the costs for this are to be paid by the firms.
11. State insurance for old age and disability.
12. Development of labor protection for women and children and the establishment of special control over production that is known to be harmful to the [workers'] health.
13. Introduction of universal, free and obligatory education in elementary schools, with the transfer of administration of school affairs to organs of local self-government. Organized assistance to those pupils in need.
14. Introduction of schools on Sundays for adult workers.
15. Establishment of criminal responsibility for the violation of laws on labor protection by both workers and firms.

Source: From *Supplication to Revolution: A Documentary Social History of Imperial Russia* by Gregory L. Freeze, copyright 1988 by Oxford University Press, Inc.. Used by permission of Oxford University Press, Inc.

This was written was written by the Russian Women's Mutual Philanthropic Society in February 1906 to the new Duma which had just been chosen in an election in which only men could vote.

- What argument is being made here?
- What does this reveal about Russian society?

III. WOMEN'S PETITION

On the great day of the opening of the State Duma, a day which all of Russia has awaited with intense impatience, when the first representatives of the Russian people gather, it will not include a single woman or a single representative directly chosen by women.

By the state acts of 6 August 1905, 17 October 1905, and 11 December 1905, half of Russia's population is deprived of the right of franchise as a duty common to all citizens; they have been deemed legally incompetent and relegated to the category of adolescents and creatures without any rights.

The Russian Women's Mutual Philanthropic Society, which in the course of its ten years in existence, has indefatigably served the interests of women, and [which has been supported] by the sympathy of the undersigned, deems itself duty-bound, in the name of justice, in the name of the defense of the human dignity of women, to place before the Duma the question of the political equality of women in Russia.

The Russian woman participates alongside men—in all spheres of work and endeavors in the cause of the development and growth of the motherland; in peasant agricultural work; in factory and industrial work; in the sphere of science, literature and art; in state, public and private institutions, and in the high service as doctor and teacher—and bears the great responsibility for the upbringing of future citizens.

Along with men, she pays taxes and assessments, and stands responsible before the law on an equal basis with all citizens. As an equal in the payment of taxes, as someone who works on the same basis as men, as one responsible in an equal degree before the law, a woman—in all fairness—should have the right to defend her interests through participation in a legislative assembly, whose decisions also directly affect her fate no less than that of men. . . .

Deputies of the Russian land! You have been summoned to a great creative work for the benefit of our motherland. Be just and dispassionate to the declaration of women, who demand equality of rights. Respond in concurrence with the numerous voices of those who are firmly persuaded of the rightness of their demands and who, among the number of reforms to renew Russia, include the regeneration of life for women by granting them equal rights to participate in service to the motherland.

Source: From *Supplication to Revolution: A Documentary Social History of Imperial Russia* by Gregory L. Freeze, copyright 1988 by Oxford University Press, Inc.. Used by permission of Oxford University Press, Inc.

The Fundamental Laws of Imperial Russia, 1906

The October Manifesto had helped to end the Revolution of 1905 by satisfying the demands of Russia's liberals. In it the Tsar promised civil liberties, a Duma (parliament), and a constitution. Elections to the Duma took place early in 1906, but it did not meet until May. The Fundamental Laws, the first Russian constitution, were promulgated by the Tsar in April 1906 to define the relations between the Duma and the Tsar's government and to define the rights of citizens.

- What is the political status of the Tsar, and what are his powers?
- What are powers of the Duma?
- What are the liberal elements of this document? How are they limited?
- Overall, how did this change the Russian political system?

1. The Russian state is unified and indivisible.
2. The Grand Duchy of Finland, while comprising an inseparable part of the Russian state, is governed in its internal affairs by special decrees based on special legislation.
3. The Russian language is the official state language and its use is obligatory in the Army, the Fleet, and in all state and public institutions. The use of local languages and dialects in state and public institutions is determined by special laws.

CHAPTER I. THE ESSENCE OF THE SUPREME AUTOCRATIC POWER.

4. The All-Russian Emperor possesses the supreme autocratic power. Not only fear and conscience, but God himself, commands obedience to his authority.
5. The person of the Sovereign Emperor is sacred and inviolable.
7. The Sovereign Emperor exercises the legislative authority jointly with the State Council and the State Duma.
8. The Sovereign Emperor enjoys the legislative initiative in all legislative matters. The State Council and the State Duma may examine the Fundamental State Laws only on his initiative.
9. The Sovereign Emperor approves laws; and without his approval no legislative measure can become law.
10. The Sovereign Emperor possesses the administrative power in its totality throughout the entire Russian state. . . .
12. The Sovereign Emperor alone is the supreme leader of all foreign relations of the Russian state with foreign countries. He also determines the direction of foreign policy of the Russian state.
13. The Sovereign Emperor alone declares war, concludes peace, and negotiates treaties with foreign states.
14. The Sovereign Emperor is the Commander-in-Chief of the Russian Army and of the Fleet. He possesses supreme command over all the land and sea forces of the Russian state. . . .
15. The Sovereign Emperor has the power to declare martial law or a state of emergency in localities.
22. Justice is administered in the name of the Sovereign Emperor in courts legally constituted, and its execution is also carried out in the name of His Imperial Majesty.

Source: Basil Dmytryshyn, *Imperial Russia: A Source Book, 1700–1917* (Gulf Stream, FL. Academic International Press, 2001), 417–425. Copyright Academic International Press, Gulf Stream, FL.

23. The Sovereign Emperor has the right to pardon the accused, to mitigate the sentence, and even to completely forgive transgressions, including the right to terminate court actions against the guilty and to free them from trial and punishment. . . .

CHAPTER II. RIGHTS AND OBLIGATIONS OF RUSSIAN SUBJECTS

28. The defense of the Throne and of the Fatherland is a sacred obligation of every Russian subject. The male population, irrespective of social status, is subject to military service determined by law.
30. No one shall be subjected to persecution for a violation of the law except as prescribed by the law.
31. No one can be detained for investigation otherwise than prescribed by law.
33. The dwelling of every individual is inviolable. . . .
34. Every Russian subject has the right to freely select his place of dwelling and profession, to accumulate and dispose of property, and to travel abroad without any hindrance. Limits on these rights are determined by special laws.
35. Private property is inviolable. . . .
36. Russian subjects have the right to organize meetings that are peaceful, unarmed, and not contrary to the law. . . .
37. Within the limits determined by law everyone can express his thoughts orally or in writing, as well as distribute these thoughts through publication or other means.
38. Russian subjects have the right to organize societies and unions for purposes not contrary to the law. . . .
39. Russian subjects enjoy freedom of religion. Terms to enjoy this freedom are determined by law.
41. Exceptions to the rules outlined in this chapter include localities where martial law is declared or where there exist exceptional conditions that are determined by special laws.

CHAPTER III. LAWS

42. The Russian Empire is governed by firmly established laws that have been properly enacted.
44. No new law can be enacted without the approval of the State Council and the State Duma, and it shall not be legally binding without the approval of the Sovereign Emperor.
45. Should extraordinary circumstances demand, when the State Duma is not in session . . . the Council of Ministers will submit such a measure directly to the Sovereign Emperor. . . . The validity of such a measure is terminated . . . if the State Duma or the State Council should refuse to enact it into law.

CHAPTER IV. THE STATE COUNCIL, STATE DUMA, AND THE SCOPE OF THEIR ACTIVITY

56. The Sovereign Emperor, by a decree, annually convenes the session of the State Council and of the State Duma.
58. The State Council is composed of members appointed by His Majesty and of elected members. The total number of appointed members of the Council called by the Emperor . . . cannot exceed the total number of the elected members of the Council.
59. The State Duma consists of members elected by the population of the Russian Empire for a period of five years, on the basis of rules governing elections to the Duma.
63. The Sovereign Emperor, by a decree, can dissolve the State Duma and release its members from their five-year tenure. The same decree must designate new elections to the State Duma and the time of its first session.

65. The State Council and the State Duma enjoy the constitutional right to submit proposals to repeal or to amend the existing laws as well as to issue new laws, except the Fundamental Law whose review belongs exclusively to the Sovereign Emperor.

69. Legislative measures that have been rejected either by the State Council or by the State Duma are considered defeated.

70. Those legislative measures that have been initiated either by the State Council or by the State Duma, but which have failed to gain Imperial approval, cannot be resubmitted for legislative consideration during the same session. . . .

Chapter V. Council of Ministers, Ministers, and Heads of Various Departments.

81. The Chairman of the Council of Ministers, Ministers, and Heads of various departments, are responsible to the Sovereign Emperor for State administration. Each individual member is responsible for his actions and decisions.

Prostitutes' Petition

In 1910, The Russian Society for the Protection of Women organized a conference to discuss the issue of prostitution (which was a legal, state-regulated profession) in hope of abolishing the practice. Representatives were invited from a wide cross section of educated society, but no prostitutes were asked to attend. A group of sixty-three prostitutes, who were aware of the conference submitted to it the following petition.

- What do the prostitutes ask for?
- What does this reveal about trends in Russian society?

Having learned from the newspaper that on April 21 of this year the All-Russian Congress for the Struggle against the Trade in Women will be convened, at which many issues concerning our unhappy life will be discussed, we the undersigned request that the esteemed members of the congress grasp our situation and do not refuse our humble request.

Many of us for various reasons became prostitutes at a very early age, when we were in tolerable health and we were not suffering from any kind of venereal diseases, of which the most horrible for us, as for everyone, is syphilis. Meanwhile, as time goes on, every one of us

Source: Robin Bishna, Jehanne M Gheith, Christine Holden, and William G. Wagner, Eds. *Russian Women, 1698–1917. Experience and Expression, An Anthology of Sources* (Bloomington, IN: Indiana University Press, 2002), 139–140. Reprinted with permission of Indiana University Press.

unfortunates becomes infected. This is due to no fault of our own, but because syphilitic men, whom it occurs to no one to examine, are indiscriminately permitted as guests. [The medical police] require us to be healthy, they make us go to examinations, they put us in the hospital for the tiniest of scratches, but nobody requires the same of our guests. They are allowed to infect us unimpeded and with impunity, and transform us in the future into miserable cripples from whom anyone would turn away in horror. Indeed, our guests are not little children, and they should understand that it is wrong to spread illness and that they do not have the right to pass on syphilis, even to loose women. We, you know, are also human beings, our health is valuable to us, and our old age will not be sweet without it.

Not daring to trouble the attention of the honored congress for long, we humbly ask you to discuss this issue and try to arrange things so that sick guests are not allowed to come to those of us who are healthy, and that health is required of them, as it is of us. They who participate in this business are no better than we.

We humbly request that you give our paper a turn and read it at the congress. Maybe it will find kind people who will understand that it is cruel and insulting to have one's health ruined when one is young, and that everything is only demanded from one side, that is, from us. We earnestly request that you look after us.

Gorky, *Mother*

In 1906, when Maxim Gorky wrote this novel, he was closely associated with the Bolshevik faction of the Social-Democratic Party. Mother *was enthusiastically received by the Russian revolutionary movement. Lenin, a close friend of Gorky, admired this book, but the relationship of the two men became more distant as Gorky became identified with "God-building," a left Bolshevik movement which identified Marxism as "the highest form of religion." Lenin insisted Marxism was science not religion.*

- What does this suggest about one of the possible motivations for participation in the revolutionary movement?
- Why might Lenin have approved of this novel, while disapproving of God-building? (Consider generational and gender issues.)

Life flowed along quickly, in a succession of varied, eventful days. Each one brought something new, and this no longer alarmed the mother. Ever more frequently her house was visited by unknown people who came in the evening to talk with Andrei in anxious, lowered voices, after which they would raise their coat collars, pull their caps down over their eyes, and disappear in the darkness with noiseless caution. She was conscious of the

---

Source: M. Gorky, *Mother* (Moscow: Foreign Languages Publishing House, 1950), 218–222, 433–435.

suppressed excitement each of them felt. It seemed that they all wanted to sing and laugh, but they had no time; they were always hurrying somewhere. Some were serious and sarcastic, others were gay and sparkling with youthful energy, still others were quiet and thoughtful. In the eyes of the mother, all of them were characterized by the same purposeful confidence, and while each of them was highly individual in appearance, for her all the faces merged into one—into a thin, calmly resolute face with deep, clear, dark eyes whose glance was at once gentle and severe, like the glance of Christ on the road to Emmaus. . . .

In all these people from the town she detected something childlike and was inclined to smile to herself condescendingly, but she was touched and happily surprised by their faith, whose profundity became more and more evident to her. Her heart was warmed and caressed by their dreams of the triumph of justice, and as she listened to them she sighed with some incomprehensible sadness. But she was particularly touched by their utter simplicity, and by a lovely, lavish indifference to their own welfare.

She already understood much of what they said about life, she felt that they had discovered the true source of human sorrow and she agreed with most of their claims. But in the depths of her heart she did not believe that they would be able to remake life, or that they would be strong enough to draw all the working people to their cause. Everyone was concerned with filling his belly today; nobody wanted to postpone it until even tomorrow.

Few people would consent to go that long and difficult road; few eyes would catch the fabulous vision of the kingdom of human brotherhood to be reached at the end. For that reason all these good people seemed to be children to her, in spite of their beards and mature faces, often worn with weariness.

"You poor dears!" she thought, shaking her head.

But now, all of them were living a fine, serious, sensible life. They spoke of doing good and did not spare themselves in their effort to teach others what they already knew. She realized how one could love such a life in spite of its danger, and with a sigh she glanced back over the dark, narrow ribbon of her past. Little by little there grew within her a calm consciousness that she herself was important to this new life. Formerly she had never felt that anyone needed her, but now she clearly saw that many people needed her, and this was a new and pleasant thing which made her lift her head.

She liked to talk to people, to hear their tales and complaints and the things that puzzled them. It always made her happy to meet a person who was deeply dissatisfied—with a dissatisfaction which, in protesting against the blows of fate, persistently sought an answer to clearly-defined questions. Before her kept unfolding the picture of human life with its restless and vainglorious struggle for satiety. Everywhere she could plainly see the brazen attempt to fool people, to do them out of something, to drink their blood and squeeze the last drop out of them for the sake of personal advantage. And she saw that there was an abundance of everything on the earth, while at the same time the masses of the people were in need, living half-starved lives in the midst of plenty. The churches of the city were, filled with silver and gold which God had no use for, while at the gates of the temple shivered beggars, patiently waiting for meagre donations to be dropped into their hands. Formerly she had also seen all this—the rich churches and the gold brocaded vestments of the priests which made such a striking contrast to the hovels of the beggars and their shameful rags. But formerly she had accepted this as a natural state of affairs, while now she found it intolerable and an insult to the poor who, as she knew, were closer to the church and had more need of it than the rich.

From pictures of Christ which she had seen and from the stories about Him which she had heard, she knew that He dressed simply and was a friend of the poor. But in the churches she saw His image adorned in flagrant gold and silk which rustled squeamishly at sight of the beggars who came to Him for comfort. . . .

Quite unconsciously she began to pray less, but to think more about Christ and about the people who, without ever mentioning His name, without seeming even to know about Him, lived, as it seemed to her, according to His precepts and in His manner, considering the earth to be the kingdom of the poor and wishing to divide all its riches equally among all people. Her mind dwelt much on this and her thoughts grew within her, becoming more profound and embracing all that she saw and all that she heard. They grew and assumed the brightness of a prayer, illuminating with their even glow the whole of the dark world, the whole of life and all of the people. And it seemed to her that Christ Himself, whom she had always loved with a vague tenderness—a complicated emotion in which fear was closely bound up with hope, and joy with sorrow—had become dearer to her. And He had changed, becoming more elevated and accessible, more bright and joyous, as though in actual fact He had become resurrected for life, laved and revived by the blood so generously shed in his name by people who modestly refrained from speaking the name of this friend of man.

Figure 14-1 Nicholas II with His family
- Compare this photograph of Nicholas II with previous representations of Russian tsars.
- What ideas does it convey?

Source: AP/Wide World Photos.

Figure 14-2 Malevich, "Reaper"

Kazimir Malevich (1878–1935) was one of the leading proponents of modernism and avant-garde art in Russia and in Europe. He experimented in a number of styles, including primitivism, Suprematism (geometric, non-objective art), and the geometric, objective style of which this work, painted in 1912, is an example.
- What is new and what is traditional in this representation of peasants?
- What does this signify regarding trends in Russian society?

Source: B. M Kustodiev Art Gallery, Astrakhan.

Figure 14-3 Poster: "Concord"

This poster, created by an unknown artist, appeared in 1914, soon after the outbreak of the war. In a caption at the bottom, the three figures are identified (from left to right) as "Love," "Faith," and "Hope."

- Which countries do these figures represent?
- What gender messages are conveyed? How does this poster "work"?

Source: Early-twentieth-century poster.

Figure 14-4 Interior of a Textile Mill in Tashkent

This photograph was taken between 1905 and 1915 in Tashkent in what is now Uzbekistan.

- What does this reveal about the level of Russian techology?
- What does it suggest about the economic relations between the center and periphery in the Russian Empire?

Source: Prokudin-Gorskii Collection, Library of Congress.

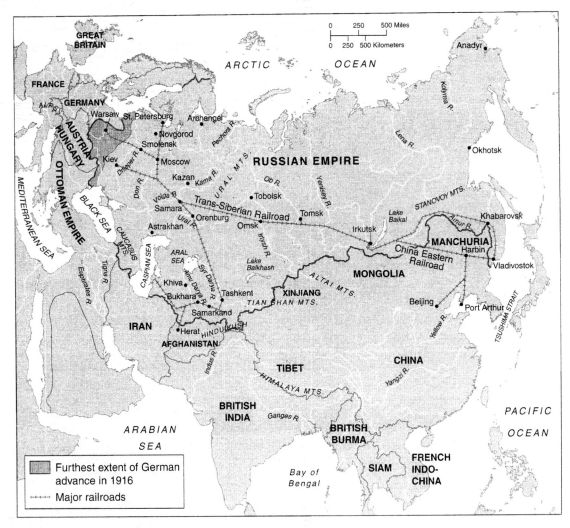

Figure 14-5 Russia in 1916

Effective transportation was important for economic and strategic regions. What does this railroad system suggest regarding Russia's plans for the future?

_____ FOR FURTHER READING _____

(In addition to the books by Engel, Hillyar, McDermid, Menning, Moon, Nathans, Rieber, Rogger, Stites, Weeks, and Wortman from the previous chapter.)

Ascher, Abraham. *P. A. Stolypin: The Search for Stability in Late Imperial Russia.* Stanford, CA.: Stanford University Press, 2001.

Figes, Orlando. *A People's Tragedy: The Russian Revolution, 1891–1924.* New York: Penguin Putnam, 1996.

Hosking, Geoffrey A. *The Russian Constitutional Experiment; Government and Duma, 1907–1914.* Cambridge: Cambridge University Press, 1973.

Lieven, D. C. B. *Russia and the Origins of the First World War.* New York: St. Martin's Press, 1983.

Manning, Roberta Thompson. *The Crisis of the Old Order in Russia: Gentry and Government.* Princeton, NJ: Princeton University Press, 1982.

Sanborn, Joshua A. *Drafting the Russian Nation: Military Conscription, Total War, and Mass Politics, 1905–1925.* DeKalb, IL.: Northern Illinois University Press, 2003.

Service, Robert. *Lenin—A Biography.* Cambridge, MA: Harvard University Press, 2000.

Stites, Richard. *Russian Popular Culture: Entertainment and Society since 1900.* Cambridge: Cambridge University Press, 1992.

Stockdale, Melissa Kirschke. *Paul Miliukov and the Quest for a Liberal Russia, 1880–1918.* Ithaca, NY: Cornell University Press, 1996.

CHAPTER FIFTEEN

REVOLUTION AND CIVIL WAR, 1917–1921

In the winter of 1917, a leaderless and unplanned revolution swept the Romanov dynasty from power. Beginning on February 23,[1] public demonstrations in Petrograd grew larger daily. When soldiers refused to fire on the demonstrators and joined the crowds themselves, the movement became an armed insurrection against the old regime. On March 2, Nicholas II abdicated, and the Romanov dynasty came to an end. However, if Russian society agreed that the autocracy had to go, it was profoundly divided on the question of what political form the new Russia should take. That question was decided only after a long and bloody civil war.

EURASIAN CONTEXT

In March 1918, Russia signed a separate peace with Germany, permitting Germany to mobilize all its forces for a final attempt to defeat Allied forces in France. This drive ground to a halt in early August 1918, leaving Germany exhausted and defenseless. The German government had also lost the support of its people. In early November, a mutiny spread in the Baltic fleet, rebellion broke out in Munich, and massive unrest spread in Berlin. Emperor Wilhelm II abdicated and fled to Holland, while the German general staff quickly set up a government of liberals and socialists. The new civilian government not only placated the population, it also relieved the military of the onus of surrender. (Militarists could later claim that the German army had been "stabbed in the back" by the liberals.) On November 11, this new government signed the armistice that finally ended World War I. Austria-

Hungary had already collapsed. Its demoralized army had ceased fighting in the summer of 1918, and its Emperor had abdicated on November 2. By the end of November, Hungary and the Slavic peoples of the Austrian empire had declared their independence.

The war was a disaster for European society. At least ten million soldiers and four million civilians had died, and thirty million had been wounded, many permanently disabled. The monetary cost of the war was also staggering. Governments across Europe were bankrupted; inflation wiped out the savings of the middle class, and wages for the working class consistently lagged behind price increases. Politics across Europe became increasingly radical. Stability was threatened by socialism (among the working class) and militant nationalism (among the middle class). Governments on the Soviet model appeared briefly in Bavaria and Hungary, and German nationalists attempted to seize power in Berlin in 1920. There was widespread labor militancy in Great Britain, two general strikes in France, and a series of massive strikes in Italy that almost brought down the government. It was not until 1921 that the radical working movement was suppressed, leaving Soviet Russia the only socialist state in Europe.

When the war was over, the victors redrew the map of Europe. Germany lost territory to Poland, and Austria lost its entire empire and was reduced to its German-speaking homeland. Hungary became independent. A new country, Czechoslovakia, was created from the Austrian territory of Bohemia (uniting the Czechs and Slovaks into one country). Rumania gained Transylvania from Hungary and Bessarabia from Russia. Serbia was made the dominant power within a new nation, Yugoslavia, which also contained the former Austrian provinces of Bosnia, Croatia, and Herzegovina. In addition, Estonia, Latvia, Lithuania, and Poland had all been detached from the Russian empire by Germany during the war, and the Great Powers now recognized their independence. Germany also lost its overseas possessions. Its Africa colonies went to South Africa, France, and Belgium; its Pacific islands were divided among Japan, Australia, and New Zealand; and its sphere of influence in China was also transferred to Japan.

The allies dismantled the Ottoman Empire according to secret treaties made during the war. Great Britain took Palestine and Mesopotamia (later to be divided into Jordan and Iraq), and France took Lebanon and Syria. Greek, French, and British forces also occupied Constantinople and parts of the Anatolian Peninsula. They restored Sultan Muhammad VI to power, forcing him to confirm the Treaty of Capitulations and the Ottoman Public Debt Administration. When General Mustafa Kemal, war hero and former Young Turk, began to organize resistance to foreign occupation, the Sultan relieved him of his command. Kemal, however, renounced the government in Constantinople, called on patriotic Turks to form a republican government in Ankara, and began a war of national liberation from Allied occupation.

When the First World War began, Britain occupied southern Iran, while Russia invaded the north. After the Soviet government came to power in 1917, it withdrew Russian troops from Iran. Britain then occupied the entire country, later using it as a base of operations to aid anti-Soviet forces in the Caucasus. By 1920, the Red Army had established Soviet power in the Caucasus, and it sponsored an Iranian Soviet government in northern Iran. In 1921, both Britain and Russia agreed to withdraw.

In China, public opinion had euphorically welcomed Woodrow Wilson's call for democracy and national self-determination. The Chinese were therefore bitterly disillusioned when they learned that instead of abrogating the unequal treaties that made China a virtual colony, Europe intended to enforce them and had furthermore given Germany's concessions in the Shandong Peninsula to Japan. In an upsurge of nationalism known as the May Fourth Movement, there were widespread demonstrations, boycotts, strikes, and shop closures. In

Beijing, the homes of the officials who had signed the Versailles Treaty were burned by out-raged students. Alienated from the imperialist west, Chinese nationalists, led by Sun Yat-sen, began to look to Soviet Russia for aid and support.

THE REVOLUTIONS OF 1917

The Russian working class was increasingly restive as the winter of 1917 began. On January 9 to mark the anniversary of Bloody Sunday, more than 100,000 workers in Petrograd went on strike. On February 11, half of Petrograd's workers were on strike, and by February 14, that figure had risen to 80 percent. On International Women's Day, February 23, the general public joined the strikers, and a popular rebellion against the autocracy began. On that day, thousands of women took to the streets to demonstrate for women's rights, many also carry-ing signs calling for more and cheaper bread and an end to the war. Some even said "down with the autocracy." On each of the next three days, the crowds of demonstrators grew larger and more militant. On the evening of February 26, Nicholas II, at army headquarters in Mogilev, was finally informed of the unrest, and he sent an order to the commanding offi-cer of the Petrograd garrison to end the disorders immediately.

It was a mistake. Soldiers in Petrograd were in complete sympathy with the demonstra-tors, and, on the morning of February 27, when they were ordered to fire on the crowd, they refused. Instead, the Petrograd garrison mutinied, opened the armory, and distributed weapons to the crowds. A Soviet of Workers' Deputies, modeled on the 1905 Soviet, was formed. The Tsar dismissed the Duma, but many liberal Duma deputies met informally and chose a committee to speak on their behalf.

Three days later, on March 2, the situation in the capital was clearly out of control. Every-one near the Tsar—the president of the Duma, the general staff, and members of the Ro-manov family—advised him to abdicate in favor of his son Aleksei, with his brother Mikhail Aleksandrovich as regent. Nicholas II first abdicated for himself then, thinking his son too frail to shoulder the burden, abdicated in his behalf. Mikhail, next in line to the throne, asked the General Staff if his security could be guaranteed, and when the answer was nega-tive, he declined to succeed his nephew. Russia was left with no Tsar and no government. The Duma had been dissolved, and the Council of Ministers had no authority except as ser-vants of the Tsar.

Two political institutions stepped forward to fill the power vacuum. On the day the Tsar abdicated, the Petrograd Soviet welcomed delegates from the army and renamed itself the Soviet of Workers' and Soldiers' Deputies. On the same day, the temporary committee formed by the dismissed Duma declared itself to be a "Provisional Government" and took upon itself the duties of the Council of Ministers. It announced that it would administer Russia until a popularly elected Constituent Assembly could write a new constitution for the country. All the new ministers were liberals, with the exception of the Socialist Revolution-ary Aleksandr Kerensky, vice-chair of the Petrograd Soviet, who accepted the post of Minis-ter of Justice.

The Provisional Government immediately granted the civil rights typical of constitutional republics: freedom of speech and conscience, equality of all citizens without regard to reli-gion, ethnicity or social status, and the right of all adult males to vote. (The right of women to vote was not recognized until July.) It granted amnesty to tsarist political prisoners, and it declared the right of unions to go on strike. It refused, however, to make any decisions re-garding land reform, workers' rights, or the status of the nations of the empire, contending that these issues could only be solved by the Constituent Assembly. Furthermore, the Provi-sional Government also continued to fight the war.

The Petrograd Soviet was organized by Mensheviks and dominated by Mensheviks and Socialist Revolutionaries. According to mainstream Marxist theory, Russia's first revolution would be bourgeois-democratic, and the Mensheviks felt it was appropriate for middle-class liberals to be in charge. The Soviet chose merely to "supervise" the Provisional government in order to protect the interests of the working people. Petrograd's Bolsheviks agreed.

The leader of the Bolsheviks, V. I. Lenin, then in exile in Switzerland, vehemently disagreed. He had opposed the Menshevik notion of a two-stage revolution since 1905, positing, instead, the possibility of a "continuing revolution" in which the working-class would not allow the democratic revolution to stop but would turn it into a socialist revolution. Lenin did not claim that Russia had reached the stage of mature capitalism which Marx said was the precondition to socialist revolution, but he argued that a working-class revolution in Russia would spark a socialist revolution in western Europe. European workers would then help their Russian comrades to build socialism.

Lenin's views on the war also distinguished him from most other revolutionary leaders. Plekhanov and many SR leaders were patriotic supporters of the war with Germany. Martov and most Social Democrats were "defensists" who opposed aggressive war but thought Russia should defend itself against foreign invasion. Lenin, however, was a "defeatist." He argued that revolutionaries should take advantage of the war to overthrow the old regime. The German General Staff believed that it was in Germany's interest to get Lenin to Russia where he would cause trouble for the pro-war Provisional Government. Consequently, they allowed Lenin and other Bolsheviks to travel by train across Germany to Petrograd.

Lenin arrived in Petrograd on April 3, and on the next day he presented his position, known as the "April Theses," to the Petrograd Soviet. He called on it to seize power from the Provisional Government, to stop fighting the war, and to confiscate all estates and turn them over to the use of the peasantry. Lenin was considered unrealistic by his own party and madly out of touch by leaders of both the Soviet and the Provisional Government.

In regard to the war, however, it was the Provisional Government that was out of touch with popular sentiment. This was revealed on April 18 when Minister of Foreign Affairs, Pavel Miliukov, sent a note to the allies promising that Russia would fight until victory and affirming war aims, which included the Russian annexation of Constantinople and the Turkish Straits. This caused massive public demonstrations and near civil war. Miliukov and other liberals resigned from the Provisional Government, and several SRs and Mensheviks accepted ministerial posts. Aleksandr Kerensky became defense minister. The new government announced war goals of "no annexation, no indemnities," but they continued to fight the war.

This led to yet another crisis in the middle of June, when the Provisional Government launched a military offensive against Austrian forces in Galicia. Antiwar demonstrations immediately broke out. The crisis peaked on July 3 to 5 when the machine gun regiment from the Kronstadt naval base joined the demonstrations and demanded that the Soviet seize power. Lenin and the Bolsheviks at first opposed the demonstrators, then supported them. The Provisional Government restored order by accusing Lenin of being a German agent, thereby causing a patriotic backlash against the Bolsheviks. Leon Trotsky, a former Menshevik who was adopting the Bolshevik position, was arrested and Lenin fled into hiding in Finland. Meanwhile the Russian army was defeated in Galicia.

Over the course of the summer the economy deteriorated, wages lagged behind prices, and the war dragged on. News from the countryside reported peasant disturbances and seizure of noble estates. The Russian army was increasingly unwilling to obey orders and to fight. There were a number of celebrated cases in which soldiers murdered their officers and deserted, but on the whole soldiers did not want to surrender: though adamantly opposed to offensive actions, they were willing to defend against German attacks. Nevertheless, workers and soldiers were becoming more radical in their mood, and Bolsheviks, the most radical political party in Russia, were elected to city Soviets in increasing numbers all across Russia and especially in Petrograd.

While workers were becoming increasingly radical, however, the Provisional Government and the industrialists were turning conservative. Over the course of the summer, factory owners seemed more self-confident and less willing to compromise with the unions. In the middle of July, General Lavr Kornilov was appointed Commander in Chief of the Russian army, and he began to restore order and discipline. At the end of July Aleksandr Kerensky became President of the Provisional Government, and he formed a political alliance with Kornilov.

On August 21, the German Army captured Riga, threatening Petrograd. Kornilov sent a cavalry corps of Cossacks toward Petrograd to protect the Provisional Government. Kerensky considered using the army to impose martial law and suppress the Bolsheviks. At the last minute, however, it appears that Kerensky became convinced that Kornilov intended to seize the capital and make himself military dictator. In a panic, he removed Kornilov as Commander in Chief. Kornilov responded by dispatching yet more troops toward the capital, convincing the population of Petrograd that he intended to suppress the revolution. This galvanized Petrograd's workers, soldiers, and revolutionary parties into action. Railroad workers refused to run the trains. Kornilov's troops refused to advance on the capital. Trotsky and other imprisoned Bolsheviks were freed from prison. Revolutionary committees spontaneously formed in the factories and armed themselves.

The moderates, including Kerensky, were now thoroughly discredited. Bolsheviks won a majority in the Petrograd Soviet, and Trotsky was elected chair on September 25. The Soviet formed a Military Revolutionary Committee, also headed by Trotsky and with a Bolshevik majority. In late September, Lenin, still in Finland, sent repeated messages to the Bolshevik Central Committee instructing them to insist that the Petrograd Soviet take power from the Provisional Government, but he was ignored. Finally on October 10, Lenin, dressed in disguise to avoid arrest, arrived in Petrograd to make his case in person. Grigorii Zinovyev and Lev Kamenev, Lenin's oldest comrades, continued to oppose him, and they even published letters arguing against the seizure of power. Only after Lenin threatened to leave the Bolsheviks and form a new party, did the Central Committee finally vote in favor of Lenin's plan.

The opportunity to seize power was provided by Aleksandr Kerensky. The Second All-Russian Congress of Soviets was to meet in Petrograd on October 25. On October 24, Kerensky sent soldiers to close Bolshevik newspaper offices, and he asked the Provisional Government for authority to suppress the Bolshevik party. That night Trotsky, as head of the Military Revolutionary Committee, called out the garrison and took control of the city. He reopened Bolshevik newspapers and sent troops to guard railroad stations and key intersections in order to protect the Congress of Soviets.

On the morning of September 25, troops loyal to the Bolsheviks occupied the winter palace and arrested the Provisional Government. When the Second Congress of Soviets met later in the day, Bolshevik leaders announced what had occurred and called on the Congress to assume power. The Mensheviks and Right (moderate) Socialist Revolutionaries opposed the idea (they thought the Provisional Government should continue to rule until the Constituent Assembly met), and they walked out. The Congress was therefore entirely made up of Bolsheviks (three hundred delegates) and Left SRs (ninety).

The first action of the Second Congress of Soviets was to create a new executive, the Sovnarkom (Council of People's Commissars) to replace the now deposed Provisional Government. The Sovnarkom included Lenin as president, Trotsky as commissar of foreign affairs, Anatoly Lunacharsky as commissar of enlightenment, and Joseph Stalin as commissar of nationalities. The Sovnarkom immediately declared a policy of peace, halted offensive operations, and called for negotiations to end the war. It also nationalized all agricultural land in the empire and declared that the land should be divided among the peasantry.

Bolsheviks all across Russia followed the lead of Petrograd. In cities where the Soviet had a Bolshevik majority, the Soviet announced that it was assuming power. Where the Bolsheviks were in the minority, they formed revolutionary committees which then claimed the authority to govern. In the first weeks of the revolution, there was comparatively little loss of life. The most violent struggle took place in Moscow where approximately two hundred people died before the Bolsheviks defeated forces loyal to the Provisional Government.

In November, elections to the Constituent Assembly took place as previously planned by the Provisional Government. Socialist Revolutionaries won 40 percent of the delegates while the Bolsheviks came in second with 25 percent. The Constituent Assembly opened on January 5, 1918, and Lenin proposed as the first order of business that it recognize the Sovnarkom as Russia's legitimate government. The Socialist Revolutionaries, however, led by Viktor Chernov, took up their own agenda. The Assembly remained in session through the night until, at 4:00 A.M., soldiers of the Petrograd Red Guard who were providing security for the Constituent Assembly requested that it adjourn. It did so. However, when the delegates returned the next morning, they found the doors locked and secured by the Red Guard. Lenin announced that the continued meeting of the Constituent Assembly would have meant the renunciation of working-class government as represented by the Soviets. The new constitution would be written under the authority of the Sovnarkom.

WAR AND CIVIL WAR

In December, negotiations for a peace treaty began at the German Army Headquarters in Brest-Litovsk, Belarus. Trotsky, Commissar of Foreign Affairs, who led the Soviet negotiating team, tried to stall, hoping that a working-class revolution would bring down the German government. The German General staff grew impatient and renewed their offensive, advancing at will against the thoroughly demoralized Russia army. Left Bolsheviks, such as Nikolai Bukharin, called for a guerrilla war of resistance that would bring revolution to Germany, but Lenin argued that the young Soviet state needed a "breathing space" and convinced his colleagues to agree to German terms. In the Treaty of Brest-Litovsk, in March 1918, the Soviet state recognized the independence, under German supervision, of Ukraine, Poland, Finland, Estonia, Latvia, and Lithuania.

This submission to German demands lost the Bolsheviks their only remaining allies, the Left SRs, who resigned from the government. The Bolsheviks now changed their name to "Communist" in order to invoke the spirit of the Parisian working class in the legendary Paris Commune of 1870 to 1871. They also moved the capital to Moscow, to the greater safety of the Russian heartland.

Even though the threat from Germany was ended, the new Soviet state now had to defend itself from the Allies and from Russian monarchist forces known as the White armies. Leon Trotsky, transformed from peace negotiator to general, was given the job of creating an army. He resisted left-Communist demands for a volunteer, revolutionary army, and created a conscripted, disciplined, modern army. He recruited tsarist military officers to command it but assigned a political commissar to each officer to guarantee his loyalty.

The Red Army, as the Soviet army was known, was faced by five major opposition groups. The first was the White Army, which was made up of former tsarist generals, aristocrats, and others who wanted to restore the old regime. The second group, Russia's former allies, Britain, France, and the United States, occupied Murmansk and Archangel in order to keep Russian military supplies out of German hands. Britain, Japan, and the United States also sent tens of thousands of troops to Siberia. (Britain supported the White army, Japan was primarily interested in the possibility of territorial expansion, while the United States wanted to restrain Japan.) The British also gave military aid to White forces in the Baltic and Black Seas and in the Caucasus. Third, Liberals and leftist parties set up alternate governments in Samara and Omsk. Fourth, many of the nations of the former Russian Empire fought for independence of both White and Red rule. The fifth opposition group, referred to as "Greens," were peasants who became disenchanted with Soviet rule and formed armies in Ukraine and the Volga region.

The Civil War can be divided into four periods. The first ran from March until November 1918. In this period, three White armies coalesced behind former tsarist generals: Nikolai Yudenich in the Baltic, Lavr Kornilov in the Northern Caucasus, and Aleksandr Kolchak in Siberia. The Red Army successfully pushed back their first attacks in the summer of 1918. The second period lasted from November 1918 until April 1920. Because of the German surrender and withdrawal from eastern Europe in November, the Whites were able to gather sympathetic forces in Ukraine and the Baltic. Nevertheless, by 1920, Yudenich and Kolchak had been defeated and Denikin (Kornilov's successor) was on the defensive. The third period, from April to November 1920, was a full-scale war between Soviet Russia and Poland that followed Poland's invasion of Ukraine. Poland was driven out of Ukraine by November 1920, but the Red Army failed in its attempt to conquer Poland. The fourth period lasted from November 1920 into the early 1920s. The Red Army finally defeated Denikin's forces, which had regrouped in the south during the war with Poland. In this period, the Red Army also defeated separatist forces in Central Asia, the Caucasus, and Eastern Siberia, and it subdued peasant rebellions in Ukraine and central Russia.

Two reasons are generally given for the victory of the Red Army. First, it controlled the Russian heartland and had the advantage of interior lines of communication. Second, the anti-Soviet movement lacked unity. White generals alienated the separatist nationalities by insisting on the preservation of the empire, they alienated liberals and socialists by their desire to restore autocracy, and they made alliance with the peasantry impossible by calling for land to be restored "to its rightful owners" (i.e., the aristocracy). There simply was no realistic alternative to Soviet rule.

By 1921, the Soviet state had managed to survive, but it was not recognized as legitimate by the international community. Soviet Russia was not invited to the Paris peace conference in 1919, and it was separated from Western Europe by a buffer zone of new countries, Estonia, Latvia, Lithuania, Poland, and Czechoslovakia, all but the last of which were former provinces of the Russian Empire. Furthermore, even though Russia had played a key role in the war, saving France from defeat in 1914 with its attack on Germany, and even though Russia had suffered as badly as France, Russia was not included in the reparations payments imposed on Germany by the Versailles treaty.

It did not help Soviet Russia's standing in the international community that the Third Communist International (Comintern) was created in 1919 with its headquarters in Moscow, with the goal of promoting worldwide communist revolution. Leftist Social-Democrats from around the world were invited to send delegates, and they were advised to model themselves on the Bolshevik pattern. They were instructed to form Communists factions, separate themselves from moderate Social-Democrats, form underground organizations, and promote working-class revolution on the Soviet model.

RELIGION AND CULTURE

The Orthodox Church was as ready for the end of the monarchy as any other segment of the population. In February, the Holy Synod actually refused the request of the Procurator to appeal to Russians to support the Tsar, and it joined the general staff in advising Mikhail not to replace his brother as Tsar. On March 4, the Synod voted to support the Provisional Government. In May, an "All-Russian Congress of Clergy and Laity" gathered in Moscow to plan Church reform, and the Synod cooperated with it, arranging for a Church Sobor, which had been forbidden by Nicholas II.

The Sobor, which opened on August 15, included clergy from all levels of the church, as well as laypeople elected by their dioceses. It separated itself from the government by declaring an end to the Holy Synod and creating an autonomous Patriarchate, and it elected Tikhon Bellavin, the Metropolitan of Moscow, to be Patriarch. The Sobor established a decentralized and democratic church: At the parish level, each community would elect its priest and local church officials. Bishops would also be elected, subject to approval by the Patriarch.

Patriarch Tikhon condemned the Treaty of Brest-Litovsk, but he otherwise avoided politics. The church refused to support one side or the other in the civil war, since there were church members on both sides. The Patriarch anathematized all who killed innocent people, desecrated churches, or killed priests. He did not, however, renounce Soviet rule.

The Church's prestige at this time was very low. In the minds of the people, it was associated with the discredited autocracy—and with the unpopular war. (As far as the church was concerned, the war to liberate the Orthodox peoples of Serbia and the Balkans was good, and parish priests had actively promoted it.) When, after the Tsar's abdication, church attendance was made optional for the military, it fell from 100 percent to only 10 percent.

As soon as it took power in October 1917, the Sovnarkom immediately began to create a secular state. All state funding for the church was ended. Religion was removed from the school curriculum. Marriage, divorce, and the definition of legitimate birth, were all made matters of civil procedure and law. Religious holidays and festivals were no longer recognized by the state, and new secular holidays (the Anniversary of the October Revolution, Aviation Day, May Day, etc.) replaced them. Christianity was replaced as the legitimizing ideology of the state by Marxism and radical egalitarianism.

The Narkompros (Commissariat of Enlightenment) took charge of all schools in the former empire and opened them to all classes. All fees and entrance requirements were eliminated. In universities, special curricula were established to provide remedial help for workers and peasants who were unprepared academically. Narkompros's plans included compulsory universal education, and a single "United Labor School" that would provide liberal arts and vocational training to students from all class backgrounds. It also declared its intention to provide instruction to all children in their native language. Lack of resources prevented the full realization of its program.

Many wealthy Russians were appalled at the idea of working-class government and culture, and at least one million people, including many of the intellectual, cultural, and artistic elite emigrated to the West. At the same time, many writers and artists greeted the revolution enthusiastically. The Futurists, led by Vladimir Mayakovsky, became propagandists for the Communist Party. A new school of poets, the "Scythians," portrayed the revolutionary masses as nomads struggling to preserve their freedom from corrupting civilization. "Cosmists" interpreted the revolution in apocalyptic terms and used images of the birth of stars and galaxies to convey its significance. A "Proletarian Culture" movement arose, organized by former left Bolshevik Aleksandr Bogdanov and sponsored by Commissar of Enlightenment Anatoly Lunacharsky. The Proletkult (as it was known) rapidly grew to a nationwide organization of local working-class clubs promoting literacy and culture. Proletkult leaders had an ideological agenda, believing that socialism would appear only after the proletariat had developed its own culture. At the grass roots, however, the Proletkult was welcomed by workers simply as an opportunity to become literate and to express themselves artistically.

WOMEN AND REVOLUTION

Over the course of the war, the proportion of women in the factory workforce had increased from 26 percent to 43 percent, and their employment in other fields also roughly doubled. An All-Russian Union for Women's Equality, founded in January 1915, called for the right to vote without regard to sex, religion, or nationality. Women played a key role in the February Revolution, as striking workers, feminist activists, and mothers demanding cheaper bread and an end to the war. However, the Provisional Government, which immediately gave civil equality to all men, ignored the rights of women. In April 1917, the Union for Women's Equality held a conference, attended by more than one thousand delegates, that demanded equality in education and employment, equality before the law, and the right to vote. It was not until July that the Provisional Government recognized women's right to vote and to serve on juries, and to equal opportunity in the civil service.

Middle and upper-class women were generally supportive of the war, and feminists advocated the right of women to serve in the military. Women's battalions were created and approximately five thousand women were allowed to enlist in the army. They worked mainly as nurses, drivers, and clerks. Only about three hundred members of the "Women's Battalion of Death" actually engaged in combat in the Galician offensive in June. The Women's Battalion also briefly defended the Provisional government during the Bolshevik seizure of power in October.

Thanks to the theoretical work of Nadezhda Krupskaya, Inessa Armand, and Aleksandra Kollontai, the Bolshevik party had a well-articulated women's rights program to implement after it came to power. Among its first reforms, the Sovnarkom required that men and women receive equal pay for equal work (this was not lived up to, however). Paid maternity leaves were required. Common-law marriages were recognized, and divorces were easy and inexpensive to obtain. The Soviet Constitution of 1918 declared the full equality of men and women. In 1920, the Sovnarkom legalized abortion and made it a state-funded medical procedure. On the other hand, the Communist party did little to promote women to responsible positions in the state and the party. Women were elected to Soviets and filled administrative positions in the party, but their numbers were small, and they were usually put in charge of issues traditionally associated with women: motherhood, family, and education.

Armand and Kollontai convinced party leaders to create a permanent Zhenotdel (Department for Work among Women) to organize grassroots women's committees across the country to mobilize women in support of the Communist program. They hoped that local Zhenotdel committees would help organize day-care centers, clinics, public laundries, and cafeterias and would pressure factories to recognize the rights of women workers. Little was achieved during the Civil War because of financial hardship.

SOCIAL REVOLUTION AND "WAR COMMUNISM"

The Bolshevik seizure of power was a revolution in the original sense of the word: It turned society upside-down. The Sovnarkom not only abolished all civil ranks and distinctions, it made workers and peasants the new privileged classes. The Soviet constitution of July 1918 gave the right to vote *only* to the laboring classes, while the nobility, middle class, clergy, and former police officials were all disfranchised. The new Soviet government had to employ experts and specialists from the old regime, but it set up institutions that kept them under popular supervision. The army was made egalitarian and democratic; uniforms did not display signs of rank, the practice of saluting superior officers was brought to an end, soldiers elected their officers, and orders, except on the battlefield, were subject to approval by the troops. The tsarist court system was replaced with courts in which ordinary citizens sat with professional judges and were allowed to vote on verdicts.

There was no systematic effort to exterminate the aristocracy or the wealthy elite, but they were persecuted, and they disappeared from sight socially. During the Civil War, when the Cheka (secret police) enforced laws against buying and selling on the black market, its officers generally showed leniency to workers, but they often summarily executed the *beloruchki* (those whose "white hands" indicated that they were members of the exploiting classes).

The decision to kill the royal family, however, *was* a conscious political decision. The Tsar and his family had been under house arrest since the abdication, and in the summer of 1918, they were living in Ekaterinburg in the Ural Mountains. In July 1918, when Kolchak's White Army was advancing toward the Volga-Ural region, Lenin ordered the local Communist Party to execute the royal family, in order to prevent them from being liberated and used as symbols of counter-revolution.

The Sovnarkom also instituted a revolution in industrial relations. In one of its first decrees it provided for workers' supervision of factory management. Then, as the economy declined and industrialists turned uncooperative, the Sovnarkom began to institute socialism. In December the Sovnarkhoz (Commissariat of the National Economy) nationalized Russian banks, and in January it took over the merchant marine, factories, and mines. By June most industrial enterprises of any size were owned by the state.

The end of the war caused an economic depression across Russia, as factories producing war supplies closed down. The population of Petrograd declined by almost three-quarters and that of Moscow by half. There had been 3.5 million industrial workers in Russia in 1917, but by 1920, that figure had shrunk to 1.5 million. The economic crisis caused a deterioration in the newly-won rights of workers, who were now subjected to forced labor and fixed wages. In October 1918, all able-bodied adults were compelled to work, and labor camps were set up for deserters and shirkers. Nevertheless, the economic collapse contributed to the Bolshevik success. Business failures caused owners and managers to abandon their factories to the control of the workers. Furthermore, although wages were low, there were other benefits to employment. Workers were allowed to use tools and materials to make goods to barter for food in the countryside. (On any given day as much as one-third of the factory workforce was out foraging for food.)

Meanwhile, a grass-roots peasant revolution was going on in the countryside. Having lost the symbol of their authority when the Tsar abdicated, the police, courts, and army also lost the will to uphold law and order. Peasants were able to realize their age-old dream of taking possession of all of Russia's arable land. At first they acted cautiously, refusing to pay rent, seizing equipment and livestock that were "underused," and intimidating nobles into abandoning their land. As they realized that the law would not be enforced, they began to loot estates, burn manor houses, and divide nobles' land among themselves. Most nobles simply fled, and the peasant revolution was relatively bloodless. Some landlords were not expropriated at all, and many of those whose estates were seized were offered the chance to keep a piece of the land if they would work it with their own labor. There were still 100,000 gentry families living on their own estates in the 1920s.

By 1919, 97 percent of all agricultural land was owned by peasants. It was distributed relatively equally: 86 percent of peasant households held between eleven and twenty-one acres, and only 2 percent had more than twenty-one acres. In addition, the Stolypin reforms were (for the most part) overturned, as separate farms were merged back into the mir and periodic redistribution of the land was revived. Demobilization of the army and the collapse of industry meant that a lot of former peasants were returning to their home villages expecting their fair share of the land. Those who had formed separate farms rejoined the commune, partly out of social pressure, partly out of the need for security. Farmers had to present a united face against the hungry cities.

Revolution in the countryside also included the democratization of the mir. Young men asserted their right to vote (traditionally, only heads of households could vote), and in some places, women were allowed to vote as well. The skhod took control of local life, setting rents and wages and providing law and order. The commune elected delegates to volost (district) committees that supplanted the administrative system set up by the Provisional Government. After October, the Communists attempted to introduce class war into the communes, calling upon poor peasants to unite against the rich kulaks. This failed, as the village maintained its traditional sense of solidarity against outsiders.

Meanwhile, city and country were in conflict. During the war, the tsarist government had held down prices for agricultural goods, thereby reducing the incentive for peasants to sell their grain. The tsarist army, therefore, began to requisition grain; that is, army patrols traveled to the black earth regions and took "surplus" grain at the point of a gun. This practice was continued by the Bolsheviks. The Sovnarkom authorized military units and factories to send armed requisition squads into the countryside. The squads were allowed to keep half of the grain they seized, provided they delivered the other half to the government. Not surprisingly, the peasants resisted. In 1920 to 1921, there were over one hundred peasant uprisings, and large Green armies formed in Ukraine, Tambov province, and western Siberia.

PEOPLES OF THE FORMER EMPIRE

The February Revolution finally freed the Jews of the Russian Empire from legal discrimination; Jews, like all religions were granted freedom of religion, and, like all national groups, were granted equality before the law, freedom of movement, and equal access to education and employment. Jews immediately began to use their new political rights and joined civic organizations and political parties. They were represented in all urban professions and occupations, and they were active members of all the center and leftist political parties. Many leaders of both the Menshevik and Bolshevik parties were Jews, and Jews made up about 20 percent of the Executive Committee of the Petrograd Soviet in the spring of 1917.

There was one great difference between the Jews and other peoples of the Empire; the Jews had no homeland in which they were a majority, and there was no political party whose exclusive purpose was to represent Jewish interests. In fact, the largest single Jewish party was the Zionists; they would have moved to Palestine had it had been possible. The Bolsheviks attempted to engage the support of the empire's Jews by creating the Yevseksia (Jewish Section), an organization within the party that fought anti-Semitism.

Poland was among the most nationalistic of any of the peoples of the Empire; Poles had revolted against Russian rule nearly every generation since the partitions of Poland by Catherine the Great. When World War I began, Poland was the first territory to be invaded by the German army, and Germany recognized Poland's independence. The Provisional Government confirmed this in March 1917, and the Sovnarkom accepted it in the Treaty of Brest Litovsk. Under Jozef Pilsudski, who became head of state and commander in chief in 1919, Poland expanded at the expense of Czechoslovakia, Ukraine, and Belarus. Soviet Russia recognized the enlarged Poland in the Treaty of Riga in 1921.

Finland was no less anxious for independence than Poland, and the Finnish Parliament declared Finland's independence in July 1917. The Provisional Government, which claimed the sovereign power previously belonging to the emperor, vetoed the declaration and dissolved the parliament. In the fall, the Finns elected a new parliament, and, by the time it declared its independence again in December, the Provisional Government had fallen. The Sovnarkom recognized Finnish independence in January 1918.

Estonia, Latvia, Lithuania, and Belarus all declared their independence while under German occupation. The Sovnarkom accepted this in the Treaty of Brest-Litovsk, but after Germany surrendered in November 1918 and withdrew from the Baltic region, the Red Army attempted to reabsorb all four countries into the Soviet state. Estonia, Latvia, and Lithuania were given military aid by the Allies, and in 1919 the Versailles peace conference formally recognized them as sovereign nations. Belarus was invaded by Poland later in the year, but the Red Army drove them out, thereby occupying Belarus and confirming Soviet rule.

Ukrainian nationalists formed a Ukrainian Central Rada (Council) immediately after the abdication of the Tsar. Ukrainian politics were complicated by the fact that Ukrainian nationalism was a rural, peasant-based movement. In six of the ten largest cities in Ukraine, Russians were the largest segment of the population, Jews were second, and Ukrainians third. Soviets were created in all Ukrainian cities, and they were dominated by Russian socialists, as was the Rada, which called for Ukrainian autonomy rather than independence. After the October Revolution, the Rada refused to recognize the Sovnarkom. In response, Ukrainian Bolsheviks called an All-Ukrainian Congress of Soviets in Kharkov, formed its own government, and declared Ukraine a Soviet republic. The Rada denounced this as illegitimate and declared Ukraine's independence under the protection of the occupying German Army.

German generals found the Rada too uncooperative, and in April they sponsored a coup d'etat in which General Pavlo Skoropadskyi seized power. Skoropadskyi's rule lasted only as long as the German occupation. His government was toppled by Ukrainian nationalists in December 1918, and in February 1919 the Rada was revived and a Ukrainian National Republic was again declared. Ukraine soon became a battleground once more: Poland invaded from the west, General Denikin (supported by the Allies) invaded from the South, and the Red Army invaded from the east. Ukraine allied with the Red Army, thinking it the least of the three evils. After the Whites and the Poles were cleared from Ukrainian soil, however, the Red Army remained, and it supported Russian elements in Ukraine who favored alliance with Soviet Russia.

In the Caucasus, the Revolutions of 1917 had little immediate practical effect, since the region was occupied by the Russian army fighting the Turks on the Caucasian front. After Brest-Litovsk, the situation changed. The Russian Army withdrew, and Azerbaijan, Georgia, and Armenia declared their independence. The Russian Civil War changed things again, as the Caucasus became a base of operations for the Volunteer Army under Denikin, supported by the British, who sent troops to Azerbaijan and Georgia by way of Iran. As had been the case in Ukraine, the peoples of the Caucasus considered the Red Army the most preferable of the available alternatives. Denikin, with his insistence on restoring the Empire, was unacceptable to everyone. In Azerbaijan, the large Georgian and Armenian minorities preferred Soviet to Azeri rule. The Armenians, now facing a possible invasion by Kemal Atatürk, declared their country to be a Soviet republic and asked for the protection of Soviet Russia. Georgia had a significant Social-Democratic element, and they welcomed the Red Army.

Ethnic conflict in the northern Caucasus also favored Soviet rule. The Don and Terek Cossacks joined Denikin and the Whites, while Russians, Armenians, and Georgians in the region, who feared Cossack domination, supported the Red Army. Once Denikin was defeated, however, Cossacks and Russians joined forces to oppose the separatist demands of Chechens and Ingush (who were Muslim traditionalists) and welcomed Soviet rule.

In Central Asia, an all-Kazakh Congress met in April 1917 and demanded the removal of all Russian and Ukrainian peasant colonists who had arrived since 1905. In July, a Kazakh-Kirgiz political party formed, calling for territorial autonomy. Bashkirs made similar demands. Neither the Provisional Government nor the Sovnarkom addressed the grievances of the Central Asian peoples, and in December 1917, Orenburg Cossacks, Bashkirs, Kazakhs, and Kirgiz rose in revolt. Russians living in Central Asia saw the revolt as a threat to their status, not as a rejection of the Bolshevik seizure of power, and Russian peasants, former tsarist administrators, military garrisons, and railroad workers all united to suppress the rebellion.

In the cities of Central Asia, a similar process occurred. In October 1917, Tashkent became the center of Bolshevism and Russian rule, and a Tashkent Soviet was formed. In December, Muslim delegates in Kokand created an Executive Committee to compete for power with the Tashkent Soviet. In January the Red Army, with the support of the Russian population, suppressed the Executive Committee. Opposition to Soviet rule then went underground, and the Fergana valley became the home of guerrilla fighters called the Basmachi who continued their struggle into the 1920s.

Russian Muslim leaders, like the Orthodox Church, took immediate advantage of the religious freedom granted by the Provisional Government. In May 1917, an All-Russian Congress of Muslims met in Moscow with over one thousand delegates, including two hundred women. Overall, the Muslim movement was western, secular, and politically liberal. Despite opposition from conservative Muslim leaders from the northern Caucasus, the Congress was the first Muslim religious body in the world to recognize the equality of women. (It also outlawed polygyny and child brides and permitted women to appear in public without veils.) The Congress asserted the right of Muslims to choose their own chief Mufti (the foremost Islamic legal authority; in principle the head of the Muslim community). It also wanted to create a single organization to represent the interests of all Muslims in the Soviet state.

CONCLUSION: THE EMERGENCE OF COMMUNIST ONE-PARTY RULE

The Soviet system of government, as established in the Soviet Constitution of 1918, violated the principle of equality of all citizens. Rights were guaranteed only to the "urban and rural proletariat and the poorest peasants;" the property-owning classes were explicitly excluded, as were those who used their rights "to the detriment of the socialist revolution." Nor did the constitution follow the principle of "one person, one vote." Delegates were elected to the All-Russian Congress of Soviets on the basis of one for every 25,000 urban voters, while in rural areas one delegate represented 125,000 voters. Nevertheless, it was a landmark in Russian history, as the first constitution recognizing the people as the source of sovereignty and providing for an elected legislature and executive.

There were five levels of elected government: volost (township), uezd (county), province, region, and state-wide (referred to as "All-Russian"). At each level, the fundamental authority to govern was vested in an elected Congress which, in turn, elected an executive committee. This executive committee decided local issues and implemented laws and decisions passed down from higher levels of government. Each Soviet congress also elected delegates to the congress at the next higher level. At the top was the All-Russia Congress of Soviets, which chose an All-Russian Executive Committee, which was the supreme legislative, administrative, and supervisory body. The Executive Committee appointed the Sovnarkom, which was in charge of the administrative bureaucracy.

The Communist Party was not mentioned in the Constitution of 1918, and one-party rule evolved only gradually. Elections to the Second Congress of Soviets (which had set the stage for the October Revolution) had been open and democratic, although, since soviets were working-class institutions, only socialists were elected. The Second Congress was made up of 300 Bolsheviks, 90 Left SRs, and 260 Mensheviks and Right SRs. Bolsheviks were in control of the new government because other parties withdrew, not because they were excluded. The list of appointments to the Sovnarkom presented by the Central Committee of the Bolshevik faction might have been revised had the Mensheviks remained to participate in the political process. In March, when the Sovnarkom approved the Treaty of Brest-Litovsk, the Left SRs withdrew their support from the Soviet government, leaving the Bolsheviks completely in control.

Over the course of the Civil War, however, one-party rule became a permanent policy. The crisis atmosphere of the Civil War contributed: A wartime mentality led the Communists to think of politics as a life-or-death struggle and their opponents as the enemy. The situation deteriorated in August 1918 when a Socialist Revolutionary shot and wounded Lenin in a failed assassination attempt. The Communist Party reacted by outlawing all opposition political parties, shutting down their newspapers, arresting their leaders, and preventing them from offering candidates for elections. Red and White reigns of terror ensued. Tens of thousands of people identified as enemies of the Soviet state were executed, and tens of thousands more were interned in concentration camps. In this environment, elections to the Soviet were uncontested and only candidates approved by the Party were elected. Real political power moved from the Soviets to the Communist Party.

NOTE

1. When Peter the Great chose to switch from the traditional Jewish calendar (that began with Creation) to the Western calendar (that used the birth of Jesus to begin the modern era), he picked the Julian Calendar. The Julian calendar lagged behind the Gregorian Calendar (which became standard in western Europe and the United States). In the twentieth century, the difference between the two calendars was thirteen days. Thus, when the calendars in Russia indicated February 23, those in the West said March 8. Russia did not begin to use the Gregorian Calendar until after midnight, January 31, 1918; the next day was February 14.

_____ TEXT DOCUMENTS _____

N. N. Sukhanov, *The Russian Revolution, 1917*

Nikolai Sukhanov (1882–1939) was an agrarian economist and a revolutionary. He was in and out of jail and Siberian exile in the tsarist period. At first, he was a member of the Socialist Revolutionary Party, but he later joined the Mensheviks, and he was a member of the Petrograd Soviet after the February Revolution. Sukhanov criticized the Bolsheviks for their violation of civil liberties after they seized power in October. He remained in Russia, however, working for the Agrarian Institute of the Communist Academy until he was fired for political reasons in 1930. He was arrested during the Great Terror and executed in 1939. In 1922, Sukhanov wrote a memoir of the revolution from which this excerpt is taken.

- What can you tell about the nature of the government and of the revolution from this account?
- How was the revolution experienced by the people of Petrograd? What was the relation between people and government?

I had been banished from St. Petersburg by May 10, 1914. At that time I was editor of the non-party but Left-wing *Sovremennik* (Contemporary), which took an internationalist line during the war . . . Though under sentence of banishment, I spent most of my time, up to the revolution itself, living underground in the capital—sometimes on a false passport, sometimes sleeping in a different place every night, sometimes slipping past the night-porter in the shadows . . . to my own flat, where my family was living.

From November 1916 on I was on the staff of Maxim Gorky's *Letopis* (Chronicle), and practically its principal contributor, keeping the entire magazine going under the Damocles' sword of police repression. Moreover, my illegal position did not stop me from working as an economist, under my own name, in a government department, the Ministry of Agriculture, in a section that dealt with the irrigation of Turkestan. . . .

I was sitting in my office in the Turkestan section [Tuesday, February 21st]. Behind a partition two typists were gossiping about food difficulties, rows in the shopping queues, unrest among the women, an attempt to smash into some warehouse.

"D'you know," suddenly declared one of these young ladies, "if you ask me, it's the beginning of the revolution!"

These girls didn't understand what a revolution was. Nor did I believe them for a second. But in those days . . . I kept thinking and brooding about the inevitable revolution that was whirling down on us at full speed. . . .

On Wednesday and Thursday—February 22nd and 23rd—the movement in the streets became clearly defined, going beyond the limits of the usual factory meetings. At the same

Source: N. N. Sukhanov, *The Russian Revolution 1917*, Joel Carmichael, Ed. and Trans. (London: Oxford University Press, 1955), 3–6, 11, 15, 25, 28–29. Reprinted with permission of Joel Carmichael.

time the feebleness of the authorities was exposed. They were plainly not succeeding—with all the machinery they had been building up for decades—in suppressing the movement at its source. The city was filled with rumors and a feeling of "disorders." . . .

On Friday the 24th the movement swept over Petersburg like a great flood. The Nevskii and many squares in the center were crowded with workers. Fugitive meetings were held in the main streets and were dispersed by Cossacks and mounted police—but without any energy or zeal and after lengthy delays. The Petersburg military commander, General Khabalov, got out a proclamation, which essentially only served to reveal the impotence of the authorities, pointing out that repeated warnings had been without effect and promising to take the sternest measures—in the future. Naturally this had no result, but it was another sign of helplessness. . . .

The mass street movement in the February days revealed no sort of purposefulness, nor was it possible to discern in it any kind of proper leadership. In general, as is always the case, the organized Socialist centers were not controlling the popular movement or leading it to any definite political goal. Of course our traditional, one might say ancient, national slogan, "Down with the Autocracy," was on the lips of all the many street orators from the Socialist parties. But this was not yet a political program; it was a negative idea that was taken for granted. The problem of *government* had not yet been put before the masses. . . .

On the other hand, the street agitators developed at great length another slogan, with extremely grave and far-reaching implications. This was "Down with the War", which dominated all the meetings of the February days.

. . . There was nothing surprising or unexpected in the fact that a revolution against Tsarism should, at least amongst the proletariat of the capital, coincide with a movement in favor of peace. On the contrary, nothing else could have been expected of the street movement during the February days. . . .

Meanwhile the movement kept growing. The impotence of the police machinery became more evident with every hour. Meetings were already taking place almost with permission, and the military units, in the person of their commanding officers, were failing to take active steps against the crowds that filled the main streets. Unexpectedly the Cossack units displayed special sympathy with the revolution at various points, when in direct conversations they emphasized their neutrality and sometimes showed a clear tendency to fraternize. And on Friday evening they were saying in the city that elections were being held in the factories for the Soviet of Workers' Deputies.

On Saturday the 25th Petersburg seethed in an atmosphere of extraordinary events from the morning on. The streets, even where there was no concentration of people, were a picture of extreme excitement. I was reminded of the 1905 Moscow insurrection. The entire civil population felt itself to be in one camp united against the enemy—the police and the military. Strangers passing by conversed with each other, asking questions and talking about the news, about clashes with and the diversionary movements of the enemy." . . .

The next day, Sunday, February 26th. . . . was given over to decisive measures and a resort to arms. The last desperate throw was being made. . . .

The siege of factories and working-class districts continued and was intensified. Great numbers of infantry units were moved out into the streets: they cordoned off bridges, isolated various districts, and set about a thorough-going clearance of the streets.

Around one o'clock the infantry trained rifle-fire of great intensity on the Nevskii. The Prospect, strewn with corpses of innocent passers-by, was cleared. Rumors of this flew swiftly about the city. The inhabitants were terrorized, and in the central parts of the city the movement in the streets was quelled.

Towards 5 o'clock it might well have seemed that Tsarism had again won the throw and that the movement was going to be suppressed. . . . [But events took a new turn in the evening.]

A small detachment of mounted police had orders to disperse a crowd that had collected along the Catherine Canal; for safety's sake the police began to fire on it from the opposite bank, across the canal. Just then a detachment of Pavlovskys [soldiers from the Pavlovsky regiment] was passing along the bank that was occupied by the crowd. It was then that an historic incident took place that marked an abrupt break in the course of events and opened up new perspectives for the movement: seeing this shooting at unarmed people and the wounded falling around them, and finding themselves in the zone of fire, the Pavlovskys opened fire at the police across the canal.

This was the first instance of a massive open clash between armed detachments. . . .

This was a terrible breach in the stronghold of Tsarism. Now, after a period of depression, we were all seized anew by a spirit of optimism, even enthusiasm, and our thoughts turned again to the political problems of the revolution. For events had again shifted our course towards revolution. . . .

Peasant Resolution

The following resolution was drawn up at a meeting of peasants in Petrograd Province on October 17, 1917. It was addressed to the Second All-Russian Congress of Soviets which was scheduled to meet on October 25.

- In what terms do these peasants analyze current events? What is the probable source of their knowledge and analysis?
- What was the relation between the Second Congress of Soviets and the Bolshevik seizure of power?
- What light does this document shed on that event?

We, the peasants of the 3rd electoral precinct, Osminsk Volost, Gdovsk Uezd, Petrograd Province, gathered for a general meeting on 17 October of this year and discussed the difficult moment for our Homeland that we are now experiencing.

The old men, women, and children left behind in the countryside are worn out by the horror going on at the present time. The insane war continues and our sons are dying fighting a foreign enemy to satisfy the whim of a tiny little handful of men—the capitalists. Our economy is collapsing because we have no strength left to labor amid such troubles. We face

---

Source: Mark D. Steinberg, *Voices of Revolution, 1917* (New Haven: Yale University Press, 2001), 246–247. © Yale University Press. Reprinted with permission.

the imminent danger of going barefoot; there is no leather for boots, no cloth, no iron, no equipment for cultivating the land; whenever an opportunity does arise to buy something, then it is only at insane prices.

The situation poses the gravest danger to the whole state. Meanwhile, the bourgeois Provisional Government has proven itself utterly incapable of carrying out the people's will. In seven months of revolution this government has allowed the capitalists to close factories and plants intentionally and thereby condemn to starvation workers who are already suffering from malnourishment; it has allowed the organization of counterrevolutionary forces that, led by General Kornilov, have come out openly against the gains of the Revolution. By an act of 3:8 June, it threw an army worn out by a three-year war under the blows of that brigand Wilhelm and his henchmen and vilely coerced the Russian army, which understood things, to attack by threatening them with the disgraceful death penalty. The Provisional Government has released all the criminals against the people, the former henchmen of the tsarist autocracy, who go about freely spreading all manner of foul fabrications against the revolution. The Provisional Government has allowed the above-cited blatant encroachments on freedom on the part of the gentlemen capitalists, despite the fact that the revolutionary people have tried with all their might to fight this kind of violence.

In view of all that has been said, we henceforth and forever will not trust any longer an authority that is not responsible to the people, and we demand that the All-Russian Congress of Soviets of W[orkers']., S[oldiers']., and P[eople's], D[eputies], take power into its own hands both in the center and in the provinces. The Soviet must immediately exercise all its powers to carry out the will of the revolutionary people, who dictated the following back in the very first days of the revolution:

1. Immediately propose to all the countries warring with us, as well as to our allies, an honest democratic peace without any seizures of foreign lands or indemnities of any kind, so that all nations can live freely without being enslaved by anyone.
2. Immediately declare all the land public and hand it over for disposal by the volost land committees.
3. Immediately institute state control over capital and production, as well as the distribution of provisions.
4. Immediately assess taxes on the propertied classes for the benefit of the state.
5. Immediately take energetic measures to provision the countryside, which at the present time is in need of kerosene, cloth, leather, iron, and nails, as well as grain, to cover the shortfall.
6. Immediately turn the profoundest attention to the people's schools, as well as to the teachers, who at present are in the direst straits; short on funds, the schools are emptying out, and the teachers must starve.
7. The rights of the cooperatives must be expanded with respect to provisioning the countryside with food products and manufactured farm goods, as well as with the export of foodstuffs to the towns from the countryside, thereby eliminating the middlemen speculators between the producer and the consumer.
8. Immediately repeal the death penalty, which brings shame upon revolutionary Russia before the revolutionary democracy of the entire world.

The resolution was passed unanimously by the assembly on 17 October.

Marriage and Family Law

The Bolsheviks quickly drew up a new law code based on secular principles and the full equality of the sexes. The following excerpt comes from the Code of Laws concerning the Civil Registration of Deaths, Births, and Marriages, of October 17, 1918.

- How does the divorce law conflict with traditional religious and social practices (in Russia, Central Asia, and practically everywhere else)? Who would benefit from this law?
- What changes does the Family Rights law make in traditional practice? Who does this benefit? Who would oppose it?

86. Marriage may be dissolved by divorce so long as both parties are living.
    Note.—All regulations of the present law relating to divorce also cover valid ecclesiastical and religious marriages contracted up to December 20, 1917.
87. The mutual consent of husband and wife, as well as the desire of one of them to obtain a divorce, may be considered as a ground for divorce.
88. The petition for the dissolution of marriage may be submitted either verbally or in writing, with the official report drawn up thereon.
92. Upon verification that the petition for divorce actually issues from both parties, the Registrar must make an entry of the divorce and at the request of the former married parties deliver to them a certificate of divorce.
93. Divorce suits are heard by the local judge sitting in public and at his own discretion.
98. The decision of the local court on the dissolution of marriage is subject to appeal in the ordinary course to the Court of Appeal . . .
133. Actual descent is regarded as the basis of the family, without any difference between relationships established by legal or religious marriage or outside marriage.
    Note I. Children descended from parents related by non-registered marriage have equal rights with those descended from parents whose marriage was registered.
    Note II. The provisions of the present article extend also to children born outside wedlock before the introduction of Civil Marriage (Dec. 20, 1917).
134. The persons registered as the parents in the register of births are considered as the father and mother of a child.
140. An unmarried woman who becomes pregnant shall give notice not later than three months before the birth of the child to the local Registrar's Office according to her place of residence, stating the time of conception, the name, and the residence of the father.
    Note: A similar notice may be given by a married woman if the conceived child does not descend from her legal husband.
141. On the receipt of such a notice the Registrar's Office shall inform the person designated as father in the notice. Such person is entitled within two weeks from the day of receipt of the information to appeal to the court against the statement made by the mother, on the ground that it is incorrect. If no appeal is made within the specified term, the person is to be considered as the father of the child.
143. Should it be established that the person designated according to article 141 has had such intercourse with the child's mother as to become, according to the natural course of events, the father of the child, the court must decide to recognize him as the father and at the same time compel him to share in the expenses connected with the gestation, delivery and maintenance of the child.

Source: *Collection of Laws and Decrees of the Workers' and Peasants' Government,* 1918. Article 818.

The First All-Russian Muslim Congress

Russia's Muslims, like all its ethnic and religious minorities, had a long history of grievances against Russian imperial rule. The end of the tsarist regime made political organization and action possible, and an All-Russian Muslim Congress was convened in Moscow May 1–11, 1917. Delegates came from all significant Muslim communities.

- What concerns are expressed here? What does this reveal about past tsarist practices?
- What does this reveal about the national aspirations and the political principles of Russia's Muslims?

THE FORM OF GOVERNMENT

The All-Russian Muslim Congress, having discussed the question about the form of government in Russia, resolved: [a] to recognize that the form of government in Russia that guards best the interests of the Muslim peoples is a democratic republic on national territorial-federal principles; moreover, the nationalities that do not possess definite territory enjoy national cultural autonomy; [b] to regulate the general spiritual-cultural questions of the Muslim peoples of Russia and their common affairs by organizing a central general Muslim organ for all Russia, with legislative functions in this sphere.

The form, composition, and function of this organ are to be defined by the first constituent congress of representatives from all autonomous units.

ON MILITARY ORGANIZATIONS

1. Military conscription must be abolished. In the event, however, that the need should arise for the existence of a regular army, because of a struggle with any kind of militarism, the army must be national.
2. Should the need for a regular army be recognized after the close of the war, separate Muslim units should be created.

CULTURAL AND EDUCATIONAL MATTERS

1. Control over educational and cultural matters must be in the hands of individual nationalities, who exercise their right through specially elected organs of each nationality.

2. Teaching in elementary schools must be conducted in the mother tongue of each group of the Turkic peoples. Teaching of the general Turkic language must be compulsory in the secondary schools. Teaching in higher schools is in the general Turkic language.
3. Universal, compulsory, and free elementary education must be introduced.
4. All elementary schools must be of one type without division into secular and ecclesiastical.
5. The system of schools must permit the free passing from the lower to the higher schools without, examinations.
6. The Russian language must be taught in schools as a separate subject.
7. Teachers and students of all nationalities in Russia should enjoy equal rights in every respect.
11. Depending on local conditions, it is desirable that boys and girls be taught together.
12. In the event that the number of Muslim boys reaches three in schools of other nationalities, they must be taught their mother tongue and religion at the expense of the state.
18. In order to prepare a teaching personnel for secondary schools, special Turkic departments must be introduced in Russian higher schools and in [teacher-training] courses.
19. With the opening of the 1917–18 academic year, teachers of national schools must be granted equal rights with the teachers of Russian schools and the same compensation.
20. Persons educated abroad should not be prohibited from teaching in Muslim schools.

The Temporary Religious Organization of the Muslims

Having discussed in several sessions the question of the religious organization of the Muslims, and having taken into consideration that the question of separation of the church from the state must be resolved at a special conference, the section on religious matters came to the following decisions:

1. It is necessary to organize a temporary religious administration to satisfy the spiritual needs of the Muslim population subject to the jurisdiction of the Orenburg Religious Council, and for the Kirghiz population should they express the wish to recognize the spiritual leadership of this administration. . . .
2. Irrespective of the question of separation or nonseparation of the church from the state, it is nevertheless necessary to outline the form and location of religious organizations.

VISUAL DOCUMENTS

Figure 15-1 Petrov-Vodkin, "1918 in Petrograd"

Kuzma Petrov-Vodkin (1878–1939), son of a shoe-maker, began his career as an icon-painter, but patrons who recognized his talent sent him to art school in St. Petersburg, and he eventually studied and painted in France and Italy. Petrov-Vodkin did not adhere to any particular school and is known for striking and original paintings that empha-size color and form.

• What ideas does this pic-ture convey?

Source: Tretiakov Gallery, Moscow.

Figure 15-2 Poster: "Fund of Free-dom"

This poster was created in 1917 after the abdication of the Tsar while the Provisional Government continued to prosecute the war. Captions (omitted here) ask for donations to defend freedom and the motherland.

• Compare this with the war poster from the previous chap-ter, what has changed?

• How have gender images changed? What might this sig-nify?

Source: Early-twentieth-century poster.

Figure 15-3 Poster of Lenin

This poster was made between 1917 and 1920. The writing says: "There is a specter haunting Europe, the specter of Communism." (A quotation from the *Communist Manifesto*.)

- Compare this with previous representations of Russian rulers.
- What qualities of Lenin does this emphasize? What does this say about Soviet society?

Source: The Art Archive/Institute of Slavonic Studies/Marc Charmet.

Figure 15-4 Tatlin, Model for the Comintern Building

Vladimir Tatlin (1885–1953) was trained as an artist, and before the Revolution of 1917 he was an avant-garde designer for the theater. His first experiment in architectural design is pictured here, a model for a building to house the Third Communist International. The building was never completed, but this model became a symbol for the Soviet avant garde.

- Compare this with previous examples of Russian architecture.
- What does this reveal about Soviet ideals and values?

Source: Vladimir Tatlin's "Model of the Monument to the Third International Communist Conference," 1919–1920. The National Swedish Art Museums. © Estate of Vladimir Tatlin/Licensed by VAGA, New York, NY.

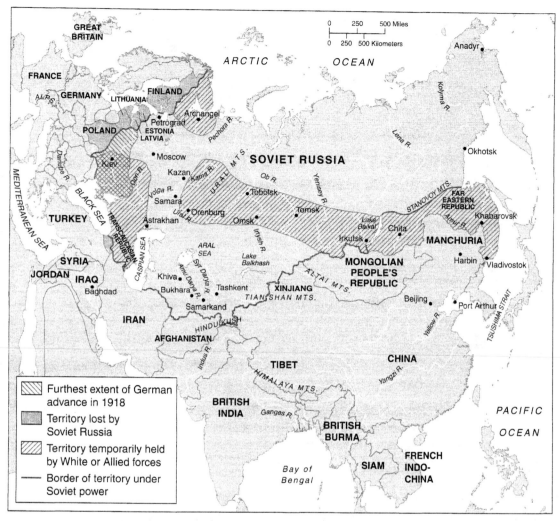

Figure 15-5 Soviet Russia in 1921

By 1921, when the Civil War had essentially been won by the Red Army, most of the old Russian Empire had come under Soviet rule. In the west, Finland, the Baltic nations, and Poland had been lost. In the east, however, the Far Eastern Republic was a temporary expedient; after Japanese forces withdrew in 1922, it was incorporated into Soviet Russia.

_____ **FOR FURTHER READING** _____

(In addition to the books by Figes, McDermid, Moon, Rieber, Sanborn, Service, and Stites from the previous chapter.)

Clements, Barbara Evans. *Daughters of Revolution: A History of Women in the USSR.* Arlington Heights, IL.: Harlan Davidson, Inc.1994.

Radkey, Oliver H. *The Agrarian Foes of Bolshevism: Promise and Default of the Russian Socialist Revolutionaries, February to October 1917.* New York: Columbia University Press, 1958.

Rabinowitch, Alexander. *Prelude to Revolution: The Petrograd Bolsheviks and the July 1917 Uprising.* Bloomington, IN: Indiana University Press, 1968.

_____. *The Bolsheviks Come to Power: The Revolution of 1917 in Petrograd.* New York : W. W. Norton, 1976.

Rosenberg, William G. *Liberals in the Russian Revolution; the Constitutional Democratic Party, 1917–1921.* Princeton, NJ: Princeton University Press, 1974.

Suny, Ronald Grigor, *The Soviet Experiment: Russia, the USSR, and the Successor States.* New York: Oxford University Press, 1998.

Wade, Rex. *The Russian Revolution, 1917.* Cambridge: Cambridge University Press, 2000.

Wildman, Allan K. *The End of The Russian Imperial Army.* 2 vols. Princeton, NJ: Princeton University Press, 1979, 1987.

CHAPTER SIXTEEN

THE EXPERIMENTAL DECADE, 1921–1928

During the Civil War (1918–1921), four developments had occurred that were produced as much by the war atmosphere as by Bolshevik planning. First, the economy was increasingly nationalized, regulated, and regimented. Second, the Communist Party suppressed its political opponents and consolidated a monopoly on political power. Third, advocates of a radical proletarian culture drowned out other voices in literature and the arts. Fourth, most of the nations of the defunct Russian Empire, whose right to freedom had been consistently declared by the Bolsheviks, had been occupied by the Red Army and given Soviet governments. When the Civil War was over, the Communist Party had the opportunity to craft more permanent and well-thought-out policies regarding the economy, the political system, culture, and the nations of the former empire. It moderated all its policies, except for the reconsolidation of the Russian Empire and the concentration of political power in the highest levels of the Communist Party.

EURASIAN CONTEXT

By 1921, socialist insurrection in Europe had been repressed, but social peace and harmony did not follow. Radicalism on the left was countered by extremism from the right. Indeed, the very places where socialist revolution had been most successful—Hungary, Italy, and Germany—were also the birthplaces of fascism. In 1919, Admiral Miklos Horthy overthrew the communist government of Bela Kun; in 1922, Benito Mussolini subverted the Italian government; and in 1923, Adolf Hitler seized power in Bavaria. Hitler's putsch was suppressed, but he and his party were only mildly punished. All three movements claimed to be nationalist *and* socialist. By socialism, they meant government regulation—not ownership—of the economy, and by nationalism they meant subordination of society to a party that claimed to represent the nation. Both Hungarian and German national socialism were viciously anti-Semitic.

Europe faced economic difficulties as well. In the peace settlement after World War I, the Allies had imposed huge reparations payments on Germany, and Germany resisted, causing an international crisis in 1923. First France invaded the Ruhr River region to enforce in-kind payment of the debt, then the German government allowed hyperinflation of the currency that quickly made it worthless. The crisis was resolved in 1924 when the United States granted huge loans to Germany which enabled Germany to begin to pay its debts to England and France. Limited prosperity returned, and in 1925, a conference of the Great Powers (including Germany) in Locarno restored stability to international relations. In the mid-1920s, Adolf Hitler was in prison (for the Bavarian putsch), neither Italy nor Hungary were expansive, and elsewhere parliamentary government and free-enterprise capitalism seemed to be making a comeback.

The First World War had sapped Europe of most of its wealth and some of its aggressiveness, and across Outer Eurasia the victims of nineteenth-century imperialism began to reassert their independence. The first and most successful was Turkey. In 1921, the Grand National Assembly in Ankara declared Turkey's independence and denounced foreign occupation. Mustafa Kemal, made commander in chief of Turkey's military forces, first signed a peace treaty with Soviet Russia, then proceeded to rid the country of foreigners. By the end of the year, he had driven Italian, French, British, and Greek forces from the Anatolian peninsula. Elected president in 1923, Kemal began a series of reforms to remove the vestiges of the Islamic Ottoman Empire and to create a modern, secular nation-state. He renounced all Ottoman imperial interests in the Middle East, and oriented Turkey toward Europe. He declared the separation of church and state, abolished religious courts and schools, and decreed that the Turkish language would be purged of Arabic and Persian words and that it would be written in the Latin rather than Arabic alphabet. Musafa Kemal instituted one-party rule and asserted government control over the economy; he nationalized banks and heavy industry, established government monopolies, and instituted centralized economic planning.

Iran had been occupied by Russian and British forces during the First World War in order to prevent German agents from organizing resistance to the Allies. The Russian army had withdrawn in 1917, but the Red Army had returned during the Russian civil war. In 1921, in the midst of bankruptcy, chaos, and foreign occupation, Reza Khan, an Iranian army officer, took control of the military and forced the Shah to recognize him as commander in chief and prime minister. He then signed a treaty with Soviet Russia, in which the Soviet regime agreed to withdraw its troops, cancel all debts and economic concessions, and turn over Russian property in Iran. British forces also withdrew, without, however, relinquishing Britain's economic privileges. In 1925, Reza Khan deposed the Shah, named himself Reza Shah Pahlavi, and began a series of reforms on the model of Mustafa Kemal. He promoted secular nationalism, limited the power of the Muslim clergy, and began to replace Islamic law with the French Civil Code. He modernized the army, built schools and railroads, and raised taxes on the Anglo-Iranian Oil Company.

Afghanistan followed a similar pattern. In 1919, the King was assassinated by anti-foreign elements who thought him too subservient to the British. His son, Amanullah, succeeded him, and, having secured the loyalty of the army and most tribal leaders, he declared Afghanistan independent of Great Britain. He repelled a British attack, and then signed a friendship treaty with Soviet Russia in 1921 and accepted Soviet financial aid and military equipment. Amanullah brought in Turkish advisers and modeled his domestic policies on Mustafa Kemal's. He modernized the army, required Western clothing in Kabul, discouraged the veiling of women, and established secular education for both boys and girls. He created a secular constitution guaranteeing civil liberties and instituted a parliament and a secular court system. Amanullah was less successful than Musafa Kemal or Reza Shah; he was opposed by tribal leaders, the military, and Muslim clerics, and he was forced to abdicate in 1929.

China was the only one of Russia's neighbors to remain a victim of imperialism. China was not partitioned by the imperial powers, but England, France, and Japan supported the regional warlords and maintained their spheres of influence and economic privileges. In 1919, the Comintern sent agents to China to aid the forces for national unity and independence. Sun Yat-sen, though a socialist, was a middle-class nationalist and did not approve of Russian "War Communism." In 1921, however, after the Soviet regime instituted the New Economic Policy, which permitted private entrepreneurship and fostered prosperity among the peasantry, Sun became willing to accept aid from the Comintern. He reorganized the Guomindang (GMD) along the lines of the Russian Communist Party, and he sent one of his lieutenants, Chiang Kai-shek, to Moscow for military training. In 1921, a Chinese Communist Party (CCP) was formed, and, under Comintern influence, CCP members were given joint membership in the GMD.

The new GMD was immediately successful in suppressing warlordism in Canton and in mobilizing nationwide support for a program of national unification and sovereignty. In 1925, however, Sun Yat-sen died and was succeeded by Chiang Kai-shek. Chiang preferred the support of industrialists and landlords to that of workers and peasants, and the friendship of the United States and western Europe to that of the Soviet Union. He, therefore, ceased to appeal to the Chinese working class and peasant movements, and he decided to suppress the Communist Party. In the course of unifying China by military force, Chiang outlawed the Chinese Communist Party and killed thousands of its members. In 1928, the GMD ruled China from Nanjing, while most of the surviving Communists fled to the countryside in southeastern China.

After World War I, Japan was one of the founding members of the League of Nations. It also played a central role in the Washington Treaties of the 1920s in which the former Allies attempted to reduce naval armaments and establish a stable international order. Japan had sent sixty thousand troops to occupy Vladivostok and the Pacific coast of Siberia in the hope of expanding its Asian empire, but the United States pressed it to withdraw, and it did so in 1922. Japan continued to industrialize, but its economy was severely hurt by the huge Tokyo earthquake of 1925. Furthermore, Japan's economy was inherently fragile; a lack of natural resources made (and still makes) it dependent on world trade both as a source of raw materials and as a market for its manufactured goods. Within Japanese society there were two competing views on how access to markets could be guaranteed. Parliamentary leaders and private industry favored free-trade and cooperation with other imperialist powers. The military, however, wanted Japan to build an empire in East Asia. Both factions supported investment in and emigration to Manchuria and continued economic penetration of China proper.

POLITICAL DEVELOPMENTS AND FOREIGN AFFAIRS

By 1921, the Bolshevik government had emerged victorious in the Civil War, but in the course of the conflict, it had alienated its principal bases of support. Forced requisitioning of grain from the peasantry produced widespread rebellions in the countryside in early 1921.

Bolshevik labor policies, including long hours, low pay, and subordination of unions to management, disappointed the working class. Opposition to one-party rule emerged in a spectacular way when the Kronstadt naval base, which had been a hotbed of Bolshevism in 1917 and was instrumental in the success of the October Revolution, revolted in February 1921. Kronstadt soldiers demanded multiparty elections that would include the Mensheviks and the Socialist Revolutionaries, and they called for an end of requisitioning grain from the peasantry. They demanded "all power to the Soviets" the very slogan that had brought down the Provisional Government and given power to the Bolsheviks.

The Communists responded with a combination of repression and concessions. Trotsky used the Red Army first to suppress the Kronstadt insurrection and then to pacify revolts in the countryside. At the same time, the Sovnarkom announced the end of "War Communism" and the beginning of a New Economic Policy (NEP). Under this program, the government would control the "commanding heights" of the economy, including banking, foreign trade, heavy industry and mines, but the rest of the economy would be returned to private ownership and the market system. Peasants were required to deliver a quota of grain to the government at fixed prices, but they were free to sell the remainder at whatever price the market would bear. Factories were put in the hands of professional managers, and workers were free to change jobs and to go on strike (for economic but not political goals). Ideological restraints were also relaxed; artists and writers were allowed creative freedom as long as they did not directly challenge the legitimacy of the Soviet regime.

In politics, however, the Communist Party refused to give up its monopoly on power and continued to prevent multiparty elections. Furthermore, two trends made the Communist Party itself less democratic. First, as the party grew in size during the Civil War and as its role in directing the Soviet state expanded, new elite institutions were formed. In late 1918, the Politburo (Political Bureau), containing the most influential members of the Communist Party—including Lenin, Trotsky, Stalin, Kamenev, Bukharin, and Zinovyev—took responsibility for formulating policy. Early in 1919, an Orgburo (Organizational Bureau) was created to organize and assign duties within the party. A Secretariat was created later that year to supervise party membership; it kept personnel files and was responsible for admitting new members and purging (rescinding Party membership from) those who did not live up to proper standards of conduct.

Second, the party leaders used the principle of "democratic centralism" to control the party. Democratic centralism meant that all policy issues were to be freely debated and put to a democratic vote, but that once the votes were counted all members were required to support and implement them. This gave inordinate influence to the leaders who were able to control the agenda of party Congresses. As the party grew (from 20,000 in 1917 to 500,000 in 1921), party congresses also grew in size, and the only way the advocates of a program could resist the status quo was to form a voting block (a faction within the party). At the Tenth Party Congress (the same congress that introduced the NEP) in 1921, however, Lenin secured approval of a rule banning factions. This effectively eliminated grass-roots movements; whoever could win power struggles at the highest level of the party would not have to worry about opposition from the rank and file.

As long as Lenin was alive, his prestige and charisma made him the acknowledged leader of Soviet Russia. His policy proposals carried immense weight. However, Lenin's health deteriorated following the attempt on his life, and by 1922, he was no longer involved in the daily affairs of party politics. In the early 1920s, four major figures were expected to compete for leadership after Lenin. Leon Trotsky was most frequently mentioned as Lenin's successor: He had been the leader of the Petrograd Soviet, the tactical manager of the October Revolution, and the military genius behind the victory of the Red Army in the Civil War. Lev

Kamenev and Grigorii Zinovyev were Lenin's oldest associates; they had been his allies since the formation of the Bolshevik faction in 1903. Zinovyev was first secretary of the Petrograd party organization and head of the Comintern. Nikolai Bukharin, considerably younger that the others, had risen to fame as a Marxist theoretician and propagandist.

It turned out, however, that all these leaders would be outmaneuvered and eclipsed by Josef Stalin, a relatively minor figure who had risen to the highest levels of the party largely because Lenin had chosen him to become the Bolshevik expert on nationality issues. Stalin had been made Commissar of Nationalities in the Sovnarkom, but he had not distinguished himself in the revolution or in the civil war. When the Secretariat was created, Stalin volunteered to become its head, a post that was considered to be a boring and thankless job. That Stalin was the only individual to serve simultaneously on the Politburo, the Orgburo, and the Secretariat did not cause any alarm among his associates at first.

In March 1923, Lenin suffered the third of a series of strokes; he could no longer speak, and his political role came to an end. At this point, Stalin began to emerge as a power broker and as the leader of centrists and moderates. Zinovyev sought him out as an ally against Trotsky, who was complaining about bureaucratism in the party and opposing the moderate policies of NEP. Trotsky insisted that Soviet Russia should attempt to spread the revolution to Europe and the world. In the course of the debate, Trotsky reminded the Party that Zinovyev and Kamenev had opposed the Bolshevik seizure of power in 1917. Stalin willingly joined Zinovyev to defeat Trotsky's program.

In January 1924, Lenin died, and the Stalin-Zinovyev clique took charge of Lenin's funeral, both sanctifying Lenin and associating themselves with his authority. They embalmed Lenin's body and enshrined it in a mausoleum on Red Square and created a cult of Lenin highly reminiscent of sainthood. Petrograd was renamed Leningrad in his honor. Stalin also used his power as head of the Secretariat to reconstruct the membership of the Communist Party. In 1922 he had begun a purge of "unreliable" members from the Party that reduced it from 500,000 to 350,000. In 1924, Stalin announced the "Lenin Enrollment," in which the party recruited hundreds of thousands of new members—all vetted and chosen by the Secretariat of which Stalin was the head. In early 1925, the Stalin-Zinovyev coalition removed Trotsky from leadership of the military, although he was allowed to keep his seat on the Politburo.

However, over the course of 1925 the intra-party rivalry changed, as a new debate over economic policy emerged. Bukharin had turned from an economic radical into a conservative and had became the leading defender of the New Economic Policy. He argued that the Soviet Union could create a socialist industrial economy, even in the absence of a revolution in Europe, by relying on the market system. He insisted that if peasants were paid fair prices for their crops, and if they were offered consumer goods to buy with the money they earned, sufficient capital for industrial development would be generated. Trotsky disagreed, arguing that not only was this "state capitalism" and therefore unacceptable on principle, but also that it would take too long; he advocated a return to state control over the economy. The government, he said, should set low prices for grain and high prices for consumer goods in order to extract the maximum possible capital from agriculture and use it to for rapid industrialization.

Stalin supported Bukharin, but Zinovyev and Kamenev suddenly changed sides and threw their support behind Trotsky. Stalin's supervision of Communist Party membership now paid off. The Fourteenth Party Congress, elected by the party in late 1925, backed Stalin and Bukharin overwhelmingly. In 1926, Stalin orchestrated the removal of Kamenev from the Politburo and the appointment of several of Stalin's close associates, including Viacheslav Molotov. Stalin also removed Zinovyev from the post of first secretary of the Leningrad party organization.

Later, in 1926, Zinovyev, Kamenev, and Trotsky realized that they had been defeated by bureaucratic methods and decided to risk their political careers by violating Lenin's rule against factions within the party. They announced the formation of a "United Opposition," which publicly denounced the economic policy and appealed to the rank and file of the party for support. Stalin punished them for violating party discipline by removing Zinovyev from leadership of the Comintern and Trotsky and Zinovyev from the Politburo. The United Opposition would not surrender, and they continued to publish attacks on Stalin and Bukharin, thus raising the political stakes. Stalin treated their behavior as sedition against the party; a number of lower-level opposition figures were arrested, and in 1927, Trotsky and Zinovyev were removed from the Central Committee. By 1928, the only member of the Politburo not to owe his appointment to Stalin was Bukharin (who would shortly become Stalin's next victim).

In foreign policy, as in economics, the beginning of NEP also marked a retreat from radicalism. Once the civil war was over, Russia began to cultivate diplomatic and commercial relations with its former enemies. In 1921, Soviet Russia signed a peace treaty with Mustafa Kemal, dividing Armenia between Turkey and Transcaucasia, and it agreed to withdraw the Red Army from Iran. In the same year, Soviet Russia established commercial relations with Great Britain, and the Comintern called for Communist parties to abandon plans for armed insurrection and to cooperate with moderate socialist parties and trade unions. The Soviet regime sent representatives to a European conference in Genoa in 1922 that attempted to normalize relations among the states of Europe. Soviet delegates negotiated a treaty with Germany in which the two countries agreed to exchange ambassadors and to cancel mutual reparations claims. They also signed a trade agreement, exchanging Russian wheat for German industrial equipment. In an additional (secret) agreement, the Soviet regime allowed Germany to train its military (outlawed by the Versailles Treaty) on Russian soil. Diplomatic relations were reestablished with France and Great Britain in 1924 and with Japan in 1925. Between 1925 to 1927, Soviet Russia signed non-aggression treaties with neighboring Turkey, Afghanistan, Lithuania, Latvia, Estonia, and Iran. Poland, however, refused.

Yet despite these efforts at diplomatic normalization, international hostility to Soviet Communism was on the rise. Relations with Germany were hurt by Comintern support of an insurrection by the German Communist Party in 1923. Furthermore, after the Dawes plan was put into effect (1924), and after the 1925 Locarno treaty among France, Great Britain, and Germany, tensions were reduced in the west, and Germany began to distance itself from the Soviet Union. In 1924, the Conservative Party in Great Britain defeated the Labour Party by publishing a forged "Zinovyev letter" that purported to promote Communist revolution in England. Across Europe, Fascism gained support in part because its leaders frightened the middle class with the dangers of communist subversion. In China, Chiang Kai-shek began an anti-Communist campaign that culminated in the Shanghai Massacre of 1927. Continued suspicion of Soviet subversion led Britain to break diplomatic relations with the Soviet Union in May 1927. In June, the Soviet ambassador to Poland was assassinated. Soviet leaders felt surrounded by enemies.

CULTURE AND RELIGION

In its educational policies, the NEP retreated from the experimental idealism of War Communism. The state education budget was cut, and local government was forced to pick up the slack. As a result, the number of schools shrank and tuition costs increased. The number of working-class children in school declined, and secondary and higher education came to be dominated by children of the professional elite. Vocational and academic schools were separated, teachers returned to traditional methods of instruction, and private schools reappeared. Education under NEP was an improvement over the tsarist era but still lagged behind the standards of modern industrial societies: In 1926, 55 percent of the rural population were illiterate and 40 percent of children between the ages of seven and eleven did not attend school, and there was only one schoolteacher for every seven hundred Soviet citizens. By comparison, higher education thrived; in the 1920s, the government spent a higher proportion of the GDP on scientific research than most Western countries.

In the Civil War period, the Communist Party followed a policy of strict separation of church and state. In the early 1920s, however, Party leaders came to feel that the Russian Orthodox Church was a rival for the hearts and minds of the population, and it began to subvert the church. In 1922, the Soviet government announced the confiscation of church wealth to feed the hungry, and when Patriarch Tikhon protested, he was put under house arrest. This provided the opportunity for a group of radical priests, who believed that Christianity was consistent with Communism, to attempt to take over the church. They tricked Tikhon into transferring his authority to them, and they announced the creation of the "Living" or "Renovationist" Church. They ended the patriarchate, created a new secular Synod to govern the church, and introduced radical church reforms, including removing distinctions between the "black" clergy (celibate monks and prelates) and "white" clergy (married parish priests).

The Soviet government soon decided that the Renovationist church, too, was a danger; although sympathetic to socialism, it was sincerely Christian in its beliefs. In 1923, Tikhon was released from detention after publicly repenting his anti-Soviet declarations, and he resumed leadership of the church. Most Renovationist congregations reaccepted the Patriarchate, and the Renovationist church declined. After Tikhon died in 1925, the Soviet government did not allow a new patriarch to be elected. The church was essentially led by its senior metropolitan, Sergei, who declared his loyalty to the regime.

The Russian peasants proved to be indifferent to church politics at the national level, but they retained religious customs. They elected their own priests, and they resisted the secularization of traditional life; they preferred religious holidays to Soviet holidays, and they thought that education was properly provided by the church. Until the end of the 1920s, almost 60 percent of all babies were christened and almost 70 percent of all funerals were presided over by a priest. No social stigma was attached to these events, since grandmothers could be "blamed" for insisting on baptisms, while the desire for church funerals could be attributed to ingrained customs of the older generation. On the other hand, Church membership was a handicap for those who wanted to advance in a career, and by 1929, only 10 percent of marriages were performed in a church.

Culturally, if not educationally, the NEP period was a time of great diversity and high achievement. There was no attempt by the government to establish a literary orthodoxy, and considerable freedom was allowed to so-called "fellow-travelers," non-Communist writers and artists who refrained from criticism of the Soviet regime. Osip Mandelshtam published his expressionist poetry through the twenties, and Anna Akhmatova and Boris Pasternak translated foreign literature. Sergei Esenin won fame for his sentimental evocations of the Russian countryside. NEP-era novelists included Isaac Babel, who is most famous for *Red Cavalry,* a series of sketches from the Civil War, and Evgenii Zamiatin, whose dystopia *We* was a prototype for George Orwell's *1984.*

In addition, many artists were active supporters and propagandists for Communism. Vladimir Mayakovsky was at his most productive, writing poems, plays, and screenplays that celebrated Soviet socialism. A few novelists set the foundation for what would be called

Socialist Realism by reviving the realistic tradition of the nineteenth century and applying it to working class and revolutionary subjects. Aleksandr Fadeev wrote *The Rout,* a novel that celebrated the proletarian consciousness of partisans who had fought in the east in the civil war. Fedor Gladkov's *Cement* told the story of an idealistic worker who revived a cement plant that had fallen idle during the civil war. Mikhail Sholokhov wrote a series of realistic novels about the revolution and civil war among the Don Cossacks.

There had been virtually no film industry in tsarist Russia, but Lenin realized the potential power of film to communicate with the people (the majority of whom were still illiterate). In 1919, the Soviet regime took charge of film making, and Nadezhda Krupskaya was put in charge of a State Institute of Cinematography which trained directors and sponsored the creation of agitational films to promote Soviet power. All Soviet directors got their start at the Institute, including Sergei Eisenstein, one of the pioneers of modern film-making. Eisenstein was an avant-garde innovator in form and technique who put his genius in the service of Communism. His series of movies made in the 1920s—*Strike, The Battleship Potemkin,* and *October*—combined high art with propaganda.

ROLES AND STATUS OF WOMEN

The Soviet government actively recruited women into the skilled labor force, the professions, and the government. It implemented propaganda campaigns to convince factory managers that women were equal to men, and it promoted the idea of equal pay for equal work. The results were mixed. Women's pay increased slightly relative to men's, from less than 50 percent before 1917 to 65 percent by 1930. Women continued to make up more than 40 percent of the urban workforce, but as men were demobilized from the Red Army after the Civil War they were favored in hiring. Men were also favored in heavy industry, and women's unemployment rates were always higher than men's. In the middle of the 1920s, women made up one-fifth of the delegates to city soviets and one-sixth of membership in the Communist Party. Although far from equality, this was considerably ahead of world trends.

Family relations were revolutionized in the 1920s. The extended, multigenerational family virtually disappeared. In the countryside, Soviet tax policies (inadvertently) favored the nuclear family. In cities, there was a huge increase in single-parent households, something practically unheard of before the revolution. This was partly the result of the feeling that monogamy was an obsolete "bourgeois" custom, partly the consequence of the idea that relationships should be built on love rather than economic interest. According to this modern view, if a husband and wife ceased to love one another, their marriage should end.

These trends were reflected in a new marriage and family law in 1926; divorce was made easier to obtain while women were given new rights in seeking child support. Court appearances were no longer necessary in divorce actions even if one of the parties objected; all that was required was a postcard informing a spouse that the marriage was over. The new law also gave women the right to claim child support from the father(s) of their children whether or not they had been married, and even if the pregnancy had occurred as the result of a brief encounter. The intent of this law was not to condone sexual promiscuity but to free the state from the obligation to provide financial support to unmarried mothers.

In the 1920s, the Zhenotdel was officially directed to give up advocating women's rights and to devote itself instead to mobilizing women in support of the Soviet regime. The Zhenotdel published a variety of women's magazines and hundreds of books and pamphlets teaching Soviet patriotism, providing Marxist analysis of current events, and attacking conservatism and religion in the countryside. The most famous magazines, *Krestianka (Peasant*

Woman) and *Rabotnitsa* (*Woman Worker*) were similar to western magazines for women, containing fiction, recipes, fashion news, child-care tips, and profiles of famous women.

The Zhenotdel also organized national conferences that brought together peasant and working-class women from all parts of the country in order to raise their political consciousness and turn them into grass roots activists and organizers. There were a number of activities Zhenotdel leaders hoped these women would engage in after they returned home: organizing courses in literacy, hygiene, birthing, and child care; campaigning for equal employment opportunities for women; and pressing local officials to set up public nurseries, day-care centers, laundries, and cafeterias.

Local activists, however, faced resistance from local (male) communist party bureaucrats and often from other women. In the countryside, at the beginning of the twenties, peasant women had little desire to liberate themselves from peasant institutions and family values, or to move to the city and become independent wage workers. The land had only recently been divided among the peasantry, and the NEP meant the possibility of a new level of prosperity for farmers. Peasant women saw no reason to leave the mir.

One region in which the Soviet regime was anxious to use the Zhenotdel to promote women's rights was Central Asia. Traditional Muslim society was particularly hostile to Soviet rule, and the Communist leadership believed that the most effective way to combat tradition would be to appeal to Central Asian women. Consequently, the Zhenotdel agitated on behalf of women's equality and encouraged Central Asian women to appear in public and to stop wearing the veil. The campaign failed. Central Asian men suppressed the women's liberation movement, by beating, raping, and murdering Zhenotdel agents and Muslim women who attended Zhenotdel meetings or who adopted western clothing and attitudes. More than eight hundred women were murdered before the Communist Party gave up.

SOCIAL AND ECONOMIC TRENDS

The New Economic Policy was declared in March 1921, but Soviet Russia had to face one more disaster before it achieved stability and a measure of prosperity. Later that year, a major famine hit the Volga region, and over the next two years five million people died of starvation and millions more from typhus and other diseases exacerbated by malnutrition. More deaths were prevented by an improved harvest in 1922 and the intervention of the American Relief Administration, which sent Soviet Russia enough food to feed ten million people. By 1923, the famine was over.

The New Economic Policy permitted private enterprise and a relatively free market. State-owned industry was decentralized, and factories were put under the control of professional managers. In the mid-twenties there were about 2,000 privately owned factories and 200,000 artisan workshops. Professionals, workers in the service and entertainment industries, and merchants were all private entrepreneurs. Nepmen (wholesalers and distributors of goods produced by private manufacturers and cooperatives) were responsible for 75 percent of trade in Russia proper and at least 90 percent of trade in Central Asia and the Caucasus region.

Nevertheless, the state was still the dominant player in the economy. The Khoznarkom (Commissariat of the Economy) continued to control banking, foreign trade, heavy industry, and mines. Privately owned factories employed only twenty-one workers on the average (as opposed to more than two hundred in state-owned factories). Moreover, in most large privately managed factories the state was in fact the majority shareholder. Nepmen did not accumulate and reinvest capital; they were not allowed to "speculate," and they paid a 50 percent tax on profits.

Economic recovery was slow. By 1924, industrial production was still only 45 percent of the pre-war level. After 1925, heavy industry began to expand; the number of workers reached pre-war levels in 1926, but in the NEP period, factory employment remained lower than it had been in 1917. Continuing migration from the countryside to the city kept unemployment levels high: in 1927, there were six million factory workers but one million unemployed urban residents.

The New Economic Policy meant a relaxation of the class warfare of the Civil War period. Toleration of "fellow-travelers" was extended to professionals as well as writers and artists, and the Soviet regime paid premium salaries to retain the services of "bourgeois specialists," particularly engineers and technical experts. At the same time, however, the government began to recruit, train, and promote individuals from working-class or peasant backgrounds, and specialists from the nobility or middle class were discriminated against whenever candidates from the laboring classes were available.

After the Civil War, life improved for workers, who were now free to change jobs and to go on strike. (Unions, however, were allowed only to negotiate for higher wages and improved working conditions; they could not interfere in management issues.) As the economy gradually recovered, workers' standard of living rose, but cities still suffered from insufficient housing, working-class slums, drug use, and prostitution.

The NEP era was a golden age for the Russian peasantry. During the Civil War, nearly all arable land had come into the possession of the commune, and separate holdings disappeared. By law, the land belonged to the state and could not be sold or rented. Nevertheless, the peasants treated the land as if the mir owned it; most mirs redistributed land periodically according to tradition. The major reason for the NEP was to get grain to the market; free trade was meant to induce farmers to grow more grain. It worked in part: by 1924, agricultural production had returned to the 1913 level. On the other hand, the cities received only 60 percent of the grain that had been delivered to cities in 1913. Russia's farmers were no longer being starved for the benefit of industrialization; they were eating more of the grain they grew.

Social stratification of the village continued. Approximately 35 percent of farmers were classified as "poor," that is, they had little land, no livestock, and had to supplement their income by working for wages. "Middle peasants," who had enough land and livestock to feed themselves, made up 60 percent of the farm population, while the top 5 percent, called *kulaks* by the government, owned enough land, livestock, and equipment so they could hire workers. Kulaks produced 25 percent of the grain that went to market.

This stratification was not the result of inherited wealth; instead it was caused by the redistribution of the land. Households with more able-bodied workers were assigned more land and were consequently better off. As in tsarist days, the pattern changed from generation to generation, and there were no permanent classes of rich and poor. The Soviet government misinterpreted the situation; it considered class divisions permanent and saw poor peasants as proletarians and kulaks as bourgeois capitalist exploiters. It established a progressive tax system in the countryside under which poor peasants paid no taxes, while rich peasants paid taxes plus a surcharge. Multigenerational households split up to reduce household income, and the number of communes increased from 100,000 in the early 1920s to 300,000 in 1928.

The mir continued to be suspicious of experts and administrators from the city, but it was no more hostile to communism than it had been to tsarism. The mir was also largely self-governing. Volost (local district) soviets were underfunded, delegates rarely attended meetings, and administration was taken over by the communes. Furthermore, there were only twenty-three thousand party cells in the countryside, less than one-tenth the number of mirs.

FORMATION OF THE SOVIET UNION

In 1921, as a result of the First World War and the Civil War, the former Tsarist empire was reconfigured. Finland, Estonia, Latvia, Lithuania, and Poland had become sovereign nation-states. Eastern Siberia had been turned into an independent Far Eastern Republic. There were six independent Soviet republics: Russia, Ukraine, Belarus, Armenia, Azerbaijan, and Georgia. To further complicate matters, Russia, officially known as the Russian Soviet Federated Socialist Republic (RSFSR) was a multiethnic state containing large national groups living in recognized homelands, including Chuvash, Bashkirs, Tatars, Yakuts, and many others. Tsarist Turkestan, which included Kazakhs, Kirgiz, Uzbeks, Tajiks, and Turkmens, had also been incorporated into the RSFSR. These homelands were organized as self-governing political units; the larger of them (such as Bashkirs, Yakuts, Crimean Tatars, and Kirgiz) were formed into Autonomous Soviet Socialist Republics (ASSRs), while the smaller ones became Autonomous Oblasts (AOs).

It was generally assumed by Communist party leaders that all of the regions with soviet governments (and ruling Communist parties) would unite to form a single state. Furthermore, even though Ukraine, Belarus, Armenia, Azerbaijan, and Georgia were technically independent, they were informally associated with one another because they had significant Russian populations, were governed by Communist parties, and were occupied by the Red Army as a result of the Civil War. There was considerable pressure for this unification both from the large Russian populations in all the old provinces of the Russian Empire who wanted to remain in a Russian-dominated state and from Communists who wanted to proletarian unity.

However, what form the new Soviet state should take was hotly debated. The more idealistic Left Communists, led by Nikolai Bukharin and Georgii Piatakov, wanted a single, unitary state that would ignore national divisions and assimilate all citizens into a Soviet, proletarian, socialist identity. Lenin and Stalin, on the other hand, considered nationalism to be an historical stage through which all peoples must pass on their way to socialist consciousness; they also believed that national separatism was caused by oppression and that Russian chauvinism was the greatest danger to Soviet unity. Lenin and Stalin, therefore, wanted a union of equal nations.

The unification of all Soviet states into a single state followed the program of Lenin and Stalin, but only after resolving a further policy dispute. In 1921, Stalin, as the Commissar of Nationalities, created a Transcaucasian Federated Republic on the model of the RSFSR, that contained Armenia, Azerbaijan, Georgia, and Chechens, Ossetians, Kabardians, and other peoples of the Caucasus region. The brutal and high-handed approach taken by Stalin's proteges in forming this republic angered Lenin, who also opposed Stalin's plan for absorbing all the soviet governments of Ukraine, Belarus, and Transcaucasia into the RSFSR as Autonomous Soviet Socialist Republics (ASSRs). Lenin feared that to absorb all national territories into the Russian Republic would mean to foster Russian power. He insisted that a new entity, the Union of Soviet Socialist Republics (USSR), be created, made up of four equal republics, the RSFSR, Ukraine, Belarus, and Transcaucasia. (Terry Martin has recently pointed out that, in fact, Stalin's plan would have promoted national autonomy more effectively, since it would have raised the status of the ASSRs rather than lowered the status of the SSRs.[1]) In December 1922, the Union of Soviet Socialist Republics was formed according to Lenin's plan.

In 1924 to 1925, the Soviet regime turned its attention to the reorganization of Central Asia, which had been divided into the Kirgiz ASSR, Turkestan ASSR, and the Republics of Bukhara and Khorazm. The Sovnarkom decided to follow the principle of nationalism and to create Soviet Republics based on the major ethnic groups: Uzbek, Turkmen, Tajik, Kirgiz, and Kazakh. These five national territories were given the form of "Autonomous Soviet Socialist Republics" within the RSFSR. (In the 1930s, they would be made independent Soviet Socialist Republics in the Soviet Union.) In the fashion typical of European colonialism, there was no attempt to draw territorial boundaries that respected ethnic divisions. Significant ethnic minorities, plus a major Russian presence in each republic, meant that the central government could play ethnic groups against one another. (This is another typical colonialist strategy.)

The new Soviet Union was, in Terry Martin's term, an "affirmative action empire." For the remainder of the 1920s, the Communist Party fostered native culture and the development of national identity in each of the Soviet Republics. In each republic or oblast, the language of the majority people (whose name was given to the republic) was made the official state language and the language of instruction in schools. Each nation was encouraged to celebrate and cultivate its folklore, history, literature, food, dress, and customs. Furthermore, in a process known as "indigenization," the Communist party worked to fill leadership positions in the party, administration, industry, and schools with members of the titular nationality of each republic or region. The goal of this affirmative-action nationality policy was to accommodate the nations of the Soviet Union to Soviet Communist rule, so they would see the union not as Russian imperialism but as a native and natural development. It did not, however, promote political autonomy; the Soviet Union was, in fact, centrally administered by the Communist party as if it were a unitary state.

A striking similarity arose between the Soviet Union and the old Russian Empire. On one hand, the unique national character of each region was recognized and the multinational character of the state was celebrated, but, on the other hand, there was an attempt to create a single civic identity for all citizens of the imperial state. The Soviet Union went further than the Russian Empire, however, both in encouraging national minorities to consider themselves to be autonomous and in indoctrinating the population in the political ideology of the ruling party. The ideal Soviet citizen was expected to have two identities, a Soviet identity as a proletarian internationalist, and a national identity as a member of a national republic. This contradiction remained unresolved for as long as the Soviet Union existed.

CONCLUSION: THE ECONOMIC CRISIS OF 1927

Soviet Communists, like the tsarist officials whom they succeeded, wanted rapid industrial development. Modernity in the late-nineteenth and early-twentieth centuries was measured by heavy industry: the production of steel and the use of steel to manufacture industrial machinery, ships, locomotives, tractors, harvesters, etc. The imperialist wars of the late-nineteenth century had demonstrated that industrial development was essential to survival: Industrial nations colonized agricultural nations. The First World War added a further concern; wars among modern industrial societies are "total wars" fought not only by soldiers on the battlefield but by workers in mines and factories. Besides these incentives, Communists had another reason to promote industrialization. In Marx's view, industrial capitalism, developed to its fullest extent, is the necessary prelude to communism. The factory system, when possessed by the proletariat rather than the capitalists, will liberate humanity from want and allow the full realization of human nature.

Imperial Russia had taken a two-pronged approach to industrialization. It had borrowed capital through foreign loans and foreign investment, and it had bought industrial equipment with the proceeds from the export of Russian wheat. Soviet Russia, however, had closed the door to foreign loans or investment by renouncing the Tsar's foreign debt and by nationalizing industry. Furthermore, whereas it was in the interests of the West in the 1920s to sponsor huge loans to prop up a democratic Germany, it was equally in their interests to starve the Soviet regime of capital and allow it to collapse. Consequently, the only option available for Soviet Russia was to export grain.

To obtain grain for export, the government could either buy it or take it by force. In the long run, requisitioning grain is counterproductive, as was proven by the famine and economic collapse that had followed the Civil War. The NEP, therefore, took the first approach, and began to provide a monetary incentive for farmers to grow more grain. But money, is not enough: There must be consumer goods for farmers to spend their money on. It was for this reason that the NEP favored light industry producing consumer goods such as textiles, rubber, matches, tobacco, and books.

Unfortunately, heavy industry of the sort required for national defense and as a foundation for communism was growing very slowly, and Soviet Communists soon ran out of patience with the New Economic Policy. In 1927, two events precipitated the end to the NEP: the war scare (discussed above) and a shortage of grain. The grain harvest in 1927 was only 10 percent less than the 1913 harvest (which had been a good year), but because of Soviet pricing policies, very little of it was delivered to market. In 1913 the Russian Empire had exported 12,000,000 tons of wheat; in 1927 the Soviet Union exported only 300,000 tons. The only alternative, if the peasantry was unwilling to sell its grain on terms acceptable to the government, was to use coercive measures. Less than three decades earlier, I. A. Vyshnegradskii had announced that "we will go hungry but we will export grain." The Communist party was about to embark on the same cruel policy.

NOTES

1. Terry Martin, *The Affirmative Action Empire: Nations and Nationalism in the Soviet Union, 1923–1939* (Ithaca: Cornell University Press, 2001), 395–397.

—————————————— TEXT DOCUMENTS ——————————————

Lenin, "On Party Unity"

The Tenth Congress of the Russian Communist Party, held in the spring of 1921, was a milestone in the emergence of party dictatorship. A key tool in this process was a resolution outlawing factions in the party. In this selection, Lenin supports the resolution.

- How does Lenin explain the need for the resolution? To what emotions does he appeal?
- What are the policies he proposes? Why might they contribute to dictatorship?

1. The Congress calls the attention of all members of the Party to the fact that the unity and solidarity of the ranks of the Party, ensuring complete mutual confidence among Party members and genuine team work, genuinely embodying the unanimity of will of the vanguard of the proletariat, are particularly essential at the present juncture when a number of circumstances are increasing the vacillation among the petty-bourgeois population of the country.

2. Notwithstanding this, even before the general Party discussion on the trade unions, certain signs of factionalism had been apparent in the Party, viz., the formation of groups with separate platforms, striving to a certain degree to segregate and create their own group discipline. Such symptoms of factionalism were manifested, for example, at a Party conference in Moscow (November 1920) and in Kharkov, both by the so-called "Workers' Opposition" group, and partly by the so-called "Democratic-Centralism" group.

All class-conscious workers must clearly realize the perniciousness and impermissibility of factionalism of any kind, for no matter how the representatives of individual groups may desire to safeguard Party unity, in practice factionalism inevitably leads to the weakening of team work and to intensified and repeated attempts by the enemies of the Party, who have fastened themselves onto it because it is the governing Party, to widen the cleavage and to use it for counterrevolutionary purposes.

The way the enemies of the proletariat take advantage of every deviation from the thoroughly consistent communist line was perhaps most strikingly shown in the case of the Kronstadt mutiny, when the bourgeois counterrevolutionaries and White guards in all countries of the world immediately expressed their readiness to accept even the slogans of the Soviet system, if only they might thereby secure the overthrow of the dictatorship of the proletariat in Russia, and when the Socialist-Revolutionaries and the bourgeois counterrevolutionaries in general resorted in Kronstadt to slogans calling for an insurrection against the Soviet government of Russia ostensibly in the interest of Soviet power. These facts fully prove that the White guards strive, and are able, to disguise themselves as Communists, and even as the most Left Communists, solely for the purpose of weakening and overthrowing

Source: V. I. Lenin, *Selected Works in Two Volumes*, Vol. 2, Pt. 2 (Moscow: Foreign Languages Publishing House, 1952), 497–501.

the bulwark of the proletarian revolution in Russia. Menshevik leaflets distributed in Petrograd on the eve of the Kronstadt mutiny likewise show how the Mensheviks took advantage of the disagreements and certain rudiments of factionalism in the Russian Communist Party actually in order to egg on and support the Kronstadt mutineers, the Socialist-Revolutionaries and White guards, while claiming to be opponents of mutiny and supporters of the Soviet power, only with supposedly slight modifications. . . .

4. In the practical struggle against factionalism, every organization of the Party must take strict measures to prevent any factional actions whatsoever. Criticism of the Party's shortcomings, which is absolutely necessary, must be conducted in such a way that every practical proposal shall be submitted immediately, without any delay, in the most precise form possible, for consideration and decision to the leading local and central bodies of the Party. Moreover, everyone who criticizes must see to it that the form of his criticism takes into account the position of the Party, surrounded as it is by a ring of enemies, and that the content of his criticism is such that, by directly participating in Soviet and Party work, he can test the rectification of the errors of the Party or of individual Party members in practice. Every analysis of the general line of the Party, estimate of its practical experience, verification of the fulfilment of its decisions, study of methods of rectifying errors, etc., must under no circumstances be submitted for preliminary discussion to groups formed on the basis of "platforms," etc., but must be exclusively submitted for discussion directly to all the members of the Party. For this purpose, the Congress orders that the *Discussion Bulletin* and special symposiums be published more regularly, and that unceasing efforts be made to secure that criticism shall be concentrated on essentials and not assume a form capable of assisting the class enemies of the proletariat. . . .

6. The Congress therefore hereby declares dissolved and orders the immediate dissolution of all groups without exception that have been formed on the basis of one platform or another (such as the "workers' opposition" group, the "democratic-centralism" group, etc.). Nonobservance of this decision of the Congress shall involve absolute and immediate expulsion from the Party.

7. In order to ensure strict discipline within the Party and in all Soviet work and to secure the maximum unanimity in removing all factionalism, the Congress authorizes the Central Committee, in cases of breach of discipline or of a revival or toleration of factionalism, to apply all Party penalties, including expulsion, and in regard to members of the Central Committee to reduce them to the status of alternate members and even, as an extreme measure, to expel them from the Party. . . .

Stalin, "Report on National Factors in Party and State Affairs"

One of the factors that had contributed to Bolshevik success in the Civil War had been the resentment of tsarist imperialism by the non-Russian nations and the demand of the White armies that the empire be restored "one and indivisible." Attempting to re-unite those same nations into a Union of Soviet Socialist Republics (declared in 1922) was bound to bring those issues back to the surface. Stalin addressed this problem at this speech given to the Twelfth Congress of the Russian Communist Party in 1923.

- Why is Stalin concerned about the success of the new Union?
- What is Stalin's understanding of the cause of national conflict?
- How does he seek to address it?
- Are there any contradictions inherent in this policy?

The fact of the matter is that the whole East regards our Union of Republics as an experi-mental field. Either we . . . within the framework of this Union, establish truly fraternal rela-tions and true cooperation among the peoples—in which case the whole East will see that our federation is the banner of its liberation . . . Or we . . . undermine the confidence of the formerly oppressed peoples in the proletariat of Russia, and deprive the Union of Republics of the power of attraction which it possess in the eyes of the East—in which case imperial-ism will win and we shall lose. . . .

The national question is also of importance for us from the standpoint of the internal situ-ation, not only because the former dominant nation numbers about 75,000,000 and the other nations 65,000,000 (not a small figure, anyway), and not only because the formerly op-pressed nationalities inhabit areas that are the most essential for our economic development and the most important from the standpoint of military strategy, but above all because dur-ing the past two years . . . as a result of the NEP, a new force is arising in the internal life of our country, namely, Great-Russian chauvinism, which entrenches itself in our institutions, which penetrates not only the Soviet institutions, but also the Party institutions, and which is to be found in all parts of our federation. Consequently, if we do not resolutely combat this new force . . . we run the risk of being confronted by a rupture between the proletariat of the former dominant nation and the peasants of the formerly oppressed nations—which will mean undermining the dictatorship of the proletariat. . . .

If the proletariat succeeds in establishing with the peasantry of the other nationalities re-lations that can eradicate all remnants of mistrust towards everything Russian, a mistrust implanted a fostered for decades by the policy of tsarism—if, moreover, the Russian prole-tariat succeeds in establishing complete mutual understanding and confidence, in effecting a genuine alliance not only between the proletariat and the Russian peasantry, but also be-tween the proletariat and peasantry of the formerly oppressed nationalities, the problem

---

Source: Joseph Stalin, "Report on National Factors in Party and State Affairs," *Works, vol. 5, 1921–1923* (Moscow: Foreign Languages Publishing House, 1953), 243–244, 245–246, 247–248.

will be solved. . . . And in order that Soviet power may become dear also to the peasants of these nationalities, it must be understood by these peasants, it must function in their native languages, the schools and governmental bodies must be staffed with local people who know the language, habits, customs, and manner of life of the non-Russian nationalities. Soviet power, which until very recently was Russian power, will become a power which is not merely Russian but international . . . only when and to the degree that the institutions and governmental bodies in the republics of these countries begin to speak and function in the native languages. . . .

The basis of this Union is the voluntary consent and the juridical equality of the members of the Union. . . . Because our national program starts out from the clause on the right of nations to exist as independent states, what was formerly called the right to self-determination. Proceeding from this, we must definitely say that no union of peoples into a single state can be durable unless it is based on absolutely voluntary consent. . . . Some people ask a purely scholastic question, namely: do the republics remain independent after uniting? That is a scholastic question. Their independence is restricted, for every union involves a certain restriction of the former rights of the parties to the union. But the basic elements of independence of each of these republics certainly remain, if only because every republic retains the right to secede from the Union at its own discretion.

Thus, the concrete form the national question has assumed under the conditions at present prevailing in our country is how to achieve the cooperation of the peoples in economic, foreign, and military affairs. We must unite the republics along these lines into a single union called the USSR. Such are the concrete forms the national question has assumed a the present time.

The Peasant Village Under the New Economic Policy

Fedor Belov was born not long after the 1917 Revolution in the village that he describes here. Belov left for advanced schooling and then served in the army during the Second World War. After the war, Belov returned to his village where he served as director of a collective farm. His army service was reactivated in 1949, and he was sent to serve in Germany. He took the opportunity to defect to the West where he turned his diaries into a book about farm life in the Soviet Union.

- What effect did the Bolshevik seizure of power and the NEP have on farm life?
- How does peasant life in the 1920s compare with life under the Tsar?

Following the Civil War, with all its anxieties and confusion, the village gradually began to revive. After the famine of 1921 (I should mention that no one in the village died of hunger during this time), the village lands were repartitioned according to the new regulations. At that time the village numbered more than three thousand inhabitants, with total holdings of 4,380 hectares [10,800 acres]. This total included the homestead strips, or individual garden plots, which averaged six to seven hectares [15–17 acres] per household.

Our land produced good crops. On an average, the yields obtained per hectare were thirty to forty centners [one centner equals 100 pounds] of wheat, twenty-five to thirty centners of rye, twenty to twenty-five centners of barley, and two hundred centners of beets. Every household had large surpluses of grain which it could dispose of as it saw fit; for the most part, the grain went to market for sale.

Since at that time the tax burden was light, the majority of the peasants were able to increase and improve their holdings. They built houses, barns and sheds, and bought agricultural implements. By 1926 the village had more than 500 cows, 300 horses, 600 swarms of bees, 2 watermills, 13 windmills, and 6 stores. More than 100 houses were fitted out with sheet-iron roofs, a sure sign of peasant prosperity. A villager who did not kill one or two pigs a year (for Christmas and Easter) was a rarity. As a rule, lard and eggs could be found in every home. These were the golden days of the NEP, which the peasants still [this was written in the early 1950s] look back upon with longing.

Church and national holidays were celebrated solemnly and joyously. During Christmas week nobody worked; everyone wore his best clothes; the best dishes were cooked for one's guests; and no one refused charity to the crippled beggars. Following the old tradition, the children went around singing carols in praise of Christ and collecting donations for the church. At Easter, the villagers greeted each other with the customary "Christ is risen!" instead of with "How do you do?" No one violated the traditions which had been established by the people and the church.

In the autumn, as a rule, two or three weddings took place in the village. They were celebrated in accordance with all the church canons and national customs. A wedding lasted six or seven days, and while it was being celebrated the relatives, friends and neighbors of the

---

Source: Fedor Belov, *The History of a Soviet Collective Farm* (London: Routledge & Kegan Paul, 1956), 3–5. Reprinted with permission of Taylor and Francis Books Ltd.

newly married pair drank copious drafts of homemade liquor, consumed a calf or a pig, and generally made merry.

A sugar refinery, which stood on the boundary between our lands and those of the neighboring village, also contributed to the well-being and prosperity of our village. Many of the households grew sugar beets and sold them to the refinery, receiving in return a good cash income as well as sugar, syrup, and mash for the livestock. The refinery belonged to a man who had owned it since before the Revolution. In 1925 the refinery workers had a disagreement with him and "had a little fun at his expense;" they forced him to carry them through the streets of the neighboring village as if he were a horse, to the general amusement of the workers. Shortly after this incident the owner left, threatening that "from now on you'll not have a refinery," and within a year the refinery was closed. We were not told why, but everybody knew—the owner had since begun to work in the main administration of the Ukrainian sugar industry. All the advantages which the refinery had brought to the surrounding villages were gone. Its equipment was hauled away and the buildings were gradually demolished. . . .

In spite of the closing of the refinery, the life of the village went on much as before. Almost the only change was that the peasants now sowed more grain and oil-producing plants and less sugar beet. Each peasant managed his farm in his own way, without any special instructions or directives, keeping to the traditions of his forefathers.

Soviet Gender Politics in Central Asia

The Communist Party made a particular effort to promote the equality of women and the liberation of women from traditional social norms in Central Asia. The following excerpt comes from a report sent back to Moscow by a Communist Party official.

- What does this reveal about gender relations in Central Asia?
- How does the author explain these offenses? What does this reveal about Soviet ideology?
- In addition to the lip service paid by Russian Communists to women's rights, can you speculate on other reasons why the Soviet government promoted the equality of women in Central Asia?

By "traditional" offenses we understand such acts of individual representatives of the population, being survivals of the past, as are in themselves socially dangerous and therefore must be fought. . . .

Source: S. Yakupov, "The Struggle against Offences Rooted in the Traditional Way of Life," in Rudolf Schlesinger, Ed. *The Family in the USSR: Documents and Readings* (London: Routledge and Kegan Paul, 1949; 1998), 188–190, 193–196, 199. Reprinted with permission of Taylor and Francis Books Ltd.

There can be no disagreement about the fact that the abolition of "traditional" crimes requires first and foremost an uprooting of those basic conditions which produce them. The economic inequality of women (especially, amongst others, in our national republics and regions such as Azerbaijan, Bashkiria, and Kazakhstan), religious and customary prejudices, (*shariat* and *adat* [Muslim religious and customary law]), cultural backwardness—all these conditions still give rise to "traditional" offences in our national regions.

At a time when the socialist offensive is developing on all fronts, the class enemies (the clergy and the big landowners in the forefront) avail themselves of every opportunity to preserve the existing social and economic relations on the basis of *shariat* and *adat.*

The measures taken by the Soviet state to promote the emancipation of women provide first and foremost for the recruitment of women into industry, the creation of special producer cooperatives for women and of special Women's Institutes . . ., the extension of a network of creches [nurseries], hospitals and canteens, easier access for Eastern women to schools and other cultural and educational institutions, the allotment of special funds to the Commissions for the Improvement of the Working and Living Conditions for Women, and so on. . . .

Although Associations for the Joint Cultivation of the Land are at present recognized as the main forms of kolkhoz economy in our Eastern Republics, the collectivization of village economy must nevertheless have introduced considerable changes in the habits of life. As kolkhoz [collective farm] economy develops and passes into higher forms (Artel and Commune), the background which produces "traditional" crime will accordingly die out. We must point out, however, that this process takes some considerable time. . . .

One cannot but agree with the opinion of the Commissions for the Improvement of the Working and Living Conditions of Women, attached to the Presidium of the All-Russian Central Executive Committee, that . . . a considerable proportion of [traditional] offences never comes before the Court. This is due, on the one hand, to a lack of initiative on the part of the organs of revolutionary law, and on the other hand to the special nature of "traditional" crimes (a girl who has been raped usually seeks to avoid prosecuting the man who has raped her; she marries him, because under the local conditions of social life it is extremely difficult for a victim of rape to marry any other man). . . .

Amongst all the various kinds of "traditional" offence which we have enumerated, *kalym* (purchase of brides) is one of the most dangerous and one which demands a special approach. Kalym is a most barbarous and despicable violation of a woman's liberty, for it reduces the women to the position of a chattel. Kalym results in a barbarous and brutal exploitation of the woman. What is more, kalym is a means to illegal enrichment. The institution of kalym makes it extremely difficult for small peasants and agricultural laborers to set up house and found a family. Kalym in rural areas enslaves the agricultural laborers and small peasants. Marriage by means of kalym is a special privilege of the clergy, the big landowners, and the kulaks. Finally, kalym is a weapon in the hands of the class enemy by which he tries to prevent the integration of Eastern women into a socialist system. . . .

Polygamy is another and equally dangerous kind of crime representing a survival of tribal life . . . polygamy under the conditions prevailing amongst the Eastern nationalities is the exclusive privilege of the propertied class. . . . Polygamy, like kalym, reduces the woman to a chattel, restricts her liberty and is an insult to her person and dignity. With the exception of those rare instances where the sexual element prevails, polygamy fundamentally pursues the aim of exploiting woman economically. . . .

We must make reference to certain regions and districts where acquittals are the rule. The reasons for this state of affairs are twofold: because there are alien elements among the organs of criminal investigation, and because court officials are insufficiently trained. . . .

Amongst the cases dismissed there, was . . . murder in the village of Zakzav-Bek in the Budinsk district: the mutilated body of one Ravat-Bida Turnova, a girl of 18, was found in a well. The evidence shows that the vicitm was an activist who worked amongst the women in the village. No proper action was taken to investigate the crime and discover the murderers. The main reason, as established by the Commission, was due to disintegration, to the penetration of elements alien to the Soviet regime into social organizations and to criminal abuse of office. In 1928, for instance, fifty court officials had to be prosecuted. . . .

During the period of intensified class struggle, especially in the Caucasian and Asiatic villages, there were outbursts of anti-feminist terrorism, particularly in connection with the discarding of the veil and the yashmak.

In Uzbekistan alone, there were 203 cases of anti-feminist murder in 1928. In the first half of 1929, such cases amounted to 165. We must place on record that the actual number of women murdered on political grounds was considerably larger, for there were also many cases which were not investigated. For instance according to a communique of the Public Attorney, sixty-eight women were murdered in Khorazm in 1928, but only twenty of the murderers came up for trial. . . .

Visual Documents

Figure 16-1 Soviet Coin
   This is the back of a Soviet-era coin.
   • Compare this with the state insignia of coins in the tsarist era.
   • What messages regarding Soviet communism are being conveyed?

Figure 16-2 A NEP-era Market
   This is a photograph of the Smolensk Market in Moscow taken during the 1920s.
   • What does this reveal about the nature of the economy in the 1920s?
   • Does it suggest anything about Soviet economic development as a result of NEP policies?
Source: Hulton Archive.

Figure 16-3 Riazhskii, "The Delegate"

Georgii Riazhskii (1895–1952) joined the Communist Party in 1924 after studying at a Moscow institute whose goal was to promote Soviet, proletarian ideals in art. Riazhskii specialized in depictions of the "new men and women" who would build Communism. He painted this portrait in 1927.

• What characteristics does the artist give this woman?
• What messages does this send regarding Communist ideals and policies?

Source: Tretiakov Gallery, Moscow.

Figure 16-4 Poster, 1927

This poster was made by an unknown artist in 1927 to celebrate the tenth anniversary of the Revolution. The writing says, "The October Revolution is a Bridge to a Bright Future."

• In symbolic terms, what ideas does this image convey?
• In practical terms, what significance did railroads have for the Soviet Union?

Source: Early-twentieth-century poster.

_____ FOR FURTHER READING _____

(In addition to the books by Clements, Figes, McDermid, Moon, Sanborn, Service, Stites, and Suny from the previous chapter.)

Ball, Alan M. *And Now My Soul Is Hardened: Abandoned Children in Soviet Russia, 1918–1930.* Berkeley: University of California Press, 1994.

Cohen, Stephen F. *Bukharin and the Bolshevik Revolution: A Political Biography, 1888–1938.* New York: Knopf, 1973.

Gleason, Abbott, Peter Kenez, and Richard Stites. *Bolshevik Culture: Experiment and Order in the Russian Revolution.* Bloomington, IN.: Indiana University Press, 1985.

Goldman, Wendy Z. *Women, the State, and Revolution: Soviet Family Policy and Social Life, 1917–1936.* Cambridge: Cambridge University Press, 1993.

Lewin, Moshe. *Lenin's Last Struggle.* New York: Pantheon Books, 1968.

Siegelbaum, Lewis H. *Soviet State and Society Between Revolutions, 1918–1929.* Cambridge: Cambridge University Press, 1992.

Tucker, Robert C. *Stalin as Revolutionary, 1879–1929: A Study in History and Personality.* New York: Norton, 1973.

Ulam, Adam B. *Expansion and Coexistence: Soviet Foreign Policy, 1917–73*, 2nd ed. New York, Praeger. 1974.

Weiner, Douglas R. *Models of Nature: Ecology, Conservation, and Cultural Revolution in Soviet Russia.* Bloomington, IN.: Indiana University Press, 1988.

CHAPTER SEVENTEEN

RUSSIA'S SECOND INDUSTRIAL REVOLUTION, 1928–1939

By the end of the 1920s, Stalin had emerged as the uncontested head of the Communist Party with handpicked clients in control of key committees and institutions. With the New Economic Policy apparently failing, Stalin began to revive the ideals of revolutionary Communism. The Party took charge of agricultural and industrial production and began an ambitious (if not utopian) program of forced economic development. While this was going on, the Great Depression hit Europe, causing a general economic and political crisis. The mutual mistrust of Communism and capitalism, exacerbated by the rise of extremism on the right, heightened the Soviet sense of encirclement and insecurity. Fear of domestic and foreign enemies, combined with the lack of institutional restraints on Communist Party leaders, produced a nightmare of violence—illegal arrests, imprisonment, and executions—known as the "Great Terror."

THE EURASIAN CONTEXT

The shaky world economy of the 1920s was shattered in 1929 by the Great Depression. Industrial production dropped by 47 percent in the United States, 44 percent in Germany, and an average of 37 percent in all industrial societies except the Soviet Union. By 1932, the unemployment rate in England had risen to 25 percent and in Germany to 40 percent. In the 1930s, the parliamentary democracies seemed helpless to recover from the economic collapse. Meanwhile, fascism flourished in Italy under Mussolini and in Hungary under

Horthy, and Bulgaria and Romania were both taken over by fascist governments. Adolf Hitler used the Depression, popular resentment at the terms of the Versailles Treaty, and fear of communism to make the Nazi Party the largest single party in Germany. Coming to power in 1934, Hitler used military rearmament as an economic stimulus to create a full-employment economy. Hitler had other goals, as well: to re-fight and win the First World War, to exterminate European Jews, to unify all Germans under one government, and to expand eastward into the Soviet Union.

In Turkey, the People's Party maintained its monopoly on power and authorized its leader, Mustafa Kemal, to appoint all candidates for elective office. Every four years, the National Assembly unanimously elected him president, and in 1935, when all Turks were required to take surnames (in the European fashion), the Assembly suggested that Mustafa Kemal take the name Atatürk, or "father of the Turks." Atatürk continued secular reforms; in 1928, he rescinded the Constitutional provision that made Islam the state religion, and in 1934, he recognized the right of women to vote and to be elected to public office. He suppressed Kurdish separatism within Turkey, but in foreign affairs he followed a policy of peace. In 1934, Turkey joined Greece, Romania, and Yugoslavia to guarantee the borders of the Balkan countries, and in 1937, Turkey signed a non-aggression pact with Iraq, Iran, and Afghanistan. Atatürk maintained good relations with the Soviet Union, even though he suppressed domestic communists.

In Iran, Reza Shah Pahlavi, who ruled until 1941, continued his program of nationalism and secularization. In 1928, he renounced the Capitulations and set higher tariffs to protect native industry. In 1932, he canceled the oil concession granted to the Anglo-Iranian Oil Company, but when Britain sent warships to the Persian Gulf and took its case to the League of Nations, Reza Shah backed down and settled for higher royalties and taxes. In 1928, he introduced a judicial system based on French law, and in the 1930s, he promoted the rights of women, permitting them to initiate divorce. In the cities, he required women to wear western clothing, and in 1938, he outlawed the veiling of women (something even Atatürk had not attempted). Reza Shah modernized the army, built railroads and schools, and fostered industry. Nevertheless, he was hated in rural areas because of his secular reforms and because he sold state land, dispossessing the agriculturalists who occupied it and creating a new landlord class.

After Amanullah abdicated as king of Afghanistan in 1929, the throne was briefly seized by a Tajik warlord. Soon thereafter, Amanullah's former minister of war, Muhammad Nadir Shah, made himself king. Nadir Shah repealed Amanullah's secular reforms, but he continued to modernize the economy. Nadir Shah was assassinated in a family feud in 1933 and was succeeded by his brother Mohammad Zahir Shah. Zahir Shah kept both Great Britain and the Soviet Union, the traditional rivals for influence in the region, at arm's length. Under his leadership, Afghanistan joined the League of Nations, and accepted economic development aid from Germany, Italy, and Japan.

After breaking with the Communists in 1927 and unifying China under Guomindang (GMD) rule in 1928, Chiang Kai-shek was recognized by the Western powers as China's legitimate ruler. On paper, the GMD government was a parliamentary democracy, but in reality Chiang was a military dictator. He stayed in power by accommodating the landlord class, allying with warlords, and cultivating the friendship of the West. In China's cities, Chiang promoted education, transportation, and industry, but in the countryside, he did nothing to limit the exploitation of the peasantry, and poverty and famine were endemic. Chiang continued his war on the Chinese Communist Party (CCP). In 1934, a series of GMD military campaigns forced the Communists to make "the Long March" to Yan'an in the north, a rural region beyond GMD control. In the course of the Long March, Mao Zedong won a power struggle with Soviet-backed officials and made himself leader of the CCP.

Japan was particularly hard-hit by the Great Depression because the economic collapse induced the Western powers to protect their Asian markets from Japanese competition. Additionally, Japan's industrial cartels (*zaibatsu*) were perceived as enriching themselves at the expense of the poor. Elements in the Japanese army, taking advantage of popular dissatisfaction with capitalism and parliamentary government, ignored the policies of civilian officials and engineered the military occupation of Manchuria in 1931. The Prime Minister was assassinated later that same year, and party government came to an end, thoroughly intimidated by the military. Japan's new leaders began to make plans for an East Asian Empire. In 1936, Japan abrogated the arms-reduction treaties of the 1920s and joined Italy and Germany in the "Anti-Comintern Pact" directed against the Soviet Union. In 1937, the Japanese army mounted a full-scale invasion of China.

THE STALIN REVOLUTIONS

As the decade of the twenties wore on, Communists became increasingly dissatisfied with the results of the New Economic Policy. Communism did not seem to be getting any nearer, and the working class was the one class not benefitting from the "proletarian" revolution of 1917. Industry was not growing, there was high unemployment, and workers were a small minority of the total population. Professional jobs in teaching, journalism, engineering, and factory management went to people from middle-class backgrounds. Peasants were doing better than ever before, but they did not seem to be promoting economic progress. The idea of large, mechanized farms (on the model of the factory) had not caught on, and peasants continued to live in self-governing communes and to practice traditional subsistence agriculture. Especially in the context of the war scares of 1927, the ability of the peasantry to withhold grain from the market was alarming and was seen as some as willful hostility toward the cities.

Stalin certainly seems to have come to that conclusion. Even as he was engineering the final defeat of Trotsky and Zinovyev in 1927, Stalin began to adopt their coercive economic program. Beginning in the fall of that year, the politburo, under Stalin's leadership, sent requisition teams to the Ural-Siberia region to forcibly seize grain (at state-set prices). Stalin also showed a new militancy toward those who appeared to stand in the way of industrialization. In Shakhty, Ukraine, some expensive coal-mining equipment had broken down, and fifty-three engineers (some of them German) were accused of sabotage. In 1928, forty-nine of them were found guilty of being agents of foreign capitalists. Five were executed, the rest imprisoned.

In 1928, Stalin advocated grain requisitioning for the entire country and proposed collectivization, that is, the creation of collective farms, which would bring peasants under state control and serve as collection points for grain. Stalin began to blame the kulaks (rich peasants), whom he called "capitalists," for waging class warfare against the Soviet state. In January 1929, Bukharin and other moderates characterized Stalin's policies as "military-feudal" exploitation of the peasantry, and they accused him of subverting democracy within the Communist party. Bukharin was removed from the Politburo and the Comintern and lost his position of editor of *Pravda*. His allies and associates were also demoted. Thus by December of 1929 none of Lenin's close associates remained on the Politburo, and the inner circle of party leaders all owed their positions to Stalin.

In the meantime, the party continued its war against the agricultural population. In 1929, 100,000 communist volunteers went out into the countryside to organize collective farms and collect grain. They collected twice as much grain as had been delivered the previous year, and in the fall the Communist party decided to enforce complete collectivization. In December 1929, Stalin announced a campaign to "liquidate the kulaks as a class," and the following year 150,000 more activists joined the effort. Approximately one million peasants were identified as kulaks and were deprived of their land, livestock, and tools. Some 60,000 were executed or imprisoned, more than 110,000 families were deported to Siberia or Kazakhstan, and roughly 800,000 were given small plots of poor land but were not allowed to join a kolkhoz (collective farm).

By the autumn of 1930, 60 percent of peasant households had joined collective farms, but there was widespread resistance. Farmers preferred to slaughter and eat their livestock rather than surrender them to the kolkhoz. Crowds of farmers would gather in front of a kulak's house to protect it or would break into storage buildings to take back confiscated grain. Sometimes kolkhoz organizers were killed, and there were sixteen hundred officially recorded incidents of armed struggle by the peasants against the invading activists, police, and soldiers. Stalin, in alarm, called off collectivization, admonished the communist activists for their excessive zeal (he called them "dizzy with success"), and announced that collectivization should be voluntary. The peasants reacted with joy, praising Stalin and thanking him for stopping the madness. Overall, the percentage of peasants living in kolkhozes fell to 20 percent.

The celebration was premature, however. Almost immediately the campaign for collectivization began again, albeit more gradually (the process took several years). This time major concessions were made: Peasant households were allowed to keep a family garden plot (less than an acre, but still significant for producing vegetables) and some livestock (chickens and cattle for both dairy and meat—but not horses). In 1930, three million tons of wheat were exported, seeming to justify the collective farm system, even though this resulted from more efficient collection and not from increased production.

Harvests were poor in 1931 and 1932, partly because of bad weather, partly because there were insufficient tractors to make up for the horses that had been slaughtered during the collectivization campaign. Nevertheless, the Soviet government imposed impossibly high grain-delivery quotas. Local communist leaders, told to make house-to-house searches for "hoarded" grain, seized not only farmers' food supplies but seed grain for the next planting season. Famines occurred in the northern Caucasus, the Volga, Kazakhstan, and Ukraine. In Ukraine, the hardest hit of all regions, the government set up road blocks to keep peasants from escaping to cities. Starving farmers ate dogs, cats, bark from trees, and even human flesh. Estimates of famine deaths range between five and ten million.

The grain harvest began to improve in 1933 and continued to rise through 1938. Average grain harvest in these years was 14 percent higher than the average of 1925 to 1929. On paper, there appeared to be a considerable increase in efficiency, since the agricultural population in the late 1930s was only two-thirds of what it had been in 1926. However, much of the increase resulted from good weather and volunteer labor. (Each fall, volunteers from factories, schools, and the army went to the countryside to help with the harvest.)

At the same time that agriculture was being collectivized, the Soviet regime began to institute central planning of the economy. Since farmers no longer had to be coaxed to produce grain by the promise of inexpensive consumer goods, the state was free to divert capital from light to heavy industry, and the Party applied the same impatient and militant attitude to economic planning and industrial development as it did to collectivization. In 1929, a five-year plan was announced that would double steel production and increase the overall GNP by 40 percent. Economists who cautioned that these goals were impossible were treated as saboteurs, and in 1930, the central planning bureaucracy was purged of economists who offered realistic estimates of possible growth. In the same year, forty-eight officials from the Trade Commissariat were found guilty of sabotaging the food industry and were executed. Between 1928 and 1932, as many as seven thousand engineers were arrested for obstructing the plan.

Industrialization was undertaken at breakneck speed without regard to economic practicality or environmental and human costs. Construction workers who built the massive steel works at Magnitogorsk, for example, lived in tents even in the cold Siberian winters and were given barely enough to eat. The plan did not provide for worker safety, and injury and death on the job was a frequent occurrence. Workers were poorly paid; real wages in 1932 were only one-tenth of what they had been in 1926. (Pay hardly mattered, anyway, since there were few consumer goods for sale.) Workers were also subjected to severe discipline. In 1930, workers were forbidden to quit their jobs without permission. In December 1932, all workers were issued passports in order to control their movement more effectively.

In 1932, after the collectivization of agriculture was largely accomplished, and after the First Five-Year Plan was declared a success (in four years!), the Communist leadership replaced the spirit of idealism, frenetic militance, and self-sacrifice with a mood of accomplishment, stability, and material reward. Collective farmers were given greater freedom on their private plots; a 1935 law allowed each family to own one cow and its calves, one sow and its offspring, four sheep, and an unlimited number of chickens and rabbits and goats. They could sell the vegetables, eggs, and livestock from these plots at market prices. Workers' lives also improved. The Second Five-Year Plan (1933–1937) allocated more resources to light (consumer goods) industry, food processing, and apartment construction. Wages were raised and labor discipline was somewhat relaxed.

However, as life was improving for ordinary workers and farmers, a time of troubles was preparing for those at the highest levels of party, state, military, and industry. In 1934, at the Seventeenth Party Congress (the "Congress of Victors"), the Party congratulated itself on its achievements, and Stalin was praised to the skies as the genius behind Soviet economic success. The party was not as united, as it appeared, however. Sergei Kirov, First Secretary of the Leningrad Party organization, was approached by adherents of "socialist legality" (a code-word for opposition to Stalin's coercive tactics) to seek election as General Secretary. Kirov refused, but in the elections to the Central Committee, Kirov actually received more votes than Stalin.

That summer, Stalin restructured the Soviet police system. The secret police and the civil police were combined into one organization, the NKVD (People's Commissariat of Internal Affairs), headed by Genrikh Yagoda, one of Stalin's proteges. The NKVD took responsibility for all prisons as well as the GULag (Main Administration of Labor Camps).

On December 1, 1934, Sergei Kirov was assassinated by a mentally ill former member of the Communist party. Stalin declared that the murder must have been organized by elements within the party, and he ordered a special prosecutor, Nikolai Ezhov, to search for those responsible. Ezhov arrested both Zinovyev and Kamenev and announced the discovery of a conspiratorial organization, the "Leningrad Center." In January 1935, the two men were found guilty of conspiring to kill Kirov and were imprisoned.

It did not end there, however. The NKVD extended its investigation to an ever widening circle of party members. All the past oppositionists who had been associated with Trotsky, Zinovyev, or Kamenev were arrested and interrogated, and each suspect was pressured to inform on past associates. In 1936, new charges were brought against Zinovyev and Kamenev. They were now charged with conspiring with Leon Trotsky to assassinate Stalin himself. At a public "show trial," the two former leaders confessed to the conspiracy and were sentenced to death. Another public trial of Old Bosheviks took place in 1937, and a third in 1938. At the final show trial, Nikolai Bukharin was sentenced to death. The Soviet Union and the world looked on in wonder as Lenin's former associates pled guilty to sabotage and assassination on behalf of the foreign enemies of the Soviet Communism. These apparently freely given confessions were, however, extorted by torture and threats to family members.

While these public trials were going on, convincing the Soviet public that a vast internal conspiracy threatened their country, purges and secret trials began to decimate the lower levels of the party and the professions. The Soviet professional elite was swept with a hysteria of denunciations and accusations. The accused informed on associates to exculpate themselves, and it is likely that subordinates sometimes denounced their superiors in the hope of promotion. Officers in the NKVD, for their part, were no doubt afraid to exonerate any of the accused for fear of being thought to be collaborators themselves.

Stalin had established a special system of secret military tribunals outside the regular court system. The accused were tried in absentia and were denied the right to face their accusers, which hardly mattered since guilt was invariably established by signed confessions extracted by torture. There was no appeal and sentences were immediately executed. Those who were not shot were sent to labor camps in the north and in eastern Siberia. Before this "Great Terror" came to an end, approximately 900,000 people had been shot and 3,000,000 had been sent to prison camps.

The highest levels of the Communist party and the Red Army were virtually annihilated. All the Old Bolsheviks (those who had known and worked with Lenin), with the exception of Stalin and his closest associates, were executed. Of the 139 people who had been elected to the Central Committee in 1934, 110 were arrested and 98 were shot. Of the 1,196 delegates to the Seventeenth Party Congress, only 59 returned to the Eighteenth. Fifteen of 16 commanders and 60 of 67 corps commanders were executed. In all, one-half of the Red Army officer corps were killed. Even the heads of the NKVD were not immune. Genrikh Iagoda was removed in 1936 and replaced by Nikolai Ezhov. Ezhov was removed (and later shot) and replaced by Lavrentii Beria in 1938.

Stalin had appointed Beria to head the NKVD in order to bring the terror to an end. The mass hysteria was quickly stifled (easy enough to accomplish, since it was largely a product of the government), but the institutions of terror remained as a deterrent to anyone who might have thought of opposing the party line. The NKVD continued to arrest political criminals, and the GULag was well supplied with forced labor.

CULTURE AND RELIGION

The Stalin economic revolution of 1928 to 1932 was accompanied by a cultural revolution. An organization calling itself the Russian Association of Proletarian Writers (RAPP) appointed itself the arbiter of Soviet culture. Its members opposed what they called "bourgeois" literature, music, and art (especially that of the "fellow travelers" of the NEP period), believing that art should denounce bourgeois values and serve the ongoing socialist revolution. New attention was paid to class background in academia and the professions. The Academy of Sciences lost its independence in 1928 and was forced to admit Communist members for the first time. University faculties were purged of professors thought to be unfriendly to Soviet power. With the same "storm the fortress" mentality that characterized collectivization and the First Five-Year Plan, a campaign was launched to produce a new generation of proletarian professionals and specialists in only four years. Intensive courses in science and technology were established with classes held in the evenings to accommodate students' work schedules. Hundreds of thousands of workers and peasants graduated from these programs. At the university level, tuition and fees were eliminated and applicants from working-class or peasant backgrounds were favored over those from the professional class.

In elementary and high schools, there was considerable educational experimentation; exams were replaced with group projects, schools were attached to factories, and students earned credit for volunteer work. Marxism-Leninism was a required subject, and students were encouraged to challenge ideologically deficient instructors. The Communist party made education mandatory for children eight to eleven in 1930 and for those aged twelve to fourteen in 1932. For the first time in Russian history, an attempt was made to extend universal education to the countryside as well as the city. Education worked hand-in-hand with collectivization to integrate agricultural communities into the Soviet political and social system.

Anti-religious activity also intensified after 1928. Priests typically supported peasant opposition to collectivization, and the same activists who organized collective farms also attacked religion. By the end of 1930, four-fifths of all village churches had been closed. Anti-religious education was required in the newly established school system. In 1929, the League of the Godless renamed itself the League of the Militant Godless, and it intensified its pro-atheist and anti-religious propaganda. In 1932, it proposed a "five-year plan" to eliminate all traces of religion from Soviet society.

The Soviet government also passed laws limiting religious activity. In 1929, religious institutions were forbidden to sponsor any activities outside church buildings, including playgrounds, recreation, and libraries. Priests could not travel to areas where there were no churches. Any religious service to be performed outside a building (with the exception of visiting the sick or dying) required the approval of the local soviet. Charity was forbidden, as was organized collection of donations, and church officials were taxed as "profit-making" businesses.

When more moderate economic policies were instituted in 1932, the cultural revolution was also brought to an end. Conservative, even "bourgeois," values returned. Experimentalism in literature was discouraged. RAPP and all other specifically "proletarian" groups were abolished and were replaced with a single organization, the Union of Soviet Writers. It was intended to include writers from all ethnic and class backgrounds, and its goal was to create a universal Soviet literature, based on the principles of "Socialist realism," which combined the tradition of nineteenth-century Russian realism with socialist optimism. Socialist realism used realistic techniques to describe the forces that blocked progress toward socialism but expressed an idealistic view of the future and a thoroughly unrealistic attitude toward people. Protagonists in works of Socialist realism were dedicated to realizing collective goals; they had no self-doubts or personal ambitions. Comradely love sometimes appeared, but passion and sex did not.

The Soviet Union developed mass media over the course of the 1930s. With the rise of literacy, daily newspapers published in the capital became national in scope. The Second Five-Year Plan provided for the production of radios, making possible a national radio industry. It also built more movie theaters. Radio dramas and movies also adhered to the requirements of Socialist Realism, providing adventure stories in the context of the struggle for socialism. Detectives uncovered plots by foreign agents of capitalism or fascism to destroy the Soviet Union, and heroic engineers overcame the resistence of slackers or kulak saboteurs.

After 1932, there was an end to experimentation in education, as well as in art. Teachers' pay and prestige were raised, and they were put back in charge of the classroom. Traditional academic subjects were reemphasized and co-curricular factory labor was eliminated. Information was conveyed in lectures, facts were memorized, and grades were earned through examination. In higher education, the intensive programs for training workers and peasants were ended. Evening classes for workers were retained, but they were part of a traditional university curriculum, and academic standards were raised. The goal of higher education was to produce technical specialists, and the government defined academic programs and set student quotas based on the economic plan.

In 1935, the Central Committee began to review history textbooks to ensure that patriotic values were being instilled in students. Previously, Marxist historians had emphasized impersonal economic forces and denied the role of "great men" and of national sentiment. Stalin, who had begun to compare himself with Ivan the Terrible and Peter the Great, wanted textbooks to praise Russian Tsars as great state-builders and to glorify Russia's military achievements.

ROLES AND STATUS OF WOMEN

In 1929, the Communist Party shut down the Zhenotdel, deeming its mission accomplished. The official function of the Zhenotdel had been to mobilize female support for the Soviet regime. It had never been intended for the Zhenotdel to advocate for women's rights, since it was assumed communism would remove all obstacles to equality of the sexes. Indeed, the Soviet government did promote equality of women in education and the paid workforce. Literacy campaigns enabled 83 percent of all Soviet women to read and write by 1939. Between 1929 and 1941, women's participation in the labor force rose from 24 to 39 percent. Women were overrepresented in light industry (about two-thirds of the light industrial workforce was female), but they also began to work in construction, machine factories, the timber industry. By 1939, women made up 57 percent of the agricultural workforce.

While women began participate in productive labor, however, they continued to bear the full burden of reproductive labor. Plans for nurseries, day-care centers, cafeterias, and public laundries were never adequately realized, nor were men encouraged to share in household tasks. Women began what came to be called the "double shift," that is, a full work day in fields, factory, office, or laboratory, plus full responsibility for child care and domestic duties. The lack of day-care centers was made up for by the donated labor of the country's grandmothers.

After 1932, as culture and education were made more traditional, so traditional values were reapplied to gender roles. A cult of motherhood was fostered, and bearing children was represented as a duty women owed to the fatherland. Mothers were given cash payments at the birth of each child and monthly payments thereafter. Family law become more restrictive and traditional; divorces were made more difficult and more expensive to obtain. Abortions were outlawed in 1936.

An exception to the "double shift" was made for the wives of the Soviet elite. Wives of party officials, soviet administrators, and factory managers were encouraged to adopt what had formerly been considered "bourgeois values": to be stay-at-home wives and mothers, and to engage in volunteer community and charity work. Kremlin wives beautified parks and public spaces, visited needy families, and taught home economics courses for women. They were helped in their own housework by hired domestic servants.

The Great Terror was overwhelmingly masculine; men staffed the secret police and the judicial system, and men were the principal victims. Some women were caught up in the terror and were either shot or imprisoned, but the principal suffering imposed on women by the terror was the loss of loved ones. Millions of women lost fathers, husbands, and sons. There was great social pressure for women to divorce husbands who were sent to the camps, but many did not.

SOCIAL AND ECONOMIC TRENDS

The beginning of collectivization, industrialization, and central planning brought the NEP to an end. In 1927, private trade began to come under attack. Taxes were raised to confiscatory levels, business were closed, and merchants were denied public services and the right to send their children to school. In 1928 to 1930 private medical and dental services were forbidden, and in 1932 private trade was made a crime punishable by up to ten years in a labor camp.

Soviet farmers considered the collective farm to be the return of serfdom. Farmers were required to perform unpaid labor on roads and construction, farm work was directed by brigade leaders, and production plans were made by outsiders appointed by the Communist Party. Farmers were tied to the land; passports, which allowed workers to change jobs and residence, were not issued to the agricultural population.

Although the average collective farm contained about seventy families, not much larger than the traditional Russian mir, they were qualitatively different from the mir. The household was no longer the basic labor unit, and land was not divided among families. Instead, all the land was held in common, the fields were consolidated, and workers were assigned individual tasks. Families owned hand gardening tools to cultivate their private plots, but plows and horses were owned by the kolkhoz. Most importantly, self-government had ended; collective farms were fully subordinated to the state. Tractors, as they became available, weren't owned by the kolkhoz. Regional Machine Tractor Stations, set up by the state, loaned tractors and harvesting machinery to local collective, and used their power of allocation to enforce Soviet policy.

After 1935, deportations of kulaks ceased, and civil rights (and the right to hold church services) were restored to rural priests. Nevertheless, kulaks, priests, and their families were still prevented from joining collective farms. Schools and medical clinics were built, but they remained inadequate and unequal to services available in cities. There was little active enforcement of the law prohibiting rural residents from relocating without permission, and many farmers escaped to the cities. Between 1926 and 1939, twenty three million peasants moved to urban areas, two million to Moscow alone.

Collectivization and industrialization caused a dramatic growth in urbanization and the working-class population. There were 9,000 industrial enterprises in the USSR in 1929 and 64,000 in 1938. In 1928, there had been 11.6 million wage laborers, while in 1937 the number had risen to 27 million. Between 1926 and 1939, the proportion of the Soviet population living in cities increased from one-fifth to almost one-third. The populations of Moscow and Leningrad doubled, and the population of Gorky (formerly Nizhnii Novgorod) tripled.

The First Five-Year Plan finally put an end to the unemployment of the NEP period, although wages and working conditions were so poor that workers tended to change jobs frequently. In 1930, there was a turnover rate of 150 percent, and the average worker spent less than a year at the same job. Unions were subordinated to the state, and the workplace was under the control of the manager who set wages and could fire workers without appeal to factory committees. Employment laws were harsh. Workers could be moved from one factory to another against their will, and they could be fired, evicted, and lose their ration card for not coming to work. In 1931, violations of labor discipline became criminal offenses, and the death penalty was introduced for theft of state property.

On the other hand, the laws were not consistently enforced. Workers used slow-downs and organized mass absences to pressure their managers to pay fair wages and to relax un-realistic production goals. Factories were generally short of labor, and managers used vari-ous stratagems to avoid firing workers for absenteeism, such as giving retroactive "permission," asking doctors to write excuses for illness, and instructing time clerks to record absent workers as actually being on the job.

The regime used rewards, as well as punishments, to encourage harder work. One method was through "shock brigades," modeled on work teams first organized by the Kom-somol in 1929 to attempt to set new production records. Members of shock brigades were given special cards that earned them extra rations. Another method was "Stakanovism," a trend named after a miner by the name of Stakhanov, who set a world record for cutting coal in 1935. He became a national hero. Across the Soviet Union workers competed to set world records in their own labor specialty. Stakhanovites were paid higher than average wages, were given preference in assignment of apartments, and had access to special stores where they could buy scarce goods such as radios, bicycles, and fur coats. In the long run, however, workers managed to make both activities routine and a perquisite of seniority. By 1936, half of all skilled workers qualified for the Stakhanovite designation.

By the end of the 1930s, two new social strata had appeared: a Soviet intelligentsia and a Soviet ruling elite. Neither can be considered a "class," since neither was based on law or on permanent possession of any significant form of property, and there was considerable social mobility (both upward and downward) in the decade of industrialization and terror. Never-theless, both strata were clearly distinguishable from the general population and both had privileges which they were largely able to pass on to their children.

The term "intelligentsia" was no doubt used to refer to Soviet scientists, academics, and producers of high culture in order to evoke the spirit of the educated and cultured segment of tsarist society that had criticized the autocracy and supplied the revolutionaries who sought to overthrow it. The Russian intelligentsia had thought of itself as "serving the peo-ple," and this concept also fit in well with the Soviet leaders' understanding of the nature of their regime. The Soviet intelligentsia, however, was neither critical nor revolutionary. Its members accepted the reality of Soviet power, shared its social ideals, and overlooked its abuses. Soviet scientists and scholars were allowed some leeway in pursuing their profes-sions; creative artists, however, had no choice but to conform to the tenets of Socialist Real-ism and to promote Soviet ideology.

During the Second Five-Year Plan, the Soviet regime rewarded the industrial and govern-ing elite with benefits far exceeding those available to the general public. Salaries of man-agers and bureaucrats were raised considerably, but even more important was their access to special amenities: luxury apartments, special stores with imported goods and luxury foods, and priority to buy scarce Soviet products such as automobiles and home appliances. The elite was also in an advantageous position for passing its status on to its children: Their sons and daughters had access to the best education, and education was the single most impor-tant requirement (after personal connections) for retaining elite status.

Two important qualifications must be kept in mind. First, the Soviet ruling elite was em-phatically not an extension of any kind of Russian elite; it was the result of upward social mobility on a massive and unprecedented scale. The generation that rose to power in the 1930s came from peasant or working-class origins. Second, the Great Terror of the 1930s ap-plied exclusively to members of the elite. Before the beginning of World War II, members of the Soviet elite paid for their privileges with constant insecurity.

By contemporary North American standards, the Soviet Union in the 1930s would have been a dismal place to live. The diet was boring and featured bread and potatoes; everything else—meat, vegetables, and fruit—was in short supply. Apartment construction was unable to keep pace with the growth of the urban population, leading to a massive housing crisis. Often several families shared a communal apartment with only one kitchen and bathroom, some families lived in hallways, and newly married couples typically lived with the parents of one of the spouses. Consumer goods were of poor quality and in very short supply. Moreover, corruption was endemic; one needed personal connections or to pay bribes to get admitted to a special school, to get a vacation in a workers' sanatorium, or to shop in a store offering imported goods.

Soviet citizens had to endure continuous propaganda and agitation. There were continual exhortations to work harder, to cultivate better manners, not to damage state property, etc. They were expected not merely to accept the Soviet regime but to show active enthusiasm for it. They lived in a one-party police state, which identified ideological nonconformity as treason. By the end of the 1930s, Stalin's secret military tribunals had sentenced more than 900,000 people to be shot and approximately 3,000,000 others (1.5 percent of the population) to prison or labor camp. The message received by the population was: Do not talk politics except around your own kitchen table.

The vast majority of the population, however, would not have seen Soviet society from this perspective. The terror of political repression existed mainly among those with power and prestige, and 98.5 percent of the Soviet population were *not* in prison camps. It is unlikely that the average worker or farmer would have had personal friends who were charged with political crimes. The director of their factory or local Machine Tractor Station might be arrested, but, given the brutal and arbitrary way in which managers treated their subordinates, the disappearance of such a person would hardly have seemed a tragedy to ordinary Soviet citizens.

Moreover, the vast majority of the population could not have measured their society by anyone's standards but their own. Many of them could remember what Russia had been like before the revolution, and even the youngest of working-age people in the 1930s were born to parents who knew the old way of life. As low as the standard of living was, it was superior to that of the tsarist era. One of the demands of workers and peasants in 1905 had been for universal, free education; that had become a reality. Social mobility was achieved by millions of peasants who made their way to a city, learned a skill, and found a (comparatively) high-paying job. Psychologically, too, the Soviet state, dedicating itself to working people and honoring manual labor, must have been an improvement over the tsarist system that despised workers and peasants. Women's lives had changed, as well. Women were overworked, but they were overworked precisely because they were accorded equal status with men in productive labor.

Life in the Soviet Union in the 1930s had many of the characteristics of a modern industrial society. Soviet citizens were entertained by radio programs and movies. Books and newspapers were plentiful and affordable. Football (soccer) had become a professional sport, and football stars became celebrities, as did movie stars and popular singers. Horse racing (and gambling on races) was popular. Public parks and recreation facilities were provided. Christmas was not celebrated, but its festivities were transferred to the New Year's holiday. There were decorated trees, gift-giving (from "Father Frost," a Santa-Claus lookalike), and festive food and drink. Easter was not officially recognized, either, but food stores were stocked with the ingredients for making traditional Easter confections. There were Soviet holidays, as well, including Red Army Day on February 23; International Women's Day on March 8; May Day; and November 7, the anniversary of the October Revolution.

PEOPLES OF THE USSR

In the period 1928 to 1932, the Soviet policy of indigenization intensified. Soviet scholars created alphabets for more than forty peoples who had never had a written language of their own. The nationhood of northern nomadic peoples was recognized. A quota system guaranteed places in Russian universities for students from all the national groups of the Soviet Union. When internal passports were introduced for urban residents in 1932, every citizen was required to choose a nationality, and this practice furthered the development of national consciousness.

When compulsory education was introduced, the Soviet regime made every effort to provide native teachers for every nation. In Armenia, Georgia, Ukraine, and Belarus more than 70 percent of teachers were native; in the Muslim regions of the north Caucasus and Central Asia, slightly more than half of the teachers were of the same nationality as their students. This had tragic consequences in Central Asia where there was strong resentment against both Russians and women as teachers: during the period of collectivization hundreds of Russian teachers were killed.

After 1932, Soviet policies toward the peoples of the Union changed. Resistance to collectivization had been particularly violent among the border nationalities, and it was frequently expressed in the language of patriotic nationalism. Furthermore, the Communist leadership began to be alarmed at the growth of Ukrainian nationalism. Ukrainians made up more than half of the non-Russian population, and Ukrainian leaders offended Russian sensibilities by promoting the Ukrainian language even in cities in which the majority were was Russian. (According to Soviet law all children had the right to an education in their native language.) In addition, Ukraine claimed the right to speak on behalf of Ukrainians who lived beyond its borders.

Beginning in 1933 and largely coinciding with the purges and the terror, the Communist party changed its nationality policy. It purged the national leadership of most republics and autonomous regions and began a more cautious policy. National identity was encouraged only within the boundaries of a national region. (Thus, Ukrainian and Belarusian were no longer allowed in schools in the RSFSR.) "Chauvinism" was closely monitored: No one (except for a Russian) was permitted to imply that his or her nation was superior to any others. A campaign was also begun to consolidate smaller nations; the 188 nationalities that had existed in 1926 were reduced to 107 by 1937.

Russian nationalism was allowed to flourish. The Russian word for motherland, *rodina*, was used to refer to the whole Soviet Union. History books began to represent Russian imperialism as the least of the possible evils that might have befallen the nations of the former Empire. In 1938, Russian language classes were required in all Soviet schools, and communities could choose to learn exclusively in Russian (and not learn their native language at all). The Cyrillic alphabet also replaced the Latin alphabet for writing the languages of Central Asian peoples. Over the course of the 1930s, about ten million non-Russians adopted the Russian nationality. (This was possible because children of mixed marriages could choose the nationality of either parent.)

In 1936 with the promulgation of a new constitution, the Soviet Union was restructured. The number of Soviet Socialist Republics was increased from five to twelve. First, the Transcaucasian SSR was dissolved, and Armenia, Georgia, and Azerbaijan were each made a Soviet Socialist Republic (SSR), that is, they were put on the same level as Ukraine, Belarus, the RSFSR, and Tajikistan). The smaller national territories of the North Caucasus (such as the Chechens and Ossetians) were transferred to the RSFSR. In Central Asia, a Tajik SSR had been formed in 1929, and in 1936 the Uzbek, Turkmen, Kirgiz, and Kazakh autonomous regions were separated from the RSFSR and turned into full republics (SSRs).

Economic "modernization" was pursued throughout the Union. Armenia, Georgia, and Azerbaijan all achieved significant gains in industrialization, urbanization, and literacy levels, while the countryside was collectivized. The agricultural populations of Central Asia were devastated by collectivization. Kazakh nomads were required to adopt sedentary lifestyles, and, in the process, an estimated 1.5 million herders died and 80 percent of the livestock was slaughtered. Afterwards, Central Asia was increasingly integrated into the Soviet system through industrialization, communication, education, health care, and by drafting its young men into the Red Army.

Consistent with the idea that every nationality in the USSR should have its own homeland, the Commissariat of Nationalities came up with a plan in 1928 to create a Jewish National District (in 1930 it was elevated to the status of an Autonomous Region). Because the Ukraine, where most Jews lived, was too heavily populated to create such a district there, the Commissariat created the Jewish National District in the Russian Far East, on the border with China, centered on the city of Birobidzhan, which became its capital. The Soviet authorities made Yiddish, not Hebrew, the official language, and hoped the Jews would develop a secular, proletarian culture. Yiddish radio stations, newspapers, and a publishing house were established. The only thing Birobidzhan lacked was a Jewish population. Between 1928 and 1934 only about 19,500 Jews moved to the District, and of those 11,500 did not acclimatize to the region and returned to where they had come from. The population was predominantly composed of Russians, Ukrainians, and Koreans.

Soviet Jews preferred not to take up agriculture in the Far East, but to take advantage of the educational opportunities provided in the 1930s. They moved to cities, began to speak Russian, and became one of the best educated segments of the population. By the end of the 1930s, Jews had largely assimilated into Soviet society, but their Jewish identity was recorded in the passport that all urban-dwellers were required to carry. The Soviet Union carried out a well-publicized campaign against anti-Semitism as part of its propaganda war with fascism in the 1930s, but anti-Semitism was only temporarily dormant.

THE ROAD TO WAR

Collectivization and industrialization had been precipitated by foreign policy crises, and foreign affairs did not cease to occupy the attention of Soviet leaders through the 1930s. Strident anti-communism was prevalent in both fascist and liberal-democratic countries, and Hitler's rise to power in Germany caused additional concern. Not only was Hitler anti-communist, in *Mein Kampf* he had announced the intention to invade the Soviet Union and carve out a territory for German colonization. When Hitler became chancellor of Germany, he crushed the Communist party and signed a German-Polish anti-aggression pact that was really an alliance against the USSR. The Soviet Union also had worries in Asia. In 1931, Japan invaded and occupied Manchuria and installed a puppet ruler.

Stalin used Russia's military "backwardness" as a spur to intensified effort to build heavy industry, and the fear of foreign agents and saboteurs contributed to the atmosphere of national emergency that justified the terror. The Soviet Union, however, continued to treat fascism as only a variety of capitalism, and not necessarily the most dangerous one. The radical turn of Soviet politics in 1928 was reflected in the Comintern, which took an uncompromising line toward moderate socialists. In 1933 the Comintern prevented the German Communist Party from cooperating with German socialists to resist the Nazis.

Although the Comintern followed a radical policy, the Soviet government sent more moderate signals. In 1930 when Boris Chicherin retired as Minister of Foreign Affairs, he was replaced with Maxim Litvinov, a man of cosmopolitan outlook who was married to an Englishwoman (both he and his wife were Jewish) and who had numerous connections in western Europe. In 1934, Litvinov endorsed the principles of collective security, and the USSR joined the League of Nations. Then in 1935 the hard-line leadership of the Comintern was replaced with moderates who held that fascism was more dangerous than capitalism, and called for cooperation with the "United Front" of liberals and socialists that was forming in western Europe. In May 1935, the Soviet Union signed defensive treaties with France and Czechoslovakia. The USSR and France pledged mutual support if either was attacked by a third party (i.e., Nazi Germany), and the USSR promised to come to the aid of Czechoslovakia if France (which had already signed a defense treaty with Czechoslovakia) acted first.

It must have seemed to the Soviet leaders that they were the only Europeans willing to stand up against fascist aggression. In 1935, when Italy invaded Ethiopia, the Soviet Union was the only country to impose economic sanctions. Then, when the Spanish Civil War broke out the following year, and Hitler and Mussolini gave military aid to the anti-democratic forces, the Western democracies did nothing more than impose a military embargo on both sides. The Soviet Union, on the other hand, sent equipment, supplies, and advisers to support the Loyalist cause.

While the Spanish Civil War was raging, crises were developing in central Europe and East Asia. In March 1936, Adolf Hitler sent troops into the Rhineland, violating terms of the Versailles Treaty, and in October he signed non-aggression and anti-Comintern pacts with Italy and Japan. In 1937, Japan invaded China from its base in Manchuria, and within six months it had occupied all of China that could be reached by railroad. Then, in March 1938, Austria and Germany merged, yet another violation of the Versailles Treaty that the West did nothing to prevent.

The crisis deepened in May, when Hitler demanded that the Sudetenland, a region of western Czechoslovakia with a predominantly German-speaking population, be annexed to Germany. The Czech army, supported by the Soviet Union, mobilized its military forces, and Hitler backed down. He continued to threaten war throughout the summer, however, and in September British Prime Minister Neville Chamberlain, consulting France but not Czechoslovakia or the Soviet Union, agreed to the annexation, on Hitler's assurance that he had no more territorial demands. England and France stood aside, and Czechoslovakia chose not to resist. Despite Hitler's promise, however, the German army invaded and occupied all Czechoslovakia in March 1939.

The Soviet Union immediately called for united action against Nazis but received no response. Instead, in April Great Britain unilaterally guaranteed the integrity of Poland, which it expected to be Hitler's next target. On May 2, Viacheslav Molotov, an ethnic Russian and one of Stalin's closest associates, replaced Litvinov as Foreign Minister. Over the summer of 1939, the Soviet Union negotiated with both Great Britain and Germany. Circumstances were unfavorable to a British-Soviet alliance, however. Public opinion in Great Britain and France was more hostile to the Soviet Union than to Germany. Poland also refused to permit the Soviet Union to come to its defense, declaring that it would rather be invaded by Germans than Russians. Furthermore, each side feared that the other would not live up to treaty obligations. Stalin feared that Britain would back down from Hitler yet again, while British and French leaders suspected that the purges had destroyed the Red Army and that the

Soviet Union would be worthless as an ally. In consequence, the USSR signed a non-aggression pact with Germany in August 1939. A secret protocol provided that in the event of a German invasion of Poland, the Soviet Union would be free to annex Estonia, Latvia, Bessarabia, and the Ukrainian and Belarusian territories in Poland. World War II in Europe began on September 1, when Hitler ordered the invasion of Poland.

TEXT DOCUMENTS

The 1936 Constitution of the USSR

Soviet leaders wrote a new constitution in 1936 in order to celebrate the changes in Soviet society that had occurred since the reorganization of the Soviet Union in 1924 and the beginning of the cultural revolution in 1928. Old class disabilities were removed (it being stated that there were only two classes, workers and peasants), direct election of all levels of government began, and government was reorganized into a single standard system throughout the Soviet Union.

- Compare the 1936 Constitution with the Fundamental Laws of Imperial Russia, 1906.
- Where is sovereignty vested? What is the highest executive authority? What is the status of the national republics?
- How is the socialist nature of the system manifested?
- What are the rights and duties of Soviet citizens? Even though those rights were not observed in practice, what might be the long-term consequences of this document?

1. The Union of Soviet Socialist Republics is a socialist state of workers and peasants.

3. In the U.S.S.R. all power belongs to the working people of town and country as represented by the Soviets of Working People's Deputies.

6. The land, its natural deposits, waters, forests, mills, factories, mines, rail, water and air transport, banks, post, telegraph and telephones, large state-organized agricultural enterprises (state farms, machine and tractor stations and the like) as well as municipal enterprises and the bulk of the dwelling houses in the cities and industrial localities, are state property, that is, belong to the whole people.

10. The right of citizens to personal ownership of their incomes from work and of their savings, of their dwelling houses and subsidiary household economy, their household furniture and utensils and articles of personal use and convenience, as well as the right of inheritance of personal property of citizens, is protected by law.

12. In the U.S.S.R. work is a duty and a matter of honor for every able-bodied citizen, in accordance with the principle: "He who does not work, neither shall he eat." The principle applied in the U.S.S.R. is that of socialism: "From each according to his ability, to each according to his work."

13. The Union of Soviet Socialist Republics is a federal state, formed on the basis of the voluntary association of Soviet Socialist Republics having equal rights . . . .

16. Each Union Republic has its own Constitution, which takes account of the specific features of the Republic and is drawn up in full conformity with the Constitution of the U.S.S.R.

17. To every Union Republic is reserved the right freely to secede from the U.S.S.R.

21. A single Union citizenship is established for all citizens of the U.S.S.R. Every citizen of a Union Republic is a citizen of the U.S.S.R.

Source: *Constitution (Fundamental Law) of the Union of Soviet Socialist Republics* (n.p.: State Publishing House of Political Literature, 1938).

30. The highest organ of state authority of the U.S.S.R. is the Supreme Soviet of the U.S.S.R.

32. The legislative power of the U.S.S.R. is exercised exclusively by the Supreme Soviet of the U.S.S.R.

33. The Supreme Soviet of the U.S.S.R. consists of two Chambers: the Soviet of the Union and the Soviet of Nationalities.

37. Both Chambers of the Supreme Soviet of the U.S.S.R., the Soviet of the Union and the Soviet of Nationalities, have equal rights.

38. The Soviet of the Union and the Soviet of Nationalities have an equal right to initiate legislation.

39. A law is considered adopted if passed by both Chambers of the Supreme Soviet of the U.S.S.R. by a simple majority vote in each.

48. The Supreme Soviet of the U.S.S.R. at a joint sitting of both Chambers elects the Presidium of the Supreme Soviet of the U.S.S.R. consisting of a President of the Presidium of the Supreme Soviet of the U.S.S.R., sixteen Vice-Presidents, a Secretary of the Presidium and twenty-four members of the Presidium. The Presidium of the Supreme Soviet of the U.S.S.R. is accountable to the Supreme Soviet of the U.S.S.R. for all its activities.

49. The Presidium of the Supreme Soviet of the U.S.S.R.: Convenes the sessions of the Supreme Soviet of the U.S.S.R.; Interprets laws of the U.S.S.R. in operation, issues decrees; Dissolves the Supreme Soviet of the U.S.S.R. in conformity with article 47 of the Constitution of the U.S.S.R. and orders new elections; . . . Awards decorations and confers titles of honor of the U.S.S.R.; Exercises the right of pardon; Appoints and removes the higher commands of the armed forces of the U.S.S.R.; In the intervals between sessions of. the Supreme Soviet of the U.S.S.R., proclaims a state of war in the event of armed attack on the U.S.S.R., or whenever necessary to fulfill international treaty obligations concerning mutual defense against aggression Orders general or partial mobilization; Ratifies international, treaties; . . . Proclaims martial law in separate localities or throughout the U.S.S.R. in the interests of the defense of the U.S.S.R. or for the purpose of ensuring public order and state security.

118. Citizens of the U.S.S.R. have the right to work, that is, are guaranteed the right to employment and payment for their work . . . .

119. Citizens of the U.S.S.R. have the right to rest and leisure. . . .

120. Citizens of the U.S.S.R. have the right to maintenance in old age and also in case of sickness or loss of capacity to work. . . .

121. Citizens of the U.S.S.R. have the right to education. This right is ensured by universal, compulsory elementary education; by education, including higher education, being free of charge . . . .

122. Women in the U.S.S.R. are accorded equal rights with men in all spheres of economic, state, cultural, social and political life. The possibility of exercising these rights is ensured to women by granting them an equal right with men to work, payment for work, rest and leisure, social insurance and education, and by state protection of the interests of mother and child, pre-maternity and maternity leave with full pay, and the provision of a wide network of maternity homes, nurseries and kindergartens.

123. Equality of rights of citizens of the U.S.S.R., irrespective of their nationality or race, in all spheres of economic, state, cultural, social and political life, is an indefeasible law. Any direct or indirect restriction of the rights of, or, conversely, any establishment of direct or indirect privileges for, citizens on account of their race or nationality, as well as any advocacy of racial or national exclusiveness or hatred and contempt, is punishable by law.

124. In order to ensure to citizens freedom of conscience, the church in the U.S.S.R. is separated from the state, and the school from the church. Freedom of religious worship and freedom of antireligious propaganda is recognized for all citizens.

125. In conformity with the interests of the working people, and in order to strengthen the socialist system, the citizens of the U.S.S.R. are guaranteed by law: freedom of speech; freedom of the press; freedom of assembly, including the holding of mass meetings; freedom of street processions and demonstrations. . . .

127. Citizens of the U.S.S.R. are guaranteed inviolability of the person. No person may be placed under arrest except by decision of a court or with the sanction of a procurator.

128. The inviolability of the homes of citizens and privacy of correspondence are protected by law.

130. It is the duty of every citizen of the U.S.S.R. to abide by the Constitution of the Union of Soviet Socialist Republics, to observe the laws, to maintain labor discipline, honestly to perform public duties, and to respect the rules of socialist intercourse.

132. Universal military service is law. Military service in the Workers' and Peasants' Red Army is an honorable duty of the citizens of the U.S.S.R.

133. To defend the fatherland is the sacred duty of every citizen of the U.S.S.R. Treason to the country—violation of the oath of allegiance, desertion to the enemy, impairing the military power of the state, espionage is punishable with all the severity of the law as the most heinous of crimes.

Speech by a Stakhanovite's Wife

The Stakhanovite movement was not only a campaign to increase productivity, it was an attempt to transform the lifestyle and culture of ordinary workers. At a conference of Stakhanovite wives, certain wives were asked to recount their experiences. The account of A. M. Piliakova, wife of a blacksmith in a timber mill, appears below.

- What attitudes and behavior are valued? With what western European class is this kind of lifestyle associated?
- What gender role messages are being sent?
- How his this related to broader changes in Soviet society?

Let me tell you about myself. After the National Conference of Stakhanovites I set the following task for myself: to work so that my husband would become a Stakhanovite. He was a shock worker, but he wasn't a Stakhanovite. I applied myself to this task and did my very best until I finally succeeded—my husband received the honorary title of Stakhanovite. It must be said that a wife plays a very important role in her husband's success at work.

Source: "Speech by A. M. Piliakova," in Sheila Fitzpatrick and Yuri Slezkine, Eds. *In the Shadow of Revolution: Life Stories of Russian Women From 1917 to the Second World War.* Copyright © 2000 by Princeton: Princeton University Press. Reprinted by permission of Princeton University Press, 362–363.

KHOROSHKO: She is a great force!

POLIAKOVA: Right. For example, if a husband comes home and his wife doesn't pay any attention to him—

VL. IVANOV: Are there such wives?

POLIAKOVA: Yes, very often. If a wife doesn't pay any attention to her husband, if she isn't nice to him—he gets upset. Before the Stakhanovite movement began, I was working in an office and doing a lot of volunteer work. My husband used to come home for dinner only. I would always gave him a good dinner, of course, but the general conditions just weren't the same as the ones I've created for him now. That was my mistake. Other women make the same kind of mistake. Meanwhile, everybody knows that if a husband has a fight with his wife or if their apartment is always dirty, he will probably be thinking while he's at work: "At home my wife nags me all the time and the apartment is always dirty. It's dirty here, too—even my overalls are dirty." Now if a wife welcomes her husband home with love and tenderness, if she respects him and talks to him, then the husband will go back to work in a good mood and think only about his work. It is obvious that in this case his labor productivity will increase. I repeat that our husbands' labor productivity greatly depends on how we treat them and on whether we are their friends and helpers.

Now I work in production and also take care of my husband. In my free time I try to do all I can for him. My husband didn't have a lot of education—he taught himself how to read. He used to read only newspapers, and even then with great difficulty. He never read books—not only did he not read them himself, but he did not even like to listen to other people reading. Every time I tried reading out loud to him, he would say: "Leave me alone. I'd rather go to bed." However, I wanted him to be a cultured person. I didn't want him to lag behind other men.

STROGANOV: Right!

POLIAKOVA: I began to look for books that would interest him. After learning that he was interested in war stories, I got the book *How the Steel Was Tempered* and read it out loud to him. I read slowly and with feeling, rather than rushing through the whole thing without stopping, the way some people do. I discussed it with him bit by bit. We would talk and argue. Afterward my husband told me: "You're right, a book is a good thing. Bring me another one."

I got in touch with the district library and, with the help of the director of the library, Comrade Lobanova, I began selecting books for him. Lobanova still sends us books—I just need to tell her which ones we want. First I read every book myself—I read fast—then I read it to my husband, and afterward we discuss it. Sometimes our daughter reads to us. Now my husband always listens attentively. I've trained him to the point where he brings home books himself and always asks me which ones are the most interesting. I give him my advice: this one is interesting, that one . . . In this way, he read *Virgin Soil Upturned* by Sholokhov, *Without Catching a Breath*, and so on. Now we are reading works by Vera Figner.

We go to the theater and to the movies quite often—we almost never miss a show. To tell you the truth, in the beginning he used to sleep in the theater. It was the same at the movies—he would sit there watching for a while and then fall asleep. I started warning him: "If you're sleepy, then you'd better sleep at home beforehand because I'm not going to let you go to sleep there." After the movies I started asking him, "Well, what did you see? Did you see this or that?" I would make things up, and if he said there had been no such thing in the movie, I would know he had been paying attention. [Applause]

Resistance to Soviet Policies in the Countryside

This comes from a Top Secret report from a regional committee to the Central Committee of the Communist Party regarding peasant resistance to collectivization in May 1929.

- Compare this with reports of peasant resistance in the tsarist era.
- How similar were peasant actions, particularly the role of women?
- How similar were official attitudes toward the peasantry?

Recently, in connection with the intensified offensive against the kulaks on two fronts–the grain requisition program and the restructuring of rural society—kulak anti-Soviet activities have increased significantly. More to the point, the kulaks no longer confine themselves to acts of individual sabotage but are beginning to adopt more sophisticated, openly counter-revolutionary tactics in the form of mass demonstrations, frequently connecting these demonstrations against the ongoing campaign to close churches, mosques, Islamic religious schools, and to remove veils, etc. . . .

A typical uprising took place in the village of Mikhailovskii on April 11 and 12, where "a mob under the control of confirmed counterrevolutionary elements ruled the village for two days. 150 armed men were required to bring the mob to heel." (Quoted from a letter dated April 15 from the representative of the grain procurement center.)

The incident can be summarized as follows. The kulaks took advantage of a mistake committed by the authorities when the latter sealed the barns of 28 farms (farms belonging to 10 kulaks, 10 wealthy peasants, and 8 middle peasants). The kulaks managed to sway the most backward segment of the population, namely the women, and through them the men, with an openly counterrevolutionary platform and managed to disrupt the grain procurement drive. They beat up the chairman of the surplus confiscation commission, shut down auctions of kulak property, seized property which had already been sold at auction, and used the threat of mob violence to compel the authorities to release prisoners under arrest, unseal the barns, and provide guarantees of no reprisals for the uprising.

A meeting called by the kulaks (attended by 900 persons, including 700 women) adopted the following platform:

1. The return of all property, livestock, and buildings sold at auction along with confiscated grain.
2. Lifting of the boycott.
3. An inventory of all confiscated seed grain and edible grain and distribution of these supplies to the needy (?!)
4. Abolition of property auctions.
5. Election of a commission to investigate the activities of the surplus confiscation commission.
6. A halt to the grain procurement drive and cancellation of the most recent measures.
7. The return of all mills to the millers.
8. Equal shares for all cooperative members.

Source: Diane P. Koenker and Ronald D. Bachman, *Revelations from the Russian Archives: Documents in English Translation* (Washington, D.C.: Library of Congress, 1997), 376–377. Reprinted by permission of Library of Congress Press.

9. Restoration of voting rights to all voters.
10. Abolition of forced communization of the peasants. Disbandment of the existing communes.

In another village in the same Mikhailovskii raion, Verkhniaia Sliudianka, on April 12 an inventory of the property of peasants caught with surplus grain led a mob of 200 individuals (primarily women) under the leadership of the kulak Rubanovich to surround the village Soviet building, lock the 24 members of the village Soviet inside, and demand a halt to grain requisition. And if the Soviet refused, the mob threatened to burn down the building. The timely arrival of a police squad kept the mob from carrying out their threat. As soon as the police arrived, the mob began to disperse. While pursuing the kulak Rubanovich, one policeman's horse got stuck in the mud, and a kulak tried to kill the policeman with a knife, but was prevented from doing so by another policeman, who shot and wounded the kulak with his revolver. Ten persons were arrested in connection with the case.

In the village of Abash in Bashelak raion of Biisk okrug, a group of women (as many as a hundred) appeared at the village Soviet building shouting, yelling, and demanding a halt to grain procurement "because if we don't have any grain, we won't have anything to eat." They pulled the chairman of the village Soviet—a day laborer—out of the village Soviet building and tried to beat him up. At that point the representative of the Biisk okrug committee rode up. The mob attacked him and tried to pull him off of his cart. After a long talk with the representative, the mob calmed down and dispersed, and two of the women admitted that some local Cossack kulaks had incited them.

Report on Ethnic Conflict

The following is a report from a Communist party member in Kabardino-Balkaria in 1940.

- What evidence of national tensions appears here? How conscious of Soviet nationality policies are the individuals involved? Who is blamed for Soviet policies?
- How does the author of the report explain the events described?
- What does this reveal about trends in Soviet society?

Manifestations of bourgeois nationalism and great-power chauvinism have been noted lately in a number of raions of the republic. . . .

Here are some of the numerous incidents that have been uncovered in recent months:

On 11 July 1940, at the Tyrnyauz Integrated Works, M. P. Kardanov beat up Comrade Sofronov, head of the food-supply department, supposedly for refusing to give him [Kardanov]

Source: Lewis Siegelbaum and Andrei Sokolov, *Stalinism as a Way of Life: A Narrative in Documents* (New Haven: Yale University Press, 2000), 265–266. © Yale University Press. Reprinted with permission.

a job because he is a Kabardin (Kardanov did not have his papers with him: no passport, labor book, etc.). He tried to stab Comrade Sofronov. Kardanov was sent to the Elbrus Raion police, but the chief of the police, Comrade Dzhaboev, released him, and he went into hiding. It was learned that Kardanov is the son of an exiled kulak.

There have also been instances of great-power chauvinism. On Navy Day a mass rally was held in which more than five hundred people took part. A plasterer named Gladkov, while inebriated, tried to gather Russians for a fist-fight among Kabardin, Balkar, and Russians. Gladkov was sent to the Elbrus Raion police, but was also released. . . .

On 16 August 1940, S. M. Divnich, Pfeifer, and Sidarenko were returning home to Chegem Pervyi while intoxicated. As they walked along the street, some young boys began to badger them, and one of them struck Divnich in the back with a rock. The latter went to chase the boy, who ran into the yard of Buzha Bogotov and hid in the corn while screaming "Urus, Urus." A Kabardin responded to the boy's screaming by running out with a stake in his hands and he stabbed Divnich in the shoulder. Pfeifer heard the screams, ran to the scene of the fight and saw Divnich surrounded already by a whole mob of Kabardin, who also attacked Pfeifer and beat him up, cracking his head open. Divnich and Pfeifer decided to complain to the village soviet, where, however, not only were the appropriate measures not taken, but they were beaten up again by the village soviet chairman Tamash Mazanovich Pekov, village soviet secretary Ibragim Makoev, Komsomol secretary Bogotov, a driver, the kolkhoz assistant manager Khabaz Kishev, and others.

During March and April of this year many Russian workers at the Eastern Akbash bast fiber factory were beaten up by Kabardin, and the methods used in the beatings were identical. The individuals would accost a Russian leaving the factory at night, ask him for a light and, upon making sure he was Russian, beat him up, saying over and over: "Now take Finland, now take the Ukraine, now take Poland and Turkey."

At 10 P.M. on 2 May a group of Kabardin attacked workers returning from the bast fiber factory and threw rocks at them, injuring Vasily Yefimovich Kvint, a driver for the factory, in the head. . . .

A group of nationalists in the village of Kenzhe, Nalchik Raion, headed by Tkhamokov, the chairman of the village soviet, destroyed the gardens of Russian workers from the Peplo-Pomzovoi mine. There have been a number of incidents in which Kabardin have beaten up Russians waiting on line at shops while they shouted out patently nationalist phrases (Leskensky, Baksan, Urvansky, Nalchik, and other raions).

In the Balkar raions and several others, schoolteachers who have resettled are persecuted even by the heads of Soviet organizations. The teachers are denied an opportunity to buy food, insulted and so forth. . . .

Figure 17-1 Poster: Stalin

Viktor Deni (1893–1946) was an artist who welcomed the Revolution of 1917 and devoted his talents to creating propaganda posters supporting Communism. He painted this in 1931.

- What messages does this send?
- How is Stalin's authority represented?

Source: Early twentieth-century poster.

Figure 17-2 Sculpture: "Worker and Collective-farmer"

Vera Mukhina (1889–1953) was the most famous sculptor of the Soviet era, and this is her most famous sculpture. Seventy-nine-feet high and made of stainless steel, Mukhina made it in 1937 to be placed on top of the Soviet pavilion at the Paris World's Fair of that year. It is now located in Moscow.

- How does this exemplify the principles of Socialist Realism?
- What gender messages does this send?

Source: Getty Images, Inc. Stone Allstock.

Figure 17-3 Collective Farmers
This is a photograph taken during the First Five-Year Plan.
- Compare it with past photographs of peasants.
- What is the same and what has changed? What does this reveal about Soviet society during the First Five-Year Plan?

Source: AP/Wide World Photos.

Figure 17-4 The Industrial Complex at Magnitogorsk
The centerpiece of the Soviet industrial revolution, this steel foundry complex is a monument to heroic labor and to the wasteful haste of the First Five-Year Plan. Perhaps as many as thirty thousand workers died in its construction. Nevertheless, it produced half the steel that was used to made Soviet tanks in World War II.
- What is the relation of this plant to the collective farm shown above?
- It what ways is this emblematic of the Soviet experiment?

Source: National Archives and Records Administration.

_____ FOR FURTHER READING _____

(In addition to the books by Clements, Cohen, Goldman, Suny, and Ulam from the previous chapter.)

Andrle, Vladimir. *Workers in Stalin's Russia: Industrialization and Social Change in a Planned Economy.* New York: St. Martin's Press, 1988.

Conquest, Robert, *The Great Terror: A Reassessment.* New York: Oxford University Press, 1990.

Dunham, Vera S. *In Stalin's Time: Middleclass Values in Soviet Fiction.* Cambridge: Cambridge University Press, 1976.

Fitzpatrick, Sheila. *Everyday Stalinism: Ordinary Life in Extraordinary Times: Soviet Russia in the 1930s.* New York: Oxford University Press, 1999.

Goldman, Wendy Z. *Women at the Gates: Gender and Industry in Stalin's Russia.* Cambridge: Cambridge University Press, 2002.

Gregory, Paul R. *The Political Economy of Stalinism: Evidence from the Soviet Secret Archives.* Cambridge: Cambridge University Press, 2004.

Haslam, Jonathan. *The Soviet Union and the Struggle for Collective Security in Europe, 1933–1939.* New York: St. Martin's Press, 1984.

Kotkin, Stephen. *Magnetic Mountain: Stalinism as a Civilization.* Berkeley : University of California Press, 1995.

Thurston, Robert W. *Life and Terror in Stalin's Russia, 1934–1941.* New Haven: Yale University Press, 1996.

Tucker, Robert C. *Stalin in Power: the Revolution from Above, 1928–1941.* New York: Norton, 1990.

Viola, Lynne. *Peasant Rebels under Stalin: Collectivization and the Culture of Peasant Resistance* New York: Oxford University Press, 1996.

CHAPTER EIGHTEEN

THE GREAT FATHERLAND WAR
AND ITS AFTERMATH, 1941–1953

The Nazi-Soviet peace pact was a temporary expedient for both sides; Hitler wanted to avoid a two-front war, and Stalin wanted more time to build up the Red Army. Peace between the two countries lasted less than two years. In June 1941, Hitler launched the largest invasion in history—three and a half million soldiers on a front one thousand miles long—overwhelming border defenses and racing into the Russian heartland. Nevertheless, the Red Army saved their capital in the fall of 1941 and began a war of attrition. After nearly four years of war, twenty-six million Soviet deaths, and unimaginable hardship and privation for the defenders, the Soviet Union prevailed. It drove out the Hitler's armies, took the war to the German homeland, and destroyed the Nazi regime.

In the course of the war, the Soviet command economy proved itself; Soviet factories out-produced their enemy in both quantity and quality. The Communist party, too, gained legitimacy among the population for its role in leading the country successfully through its life-or-death struggle. Postwar life remained grim, however. The Soviet economic infrastructure had been seriously damaged, and the government continued to fund heavy industry at the expense of consumer goods and housing. Nor did the Communist Party retreat from its desire to control all aspects of political, social, and cultural life. Sporadic purges continued. Furthermore, victory over Germany did not mean an end to national security concerns; mistrust between the Soviet Union and the United States led to the diplomatic confrontation and arms race known as the Cold War.

EURASIAN CONTEXT

From the invasion of Poland in September 1939 until they entered the city of Stalingrad in September 1942, the German army seemed invincible. Hitler's forces had overrun Norway, Denmark, France, eastern Europe, the Balkan Peninsula, and all of the western Soviet Union, from the outskirts of Leningrad in the north to within one hundred miles of the Caspian Sea in the south. Nevertheless, this was the furthest extent of Nazi expansion. After the victory of Soviet forces in the Battle of Stalingrad in January 1943, the Germans and their allies were steadily pushed back. In June 1944 when Anglo-American forces invaded at Normandy, the Soviet army had already cleared their country of the German army and were preparing to liberate eastern Europe. One year later, the Allies were victorious; in early May 1945, Germany surrendered unconditionally.

The Second World War in the Pacific roughly paralleled the war in Europe. Japan had easily occupied the modern, coastal regions of China in 1937, and in September of 1940 had begun to invade French Indo-China (Vietnam). The United States historically opposed Japanese expansion and imposed trade sanctions, which became increasingly severe as Japan moved south toward the Dutch East Indies (Indonesia). After the United States put an embargo on the sale of oil to Japan, Japanese leaders decided that war with the United States could not be avoided. In surprise attacks in Hawaii and the Philippines, the Japanese destroyed America's Pacific air and naval forces, and then quickly overran all of Southeast Asia and the East Indies. Japan reached its furthest expansion by the summer of 1942, but, beginning with the U.S. victory in the battle for the Pacific island of Midway, Japan was slowly but relentlessly pushed back. Japan lacked the population, industrial base, and natural resources necessary to realize its imperial ambitions. By the summer of 1945, while elements in the Japanese government were trying to arrange a surrender, the United States dropped atomic bombs on Hiroshima and Nagasaki. Japan then surrendered.

In October 1939, one month after the war began, Turkey signed a defense treaty with Britain and France, but when the Allies seemed powerless to resist German expansion, Turkey did not join the fighting. Instead, in June 1941, four days before Germany invaded the Soviet Union, Turkey signed a non-aggression pact with Germany. The possibility that the Soviet Union might be defeated encouraged many Turks to dream again of a pan-Turkish state in Central Asia. Turkey nevertheless remained neutral, and, in February 1945, when the defeat of Germany was imminent, it changed course again and entered the war on the side of the Allies. Turkey joined the United Nations, and, in the postwar era, aligned itself with the United States.

Iran's Reza Shah Pahlavi was very sympathetic to the Nazis, partly because Iranians were Aryan and Nazi ideology was appealing, but mostly because Germany was the enemy of Iran's historical predators, Russia and England. Reza Shah maintained economic and diplomatic ties with Germany. In 1941, British and Soviet forces invaded Iran and forced Reza Shah to abdicate in favor of his twenty-one-year-old son, Mohammed Reza Pahlavi. The Allies then arrested German agents and used Iran as a supply route to the Soviet Union.

The same process occurred in Afghanistan, which had also maintained friendly relations with Germany. King Zahir Shah attempted to remain neutral, and he did not comply with British and Soviet demands that he expel German agents. Britain and the Soviet Union then invaded Afghanistan and occupied it until the end of the war.

In 1937, China had been no match for Japan's modern military forces, and Japan had quickly captured China's major port cities and all of eastern China accessible by railroad. Neither the GMD nor the CCP were defeated, however. From its rural base in Yan'an in northern China, the CCP mobilized peasant support and waged guerrilla war against Japan. The GMD had fled to Zhangsha in southeast China, and continued to be recognized by the Allies as the legitimate government of China and received military supplies via Burma. Some estimates place Chinese military and civilian casualties at levels nearly as high as Soviet losses.

THE SOVIET UNION IN WORLD WAR II

The Soviet Union began the war as one of the aggressors. The German army invaded Poland on September 1, 1939, and, sixteen days later, the Soviet Union invaded from the east. The two armies met at Brest-Litovsk, where the border between Belarus and Poland had been drawn at the end of World War I. The Soviet Union also demanded the right to establish military bases in Estonia, Latvia, Lithuania, and Finland. The Baltic countries capitulated, but Finland did not. The Finns refused, and they resisted the ensuing Soviet invasion for three months, inflicting heavy losses on the Red Army. In the end, however, Finland ceded a strip of land extending fifty miles north of Leningrad and including the port of Hango.

Hitler had long intended to invade the Soviet Union, but his plans were accelerated by what he considered aggressive expansion by the Red Army. The Soviet Union actually seized more territory from Poland than Germany had, it occupied the Baltic countries and began to deport its citizens (including Germans) to the east, and it invaded and occupied Bessarabia (now Moldova, another former province of the Russian Empire). Hitler invaded the Balkan Peninsula in the spring of 1941, and then, on July 22, 1941, he sent his armies into the Soviet Union.

The Soviet Union had begun to reorganize its army and to gear up its defense industries, but it was woefully unprepared for the German invasion. The Soviet leadership had dismantled defenses on the pre-war border with Poland but had not yet established defenses for its new western border. Deliveries of grain, cotton, oil, lumber, and metals to Germany continued. To make matters worse, the Red Army did not have a plan for retreat; official policy declared that an attack could only be answered by counter-attack. Furthermore, in the weeks leading up to the invasion, Stalin ignored warnings from the United States and Great Britain and intelligence from German deserters and Soviet spies. Consequently, when the German armies poured across the border with Poland on June 22, 1941, they met no organized resistance. For the first few hours, the Soviet military command believed it was some sort of misunderstanding, and ordered the troops not to fight back, so as not to "provoke" the Germans. Then, once the leaders realized that war had begun, they gave the order to attack and not to retreat. During the first months of the war, about one million soldiers were captured by the Germans.

Luckily for the Soviet leaders, Hitler did not plan for a concentrated, rapid advance on Moscow. Instead, he ordered a three-prong attack on a broad front, heading towards Leningrad in the north, Moscow in the center, and the Don River in the south. Within a month, German forces occupied Poland, western Ukraine and Belarus, and the Baltic states, but, spread out in this way, they advanced slowly enough to give the Red Army a chance to regroup. On July 16, at the Battle of Smolensk, the advance of a German army was halted for the first time since the war had begun. After a three-week stalemate, Hitler decided to concentrate his forces on the conquest of Kiev and the remainder of Ukraine before returning to attack Moscow.

Knowing the attack was coming, many Muscovites fled in panic, but Stalin and the Communist leadership remained in the capital preparing a defense. The German attack came in November, and once again the Red Army protected Moscow. In the Battle of Moscow, 1,000,000 Russian and 800,000 German soldiers died, but the German army was defeated and was forced to withdraw. This was the first major defeat and retreat of German forces; Hitler's plans, his blitzkrieg tactics, had failed. The conflict become a war of attrition, and, since the Soviet Union had a larger population and more natural resources, Soviet victory now depended on the will of the people to keep fighting.

That will was sorely tested. By the end of 1941, nearly four million Russian soldiers had been killed and almost three and a half million had been taken prisoner. In addition, the German army had seized the industrial and agricultural heartland of the Soviet Union: they controlled 70 percent of the Soviet iron and steel industry, 75 percent of its tank manufacturing capacity, and 40 percent of its grain production. Furthermore, German successes continued in the new year. In 1942 the German army repelled a major Soviet offensive to retake Kharkov and took more than a quarter of a million prisoners. It also advanced along a broad front in the south, capturing the Crimean Peninsula and the lower Dnieper and Don regions. In September, German forces began to enter Stalingrad.

Possession of Stalingrad meant control of the Volga River and access to the Caspian Sea and the Baku oil fields. Stalingrad also guarded the route to the Soviet steel works and munitions factories that were sheltered behind the Ural Mountains. There was also, of course, the symbolic significance of the city's name; Hitler wanted very badly to take possession of a city named after the Soviet leader, while Stalin was just as anxious to defend it. There was no question of surrendering the city, therefore, and the German army had to take it one building at a time.

Up to this point, German military superiority had been based on its mastery of tank warfare, but tanks are of little use in street fighting. Hitler's refusal to permit his troops to retreat from the city and engage the Red Army on a battlefield played into Stalin's hand. Soviet willingness to sacrifice life for life (more than 1,100,000 Soviet and 800,000 German soldiers died in the battle) meant victory; no reinforcements were forthcoming, and, as German forces dwindled, the Red Army was able to surround and destroy them. In the end, the German commander surrendered, and 91,000 Axis soldiers (all that were left of an army of a quarter of a million) were taken prisoner.

Victory at Stalingrad was a tremendous boost to Soviet morale, and it was the turning point of World War II in Europe, but it did not end the war. The main body of the German army was able to regroup and mount the last successful German offense of the war, at Kharkov in the spring of 1943. When the Germans then marched toward Moscow, however, they were met by Soviet forces at Kursk, where, in the biggest tank battle of the war the Red Army was victorious. There would be no more German advances. After Kursk, the Red Army began an inexorable march toward Berlin. Kharkov was liberated in August, Smolensk in September, and Kiev in November, and the siege of Leningrad was lifted in January 1944. In June 1944, when the Allies mounted their invasion of Normandy, the Red Army had begun to pursue the retreating Germans into the Balkans and had almost completely liberated western Ukraine and Belarus from Nazi occupation. In the fall of 1944, Soviet forces entered Poland, and in the spring of 1945, they liberated Czechoslovakia and invaded Austria. U.S. and Soviet troops met on the Elbe River in April 1945, and on May 1, the Soviets began the Battle of Berlin. On May 7, the Germany army surrendered to the Americans, and the next day, the Red Army insisted on another formal surrender to the Soviet Union.

THE COLD WAR

The wartime alliance of the Soviet Union, Great Britain, and the United States had been created only by Adolf Hitler's decision to make war on them all. The mutual mistrust that had made an alliance against Hitler impossible in the 1930s, however, also stood in the way of continued cooperation once the war was won. The Soviet Union had feared that if it joined the war, it would bear the brunt of the fighting, and its fears were realized. The Normandy invasion did not begin until three years after Germany had invaded Soviet territory, and the Allied forces were opposed by only 27 German Divisions, while the Red Army was fighting 181 German divisions. Eighty percent of all German battle deaths occurred in the Soviet Union. Twenty-five million Russians died, while Great Britain lost 357,000 and the United States lost 298,000. On the other hand, Great Britain had feared that, in the event of a war with Germany, the Soviet Union would take advantage of its occupation of eastern Europe to impose Soviet communism there. These fears also were realized. By 1948, Eastern Europe (Bulgaria, Albania, Yugoslavia, Romania, Hungary, and Poland) were all ruled by socialist governments installed by Stalin.

Neither side trusted the motivations behind the other's actions. Stalin suspected that the Allied delay in mounting a second front in the West was not the consequence of the need to marshal the necessary resources but was intended to weaken the Soviet Union. Western leaders believed that Soviet hegemony in Eastern Europe was not just an attempt to create a friendly buffer-zone on the Soviet border but was the first stage of a campaign to spread communism throughout Europe. Furthermore, the United States, the leader of the western Allies, had decided that the future prosperity and peace of the world depended on the global spread of free-enterprise capitalism, while the Soviet Union remained committed to the Marxian notion that capitalism must inevitably collapse in Communist revolution. Thus, the United States and the Soviet Union both expected that one day the entire world would be modeled on its system, and both interpreted each strategic move of its opponent as offensive rather than defensive.

Germany played a key role in the development of the Cold War. Until the allies could decide on Germany's future, it was divided into four sectors and occupied by U.S., British, French, and Soviet troops. The Soviet Union, arguing that it could not afford to fight Germany every generation, wanted Germany to be deindustrialized and divided into several agricultural countries. The Soviet Union also demanded ten million dollars in reparations to be paid in the form of factories, which would be dismantled and shipped to the Soviet Union to replace industry destroyed in the war. At first the Allies were sympathetic to the Soviet position, but once they fully realized the power of their new atomic weapons, American leaders changed their attitude. With such awesome military power at their disposal, they no longer feared Germany. Quite the reverse, they felt that a prosperous and united Germany would be a valuable addition to the free world economy, and that it would also serve as a buffer between the West and the Soviet Union. In the summer of 1945, U.S. president Truman had announced that Soviet reparations would be limited to the Soviet sector plus twenty-five percent of the "excess capacity" in the remainder of Germany. The following year Truman declared an end to reparations and said that there was no excess capacity.

In March 1948, England, America, and France decided that a compromise could not be reached, and they announced their intention to form a West German government. In April, the Allies created a West German currency, the Deutschmark, which they also introduced into Berlin. Berlin, the former capital of Germany, was in the Russian sector, but the western half of the city was occupied by the Allies. In June, to protest the use of the new currency, the Soviet Union declared a blockade of Berlin and closed the highway that connected it with the west. The Allies, refusing to back down, began to supply Berlin by air. The confrontation— in which the United States signaled its willingness to use atomic weapons, if necessary— lasted for almost a year.

In April 1949, the Allies created the North Atlantic Treaty Organization (NATO), a military pact among the nations of western Europe intended to resist Soviet aggression. In May, the

Berlin crisis was resolved, and Stalin lifted the blockade. There was no more hope of an agreement on Germany, however. In September 1949, the Allies declared the creation of the Federal Republic of Germany, which would join both NATO and the United Nations. The Soviet Union followed suit the following month and created the German Democratic Republic.

While the confrontation over Germany had been developing, Soviet policies in eastern Europe, which had originally been quite moderate became increasingly radical. The Red Army had been welcomed as liberators by a significant proportion of the population of eastern Europe, and native Communist parties gained in popularity. At the beginning of the Soviet occupation, non-Communist political parties were allowed to form and were given representation in coalition ministries. As time went on, however, political harassment and military intimidation broke up the liberal parties. Socialist parties were forced to merge with the Communist party. After 1948, the nations of eastern Europe were sovietized: Communist parties were purged, leaders of opposition parties were arrested and executed, industry was nationalized, central economic planning was imposed, and agriculture was collectivized. Workers and peasants were regimented and impoverished. In 1953, when East German workers demonstrated against increased production quotas, they were suppressed by the Red Army.

An exception to this pattern occurred in Yugoslavia. There, an independent native Communist movement had won widespread popularity as a result of its resistance against Nazi occupation. Yugoslav partisan forces, led by Communist leader Tito, had driven the Germans out, and they were therefore not beholden to the Red Army. Tito spoke of independent, "national" roads to socialism and refused to follow the Soviet model. Factories were supervised by councils elected by the workers, private property was permitted in agriculture, and the system was more decentralized and less coercive than the Soviet Union. When Stalin attempted to interfere in Yugoslav politics, Tito purged Stalinists from the Party. Stalin broke relations with Yugoslavia but did attempt military action against it.

The Sovietization of eastern Europe occurred in the context of U.S. trade policy. In 1944, the United States had convened a conference in Bretton Woods, New Jersey, to formulate plans for fostering free-enterprise capitalism around the world and creating a global system of free trade. In 1945, the conferring nations set out the rules of free trade in the General Agreement on Tariffs and Trade, and they established two global financial institutions, the International Monetary Fund (IMF), to stabilize exchange rates of currency, and the World Bank, to provide loans for long-term economic development. Both the IMF and the World Bank loaned money only on the condition that the borrowing nations adhere to the principles of free trade. This was perceived by the Soviet Union as a weapon in the war of capitalism against socialism, and the perception was confirmed when they were offered a $1 billion reconstruction loan on condition that the West be allowed to supervise elections in eastern Europe. The American Marshall Plan, which offered reconstruction grants to help Europe rebuild, was also predicated on participation in the global free-enterprise economy. Stalin refused the offer of aid, and he pressed his client states in eastern Europe to turn it down as well.

These events were paralleled by Soviet actions in Asia that were interpreted by the United States as evidence of aggressive expansionism. In the summer of 1945, as U.S. victory in the Pacific became certain, Truman began to regret having pressured Stalin to join the war with Japan three months after Germany surrendered. Stalin lived up to his promise, and on August 8 (two days after the first atomic bomb was dropped), the Soviet Union declared war on Japan. The Red Army drove Japanese troops out of Manchuria and northern Korea; it also took possession of two pieces of territory that had been lost to Japan in 1905, the southern half of Sakhalin Island and Port Arthur. Stalin wanted to occupy the northern Japanese island of Hokkaido, but the United States refused. Simultaneously, the Red Army occupied northern Iran and Stalin demanded that Turkey cede territory adjacent to Georgia and Armenia. Truman applied strong diplomatic pressure on Stalin to retreat. The atmosphere of alarm in the west was heightened in March 1946 when former British Prime Minister Winston Churchill announced in a speech in Fulton, Missouri, that an "Iron Curtain" was being lowered between the Communist east and the free west.

In these cases, Stalin yielded. He rescinded his demand for territory in eastern Turkey, withdrew Soviet troops from Iran, and prepared to pull out of Manchuria. This did nothing to allay Truman's fears, however. In 1947, there were active Communist insurgency movements in Greece and Turkey, and both countries appealed to the United States for aid. The Soviet Union was not, in fact, supplying aid to Greek or Turkish Communists. Nevertheless, Truman convinced the U.S. Congress that the two insurgencies were part of an international communist movement directed by Moscow. To counter the perceived threat, he initiated the Truman Doctrine, declaring that it would be U.S. policy to help defend free nations from subjugation by armed minorities or outside pressure. He justified this policy by what came to be called the "domino theory," the idea that if one country (Greece or Turkey, for example) succumbed to communism, its neighbors would also fall. The United States also began to establish military bases across Outer Eurasia, from Okinawa to Manila to Turkey.

Simultaneously with the emergence of a Cold War in Europe, momentous events were taking place in China. Chiang Kai-shek and the Guomindang (GMD, the Nationalist Party) had let the United States fight the war against Japan in China, while stockpiling weapons to use against the Communists when the war was over. The GMD had long since given up plans for land reform, and the countryside was starving and alienated from Chiang's regime. After the war was over, and as the Japanese retreated, Chiang's forces quickly moved into the cities, where the GMD's principal supporters lived. However, the GMD administration had become corrupt: It extorted bribes from business, granted monopolies to cronies, and raised taxes to ruinous levels. Deficit spending by Chiang (and the printing of currency by the Japanese during the war) created a runaway inflation that bankrupted the middle class, demoralized the cities, and deprived Chiang of his last support.

In the meantime, the Chinese Communist Party (CCP) was riding a wave of popularity. It had actively fought a guerrilla war of resistance against the Japanese, and it had promoted moderate land reform (dividing land of traitors and absentee landlords among landless peasants). The Chinese Communists provided law and order and honest local government in which workers, peasants, and the middle class had the right to vote. After the Japanese surrender, the CCP steadily advanced against the hapless GMD, which was not only corrupt and demoralized but thoroughly incompetent. On October 1, 1949, the People's Republic of China was declared. Chiang Kai-shek and his army fled to Taiwan, where they were protected by the U.S. Seventh Fleet, and where they established the Republic of China.

The victory of the CCP appeared to many in the West to be proof of a monolithic communist movement, but the reality was quite different. Stalin had invaded Manchuria in order to loot Japanese factories, not to spread communism. Stalin actually tried to convince Mao Zedong not to seize power, arguing that GMD was too powerful and that the CCP should bide its time. Despite this advice, however, Stalin ordered the Red Army, when it evacuated Manchuria at the end of the war, to leave stockpiles of weapons where the Peoples Liberation Army, and not the GMD, would be able to recover them. Stalin granted China a loan of $300 million, but in exchange he demanded that Mao confirm the independence of Mongolia, permit Soviet exploitation of natural resources in Xinjiang, and share with the Soviet Union the administration of the former Chinese Eastern and Southern Manchurian Railways (until 1953) and Port Arthur (until 1955).

For his part, Mao had no intention of taking orders from Stalin or of following the Stalinist model. At first, Mao instituted a system that had much in common with the Soviet New Economic Policy of the 1920s. The government controlled banking, heavy industry, international trade, and natural resource extraction, but granted private property rights to small businesspeople and farmers and permitted a limited market to function. This all changed, however, after the beginning of the Korean War (1950–1953). Under the protection of the Red Army, Korean Communist Kim Il-Sung had established the Democratic People's Republic of Korea north of the thirty-eighth parallel, while the United States had supported a western-oriented Republic of Korea in the south. In June 1950, the North Korean army invaded and advanced rapidly southward. The United States, under the auspices of the UN, quickly came to the defense of the South, but General Douglas MacArthur was not content with liberating the South from Communist occupation. Instead, he invaded the north with the intention of overturning Communist rule. This drew China into the conflict, and in October 1950, Mao launched a massive invasion that pushed the United States back south of the thirty-eighth parallel. The war then turned into a stalemate that dragged on until an armistice was arranged in 1953.

War with the United States made Communist China xenophobic and drove it into closer relations with the Soviet Union. China forced Westerners to leave the country, accepted military aid from the Soviet Union, and began to suppress independent thought and economic freedom for the middle class. In 1953, in exchange for development loans, China adopted the model of its Soviet benefactor and began to collectivize agriculture, nationalize economic enterprises, and begin a five-year plan of industrial expansion.

Meanwhile, an arms race between the United States and the USSR was under way. In 1948, the United States instituted a peacetime draft for the first time in its history, and began to rearm. The Soviet Union followed suit. In August 1949, the Soviet Union detonated its first atomic (fission) bomb; in October 1952, the United States tested a far more powerful hydrogen (fusion) bomb; and in August 1953, the Soviet Union proved that it, too, could make a hydrogen bomb. Both sides began developing delivery systems: intercontinental jet bombers and missiles.

POST-WAR DOMESTIC POLITICS

World War II profoundly affected both the Communist Party and the attitude of Soviet citizens toward the state and the party. The war had brought the purges and the terror to an end, and the invasion seemed to justify the crisis atmosphere of the 1930s: The foreign threat had not been imaginary. When the war was over, the Communist Party was credited with the victory. Patriots were impressed by their country's military success. Where tsarist Russia had failed only a generation earlier, Soviet Russia had succeeded. The Soviet Union regained the Baltic states, Bessarabia, and the western parts of Ukraine and Belarus that had been annexed by Poland after World War I. Of Russia's traditional rivals for hegemony in Eurasia, Japan had been utterly defeated, and Great Britain was so weakened that it could not retain its empire. Soviet influence over the Balkans realized the dreams of Catherine the Great.

Stalin was perceived as an effective war leader. He had been the chair of the State Defense Committee (made up of the highest party officials), chair of the Stavka (the supreme military command), General Secretary of the Party, chair of the Politburo, chair of Council of Ministers, and the Commissar of Defense. Stalin has since been charged with wasting lives by ordering suicidal attacks and by refusing to permit retreat, but at the time, those deaths were blamed not on Stalin but on the invading Germans. Stalin was also credited with the decision to move workers and factories to the east, beyond the reach of Nazi forces. More than 16.5 million people and 2,500 factories were moved to the Volga, Urals, Siberia, and Central Asia. Stalin had also raised the morale of the people. He had stayed in Moscow in the fall of 1941 and had appealed to the patriotism of the Russian nation, invoking the memory of Russian military heroes, and referring to his audience not only as "comrades" but as "brothers and sisters."

The Soviet *system* also proved itself. Centralized economic planning permitted a rapid shift to wartime production and the immediate mobilization of resources for the war effort. The five-year plans had been undertaken in an atmosphere of crisis and emergency, and workers were accustomed to heroic labor and the idea of overfilling plans. Soviet industry outproduced Germany in aircraft, tanks, and artillery, and the Soviet T-34 tank and Katiusha rocket launcher were superior to the German equivalents.

Despite the good will and patriotism on the part of the Soviet people, when the war was over Stalin did not allow the somewhat freer and more open atmosphere of the war years to continue. Just the opposite, he returned to the repressive atmosphere of the 1930s. Centralization and discipline were restored to the Party. Policies regulating admission to the Party were made more stringent, and there were sporadic, localized purges. The Central Committee, which had been eclipsed by the State Defense Committee, was restored as the supreme policy-making institution in the country.

A new terror was applied to prisoners of war. Stalin had made it illegal to surrender to the enemy, and therefore all prisoners of war were considered criminals. As such, they were sentenced to prison camps when they were repatriated. This was also the case with officers or soldiers who had formed friendships with foreigners in the course of the war. The population of prison labor camps rose from 1.5 million in 1945 to 2.2 million in 1953. In addition, an estimated 3.7 million German POWs were held in Soviet labor camps. (In 1955, when they were finally allowed to return to Germany, only 20,000 were still alive.)

CULTURE AND RELIGION

On the very first day of the invasion, the Metropolitan Sergeii announced that the Orthodox Church would support the nation in the trials that were to come. In regular sermons, published and distributed by the Church for the duration of the war, Sergeii rallied the support of all Orthodox believers for the struggle against Nazism. He offered prayers for victory, prohibited any collaboration with the Nazis in occupied territories, and he called on Orthodox Christians in the Balkans to resist. Under his leadership, the church raised millions of rubles in contributions to the war effort. In these circumstances, priests could not be treated as individual, profit-making businessmen, and, when Stalin permitted the Church to open bank accounts in the name of the Church, he tacitly recognized the existence of the Church as a corporate institution. In 1942, Stalin allowed some churches to reopen, and in 1943 he permitted the calling of a Church Sobor to elect a Patriarch, as well as the opening of seminaries and the publication of a monthly journal. Stalin offered to fund the Sobor and to give the church annual subsidies, but Sergei and other metropolitans refused in order to preserve the independence of the Church.

The Sobor, made up of only nineteen bishops, unanimously elected Sergeii Patriarch. Sergeii then created a patriarchal synod to administer the church. For the remainder of Stalin's life, the Church was allowed a space in Soviet society in which to function. Church services were permitted, and taxes on priests were lowered. In addition, Church officials were released from prisons and labor camps (provided they recognized Sergeii as Patriarch and accepted the legitimacy of the Soviet regime). When Sergeii died in 1944, there were forty-one bishops to elect his successor.

When the war was over, life was not easy for the Church. Priests who were active in re-cruiting members were harassed. Church attendance made any kind of career advancement impossible. In addition, the "All-Union Society for the Promotion of Scientific and Political Knowledge" actively promoted atheism. Nevertheless, churches and seminaries were not closed, and the Church hierarchy was not persecuted. Furthermore, it appears that the Church grew significantly. During Lent in 1947 approximately 400,000 believers attended the main cathedral in Leningrad, and attendance in Moscow was comparable. By 1953, approximately 30,000 priests served more than 20,000 parishes.

During the war, writers served the cause by acting as war correspondents at the various fronts, or by writing patriotic novels. There was some relaxation of control over literature. Anna Akhmatova and Boris Pasternak published their first new poetry in decades, and Mikhail Zoshchenko and Konstantin Fedin were able to publish memoirs. However, most writing dealt with the war. The poet Aleksandr Tvardovskii won both a Stalin Prize and popular acclaim for an epic poem, "Vasilii Terkin," a serialized work that followed the expe-riences of a simple Russian infantryman from the invasion to victory.

After the war, however, the Party regimented culture once again under the direction of Andrei Zhdanov, head of the Leningrad party organization, member of the Central Commit-tee, and close associate of Stalin. Socialist realism was reaffirmed, and "art for art's sake" and imitation of foreign trends were forbidden. Fedin, Zoshchenko, and Akhmatova were reviled for discussing personal issues and ignoring social concerns. Zoshchenko and Akhmatova were expelled from the Writers' Union in 1946 for decadence, and the editors of the journals who had published their work were fired. Even patriotic, socialist realist novels were criticized if they focused too much on individual heroes and did not sufficiently cele-brate the role of the party. *Zhdanovshchina* was used to refer to the narrow-minded, philis-tine, and xenophobic standards for art.

Stalin had begun to celebrate Russian nationalism during the war. He had replaced the "Internationale" with a new national anthem that referred to the unity of nations under Russian leadership. In a famous speech in May 1945, Stalin singled out the Russians as the most outstanding of all the Soviet peoples and as deserving the lion's share of credit for the victory over Germany. Under Zhdanov's influence, Russian chauvinism reached exagger-ated and even absurd levels. Russian civilization was represented as unquestionably the greatest in the world, and it was claimed that Russians had invented synthetic rubber, the first airplane, the lightbulb, radio, and even baseball!

Universities were also subjected to Zhdanovshchina. Scholars and scientists were ex-pected to subordinate their work to the requirements of Russian chauvinism and socialist propaganda. "Rootless cosmopolitans" (a term which could stand for Jews or for anyone re-vealing any sympathy for a western idea) were purged from university faculties. The most bizarre development was the promotion of a geneticist, T. D. Lysenko, who believed in the inheritance of acquired characteristics and who claimed to make wheat seeds hardier by freezing them. He was put in charge of the highest agricultural institute in the Soviet Union and was allowed to purge the genetics departments of Soviet Universities of any scientist who disagreed with him.

ROLES AND STATUS OF WOMEN

Soviet women were involved in every aspect of the war. One million women served in the military, making up 8 percent of total troops, by far the largest proportion of any nation in the war. Women were not drafted, so all female soldiers were volunteers. They were typically young, unmarried, and from Ukraine or Russia. Women were actively discouraged from serving in combat, and many male soldiers believed it was unlucky to have women in their unit. Nevertheless, several thousand women managed to serve in the infantry, operate machine guns, drive tanks, and fly bombers. Women also served as saboteurs, snipers, spies, and double-agents in partisan units in occupied regions. Most women, however, served in support roles, as political officers, communication specialists, transportation workers, or as nurses and doctors. Forty-one percent of physicians at the front were women. In fact, most women who ended up in combat roles had managed to get to the front in other capacities and became fighters out of necessity. Over the course of the war more than 100,000 women were given military decorations.

Since more than eight million men were drafted, the burden of labor on the farm and in factories fell increasingly to women. Women made up 57 percent of the non-agricultural labor force, including 90 percent of workers in light industry and 41 percent of coal miners. Women had the opportunity to take jobs (such as mechanics, technicians, and accountants) that had previously been monopolized by men. In addition, women achieved upward mobility as they acquired greater skills and moved into managerial positions. Women also dominated agricultural labor, making up 80 percent of collective farm workers. Work on collective farms became even more difficult. Since tractor factories were converted to the production of tanks, and horses were needed for the military, women actually had to pull plows by hand in many cases.

The war had devastating effects on the family: The marriage rate and birthrate declined, and there were millions of orphans. In 1944, a new marriage law was implemented that attempted to raise the birthrate. Divorces were made prohibitively expensive, bachelors were required to pay extra taxes, financial aid was given to unmarried mothers (in addition to the monthly stipend paid to all mothers), and cash premiums were paid for the birth of each child after the first two. The payments increased with the number of children in the family; for her tenth child a women was awarded five thousand rubles. Medals were also issued for mothers of large families. A women with seven or more living children earned the award "Hero Mother of the Soviet Union." The law had little effect, while the war lasted, however; the birthrate did not rise until after the war ended and the economy improved.

In the postwar period, women's lives continued to be difficult. Returning veterans were favored for employment, and many women were demoted. (They were not fired, however, and the number of women workers continued to rise.) In addition, while about seven million women had died during the war, some twenty million men had died, leaving far fewer men than women of marriageable age. This was a social calamity for women who had been raised to believe that a woman's natural function, and most important role, was that of wife and mother. At least one-third of women could not hope to marry. Many single women managed to get pregnant (there was no risk to men, since the 1944 marriage law made it impossible for women to sue for paternity), but the life of a single mother, even with monthly payments from the government, was difficult. Finally, public opinion effectively denied women war heroes the satisfaction of participating in public celebrations of the great victory over Nazi Germany. Women who had fought at the front were thought to have been either sexually promiscuous or to have become masculine, so most female soldiers kept their war records secret.

ECONOMIC AND SOCIAL TRENDS

The war devastated Soviet society. The total population of the USSR declined from 194 million in 1939 to 178 million in 1950. Approximately 27 million died as a result of the war, including 8 million soldiers who died in battle, 9 million civilians who were killed by military actions, 2 million Jews killed by Nazi extermination units, and 8 million more whose lives were shortened by malnutrition, disease, and starvation. In the course of the war, cities were devastated, and 1,700 towns and 70,000 villages were destroyed. The war left 25 million people homeless. In addition, 31,000 factories were destroyed, including 80 percent of the industrial base of Ukraine, Belarus, and western Russia. At the end of the war, industrial output had fallen to 75 percent of prewar levels and agricultural production had fallen to 60 percent.

Life in cities in the post-war period was miserable. The acute lack of housing meant severe overcrowding. Apartments intended for single families were turned into communal living quarters, each room often containing more than one family. The Soviet leaders preferred to rebuild government buildings rather than apartments, and the housing crisis lasted for many years. Food was both rationed and very expensive until 1947 when rationing ended and prices began slowly to fall. Soviet leaders continued the pre-war emphasis on heavy industry, and consumer goods were in short supply. There was a gradual increase in wages, but labor continued to be highly regimented. During the war, tardiness was made a criminal offense and workers had to obtain permission to change jobs.

Despite the increased workload for the agricultural population in the war years, farmers had actually prospered. In order to foster maximum production, the state had allowed farmers to expand their private plots at the expense of collective farmland and to sell their produce at market prices. These policies had been so successful that some within the government proposed a permanent reversion to a NEP system after the war. Stalin and the Communist leadership disagreed, however, and in 1946, the government mounted an assault on the private farm economy. Farmers were forced to return to the collective all land in excess of the small private plots that had been allowed in the 1930s.

In addition, farmers were exploited financially. Taxes were raised on private plots, and a currency reform was implemented that wiped out farmers' savings. New rubles were exchanged for old at the rate of one to ten. Savings accounts up to 3,000 rubles were exchanged on a one-to-one ratio, but peasants mistrusted banks and generally kept their savings in cash, and as a result, the currency exchange expropriated 90 percent of their wealth. In addition, prices on agricultural products were brought under state control once again and were cut often below production cost. Low prices, combined with rising taxes, caused extreme poverty in the countryside. By 1948, farmers were earning only half the income they had earned in 1929.

Women continued to make up most of the agricultural labor force. Not only had a disproportionate number of men died in the war, but demobilized soldiers preferred to live in cities rather than return to the farm. Even after the government required ex-soldiers to return to their pre-war residence, veterans ignored the law, and factory managers, anxious for workers, overlooked the absence of proper documentation. Collective farmers also escaped to cities whenever they could. Between 1939 and 1959, the proportion of agricultural workers fell from 61 to 56 percent of the population.

PEOPLES OF THE USSR

In the first months of the war, in accordance with the Nazi-Soviet pact, the Soviet Union had invaded and occupied eastern Poland, Bessarabia, and the Baltic nations of Lithuania, Latvia, and Estonia. The NKVD then rounded up 900,000 people it considered politically dangerous and sent them to Russian labor camps. In Poland, about 20,000 Polish army officers were shot, more than 4,000 in the Katyn Forest massacre. In 1941, the invading German army had driven Soviet forces from all these regions, but in 1944, the Red Army and Soviet rule returned. Ultimately, Bessarabia, Estonia, Latvia, and Lithuania, were incorporated into the Soviet Union as Soviet Socialist Republics (Bessarabia was renamed Moldavia, and is now known as Moldova). The Soviet regime encouraged Russians and non-Balts to move to the Baltic nations in an attempt to make them less homogenous and to attempt to counter nationalism.

Western Ukrainians had actually welcomed the Germans. They hated collectivization, they blamed Stalin for the terrible famine of 1932 to 1934, and they thought that the war might give them independence. It turned out, however, that Nazi rulers were not preferable to Communists. German soldiers were taught that Slavs were subhuman, and they were not punished for crimes against civilians. Nazi administrators did not disband collective farms but used them to collect even more grain than the Soviets had demanded. Ukrainians were used as slave labor and lived in semi-starvation. Some Ukrainians continued to support the Nazis, and Andrei Vlasov, a former Red Army general volunteered to lead Ukrainian prisoners of war against the Soviet Union. However, many Ukrainian patriots joined the partisan resistance movement in occupied territory. Some worked with the Red Army, others in western Ukraine were simply anti-Nazi. After the war, excessive grain collection led to yet another famine beginning in 1946. In western Ukraine, a national liberation army of 90,000 partisans that had formed to fight the Germans continued to exist after the war and to resist the return of Soviet Rule. It was not suppressed until the late 1940s, when the partisans were executed or imprisoned and approximately 200,000 suspected sympathizers were deported to the east.

The Soviet regime doubted the loyalty of many of the Soviet peoples and feared they would collaborate with the invading Germans. Approximately 400,000 Volga Germans and 1,000,000 Crimean Tatars and Caucasian peoples (Chechens, Ingush, Kalmyks, Meskhetians, etc.) were forcibly relocated to Siberia, Kazakhstan, and Central Asia. These wartime deportations had a drastic effect on the ethnic composition of Kazakhstan; the Kazakhs became a minority in their own republic.

During and after the war, the Soviet government made a number of well-publicized gestures toward Soviet Jews. When evacuating Soviet citizens from the west to safety in the east, Jews were given priority. (Despite this, the Nazis still managed to kill 2.2 million of the total 5.2 million Soviet Jews.) In 1947, Andrei Gromyko, the Soviet delegate to the UN, supported the creation of the State of Israel, and the USSR was one of the first countries to recognize Israel after its declaration of independence in 1948. After the war, the idea of a Jewish homeland in Birobidzhan was revived, and for a time one-third of the population was Jewish.

Jews had proved themselves to be loyal and patriotic citizens. Half a million Jews served in the army, and probably a greater percentage of Jews died than any other nationality. Nevertheless, the rise of chauvinism and xenophobia after the war was accompanied by an increase in anti-Semitism. Rumors were spread that Jews had avoided military service and even collaborated with the Germans. Andrei Zhdanov's campaign against "rootless cosmopolitans" had anti-Semitic as well as anti-foreign overtones. Furthermore, after Israel chose to align itself with the United States and global capitalism, the Soviet regime began to attack Zionism. Anti-Zionism became a surrogate for anti-Semitism.

CONCLUSION

From the time of the German invasion until the end of his life, Stalin seems to have been highly revered by Soviet citizens. He had become a symbol of Soviet power and an object of patriotic pride. Among the highest circle of Communist Party leaders, however, Stalin caused high anxiety. In August 1948, Zhdanov unexpectedly died, and the Leningrad party organization, which had been his base of support, was purged. Lavrentii Beria's position was weakened by the division of the NKVD into the MGB (Ministry of State Security, the security police) and the MVD (Ministry of Internal Affair, in charge of the regular police and the prison system). Beria headed the latter and lost control over the security police. Viacheslav Molotov, once Stalin's closest associate, was no longer invited to Stalin's dacha, and his colleagues thought his days were numbered. At a party congress in 1952, Stalin dissolved the Politburo and Orgburo and created a Presidium which included the ten old members of the politburo, but added twenty-six new members, all expected to be subservient to Stalin. In January 1953, it was announced that a "Doctor's Plot" had been discovered in which nine doctors (six of whom had Jewish-sounding names) were accused of poisoning Zhdanov as part of a foreign conspiracy against the Soviet state. Parallels with the beginning of the purges of the 1930s were obvious.

On March 1, however, before a purge could begin, Stalin was incapacitated by the first of a series of strokes. He died on March 5. The general Soviet population showed real grief at Stalin's death, but Communist party leaders must have had very mixed emotions. They would have been relieved that the anticipated purge did not occur, but also anxious about a possibly dangerous competition for power. Would a new Stalin appear?

_____ TEXT DOCUMENTS _____

Metropolitan Sergii, "Letter to Shepherds and Flock"

On June 22, 1941, the day the German army invaded the Soviet Union, Sergii, Metropolitan of Moscow (later Patriarch of all Russia), addressed this message to the Orthodox community.

- In what terms does Sergii appeal to Orthodox believers?
- What is his attitude toward to the Soviet regime?
- To whom is this likely to appeal?

In recent years we who live in Russia have consoled ourselves with the hope that the conflagration of war, which has enveloped nearly the whole world, would not touch our country. But fascism, which recognizes the law only of naked force and is accustomed to desecrate the high demands of honor and morals, has turned out to be true to itself. The fascist robbers have fallen on our motherland. Trampling on all agreements and promises, they suddenly attacked us, and the blood of peaceful citizens has already watered the soil of our motherland. The times of Batu, the Teutonic Knights, Karl the Swede, and Napoleon are repeating themselves. The wretched offspring of the enemies of Orthodox Christianity want yet again to attempt, by the use of naked force, to put our people on their knees before falsehood, compelling our people to sacrifice for the well-being and unity of the country in a bloody testament to their love for the fatherland.

This is not the first time that the Russian people have gone through such ordeals. With God's help this time, as well, it will blow away as dust the power of the fascist enemies. Our ancestors did not give up heart in the worst situations because they thought not of personal dangers and benefits but of their sacred obligation to motherland and faith, and they came through as victors. We Orthodox will not now disgrace their glorious name; they are our brothers and sisters in flesh and in faith. The fatherland will be defended with arms and by the heroism of the whole people, by the general readiness of all who are able to serve the fatherland in this difficult hour of trial. This is a matter for workers, peasants, the learned, women and men, young and old. Each can and must devote to the general heroic struggle his or her own portion of labor, care, and skill.

Let us remember the holy leaders of the Russian people, for example Alexander Nevskii and Dmitrii Donskoi, who put their hearts in service of the people and of the motherland. Not only leaders did this. Let us remember the innumerable thousands of ordinary Orthodox warriors with unknown names whom the Russian people have immortalized in their glorious legends . . .

Our Orthodox Church always shared the fate of the people. It endured their ordeals and took joy in their successes. It will not abandon its people today. It blesses with heavenly bene-

Source: *Russkaia pravoslavnaia tserkov' i velikaia otechestvennaia voina; sbornik tserkovnykh dokumentov* (Moscow: 1-ia Obraztsovaia tipografiia Ogiza, 1944), 3–5. Translated by the author.

diction the coming heroic exploit of all the people. We must all remember the precept of Christ: "Greater love hath no man than this, that he lay down his life for his friends." They lay down their lives not only those who will die on the field of battle but also those who sacrifice their health or their possessions for the sake of their motherland. It would be unworthy of us shepherds of the Church, at this time when the fatherland summons all to heroism, silently to look out on all that is going on around us, and to fail to encourage the faint-hearted, console the afflicted, and to remind those who hesitate of their duty and of the will of God. Above all, the silence of the pastorate and a lack of connection to the suffering of the flock, would seem to confirm the cunning hints about possible benefits on the other side of the border. This would be a direct betrayal of the motherland and of our pastoral duty, inasmuch as the Church needs a pastorate that truly serves "for the sake of Jesus and not for the sake of a morsel of bread," as expressed by the prelate Dmitrii Rostovskii. We put our hearts together with our flock. Countless thousands of our Orthodox warriors have taken the part of selflessness, laying down their lives for the motherland and the faith, whenever enemies have invaded our country. They were not thinking of glory but only that their motherland needed sacrifice from all quarters; they humbly sacrificed everything, including their very lives.

The Church of Christ gives it blessing to all Orthodox for the defense of the sacred borders of our motherland.

God give us victory.

[Signed] The humble Sergii, Patriarch *locum tenens* and Metropolitan of Moscow and Kolomna.

Aleksandr Fadeev, "Children"

One of the ways Russian writers contributed to the war effort was to serve as war correspondents. Fadeev (1901–1956) was one of the pioneers of Socialist Realism, writing several novels of the Civil War in the 1920s, of which The Rout *is most famous. He won the Stalin Prize during the war for a novel about partisan resistance to the Nazi occupation of Ukraine. He submitted this newspaper dispatch from Leningrad during the seige.*

- What does this reveal about the seige of Leningrad?
- How does this work to shape Russian attitudes toward the war?
- What is its gender message?

Leningraders and particularly Leningrad women can be proud of the fact that under blockade conditions they saved the children. . . .

Leningrad founded a wide network of children's homes, to which the starving city gave the best of what it had. . . . In April, when I first saw Leningrad's children, they had already come out of the most difficult period of their lives, but the stamp of the difficult winter still lay on their faces and showed in their games. It showed in the way so many children played alone and in the way the children played even group games in silence, with serious faces. I saw children's faces so full of adult seriousness, I saw children's eyes so full of thought and sorrow that those faces and those eyes could say more than all the stories of the horror of starvation.

In July there were not many such children left, mostly orphans whose parents had recently died. The great majority of the children seemed completely healthy, and in their behavior, games, laughter, and merriment they did not differ from any other normal children.

This was the result of the great and holy work of Leningrad women, many of whom volunteered their energy and time to save and bring up the children. The average Leningrad woman displayed so much maternal love and self-sacrifice that we can only bow before the magnificence of her exploit. . . .

I will let one of them speak:

On February 24, 1942, in the severe conditions of blockaded Leningrad our preschool children's home No. 38 of the Kuibyshev Region began its existence. We have one hundred children. Recently, very recently, we saw sad, stooped children. All of them huddled close to the stove and like fledglings tucked their heads into their shoulders and collars, the sleeves of their robes dangling past their wrists, crying and struggling for space by the stove. The children could sit silently for hours at a time. Our work plan the first day was unsuccessful. The children were irritated by music, they didn't need it. The children were also irritated by adult smiles. This was made clear to us by Lerochka, seven. When a teacher asked her why she was so glum, Lerochka replied: "And why are you smiling?" Lerochka stood by the stove, hugging it with her tummy, chest and face, stopping her ears with her hands. She did

---

Source: S. Krasilshchik, *World War II: Dispatches from the Soviet Front* (New York: Sphinx Press, 1985), 78–84. Reprinted by permission of International Universities Press, Inc.

not want to hear the music. The music interrupted her thoughts. We were convinced that we had not thought things through: our whole approach, the music, the new toys—it all made things worse for the children.

The sharp general decline was expressed not only in physical manifestations, but in their whole psychological activity; everything upset them, everything was difficult. Can't tie the robe, makes a face. Has to move a chair—sudden tears. Kolya picks up a chair and wants to move it, but Vitya, standing by the table, is in his way. Kolya pushes the table onto his feet. Vitya starts to cry. Kolya sees his tears, but they don't move him. He's crying himself. It was hard for him to move the chair and it was just as hard for him to speak. . . .

Children in the young and middle groups express all their requests and demands in tears, tantrums, and whining, as if they had never learned to speak. . . .

[Several accounts of children are omitted.]

Here is a wonderful boy, called Erik. Children and adults love him for his exceptional gentleness, which he shows to everyone. But Erik does not like any studies or activities. He says: "I just don't feel like it," or "I don't feel well." Taciturn, he often stands by the window or goes out on the balcony. His eyes immediately fasten onto the house opposite from where he was brought to us and where he lost his mother. One day during nap time Erik hides under the covers and cries. The teacher is worried that he is sick, but Erik explains: "I remembered how our mama died, I feel sorry for her, she went for bread early in the morning and didn't come back all day until nighttime, and it was cold in the house. My brother and I lay in bed, we kept listening for mama to come. Whenever a door slammed, we thought it was mama. It got dark, and mama didn't come, and when she did, she fell on the floor. I ran through the house to get water and I gave her the water, but she wouldn't drink. I dragged her up on the bed, she was very heavy, and then the neighbors said she was dead. I was so afraid, but I didn't cry, and now I can't help it, I feel so sorry for her."

This official report by the head of children's home No. 38 is one of those great and horrible bills that our people should present, and will present, to the enemy.

The shame of the crime against the life, happiness, and souls of our children must lie for centuries as a curse on the heads of the killers. All the vile animal lives of all those Hitlers and Goerings and hundreds of thousands and millions of Germans, who were perverted by them and brought by them to the last degree of degeneracy and bestiality, are not worth a single tear of our children. For each tear they must pay and will pay with rivers of their black blood.

And the memory of humanity will retain forever the beautiful and majestic image of the Leningrad woman and mother as symbol of the great and immortal universal love that will reign—and the time will come!—over the whole world.

Ilia Erenburg, "Three Years"

Erenberg (1891–1967) joined the Bolshevik faction in 1906 and after several arrests, fled to Europe. He turned from politics to poetry, literature, and journalism, and spent most of his time in Europe until after the Second World War. He served as a war correspondent in the First World War, the Spanish Civil War, and the Second World War. This dispatch is dated June 20, 1944.

- What messages is Erenburg sending to the Soviet Union? Germany? the West?

One would think that we would be exhausted by three years of bloody war, but even in the most brilliant eras, when Voltaire flattered Catherine or when Napoleon fell under Russian pikes, even then Russia did not seem as strong to the world as it does now. Three years have changed many things. We were the first soldiers of the Resistance, and we will be the first blacksmiths of victory.

This victory did not come easy. We paid for it with the blood of our best. We had denied ourselves many things for our children. We had thought that their lot would be happiness. Their lot was terrible battles.

We built our country with the sweat of our brow. We were proud of our cities. Our life was not worn in yet, like a new apartment, it smelled of plaster, glue, and lacquer. The Germans turned to ashes the labor of a generation. They called the "desert zone" the "highest achievement of German military genius."

They took away our reliquaries. They took care of the house where Leo Tolstoy lived in Yasnaya Polyana. They turned it into a stable. They set up a pesticide chamber in the Tsarskoe Selo Museum. They made glasses and ashtrays from the gold of the Novgorod Kremlin. They stole our trust and kindness. They forced the most peaceful of men to bless weapons. We have become wise and that wisdom is as heavy as a rock. . . .

In 1940 the British could staunchly expect invasion: they knew they were defending their island, their rights, their freedom. When the Germans reached the Volga, we did not despair: we were defending Russian soil and the Soviet state. The Germans cannot have that high consciousness that permits you to remain cheerful even in disaster. No one attacked Germany. We are coming to them as plaintiffs and judges. You cannot be an ascetic with a skeleton key in your pocket and children's blood on your hands. Germany was strong while it was conquering, her children grew to make raids. But Hitler is mistaken to depend on the spiritual strength of unsuccessful highwaymen.

A year ago the Germans still did not understand the full meaning of Stalingrad. They were preparing to attack the Kursk arc. They thought they would win with their Tigers and Panthers. That attack did not last long and it was Germany's last attack. Now the Germans try to guess grimly: where will the next blow come? Our offensive near Vyborg and our victory there were yet one more reminder that the time of decisive stormings had come.

Source: S. Krasilshchik, *World War II: Dispatches from the Soviet Front* (New York: Sphinx Press, 1985), 265–270. Reprinted by permission of International Universities Press, Inc.

Three years of war on our front have prepared the way for Allied operations in Normandy. American correspondents remark in surprise that there are teenagers and elderly men among the German prisoners. That is not because the Germans did not give birth to sons twenty-five years ago. That is because the twenty-five-year-old Germans were killed in Russia. Now nothing will save Germany from being surrounded. French partisans are destroying the occupiers. In Italy the Germans are beginning to resemble Italians in their ability to be captured and in their ability to run. This is only the beginning, but how close this beginning is to the end!

I'm not saying that the resolution will be simple. We are not dealing with an abstract German race, but with a fully real multimillion band of killers. . . . We are dealing with fascists held on bail. They are looking for a loophole. They want to play a draw. They dream of putting off the match by twenty years. They will fight back ferociously, and the final "quarter hour" will be a heavy one. But nevertheless we will be in Berlin: that was determined on June 22, 1941, at the very minute that the Germans attacked us.

We are led there by righteous anger. Our land had seen invaders before. Peter drank to the vanquished Swedes. Russians entered Paris and played with the children of Napoleon's soldiers. Can the Nazis be compared to Karl's Swedes or Bonaparte's Frenchmen? The Germans performed their inhuman deeds with forethought, calm, and precision—to clear Russians out of Russia, to demonstrate their racial superiority, to amuse themselves. It is possible to forgive a live man, but not a robot, a master of gas chambers. You can forgive for yourself, but not for the children. In Mariupol on October 20, 1941, the Germans led several thousand residents to be executed. The victims were ordered to undress. Tiny Vladya, who did not know what awaited him, shouted: "Mama, are we going swimming?" Who would dare forgive them for Vladya?

The Germans set up a stable at the Simeizsky Observatory and soldiers used the platform where astronomers studied the movements of the heavenly bodies for a toilet.

We do not want to smash the telescopes of Jena. We do not want to burn down Goethe's house. We do not want to smear prussic acid on German children's lips. We want to put a straitjacket on Germany. We want to come to them so that they never again come to us. In that way we will save not only Russian children and the Soviet Union, but all humanity.

My country has suffered for three years. . . . I don't know what the weather will be on the day we enter Berlin—hot, rainy, or chilly, but I do know that as we walk along the dreary, barracks-like streets of the German capital, each of us will recall the June morning and a life chopped in half. Raising the sword over Germany's head, we will say: Never again!

Family Law of July 8, 1944

A new family law was enacted late in the war. It paid cash premiums to women for the birth of each child after the first two, it raised the monthly stipend paid to mothers with young children, and it gave medals to the mothers of particularly large families. It also changed the laws regarding divorce.

- Compare this with the marriage and family laws of 1918.
- How do you explain the differences? How might they be connected with the war?

19. To establish that only registered marriage produces the rights and obligations of husband and wife laid down in the Code of Laws on Marriage, Family and Guardianship of the Union Republics. Persons having *defacto* matrimonial relations before the publication of the present Decree may formally establish their relationship by registering their marriage, indicating the period they have in fact been living together.

20. To abolish the existing right of a mother to appeal to the court with a demand for the establishment of paternity and obtaining alimony for the support of a child, born of a person with whom she is not living in registered marriage.

21. To establish that, when registering with the offices which register births, deaths and marriages the birth of a child by a mother whose marriage is not registered, the child is registered in the mother's surname, the patronymic to be given according to the wishes of the mother.

24. In bringing a court action for dissolution of a marriage, the following conditions to be compulsorily observed:

    a. Presentation to the People's Court of a notice of the desire to dissolve the marriage, indicating the motives for the dissolution, and also the surname, name, patronymic, year of birth, and place of residence of the husband or wife. Upon presentation of the notice for the dissolution of the marriage, 100 rubles is payable.

    b. The husband or wife to be summoned into court to become acquainted with the divorce statement of the wife or husband, and for the preliminary establishment of the motives of the divorce, and also for the establishment of witnesses to be summoned to court for examination.

    c. Publication in the local newspaper of the notice on the bringing of a court action for dissolution of marriage, the cost of publishing the notice to be borne by the husband or wife who gives notice of dissolution of marriage.

25. The People's Court is obliged to establish the motives for notice of dissolution of marriage and take measures to reconcile the husband and wife, to which end both the divorcing parties must absolutely be summoned, and, where necessary, witnesses. . . .

Source: Rudolf Schlesinger, Ed., *The Family in the U.S.S.R. Documents and Readings* (London: Routledge, 1949, 1998), 373–375. Reprinted with permission of Taylor and Francis Books Ltd.

27. On the basis of the decision of the Court, the office for registering births, deaths and marriages writes out a certificate of dissolution of marriage, on the basis of which an entry concerning the divorce is made in the passport of husband and wife and, by decision of the Court, from 500 to 2,000 rubles is charged to one or to each party.

Figure 18-1 Poster, "The Motherland Calls"

Iraklii Toidze (b. 1902), a Georgian artist, painted what is probably the most famous Soviet poster from World War II, in 1941.

- To what emotions and traditions does this appeal?
- What does it indicate about Soviet society during the war?

Source: N. I. Baburina, *Rossiia 20vek: Istoriia Strany vplacate* (Moscow: Panorama, 2000), 130.

Figure 18-2 Fighting in Stalingrad

- What does this reveal about the nature of the Battle of Stalingrad?

Source: Getty Images Inc.—Hulton Archive Photos.

Figure 18-3 Homeless Family
   This photo shows a collective farm family whose house was destroyed during the war.
- What messages does this photograph send?
- Taken with the previous photograph, what can you tell about the effect of the war on the Soviet Union?

Source: Getty Images Inc.—Hulton Archive Photos.

Figure 18-4 Moscow State University

What is now the central building of the Moscow State University campus was built between 1949 and 1953. It is thirty-six stories tall (more than eight-hundred feet) and everything about the building is massive and imposing. The building's facade is ornamented with giant statues, clocks, and Soviet insignia, and the star on the top weighs twelve tons. The foyer is lavishly decorated in green marble walls and colonnades.

- Compare this with previous examples of Russian and Soviet architecture.
- What messages are being sent by the appearance of this building?
- What does the fact that construction began in 1949 reveal about Soviet society? (What else could have been built?)

Source: Getty Images Inc.—Hulton Archive Photos

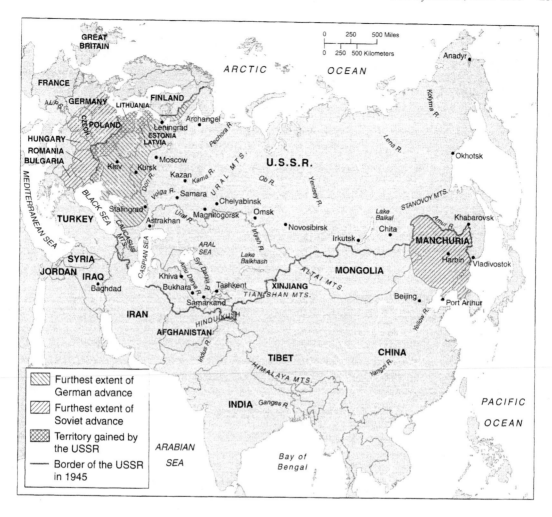

Figure 18-5 The USSR in 1945

Although the German army drove deep into the Soviet Union in World War II, by the time the war was over, the Red Army itself occupied a great deal of territory beyond its borders. The U.S.S.R. soon withdrew from Manchuria, but it exercised hegemony over Eastern Europe for the next half-century.

_____ **FOR FURTHER READING** _____

(In addition to the books by Clements, Suny, and Ulam from the previous chapter.)

Alperovitz, Gar. *Atomic Diplomacy: Hiroshima and Potsdam: The Use of the Atomic Bomb and the American Confrontation with Soviet Power,* 2nd expanded ed. London: Pluto Press, 1994.
Barber, John and Mark Harrison. *The Soviet Home Front, 1941–1945: A Social and Economic History of the USSR in World War II.* London: Longman, 1991.
Erickson, John. *The Road to Stalingrad.* London: Weidenfeld and Nicolson, 1975.
_____. *The Road to Berlin: Continuing the History of Stalin's War with Germany.* Boulder, CO: Westview Press, 1983.

Gaddis, John Lewis. *We Now Know: Rethinking Cold War History.* New York: Oxford University Press, 1997.

Mastny, Vojtech. *Russia's Road to the Cold War: Diplomacy, Warfare, and the Politics of Communism, 1941–1945.* New York: Columbia University Press, 1978.

Salisbury, Harrison E. *The 900 Days: The Siege of Leningrad.* New York: Harper & Row, 1969.

Weiner, Amir. *Making Sense of War: The Second World War and the Fate of the Bolshevik Revolution.* Princeton, NJ: Princeton University Press, 2001.

Werth, Alexander. *Russia at War, 1941–1945.* New York: Dutton, 1964.

Zubkova, Elena. *Russia after the War: Hopes, Illusions, and Disappointments, 1945–1957.* Armonk, NY: M. E. Sharpe, 1998.

CHAPTER NINETEEN

NEW EXPERIMENTS IN SOCIALISM, 1953–1964

In the first two decades of the Cold War, western social scientists, trying to make sense of the illiberal politics of fascism, Nazism, and communism, created an explanatory model they called "totalitarianism." A totalitarian regime, according to their definition, attempted to force its people to behave in accordance with a comprehensive ideology. Totalitarian societies are characterized by a single political party (made up of those who believe in the ideology), secret police, secret political trials, executions, and prison camps. The party seeks monopolistic control over all aspects of society including politics, media, education, and the economy. These social scientists assumed that such a totalitarian ideology must be contrary to human nature, since if it were "natural" it would not have to be imposed by force and fear. They concluded that a totalitarian system was incapable of reforming into a government that respected individual rights and that ruled by the consent of the governed; if a totalitarian regime loses the will to use force, they reasoned, it would be rejected by the population.

Yet, even as this model was being elaborated in the West in the 1950s, the Soviet system was proving it wrong. The Communist regime was, in fact, beginning a long and slow process of reforming and accommodating itself to the population. This was missed by many observers, in part because Stalin's successor, Nikita Khrushchev, used some of Stalin's political techniques in his own rise to power. In retrospect, however, it is evident that Khrushchev transformed the Soviet system in qualitative ways. He ended the system of terror-purges, and he began to implement the rule of law. Life in the Soviet Union in the late 1950s and 1960s was more regimented and artistic expression was more inhibited than in the West, but Soviet society was far more open and free than it had been in the Stalin era.

THE EURASIAN CONTEXT

At the end of World War II, Europe was in ruins: millions were dead, tens of millions were homeless, and the economic infrastructure had been largely reduced to rubble. The United States, unscathed by the war and with a booming economy, took over western Europe's former role of world leadership. U.S. leaders decided that the postwar world had to be rebuilt on the basis of international capitalism (that is, the free flow of goods and capital among the nations of the world) in an international system of independent, sovereign nations associated in the United Nations. In 1945, the International Monetary Fund was established to stabilize national currencies by setting fixed exchange rates based on the dollar, and the World Bank was set up to loan money for the reconstruction of Europe and the development of former colonies. GATT (the General Agreement on Tariffs and Trade) sought to eliminate protective tariffs and other restrictions on free international trade. In addition, in 1948 the Marshall Plan was put into effect, providing further financial assistance for European reconstruction. Recipients were required to balance their budgets, free prices, and open their markets to world trade.

By 1953, western Europe, thanks in large part to the Marshall Plan, had recovered from the devastation of the Second World War and was experiencing a rapid economic growth that lasted through the 1960s. The economies of western Europe combined socialism and capitalism in varying degrees. In England and Sweden, major industries were nationalized; in Germany and France, private enterprise predominated. Nevertheless, all western European governments fostered free enterprise at the grass-roots level, and all regulated the economy to some extent, both to stimulate growth and to provide a social safety-net. The governments of western Europe fit the definition of formal democracy: All adults were free to vote and to run for public office. Class lines began to weaken, and universal education contributed to social mobility. Prosperity was spread widely enough to foster a consumer society. By end of the 1960s, automobiles, television sets, and automatic washers and dryers were no longer luxuries for the few.

Western Europe's prosperity did not mean it had the resources necessary to retain its overseas empire. Colonial peoples had been through two world wars supposedly fought on behalf of democracy and freedom. They had been educated in the language of liberalism by their European masters. They were now ready to fight for independence. England had begun the process by recognizing India's independence in 1947, and, one by one, the colonial powers were forced to let go of their colonies. By the end of the 1960s, only a handful of colonies remained. Europe also lost control over world politics. International relations were now dominated by the superpower rivalry between the United States and the USSR, and western European governments accepted U.S. leadership in the Cold War.

The USSR had been involved in the initial conference at Bretton Woods, New Hampshire, at which plans for the IMF and World Bank had been worked out, but Stalin soon opted out of the new system. The United States offered the Marshall Plan to the USSR, but Stalin found the conditions incompatible with communism, and he refused to accept aid. He also refused to permit the nations of eastern Europe to benefit from U.S. aid. Consequently, eastern Europe lagged far behind the West in economic growth.

Instead, the nations of eastern Europe were required to follow the Soviet model, which emphasized heavy industry over consumer goods and collectivized agriculture over family farms. Collectivization was carried out with less violence than the Soviet Union had experienced, but it was nevertheless a process that distressed the agricultural population. As in the Soviet Union, farmers devoted far more attention to their private plots than to collective land, and economies of scale did not result. In addition, the Soviet Union's planning bureaucracy set prices for the eastern block countries; reversing the typical colonialist practice, they set low prices for manufactured goods from eastern Europe and high prices for raw materials exported from the Soviet Union. Soviet economic exploitation and military occupation of eastern Europe caused resentment and the steady rise of nationalist sentiments.

After World War II, Turkey increasingly sought to associate itself with Europe and distance itself from its former Arab provinces. Turkey joined NATO in 1951 and served as a front line in the containment of the Soviet Union. The United States had prevented Soviet expansion into eastern Turkey after the war. In 1960, U.S. military bases in Turkey were stocked with nuclear missiles aimed at the Soviet heartland. Turkey was beset with economic difficulties as well as a national separatist movement among its Kurdish population. Power ultimately rested with the military; at several points, it stepped in to remove governments it thought corrupt and to refashion the political system.

Iran had been occupied by Great Britain and the Soviet Union during the Second World War, and the Red Army lingered in the north, supporting a native communist movement. Fearing that the Soviet Union was attempting to make Iran a satellite similar to the nations of eastern Europe, the United States pressured Stalin to withdraw. The young Mohammed Reza Pahlavi ruled cautiously, respecting the rights and powers of the Majlis (parliament), until it nationalized the Anglo-Iranian Oil Company in 1951. After pressure from Great Britain, the Shah removed the prime minister, but this caused such popular unrest that the Shah was forced to flee the country. At this point, the United States, under the pretext of stopping communist subversion, sponsored a coup, which brought the Shah back. U.S. leaders then chose Iran to be a major ally in southern Asia and sent hundreds of millions of dollars of military and economic aid.

Afghanistan and India had historically contested the border that separated them, and this conflict was continued by West Pakistan after that country was created in 1947. To press its claim, Pakistan cut off shipments of oil to Afghanistan, upon which Afghanistan turned to the Soviet Union, trading Afghan wool and cotton for Soviet oil, textiles, and manufactured goods. Afghanistan also relied on Soviet air and rail transportation to reach the outside world. Close ties with the Soviet Union put pressure on the Afghan government to tolerate an Afghan Marxist party. King Muhammad Zahir Shah sought to limit Soviet influence by accepting aid from the United States and by reestablishing diplomatic and trade relations with Pakistan in 1963. As long as the border conflict continued, however, he could not break with the USSR. King Zahir promulgated a constitution in 1964, which recognized Islam as the official religion, confirmed individual equality before the law, and established an independent judiciary and an elected parliament. The King outlawed political parties but did not actively suppress them, and Afghan Marxists regularly elected a handful of delegates to the parliament.

After China's leaders adopted the Soviet model of collectivization and five-year plans in 1953, the USSR began a major program of economic and military aid to China, including the development of a facility to produce nuclear weapons. Conflict between the two countries soon arose, however. Mao felt that Khrushchev's public attack on the memory of Stalin and the "cult of personality" was an attack on himself. He also resented Khrushchev's unilateral declaration of "peaceful coexistence" with the West; he felt that he should have been consulted first, as the elder statesman of communism. Mao declared his independence of Moscow by calling for "people's wars" against imperialism and by abandoning the Soviet economic model. In 1958, Mao proposed the "Great Leap Forward," which envisioned an entirely new way of industrializing an agricultural society. Instead of building industry in cities, huge agricultural communes would be formed that would, themselves, build steel foundries and factories. Mao announced that China was on the verge of communism, a goal that Soviet leaders had postponed indefinitely.

Khrushchev was thoroughly alarmed at Mao's radicalism, and in 1959, he cut financial aid to China and withdrew Soviet scientific and technical advisers. Factories were left unfinished, including the nuclear weapons plant. The Great Leap Forward was a disastrous failure, which actually set back China's economic development, and Mao's opponents forced a return to a moderate, Soviet-style approach to economic development. In the middle of the sixties, however, in a bid to remove his enemies, Mao initiated the "Great Proletarian Cultural Revolution" which amounted to a civil war between young and old generations of Communists. By the time Mao brought the movement to an end in 1969, he had established himself as a cult figure, but he also had to permit a return to conservative (Soviet-style) economic planning.

Japan, a rival of both China and Russia since the late-nineteenth century, benefitted enormously from the Cold War. The United States had chosen Japan to be a major ally in the Cold War and had located U.S. military bases there. The United States gave Japan reconstruction grants and loans, encouraged pro-business policies, gave Japan access to world markets including its own, and permitted Japan to protect its domestic market. Japan benefitted, as well, from the U.S. purchase of billions of dollars' worth of supplies during the Korean and Vietnamese wars.

POLITICAL DEVELOPMENTS AND FOREIGN AFFAIRS

Immediately after Stalin's death, the most powerful figures in the Communist Party appeared to be Georgii Malenkov, Chair of the Presidium and of the Council of Ministers, Lavrentii Beria, head of the MVD, and Viacheslav Molotov, a member of the Presidium despite having fallen out of favor with Stalin. Lavrentii Beria was the first to make a bid for leadership, immediately merging the MGB back into the MVD thereby taking personal control over the police forces. Beria presented himself as a reformer: He arranged for a major amnesty program for political prisoners, and he pardoned those who had been arrested in connection with the Doctors' Plot. He also proposed that Germany should be reunited and (provided it remained neutral) that the Soviet Union should withdraw its troops.

A relative political newcomer, Nikita Khrushchev, who had been promoted to the Presidium in Stalin's last years, was able to convince Malenkov and other party leaders that Beria was a threat: the MVD was independent of the Party bureaucracy, and Beria, therefore, could easily destroy his enemies. A conspiracy to remove Beria from power was formed; Marshal Zhukov and other generals were brought in to circumvent and, if necessary, to control the MVD. In July 1953, at a joint meeting of the Presidium, Council of Ministers, and General Staff, Beria was denounced and arrested. Under the cover of darkness he was spirited out of the Kremlin past his MVD guards and placed in prison. He was executed in December. Although no one could have known it at the time, this would be the last time execution was used to remove a Soviet leader from office.

Now Malenkov and Khrushchev began to compete for the allegiance of the Communist party. Malenkov proposed cuts in the budgets of military and heavy industry and an increase in the production of consumer goods. Khrushchev called for an increase in the military budget and for greater investment in agriculture. Khrushchev arranged for a 50 percent tax cut on collective farmers, and he sponsored a "virgin lands" program in the Volga, Urals, Siberia, and Kazakhstan to bring more land under cultivation. Grain production increased significantly, as did Khrushchev's prestige in the party. Khrushchev also benefitted from the fact that his opponents, Molotov, Kaganovich, and Malenkov, had all been close associates of Stalin during the great purges. Although he, too, had participated in the purges, Khrushchev was younger and was perceived as a follower rather than a leader. Furthermore, as head of the Secretariat, Khrushchev was able to promote his supporters to leadership positions. When the Twentieth Party Congress convened in 1956, one-third of the Congress were new members, and almost half of those had served under Khrushchev when he had been first party secretary in Ukraine.

Khrushchev also discredited his older colleagues by exposing Stalin's crimes and, by implication, theirs as well. At the Twentieth Party Congress in 1956, he asked reporters to leave and then delivered a "Secret Speech"—which was rapidly publicized around the world. In his speech, he disclosed the illegality of the terror purges after 1934. The revelation that the case against the Old Bolsheviks was a complete fabrication, and that millions of Communist party members had been forced to confess crimes they had not committed, created a sensation. (Khrushchev ignored the murder of kulaks during collectivization, the terrible famine in Ukraine, the persecution of non-Communists, and the deportation of national groups.) Khrushchev denounced the "cult of personality" that had permitted this, and called for "Leninist collective leadership." Khrushchev demoted Molotov and Kaganovich, and he arranged for more of his own supporters to be appointed to the Central Committee.

In 1957, Malenkov attempted to strike back. Khrushchev's rapid destalinization and concessions to the West (to be discussed below) had caused dissatisfaction in the Presidium, and Malenkov used this to orchestrate a vote to remove Khrushchev as head of the Secretariat. Khrushchev, however, insisted that he had been elected by the Central Committee and that it alone had the authority to remove him from office. He therefore summoned a meeting of the Central Committee (Marshal Zhukov used military aircraft to fly distant members to Moscow), which supported him. Khrushchev was then able to purge his opponents from the upper levels of the party.

However, a new era had dawned. It was notable that Malenkov and his fellow-conspirators did not have Khrushchev arrested and executed as Beria had been. In fact, their plan called only for his removal as first secretary of the party; he had been offered the position of Minister of Agriculture. In the same spirit, Khrushchev did not execute them, choosing instead to demote them. Molotov was made ambassador to Mongolia (not an insignificant appointment given Mongolia's strategic location on the border with China), Malenkov was appointed director of a cement factory, and Kaganovich became director of hydroelectric power station. Furthermore, all three kept their privileged social status and their pensions.

In 1958, Khrushchev took the post of Premier, uniting in himself the highest positions in both the government and the Party, but although Khrushchev dominated Soviet politics, he respected the political system. He submitted policy proposals for votes in the Presidium, formed coalitions, and compromised with opponents. Furthermore, Khrushchev restored what he called "socialist legality" to the party and to the country. He subordinated the KGB to the Party by appointing its leaders from the upper levels of the Communist party (instead of permitting them to rise by promotion from within the KGB, itself), and he dismantled the Stalinist system of secret military tribunals for political offenses. Khrushchev required the courts to look into past cases, and the prison camps were practically emptied; tens of thousands of political convicts were absolved of crimes and released.

Socialist legality meant that the judiciary was made independent of the police, and those arrested could only be held for a short time without being formally charged. People could no longer be accused of being an "enemy of the people" or of engaging in "counter-revolutionary activity"; they had to be charged with an actual crime. In addition, conviction depended on the presentation of evidence; the police could no longer rely on confessions extracted by torture. This did not mean that the Soviet Union became an open society with freedom of speech and political activity. "Anti-Soviet agitation," for example, remained a crime; critics of the regime could still be convicted and sent to labor camps. Nevertheless, the principle of the rule of law was established.

Khrushchev revised a number of Stalin's doctrines, including the notion that the class struggle would intensify as the final construction of socialism grew nearer. Instead, Khrushchev announced that the Soviet state represented all the people, and that there was only one class, a laboring class which included both manual and intellectual workers. Khrushchev did not, however, retreat from a firm commitment to Marxism-Leninism, which he regarded as scientific truth and the sole guide to progress. He continued to have faith in economic planning, scientific organization of labor, and the application of the factory model to agriculture. Khrushchev also exhibited Stalin's penchant for big reforms and mobilization campaigns; he talked about "catching up and surpassing" the West, and he predicted that the foundations of communism would be laid by 1980.

In the Khrushchev era, the Soviet Union faced rebellions from two of its eastern European satellites, Poland and Hungary. In Poland the head of the Communist party, a hard-line Stalinist who had brutally repressed striking workers, died in 1956, and reform-minded members of the Polish Communist Party elected Wladislaw Gomulka its leader. Gomulka was a moderate who had been imprisoned in the past as a "Titoist." He promised a "Polish road to communism," but he also assured Khrushchev that he remained committed to communism. The Polish government retained possession of large industry, finance, and economic planning, but it allowed collective farms to break up into individual farms, and it permitted a private small-scale trade and service sector. It also allowed workers' committees to play a role in factory management. In addition, the Catholic Church (in exchange for recognizing the legitimacy of the Communist state) was allowed to teach religion in the schools and to nominate deputies to the Sejm (parliament). Gomulka did not continue on this path; on the contrary, by the late 1960s he was restricting Church activity and suppressing movements among students and workers.

In Hungary, the example of Gomulka in Poland precipitated an anti-Stalinist reform movement led by Imre Nagy. The Soviet Union backed Nagy in the power struggle that ensued, but this encouraged an even more radical movement among students and intellectuals. The radicals called for an end to the secret police, the withdrawal of the Red Army, freedom of the press, and multiparty elections. Nagy, responding to the popular movement, proclaimed Hungary neutral, withdrew from the Warsaw Pact, declared a multiparty system, and proposed a coalition government. This went far beyond the Polish reforms, which were in line with the NEP and did not reject communism. Khrushchev would not accept the situation, and in November 1956 he sent the Red Army to subordinate the Party and reimpose communism. As many as twenty thousand Hungarians and seven thousand Soviet soldiers may have been killed in the struggle that followed; in the end, the Soviet Union prevailed.

In regard to western Europe, Khrushchev was conciliatory. In 1955, he established diplomatic relations with West Germany, and, in July of that year, at a summit conference with the United States, Great Britain, and France in Geneva, he talked of the possibility of "peaceful coexistence" of capitalism and communism. He established friendly relations with Yugoslavia, returned a port to Finland, and surrendered territorial claims in Turkey. Most importantly, he withdrew the Red Army from the eastern half of Austria on condition that Austria declare itself neutral and not become a member of NATO.

Nevertheless, the Cold War continued. In 1955, a remilitarized West Germany joined NATO, and in response Khrushchev created the Warsaw Pact, a defensive military alliance among the communist nations of eastern Europe. Both the United States and the USSR had developed hydrogen bombs (the United States in 1952 and the Soviet Union in 1953), and by 1955, the United States had more than two thousand nuclear bombs and had begun to build

B-52 bombers capable of striking the Soviet Union from bases in the United States. The Soviet Union chose to develop intercontinental ballistic missiles (ICBMs), and tested its first in 1957. By 1962, Soviet missiles were aimed at targets in the United States, but only four of them could reach targets in the United States. Meanwhile, the United States had expanded its bomber fleet and developed ICBMs of its own, both land- and submarine-based.

The greatest threat to the Soviet Union, however, was not long-range ballistic missiles on U.S. soil, but medium-rage missiles deployed in Europe. In 1954, the United States installed tactical nuclear weapons in Germany, and by 1957, the Soviet Union had followed suit. Then, in the late 1950s, the United States installed nuclear missiles in Turkey that could reach the cities of the European USSR. The Cold War intensified in 1960, when a U.S. U-2 spy plane was shot down over Soviet territory, and again in 1961, when the Soviet Union built a cement wall on the dividing line between East and West Berlin in order to prevent defections. This "Berlin Wall" immediately became a symbol of the Cold War.

In an attempt to counter the threat from U.S. missiles in Turkey, Khrushchev decided to install similar missiles in Cuba. In 1959, Fidel Castro had led a popular revolution against the dictatorship of Fulgencio Batista, and the following year, after the United States denounced the Cuban revolution and refused to recognize the new government, Castro became a Communist. A failed CIA-backed invasion of Cuba in 1961 convinced Castro that he needed protection from further U.S. attacks, and in August 1962, the Soviet Union began to install nuclear missiles in Cuba. President John F. Kennedy and his administration decided that it could not permit these missiles to remain, and in October Kennedy presented Khrushchev with an ultimatum: remove the missiles or face a nuclear attack. Khrushchev backed down, and agreed to dismantle the missile system. Kennedy, for his part, made a public promise not to invade Cuba and a secret promise to remove U.S. missiles from Turkey.

CULTURE AND RELIGION

In the first half of the Khrushchev era, the Russian Orthodox Church continued to expand, but Khrushchev was laying the groundwork for an attack. Articles in the press declared that religion would not wither away as communism drew nearer but would have to be combated through education; in 1957, courses in scientific atheism were made a part of the required curriculum in schools and universities. Then in 1959, Orthodox parishes were reorganized; the parish priest was limited to performing religious services, while the administration of other church affairs was put in the hands of an elected committee subordinated to the local soviet. The religious laws of 1929 were reinstituted, depriving the church of corporate existence and treating priests as profit-making entrepreneurs. Even the sale of candles was made illegal. The only way a priest could maintain his church was by concealing income, and this provided a convenient pretext for the state to arrest priests and close churches.

The Soviet regime fought the war against the Church on a number of fronts. It imposed such heavy taxes on monasteries that the number fell precipitously (from ninety in the mid-fifties to fewer than twenty in the mid-sixties). Parish churches were harassed to such an extent that only eight thousand remained in 1965 (down from twenty thousand to twenty-five thousand in 1958). Five of eight seminaries were closed; seminary students and monastery novitiates were persecuted, many by being drafted into the army. Holding unauthorized church services was made a crime punishable by five years in a labor camp, and children of those who attended church were often sent to boarding schools or forced to join the Young Pioneers or Komsomol (Communist youth organization).

Khrushchev took a populist approach to education. He eliminated fees for high schools and universities and gave students stipends to cover living expenses. In an effort to promote practical labor-oriented education, high schools were required to be associated with factories, in which students were expected to work part-time, and Khrushchev pushed for the creation of polytechnic secondary schools in which students would learn an industrial skill as a part of their academic program. Khrushchev encouraged students to spend two years as manual laborers in between high school and university by requiring universities to reserve sixty percent of their admissions to students who had done so. Parents in the white-collar elite did not want their children subjected to these requirements, and Khrushchev made concessions to this interest group by permitting the establishment of special schools in foreign languages, mathematics, and science for qualified students.

Most people affected by these reforms opposed them. Neither students nor their parents wanted the extra work requirements, it was difficult for school administrators to find factories to associate with, and factory managers found student labor inefficient and pointless. Furthermore, the reforms did not work. The number of skilled workers did not increase, and universities remained the preserves of children from well-to-do, white-collar families.

Immediately after Stalin's death, Soviet literature, under the leadership of the poet Aleksandr Tvardovskii, editor of the journal *Novyi Mir (New World)*, began to violate the prescriptions of Socialist Realism. In 1953, Vladimir Soloukhin wrote a series of articles, later published under the title *Country Roads of Vladimir*, which described a hiking trip through the countryside. Soloukhin celebrated Russia's native culture, old churches, religious art, and pre-Petrine literature. The following year Fedor Abramov published an article calling for truthful and un-idealized portrayals of the Russian countryside, implying an end to Socialist Realism (since the Soviet system had been a disaster for the countryside). These two writers inspired a movement known as the "village prose" writers (*derevenshchiki*).

In 1954, Ilia Erenburg's novel *The Thaw* (serialized in *Novyi Mir*), describing a society in which living conditions were poor and progress was inhibited by authoritarian factory directors and conforming artists, implied that only the reemergence of human creativity and spontaneity could make progress possible. "The Thaw" came to refer to greater freedom of expression, but it was not immediately embraced by the Communist party. Aleksandr Tvardovskii was fired, and a more conservative line was imposed.

Nevertheless, in 1956 the new editors of *Novyi Mir* published *Not by Bread Alone* by Vladimir Dudintsev, written in the style of a typical Socialist Realist production novel, except that the hero was a lone scientist opposed by complacent and venal managers and party officials. The villains of the novel were presented not as exceptions but as typical of the system, and Dudintsev implied that the Soviet System was in need of fundamental reform. Dudintsev was severely criticized by those who held to the party line, but Khrushchev supported Dudintsev and used *Not by Bread Alone* to criticize Stalinism. In 1958, Khrushchev signaled his willingness for the Thaw to continue by reinstating Aleksandr Tvardovskii as editor of *Novyi Mir*.

The Thaw did not extend to writers who were critical of the Soviet experiment in general, as Boris Pasternak discovered when he attempted to publish his novel, *Dr. Zhivago*. Pasternak's novel dealt with the relation of the intelligentsia to the revolution and presented the revolution, civil war, the rise of Stalin realistically and unsentimentally. In 1955, *Novyi Mir* and two other publishers turned it down, and the following year Pasternak gave it to an Italian publisher to read. When it was published in the West, without Pasternak's permission, *Dr. Zhivago* became an international best-seller, and in 1958, it was awarded the Nobel Prize for literature. The Soviet establishment bitterly criticized the novel and condemned the award and did not allow Pasternak to leave to accept the prize.

Pasternak became a symbol of freedom of thought within the Soviet Union, and *Dr. Zhivago* was one of the first examples of *samizdat* (self-publication), in that literature that could not be published was typed, circulated, and re-typed by individuals. In addition, his death in 1960 provided Soviet society the opportunity to register its opposition to Soviet repression of free thought and speech. The pallbearers and the funeral attendees ignored government plans for an official procession and carried his casket across fields to the cemetery. No speeches critical of the regime were given, but the protest was clear.

The most famous and influential of the works produced during the Thaw was the story "One Day in the Life of Ivan Denisovich" by Aleksandr Solzhenitsyn. Solzhenitsyn had been arrested during the Second World War for anti-Soviet activities (he had written a letter to a friend criticizing Stalin and advocating changes in Soviet government), and he had spent eight years in prisons and labor camps. "One Day in the Life of Ivan Denisovich" was a straightforward and unsensational description of a normal day in a labor camp that exposed the injustice of the legal system and the inhumanity and brutality of the camps. Aleksandr Tvardovskii recognized Solzhenitsyn's story as a work of art, but he was afraid to publish it without the approval of the party. It was ultimately referred to Khrushchev who read it and welcomed it as another useful work in combating Stalinism. Solzhenitsyn's story was a literary sensation, and Solzhenitsyn became a celebrity overnight.

Novyi Mir and other journals and publishing houses were quickly inundated with hundreds of prison-camp memoirs, but the regime felt that one was enough. Khrushchev saw nothing more to be gained politically by dwelling on the past. Solzhenitsyn himself had plenty more prison experiences he wanted to write about however, and he soon ran afoul of the regime. His *Cancer Ward* and *The First Circle* were polyphonic novels, like Dostoyevsky's, that presented many different points of view, from loyal Stalinist to outright rejection of communism. Moreover, it became clear that Solzhenitsyn did not think of the prison camps as merely an aberration associated with Stalin but as symptomatic of Soviet society. Solzhenitsyn became increasingly frustrated at his inability to publish his work, and he began to disseminate his novels through samizdat. In 1963, he was permitted to publish a short story, "Matrena's Place," which brought to a culmination the themes of the "village prose" movement. He used an old peasant woman to symbolize the purity of Old Russia and her treatment to reveal the destructive effects of Soviet industrial society.

Ideological conformity aside, the regime also disapproved of any literature or art that was irreverent, iconoclastic, or experimental. Khrushchev's attitude toward art was quite unsophisticated, and in 1962, he made a scene at an art exhibition where he publicly abused modern artists whose work he failed to understand. Poets, regularly meeting on Mayakovsky Square to read their avant-garde works in public, were harassed by police, beaten by hooligans, and occasionally prosecuted for using drugs.

ROLES AND STATUS OF WOMEN

Khrushchev seems to have had a sincere desire to make good on communism's promise to make life better for ordinary people, and he did a great deal to improve conditions for women. Maternity leave was doubled to seven months at full pay, personal sick leave was doubled to allow workers time off to care for sick children, and it was made illegal to fire working mothers with small children. Women were also "protected from dangerous work" (in mines or on fishing boats, for example), although this deprived women of the opportunity to apply for some of the highest-paid jobs in manual labor. Khrushchev increased the numbers of cafeterias, clinics, daycare centers, and public laundries. Stalin's restrictions on marriage and reproductive rights were also relaxed. Abortion was legalized in 1955, and divorce was made easier; courts were involved in divorce proceedings only in disputed cases.

Women were also given a greater role in political life. It was required that one-third of deputies to the Supreme Soviet be women, and quotas of 30 to 40 percent were set for the appointment of women to professional organizations, party committees, and organs of the Soviet government. Valentina Tereshkova became the first female cosmonaut in 1963. Women were also given equal access to education.

Nevertheless, Khrushchev promoted the rights of women in the same way that he reformed education and encouraged literature: from the top down and according to his own political agenda. The patriarchal essence of Soviet society remained. The highest positions in government, science, management, and academia were dominated by men (with a few exceptions), and women continued to earn two-thirds as much as men. Discussion of feminism was not allowed, and despite many advertising campaigns to make Soviets better citizens and more efficient workers, little effort was made to convince husbands that they should take an equal share of housework or childcare.

ECONOMIC AND SOCIAL TRENDS

Despite Khrushchev's populism, a permanently stratified society emerged while he led the Communist party. The introduction of socialist legality and the end of periodic purges permitted Communist party members and the upper echelons of government and industry to pass their status on to their children. The Soviet system was in theory a meritocracy, but those in power were able to pull strings to secure favors for children and relatives. Moreover, as in any society in which education is the key to social mobility, the children of the affluent and educated had an automatic advantage over children from working families.

The same was true of the intelligentsia, which had grown enormously as the Soviet Union had industrialized and urbanized. By the 1950s, the intelligentsia had become self-perpetuating, dominated by those with a second-generation higher education. A highly educated elite, the Soviet intelligentsia embraced liberal values of intellectual freedom, scepticism, and cosmopolitanism, but it differed from the intelligentsia of the tsarist period because it was employed by the state and its economic well-being depended on conformity. It was not revolutionary, and its most subversive activity was to read and reproduce forbidden literature (samizdat), which included not only works by dissident Soviet writers but banned western authors, as well.

Nikita Khrushchev, himself a child of farmers, did much to improve the lives of Soviet collective farmers. He allowed farm workers to apply for passports, making it possible for them to move and change jobs. It then became necessary to raise farm incomes in order to keep farmers from leaving for the cities in droves. Prices for agricultural goods were steadily raised until by 1958 they were double what they had been immediately after the war. In addition, restrictions on the size and use of private plots were reduced, taxes were lowered, and farmers were included in the social security system. Collective farms were given more autonomy in decision making; Machine Tractor Stations were dissolved, and the farm equipment divided among the local collective farms. The state's annual capital investment in agriculture in 1964 was 74 percent higher than it had been in 1953.

Despite his good intentions, however, agriculture was also the area in which Khrushchev experienced his greatest failures. His Virgin Lands campaign appeared to be tremendously successful at first, and had been a major factor behind his popularity in the party in 1957. Unfortunately, success was largely the product of luck; the usually arid steppes of northern Kazakhstan had a higher than average rainfall in the 1950s. In the early 1960s the normally dry, windy climate returned, causing an environmental disaster. No shelter-belts of trees had been planted to prevent wind erosion of the newly plowed land, and huge dust storms carried away the topsoil. Grain production fell precipitously.

At the same time, Khrushchev was promoting corn production in the western USSR. On a visit to the United States in 1959, Khrushchev had spent time on an Iowa corn farm, where he was impressed with the great productivity of corn. When he returned home, he intensified a campaign, previously begun, to increase corn and beef production. He ordered corn to be planted everywhere, on the assumption that it could be harvested as grain in regions where the growing season was long and as silage (to be fed to livestock) where the growing season was too short to ripen the grain. Khrushchev predicted that in 1962 the USSR would outproduce the United States in meat, milk, and butter.

Khrushchev's prediction was not realized. The climate of western Russia is colder and drier than the climate of the north American heartland, and the corn harvest was a disaster. Very little corn ripened, and much of the fodder rotted or was otherwise useless for feeding cattle. Because this occurred at the same time as the Virgin Lands campaign was failing, in 1962 food was in short supply and prices had to be raised. In fact, Russia, a wheat-exporting country since the reign of Catherine the Great, was forced to buy wheat from the United States. It was greatly to Khrushchev's credit that he accepted the humiliation; in similar circumstances, Stalin had preferred to allow Soviet citizens to starve to death by the millions.

Khrushchev tried to improve the lives of workers just as he had done for farmers. He decriminalized absenteeism and permitted workers to quit their jobs and seek employment elsewhere. He limited mandatory overtime, reduced the workweek from forty-eight to forty-one hours, and made it more difficult for managers to fire workers. Wages for workers increased almost 75 percent between 1952 and 1964, and the quality of life also improved. Between 1956 to 1964 almost twenty-three million new apartments were built, providing new housing for 40 percent of the population. Khrushchev continued to instigate campaigns to increase efficiency and productivity, but they lacked the coercive and threatening atmosphere of the Stalin era. Instead of fostering a mood of combative struggle against saboteurs or slackers, Khrushchev's campaigns were characterized by a sense of common striving to apply science and technology to production.

The traditional problems of a planned economy continued. Unanticipated production problems caused bottlenecks, and factory managers overestimated requirements and hoarded unused materials. Output goals were usually given without regard to quality, but because of the severe shortage of consumer goods, all goods produced was sold. The market did not punish the producers of shoddy goods. Nor was there any incentive for planners to innovate or pay attention to consumer wants. Khrushchev spoke publicly of the importance of consumer goods production, but he was unable to change the traditional Communist preference for heavy over light industry.

One of Khrushchev's campaigns that was a brilliant success was the Soviet space program. In 1957, the Soviet Union launched the first missile to leave the Earth's atmosphere and put the first artificial satellite into orbit. In 1961, Iurii Gagarin became the first human to travel into "outer space" and orbit the earth.

PEOPLES OF THE USSR

Khrushchev was not particularly concerned with nationality issues, apparently believing that nationality would "wither away," and that one day a common Soviet identity would drown out all national distinctions. In this spirit, he reemphasized the teaching of the Russian language in all Soviet schools; he was not a Russian nationalist, but he believed that the

Soviet "people" needed a single language to unite them. In the same vein, Russian language-speakers who lived in any republic other than the RSFSR were no longer required to learn the language of that republic.

Khrushchev ended the forced exile of North Caucasian peoples, including Chechens and Ingush, and allowed them to return to their traditional homeland. As if to prove the insignificance of nationality, however, Khrushchev refused to allowed the deported Crimean Tatars to return, and he attached the Crimean Peninsula, the population of which was now mostly Russian, to Ukraine. He allowed Volga Germans to return to their homeland, but he did not restore their status as an Autonomous Region. The greatest repression of a popular movement in a national republic in Khrushchev's era was in Georgia, where, in 1956, there were demonstrations against de-Stalinization in which hundreds of Georgian protesters were killed.

The republic most seriously affected by Khrushchev's policies was Kazakhstan, where huge tracts of grazing land were plowed and planted with wheat during the Virgin Lands campaign. This was devastating to Kazakh herders, who lost their livelihood, and, since the new grain farmers were mainly Ukrainians and Russians, Kazakhs became a minority in their own republic. Migration of Slavs to Kazakhstan continued into the 1970s.

Khrushchev's aggressive promotion of atheism affected Jews as well as Russian Orthodox and Baptists. Synagogues were closed, as was the only rabbinical training school in Moscow. In Khrushchev's last years in office, even the baking of unleavened bread for Passover was outlawed. The Hebrew language could not be published, and the Hebrew Bible, even in Russian translation, was forbidden. (It was included in the form of the Old Testament in the Christian Bible, but even those were in short supply). In addition, Zionism was repeatedly attacked in the press, and Soviet Jews were not permitted to emigrate.

KHRUSHCHEV'S FALL

Khrushchev had saved the Communist party and the Soviet system from the irrationality, illegality, and inhumanity of Stalinism. He had relaxed the regimentation of Soviet society in general, he had raised the standard of living of both factory workers and farmers, and he had permitted greater artistic freedom. By 1964, however, he had alienated the Communist party, and his populism offended the new meritocracy. The elite did not appreciate Khrushchev's emphasis on real work experience for high school and college students; they resented admissions policies that benefitted the children of workers, and they especially opposed Khrushchev's imposition of term limits for officials in the party and government. Many in the party believed that his destalinization had gone too far, too fast, and had destabilized eastern Europe. They were embarrassed by his naive claim that the basis for communism would be built by 1980 and by the need to buy wheat from the leader of the capitalist world.

In international relations, Khrushchev was also found lacking. Many Communist leaders felt that Khrushchev had made too many concessions to the West and had received nothing in return. The Cuban Missile Crisis was yet another of his rash actions followed by a humiliating retreat. In 1960, while addressing the United Nations, he had taken off a shoe and used it as a gavel. Khrushchev's colleagues thought this was boorish behavior typical of an uncultured peasant and not befitting the leader of a superpower.

In the summer of 1964, the Presidium concluded that it was time for Khrushchev to go. Having learned from the debacle of 1957 that Khrushchev would insist on a vote by the Central Committee, Khrushchev's opponents called a meeting of the Central Committee for October 1964. At the meeting, a long list of Khrushchev's failures was read to the members of the committee, and they voted him out of office. However, the very manner in which he left office reveals how successful his advocacy of socialist legality had been. Although Khrushchev disappeared completely from public life, he was not shot, imprisoned, or even exiled. He was given a house in Moscow and a comfortable pension. Retired at the age of seventy, Khrushchev settled down to write his memoirs.

—————————— TEXT DOCUMENTS ——————————

Khrushchev, "Secret Speech"

A crucial point in Nikita Khrushchev's campaign to consolidate his power and to establish "socialist legality" was a speech to a closed session of the Twentieth Congress of the Communist Party of the Soviet Union on February 25, 1956, in which he described the crimes committed under Stalin's leadership during the great terror of the 1930s.

- What does Khrushchev say about Stalin, positive and negative? What crimes does he leave out? Why?
- How does Khrushchev separate Stalin's crimes from the Soviet system? How sincere a Communist do you think Khrushchev was?
- How might this serve socialist legality? Khrushchev's political career?

The objective of the present report is not a thorough evaluation of Stalin's life and work. Concerning Stalin's merits, an entirely sufficient number of books, pamphlets and studies had already been written in his lifetime. Stalin's role in the preparation and execution of the socialist revolution, in the Civil War, and in the fight for the construction of socialism in our country is universally known. Everyone knows this well. At present we are concerned with . . . how the Stalin cult gradually grew, the cult which became at a certain specific stage the source of a whole series of exceedingly serious and grave perversions of Party principles, of Party democracy, of revolutionary legality. . . .

Stalin originated the concept "enemy of the people." This term automatically rendered it unnecessary that the ideological errors of a man or men engaged in a controversy be proved; this term made possible the use of the most cruel repression, violating all norms of revolutionary legality, against anyone who in any way disagreed with Stalin, against those who were only suspected of hostile intent, against those who had bad reputations. This concept, "enemy of the people," actually eliminated the possibility of any kind of ideological fight or the making of one's views known on this or that issue, even issues of a practical nature. In the main, and in actuality, the only proof of guilt used, contrary to all norms of current law, was the "confession" of the accused himself; and, as subsequent investigation has proved, "confessions" were obtained through physical pressures against the accused.

This led to glaring violations of revolutionary legality, and to the fact that many entirely innocent persons, who in the past had defended the Party line, became victims.

We must assert that, in regard to those persons who in their time had opposed the Party line, there were often no sufficiently serious reasons for their physical annihilation. The formula "enemy of the people" was specifically introduced for the purpose of physically annihilating such individuals.

Source: Thomas P. Whitney, Ed. *Khrushchev Speaks: Selected Speeches, Articles, and Press Conferences, 1949–1961* (Ann Arbor: University of Michigan Press, 1963), 212–217. Reprinted with permission of the University of Michigan Press.

It is a fact that many persons who were later annihilated as enemies of the Party and people had worked with Lenin during his life. Some of these persons had made mistakes during Lenin's life, but, despite this, Lenin benefitted by their work, he corrected them and he did everything possible to retain them in the ranks of the Party; he induced them to follow him. . . .

Lenin's wisdom in dealing with people was evident in his work with cadres.

An entirely different relationship with people characterized Stalin. Lenin's traits—patient work with people; stubborn and painstaking education of them; the ability to induce people to follow him without using compulsion, but rather through the ideological influence on them of the whole collective—were entirely foreign to Stalin. He [Stalin] discarded the Leninist method of persuading and educating; he abandoned the method of ideological struggle for that of administrative violence, mass repressions and terror. He acted on an increasingly larger scale and more stubbornly through punitive organs, at the same time often violating all existing standards of morality and of Soviet law.

Arbitrary behavior by one person encouraged and permitted arbitrariness in others. Mass arrests and deportations of many thousands of people, execution without trial and without normal investigation created conditions of insecurity, fear and even desperation.

This, of course, did not contribute toward unity of the Party ranks and of all strata of the working people, but, on the contrary, brought about annihilation and the expulsion from the Party of workers who were loyal but inconvenient to Stalin.

Our party fought for the implementation of Lenin's plans for the construction of socialism. This was an ideological fight. Had Leninist principles been observed during the course of this fight, had the Party's devotion to principles been skillfully combined with a keen and solicitous concern for people, had they not been repelled and wasted, but rather drawn to our side, we certainly would not have had such a brutal violation of revolutionary legality and many thousands of people would not have fallen victim of the method of terror. Extraordinary methods would then have been resorted to only against those people who had in fact committed criminal acts against the Soviet system. . . .

Lenin used severe methods only in the most necessary cases, when the exploiting classes were still in existence and were vigorously opposing the revolution, when the struggle for survival was decidedly assuming the sharpest forms, even including a civil war.

Stalin, on the other hand, used extreme methods and mass repressions at a time when the revolution was already victorious, when the Soviet state was strengthened, when the exploiting classes were already liquidated and socialist relations were rooted solidly in all phases of national economy, when our party was politically consolidated and had strengthened itself both numerically and ideologically. It is clear that here Stalin showed in a whole series of cases his intolerance, his brutality and his abuse of power. Instead of proving his political correctness and mobilizing the masses, he often chose the path of repression and physical annihilation, not only against actual enemies, but also against individuals who had not committed any crimes against the Party and the Soviet government. Here we see no wisdom but only a demonstration of the brutal force which had once so alarmed V. I. Lenin. . . .

Solzhenitsyn, *One Day in the Life of Ivan Denisovich*

Aleksandr Isaevich Solzhenitsyn (b. 1918) spent eight years in the GULag in the late Stalin era for writing a letter to a friend in which he criticized Stalin. After he was released, Solzhenitsyn began to write a series of novels about prison camp life. One Day in the Life of Ivan Denisovich, *personally approved for publication by Nikita Khrushchev, made Solzhenitsyn an instant celebrity, not only in the Soviet Union but around the world. The Brezhnev regime did not allow his other novels to be published, and because he published them abroad (winning the Nobel Prize for Literature in 1970), Solzhenitsyn was charged with treason and deported to the West in 1974. He lived in the United States until 1994, when he returned to Russia.*

The following selections come from the final pages of One Day in the Life of Ivan Denisovich.

- What characteristics of prison camp life are represented here?
- Why might Solzhenitsyn have made Alyoshka a Baptist rather than a member of the Russian Orthodox Church?
- What points might Solzhenitsyn be making about life in Soviet society in general?

Shukhov lay down with his head to the window, and Alyoshka was on the other side of the bunk with his head the other way so he got the light from the bulb. He was reading the Gospels again.

Alyoshka'd heard Shukhov thank the Lord and he turned to him. "Look here, Ivan Denisovich, your soul wants to pray to God, so why don't you let it have its way?"

Shukhov looked at Alyoshka and his eyes were narrow. They had a light in them and they were like two candles. And he sighed. "I'll tell you why, Alyoshka. Because all these prayers are like the complaints we send in to the higher-ups—either they don't get there or they come back to you marked 'Rejected.'"

In front of HQ barracks there were four boxes with seals and one of the security guys came along every month to empty them. A lot of fellows put slips in those boxes and they counted the days—a month or two months—waiting to hear.

Either there was nothing or it was "Rejected."

"The trouble is, Ivan Denisovich, you don't pray hard enough and that's why your prayers don't work out. You must pray unceasing! And if you have faith and tell the mountain to move, it will move."

Shukhov grinned and made himself another cigarette. He got a light from one of the Estonians.

"Don't give me that, Alyoshka. I've never seen a mountain move. But come to think of it, I've never seen a mountain either. And when you and all your Baptists prayed down there in the Caucasus did you ever see a mountain move?"

The poor fellows. All they did was pray to God. And were they in anybody's way? They all got twenty-five years, because that's how it was now—twenty-five years for everybody.

Source: Alexander Solzhenitsyn, *One Day in the Life of Ivan Denisovich,* trans. Ronald Hingley and Max Hayward (New York: Bantam Books, 1963), 195–199, 202–203.

"But we didn't pray for that, Ivan Denisovich," Alyoshka said, and he came up close to Shukhov with his Gospels, right up to his face. "The only thing of this earth the Lord has ordered us to pray for is our daily bread—'Give us this day our daily bread.'"

"You mean that ration we get?" Shukhov said. But Alyoshka went on and his eyes said more than his words and he put his hand on Ivan's hand.

"Ivan Denisovich, you mustn't pray for somebody to send you a package or for an extra helping of gruel. Things that people set store by are base in the sight of the Lord. You must pray for the things of the spirit so the Lord will take evil things from our hearts. . . ."

"But listen. The priest in our church in Polomnya . . ."

"Don't tell me about that," Alyoshka begged and he winced with pain.

"No. But just listen." And Shukhov bent over to him on his elbow. "The priest is the richest man in our parish in Polomnya. Suppose they ask you to build a roof on a house, your price is thirty rubles for plain people. For the priest it's a hundred. That priest of ours is paying alimony to three women in three towns, and he's living with a fourth. And he's got the bishop under his thumb. You should see the way he holds that fat greasy hand of his out to the bishop. And it doesn't matter how many other priests they send, He always gets rid of 'em. He doesn't want to share the pickings."

"Why are you telling me about this priest? The Orthodox Church has gotten away from the Gospel. And the reason they don't put them in prison is because they have no true faith."

Shukhov looked straight and hard, and went on smoking. "Alyoshka," he said, and he moved the Baptist's hand away and the smoke from his cigarette went in Alyoshka's face. "I'm not against God, understand. I believe in God, all right. But what I don't believe in is Heaven and Hell. Who d'you think we are, giving us all that stuff about Heaven and Hell? That's the thing I can't take."

Shukhov lay back again and dropped the ash off his cigarette between the bunk and the window, careful so's not to burn the Captain's stuff. He was thinking his own thoughts and didn't hear Alyoshka any more, and he said out loud: "The thing is, you can pray as much as you like but they won't take anything off your sentence and you'll just have to sit it out, every day of it, from reveille to lights out."

"You mustn't pray for that." Alyoshka was horror-struck. "What d'you want your freedom for? What faith you have left will be choked in thorns. Rejoice that you are in prison. Here you can think of your soul. Paul the Apostle said: 'What mean you to weep and to break my heart? for I am ready not to be bound only, but also to die for the name of the Lord Jesus.'"

Shukhov looked up at the ceiling and said nothing. He didn't know any longer himself whether he wanted freedom or not. At first he'd wanted it very much and every day he added up how long he still had to go. But then he got fed up with this. And as time went on he understood that they might let you out but they never let you home. And he didn't really know where he'd be better off. At home or in here.

But they wouldn't let him home anyway. . . .

Alyoshka was talking the truth. You could tell by his voice and his eyes he was glad to be in prison.

"Look, Alyoshka," Shukhov said, "it's all right for you. It was Christ told you to come here, and you are here because of Him. But why am I here? Because they didn't get ready for the war like they should've in forty-one? Was that my fault?". . . .

Shukhov went to sleep, and he was very happy. He'd had a lot of luck today. They hadn't put him in the cooler. The gang hadn't been chased out to work in the Socialist Community Development. He'd finagled an extra bowl of mush at noon. The boss had gotten them good rates for their work. He'd felt good making that wall. They hadn't found that piece of steel in the frisk. Caesar had paid him off in the evening. He'd bought some tobacco. And he'd gotten over that sickness.

Nothing had spoiled the day and it had been almost happy.

There were three thousand six hundred and fifty-three days like this in his sentence, from reveille to lights out.

The three extra ones were because of the leap years. . . .

"'I Hate Mother'—A Girl's Letter and Some Replies"

The newspaper Komsomolskaia Pravda *initiated a feature, called "Letters on the Round Table: When you are 18," in which they invited young people to write "letters of reflection, letters of confession of questioning and doubt," to be discussed by "elder comrades, people of various occupations, rich in experience and generous with good advice." This is one such letter, followed by a summary of the reaction to it.*

- Why do you think this letter was published?
- What does this reveal about developments in Soviet society?
- What gender issues are involved?

Esteemed editors! I read your article "Can Mother Be Forgiven." I have never had the desire to write to a newspaper. I know they print only those articles that propagandize copybook maxims of various kinds, such as "It is noble to labor," "You mustn't steal," "You must love your mother," and so on. But today I cannot refrain from writing. Perhaps you would be interested in knowing that there are people who think differently from your esteemed authors.

Can Mother be forgiven? I have no reason to forgive her. I am speaking about my own mother. She is a teacher, she pores over notebooks for days on end and, since she has been teaching her whole life, she imagines that there is no one smarter than she. And she thinks the fashions now are hideous and the hairstyles awful and the morals low. I hate my mother because she doesn't let me live as I please. It is indecent to go to the movies late at night. It is in bad taste to wear a black sweater. I wear my hair in an ugly style. Why do I let it hang down over my eyes? In her opinion, one's face and eyes must be uncovered. All the girls in the films and in the fashion magazines wear bangs, but I can't. I can't come home late. My girl friends are bad, they look vulgar: bright lips and mascaraed eyelashes. A girl should be

Source: "'I Hate Mother'—A Girl's Letter and Some Replies." *The Current Digest of the Soviet Press.* Vol. 16, no. 24 (1964): 18, 19. Translation copyright by *The Current Digest of the Soviet Press,* published weekly at Columbus, Ohio. Reprinted by permission of the *Digest.*

modest and shy. There is a row at my house if I put on a narrow skirt. Like everyone else, I want to wear beautiful, elegant sandals with spike heels, but she has different views. These sandals are harmful. Everyone else is wearing such shoes, but for me they are harmful. She is always referring to the fact that she can't buy expensive things. But she buys so many books there is no place to put them. She has worn my little sister to death with music. My sister doesn't even go for walks, just does her endless practicing.

We can listen only to classical music. All the rest is vulgarity, muck. Vertinsky is muck. Esenin is decadent. Don't read Zola, he corrupts the mind. Don't read Remarque. Turgenev—that's what you can read. His garnet crucifix, beslobbered and old-fashioned, inspires noble sentiments.

But look in a streetcar or a trollybus—does anyone admire a modest, shy girl? They all look at the fashionable, good-looking girl with the mascaraed eyelashes. And [at school] the modest girls don't attract anyone with their modesty; on the contrary, it is the informal, forward and gay ones that gather crowds of young fellows around them. But mama says "They look vulgar," "They are ill-bred." All my life it has been as though I were in a vise; I am so fed up with my mother's tutelage I would run away to anywhere. Don't stand that way, don't sit that way, don't comb your hair that way, don't read that. I hate her! I hate her!

Everyone else I know reads what she wants, uses lipstick, goes to the movies and comes home late, wears fashionable shoes and fashionable skirts, but I am like a nun. We have eternal arguments. I hate my mother! I hate her because with her wretched teaching she can't even provide decently for her family; even though other people, without a higher education, without this superzealaus labor, earn enough for fashionable shoes and beautiful furniture, "We can't, we have no money." Others have it, but not us. To sit up nights poring over notebooks, to solve endless problems and then to have no money! It must be that she isn't smart enough to earn a decent salary.

I don't want to go home. Everything there disgusts me; but you ask if I can forgive my mother. I can't forgive my mother's stupidity, her inability to appreciate the new, modern music and the new fashions, her incomprehension of new people and moods, as though she never went to the movies, never read a newspaper and were living 30 years in the past.

I can't forgive my mother for our father's leaving us. She was always busy and always dowdy; she wears the same suit for almost ten years. She thinks that if everything is clean and neat it must be beautiful. But another woman—red-haired, bright, wearing makeup and fashionable shoes and a dress with a plunging neckline—whom our modest mama blames, turned out to be more attractive and attentive, and our father left us, two daughters, for the sake of this vulgar—from Mama's point of view—woman. Mama says she was a blockhead, this woman, but it turned out that no one paid any attention to our oh-so-intelligent mama with her great mind.

I am interested in hearing what you will say in connection with all this.

[Signed] Irina A.

[The following excerpt from the roundtable discussion which followed encapsulates the general response:]

The "I hate her" that Irina hurls at her mother contradicts our morality, the essence of which lies in love and gratitude toward the person who gave you life, toward the land that fed you, the motherland that reared you.

Forced Marriage in the Northern Caucasus

The following report was published in Pravda *on July 2, 1964.*

- What does this reveal about the Soviet modernizing project? About relations between center and periphery in the USSR?
- What might the motives of Communist party leaders have been? The motives of the local Communists?

In early May the Chechen-Ingush Province Party Committee received an alarming letter from the young Communist Rimma Khashagulgova. "Black storm clouds," the mountain girl, an upper-class student, wrote, "have gathered over me. Against my will and desire, I have been betrothed to Citizen Yusup Madigovich Kuzgov from the village of Achaluki. I don't even know this man. Despite my resistance, my father, Elmurza Elmurzayevich Khashagulgov, sold me for 800 rubles of bride money. The wedding is to be held in two weeks. I demanded of my father that he cancel this unworthy transaction. But father says he will bind me with ropes and send me to Kuzgov.

"I am asking you to intervene in this matter before the wedding is held and protect me. Otherwise my life will be ruined."

The girl's letter alarmed the officials of the province Party committee. Roza Markhiyeva, an instructor of the department for work among women, went to the locality. Rimma had been permitted to complete the eleventh grade. Her dream is to become an educator of children, a pedagogue.

The "contract" between Rimma's father and her fiance, concluded according to the laws of the Sharia, was dissolved. The fire has been temporarily extinguished. But there is still a smell of burning. A new warning signal has been revived by the province Party committee's department for work among women. Another mountain girl is now calling for help. She is a secretary of a Y. C. L. organization, and is graduating from an institute. The student girl caught the eye of Bashir Tangiyev, a militia lieutenant and a Communist, for whom she has no feeling, whatsoever. He obtained the consent of the girl's father to give him his daughter in marriage. True, later the father took pity on his daughter and went back on his word. But Tangiyev continues to blackmail the girl.

Why are such cases frequent in Chechen-Ingushetia? Why do even Party members here still display feudal-bey attitudes toward women?

An acquaintance with ideological work in the Chechen-Ingush Autonomous Republic permits one to conclude that the republic's ideological forces and Communists are not mobilized for the struggle against feudal-bey survivals and religious prejudices, that they do not wage a resolute offensive against those who flout our Soviet laws and morality and poison people's lives. Officials of several Party committees rather operate from defensive positions. They merely react to the alarming warning signals they receive. Administrative agencies

Source: "Be on the Attack, Not the Defensive!" *Current Digest of the Soviet Press.* Vol. 16, no. 27 (1964): 27–28. Translation copyright by *The Current Digest of the Soviet Press,* published weekly at Columbus, Ohio. Reprinted by permission of the *Digest.*

make the "fiances" sign releases. But the "fiances," following old customs, consider themselves disgraced and look for occasions to avenge themselves against the "offenders."

I think it would be more correct if the province Party committee's ideological department and the Party committees would send influential Communists of the basic nationality who are qualified lecturers on atheism hot on the trail of such instances, and if the latter would gather together the residents of villages for a discussion of these facts. Party and Y. C. L. organizations must react sharply to such phenomena and construct their educational work with a view to preventing manifestations of feudal-bey attitudes toward women. . . .

In March, 1964, the bureau of the province Party committee discussed the state of atheistic propaganda among the republic's population. It was noted that the majority of the members and candidate members of the Nazran and Grozny Party Committees and of the October District Party Committee do not participate in this important matter. Out of 52 activists of the Shalin District, almost no one reads books, goes to the movies with his wife or helps the meanders of his family to become literate.

"The explanation for this," it is stated in the decision of the bureau of the province Party committee, "is the harmful view, which is widespread in the republic, that leaders of cadres would lose authority among the basic population if they engaged in antireligious indoctrination." . . .

The struggle against survivals of the past will be successful when the Party aktiv, Communists and the intelligentsia march in the forefront of the offensive. They must set a standard of Communist relations in everyday life. . . .

The Chechen-Ingush Party organization has more than 20,000 Propagandists and agitators and a huge army of specialists and the intelligentsia. No force, however dark, can withstand them if they all militantly enlist in the struggle against survivals of the past.

VISUAL DOCUMENTS

Figure 19-1 Khrushchev
   This is a photograph of Nikita Khrushchev addressing the General Assembly of the United Nations.
- Compare this with previous representations of Russian and Soviet leaders.
- What does the context signify? What did Khrushchev want to convey? What might this mean to a Soviet audience?

Source: Corbis/Bettmann.

Figure 19-2 The New Arbat

Old Arbat Street was a formerly fashionable residential district favored by the intelligentsia in the Soviet era. In 1962, part of it was demolished to make a wide street to facilitate parades on Red Square. Apartment buildings, nightclubs, and shops were built there, and it became one of the trendiest parts of Moscow. The building shown here was built for the "Palace of COMECON" (Council for Mutual Economic Assistance). This photo was taken in 1967.

- What does this reveal about architectural and social trends in Soviet society?
- How does the Soviet Union compare with world trends?

Source: Marc Garanger/CORBIS.

Figure 19-3 Harvesting on the Kuban

This photograph shows combines harvesting wheat in the Kuban region north of the Caucasus mountains.

- Compare this with previous images of agricultural activity.
- How is this related with previous images of industrial activity? What does it suggest about the Soviet economy?

Source: AP/Wide World Photos.

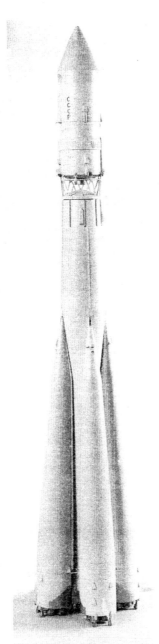

Figure 19-4 A-1 Rocket
   This is a photograph of the rocket (also known as the Vostok, or "East") that was used to launch the Sputnik satellites in the late 1950s and early 1960s.
* What does this reveal about the Soviet economic system?
* About Soviet technology?
Source: Dorling Kindersley Media Library

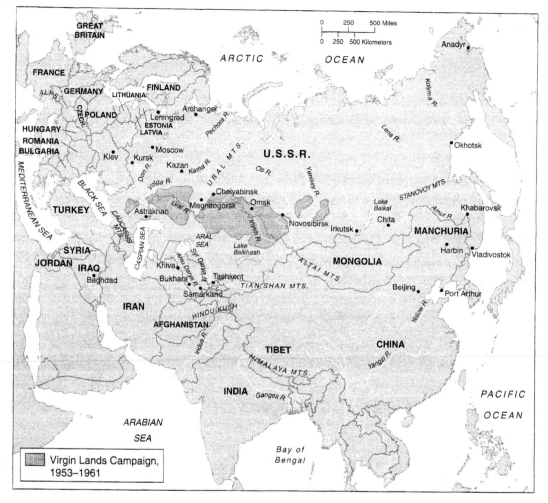

Figure 19-5 Khrushchev's Virgin Lands Campaigns
Khrushchev's Virgin Lands campaigns were an ambitious attempt to farm vast regions of the Central Asian steppe that for millennia had only provided pasture for nomadic herders. The initial success was due to better than average rainfall; when normal dry weather returned, the wisdom of the nomads was vindicated.

_____ FOR FURTHER READING _____

(In addition to the books by Clements, and Suny from the previous chapter.)

Beschloss, Michael R. *The Crisis Years: Kennedy and Khrushchev, 1960–1963*. New York: Edward Burlingame Books, 1991.

Brown, Deming. *Soviet Russian Literature since Stalin*. Cambridge: Cambridge University Press, 1978.

Burlatsky, Fedor. *Khrushchev and the First Russian Spring*. London: Weidenfeld and Nicolson, 1991.

Filtzer, Donald. *The Khrushchev Era: De-Stalinisation and the Limits of Reform in the USSR, 1953–1964*. Basingstoke: Macmillan, 1993.

Hosking, Geoffrey. *Beyond Socialist Realism: Soviet Fiction since Ivan Denisovich.* New York: Holmes & Meier Publishers, 1980.

Ilic, Melanie, Susan Reid, and Lynne Attwood. *Women in the Khrushchev Era.* Basingstoke: Palgrave Macmillan, 2004.

Khrushchev, Nikita S. *Khrushchev Remembers.* Boston: Little, Brown, 1970.

McCauley, Martin. *The Khrushchev Era: 1954–1964.* London: Longman, 1995.

Taubman, William. *Khrushchev: The Man and His Era.* New York: W.W. Norton, 2003.

CHAPTER TWENTY

SOVIET INDUSTRIAL SOCIETY, 1964–1979

Nikita Khrushchev had ended the terror and lawlessness that had characterized Stalin's rule, but he did not give up Stalin's penchant for radical reforms, drives, and campaigns. The new generation of Communist leaders approved of the former and therefore supported Khrushchev in 1957, but they objected to the latter and removed him from office in 1964. The men who ruled the Soviet Union for the next two decades wanted stability and security above all. They were satisfied with the ability of a planned economy to direct resources toward heavy industry, the military, and space exploration, and they apparently felt that progress in these areas was worth a low standard of living for the population as a whole. They were not Communist utopians but practical rulers of an imperial superpower intent on preserving order at home and projecting influence abroad.

EURASIAN CONTEXT

By the mid-1960s, western Europe had fully recovered from the devastation of World War II. Its economy was booming, and the newly formed Common Market (France, Germany, Italy, Belgium, Holland, and Luxembourg) was actually exporting more goods than the United States. When Great Britain, Ireland, and Denmark joined the Common Market in 1973, it was clear that the old Europe had been transformed. Economic competition, military rivalry, and imperial ambition was gone, and Europeans allowed the United States to take over the task of preserving global order. The edge was also taken off the traditional conflict between labor and capital. The Common Market provided ground for the development of multinational corporations and a wealthy capitalist elite, but European governments also sponsored the sort of cradle-to-grave social welfare system that working-class activists of the late-nineteenth century might have mistaken for socialism.

The western European economy suffered a setback beginning in 1973 when the Organization of Petroleum Exporting Countries (OPEC) imposed a temporary oil embargo to punish the friends of Israel. OPEC then steadily increased the price of oil until by 1979 it cost ten times more than it had in 1973. Europe suffered from high unemployment and inflation, and found it difficult to compete on the world market with nations such as Japan, Taiwan, South Korea, Brazil, and Mexico, which benefitted from newer and more technologically advanced equipment and lower labor costs.

The new European society faced criticism from both the left and the right. Leftist environmentalists resisted the expansion of industrialization and urbanization, feminists pressed for equal pay and equal rights, and peace activists worked for reconciliation of east and west and an end to the arms race. Right-wing advocates of the free market feared that capitalism was not winning the struggle with communism but was converging toward it, and they blamed the labor movement and the welfare system for Europe's economic decline. These divisions crystalized in 1979 when the Green Party, representing the left, was formed in Germany, and Margaret Thatcher, on the right, became Prime Minister of Great Britain.

The nations of eastern Europe remained in the Soviet sphere of influence, but they attempted to pursue their own paths to communism. In 1964, Romania withdrew from COMECON, because it thought that central planners paid too little for its oil and did not permit it to develop an industrial economy. Romania began to trade with the West. Because the Romanian Communist Party preserved its authoritarian monopoly on power, the Soviet Union did not interfere. Czechoslovakia, however, had a different experience. In 1968, Alexander Dubcek, First Secretary of the Czechoslovak Communist Party, proposed a number of reforms: decentralization of the economy, electoral competition within the Communist party, and a role for non-Communist parties in nominating candidates for public office. Although Dubcek stressed that Czechoslovakia was to remain a socialist society and would not withdraw from the Warsaw Pact, the Soviet Union did not permit the reforms to proceed. The Red Army invaded and forced Dubcek to rescind his reforms, suppress free speech, and purge liberals from the party and the universities.

Learning from the Czech example, the Communist Parties of eastern Europe maintained their monopoly on politics, media, and culture, even as they diverged from the Soviet model in other respects. Poland, Yugoslavia, and Romania were granted "most favored nation" status by the United States and received economic development loans through the U.S. Agency for International Development (USAID). Poland and Yugoslavia turned almost all farmland into private family farms. The Polish regime increasingly accommodated the Catholic Church. Hungary allowed factories greater flexibility in planning and setting prices and allowed peasants to sell some of their produce on the private market. Albania aligned with China. Yugoslavia continued to follow its own foreign policy and fostered a mixed socialist-market economy. Only Bulgaria followed the Soviet model in most regards.

In the Middle East, the most striking development was the dramatic rise of Islamism. Over the course of the twentieth century, as Arab societies liberated themselves from European colonialism, they were typically led by military officers who admired and imitated Kemal Atatürk's program of modernization and secularization. Many Muslims objected not only to imperialism but to the atheism and materialism of western civilization, and they opposed the secular nationalist leaders who followed modernizing programs. These Islamists proposed a return to Islamic theocracy and Islamic law as the only way to true independence. The newly independent Arab states were military dictatorships, and Islamist organizations were outlawed, suppressed, and marginalized. Islamism flourished nevertheless, especially when secular governments appeared to be subordinate to the West.

The most fertile soil for Islamism was Iran, where the Shah used the huge profits from the rising price of oil to sponsor industrialization, urbanization, and secularization. He nationalized land belonging to religious institutions, he promoted women's rights, and he directed that secular, not religious, works be used in government literacy programs. In addition, Iran became an ally of Israel in fact, if not in law: The Shah sold oil to Israel, bought Israeli military hardware, and sent secret police and military officers to Israel for training. Additionally, as a close ally of the United States, Iran served as a guarantor of the status quo in the Middle East, including continued Israeli occupation of the West Bank, Golan Heights, and Gaza Strip. When faced with rising opposition to his dictatorship, the Shah employed a secret police to stifle free speech and imprison dissidents. In 1979, the Shah was swept from power by a massive popular revolution, which was quickly taken over and harnessed by the Islamist followers of an exiled imam, Ayatollah Khomeini. Khomeini led the creation of an Islamic theocracy.

In Afghanistan, King Muhammad Zahir Shah established a constitutional monarchy with an elective parliament in 1963. Politics quickly became polarized between an Islamist party on the right and a Communist party on the left, and the king frequently dismissed the parliament. In 1973, Muhammad Daud Khan, a former prime minister, came to power with the support of leftist military officers and the Soviet Union, forcing the King to abdicate and declaring Afghanistan a republic. Once in power, Daud Khan both suppressed militant Islamists and purged leftists from his government, and in 1977, he declared one-party, presidential rule, distanced himself from the Soviet Union, and sought aid from Iraq and Saudi Arabia. Continued repression drove two Marxist parties together, and in 1978, they mounted a successful coup against Daud's dictatorship. The new government denied it was a puppet of Moscow and claimed to stand for nationalism, Islam, and social justice, but it undertook secular reforms, recognized the equality of women, and instituted social and economic programs that were interpreted by Islamists as Communistic. Many Islamist tribal leaders fled across the border into Pakistan to organize opposition to the new regime, and sporadic revolts broke out.

By 1968, the Chinese Cultural Revolution had exhausted itself. The economy was in crisis, and China's social fabric had nearly unraveled. When stability was restored in the late sixties, China had a split personality: Mao was an idol, and the government spoke the language of radical communism, but it practiced conservative Soviet-style economics. Abandoning ideology in foreign policy, the regime embarked on old-fashioned power politics. Soon after the split between China and the Soviet Union in the 1950s, China had argued that the mid-nineteenth century Treaties of Aigun and Beijing (which had transferred to Russia the territory north of the Amur River and east of the Ussuri River) were part of the imperialist, unequal treaty system and therefore invalid. By the late 1960s, Russian and Chinese troops engaged in border skirmishes on the Amur, and the danger of war did not subside until the middle of the 1970s. In the meantime, China's relations with the United States improved. In 1971, they exchanged ambassadors, and President Richard Nixon agreed that Communist China should replace Taiwan on the UN Security Council. Mao Zedong died in 1976, and Communist moderates were finally able to begin a clean break with the past.

POLITICAL DEVELOPMENTS AND FOREIGN AFFAIRS

In 1964, the two principal leaders of the movement that forced Khrushchev into retirement divided Khrushchev's titles between them, Leonid Brezhnev becoming First Secretary of the party and Aleksei Kosygin Chair of the Council of Ministers, and they began to rescind many of Khrushchev's reforms. They restored the old, centralized planning system. They canceled the term limits Khrushchev had proposed and reduced the vocational component of high school education. Most notably, they began to refer to the Soviet system as "developed socialism," as if it were an end point rather than a temporary stage on the road to Communism. The Soviet planning bureaucracy continued to favor the production of coal, steel, and heavy machinery, the exploration of space, and the expansion of the military establishment.

Though Brezhnev was pragmatic and lacked any hint of communist idealism, he was hard and unyielding when it came to political power at home or military prestige abroad. In the first years of his rule, Brezhnev gave notice to Soviet society and the world at large that a new era of realpolitik had begun. In 1965, as part of the celebration of the Twentieth Anniversary of the victory in the Second World War, Stalin was hailed as the architect of that victory. The following year, two Soviet writers, Andrei Siniavskii and Iulii Daniel, were charged with "anti-Soviet propaganda" for publishing abroad satires of Soviet life. Their well-publicized trial was a message to the literary establishment that the thaw was over and criticism of the Soviet system would not be tolerated. In 1968, Brezhnev sent the Red Army into Czechoslovakia to suppress the progressive movement there. As part of his determination not to back down from any military confrontations, Brezhnev began a huge military buildup, countered American containment of communism in Vietnam by sending aid and advisers to the North Vietnamese, and reinforced Soviet defenses on the Chinese border.

There was very little political activity of note between Khrushchev's forced retirement in 1964 and Brezhnev's death in 1982. The Twenty-third Party Congress (spring 1966) confirmed Brezhnev's status as the dominant figure in the party by giving him the title of General Secretary. It also renamed the Presidium the Politburo. (Both changes were reversions to Stalinist usage.) In 1964, Brezhnev made Konstantin Chernenko his chief of staff; he became a full member of the Central Committee seven years later. In 1967, Iurii Andropov was made head of the KGB, where he remained through the Brezhnev era.

The only competition even remotely resembling a power struggle was competition among Leonid Brezhnev, Aleksei Kosygin, and Nikolai Podgornyi, Chair of the Presidium of the Supreme Soviet (the Soviet "head of state"). In 1965, Kosygin led a group of economic reformers in the party who proposed more decentralized planning, the introduction of profit accounting as an incentive to higher quality, and the production of more consumer goods. Brezhnev, who represented the Soviet Union's military-industrial complex, blocked the reforms and discredited Kosygin. Nevertheless, Kosygin retained his titles until his retirement attributed to poor health in 1980 (he died soon after). In 1977, Brezhnev engineered the only significant shake-up of his time in office by forcing Podgornyi into retirement and taking his title as head of state. This was the only time in Soviet history that one person was head of both party and state.

The new regime was determined to confront Europe, China, and the United States from a position of strength, and it annually allocated at least 15 percent of the Soviet GNP to the military. The Soviet leaders aimed at parity with the United States in submarines and ICBMs, and they expanded their conventional military forces to five million soldiers to guard their long borders. They decided to confront the United States indirectly by supporting North Vietnam's effort to unite all Vietnam under Communist rule, providing Hanoi with $1.5 billion in financial and military aid. They also were determined to resist China's demands to renegotiate the border between the two countries, and in 1969, Soviet forces held the line against Chinese attacks along the Amur and Ussuri Rivers and the Xinjiang border.

Enhanced Soviet power gave the West an incentive to seek accommodation with the Soviet regime and made Soviet leaders confident that their willingness to negotiate would not be perceived as an indication of weakness. In 1970, the Soviet Union signed a nonaggression treaty with West Germany, and in the spring of 1972, it signed the first Strategic Arms Limitation Treaty (SALT I) with the United States. This began a period known in the United States as "detente" during which the United States followed "realism" in foreign policy, relaxed its anti-communist rhetoric, and scaled back its commitment to "containment."

In the mid-1970s, the Soviet Union was at the peak of its power and influence in world affairs. Eastern Europe was docile. In 1974, China proposed a non-aggression pact, which the Soviet leaders accepted. In 1973, the United States withdrew from Vietnam, and in 1975, North Vietnam completed its conquest of the south. By the end of the 1970s, Cambodia and Laos were ruled by pro-Soviet communist regimes, and Soviet-backed insurgencies had seized power in Angola, Mozambique, and South Yemen. In June 1979, U.S. President Jimmy Carter and Leonid Brezhnev signed a second arms limitation treaty (known as SALT II).

CULTURE AND RELIGION

The Russian Orthodox Church, under the leadership of the aged Patriarch Aleksii (who was eighty-six years old in 1964) changed little after Khrushchev's retirement. Khrushchev's treatment of the church was one initiative Brezhnev had no desire to overturn. Aleksii died in 1970, and a Church Sobor convened in the spring of 1971 to elect a new Patriarch, Pimen. The most notable achievement of the Sobor of 1971 was to invite the Old Believers back into the Church; it rescinded all the anathemas of the seventeenth century and recognized the validity of the old rites. (It did not end the schism, however, since the Old Believers have not yet accepted the invitation.) The Sobor did not attempt to reverse the 1961 Church Statutes that had deprived priests of a role in administering local parishes, nor was it allowed to reopen the seminaries closed by Khrushchev.

Critics have accused Church leaders of excessive timidity. Occasional public demonstrations by dissidents had revealed that there was a space in Soviet society for independent social action (for those who could endure police harassment, employment discrimination, and brief jail terms); martyrdom was no longer the price paid for resistance to the regime. Nevertheless, even though the number of urban believers approximately doubled over the 1970s, the Orthodox Church made little effort to open new churches. In the same time period, the Patriarch of the Georgian Church managed to double the number of churches, reopen seminaries, and attract young people to the church. Between 1974 and 1978, the Russian Baptist Church registered 170 new parishes compared with 10 registered by the Orthodox Church. Indeed, the Orthodox Church cautioned priests not to engage in politics, and Patriarch Pimen gave speeches in the West declaring that Soviet citizens enjoyed full human rights, including religious freedom. Dissidents began to accuse the Church of being run by the KGB.

In mainstream literature, the most notable and influential writers were the poets Evgenii Evtushenko and Andrei Voznesenskii, who revived the vibrant, declamatory style and striking diction of Mayakovsky and Esenin and turned poetry-readings into public events. Evtushenko rose to fame as an iconoclast and anti-Stalinist during the thaw, but after the fall of Khrushchev both he and Voznesenskii stayed within the bounds of what was officially acceptable and were considered as "sell-outs" by some dissidents. Socialist Realism remained the only approved literary school, but its canons were violated to a greater or lesser extent. The "village prose" movement continued to celebrate and romanticize the Russian countryside and folk culture, and mainstream literature concentrated on the problems faced by ordinary men and women in modern (Soviet) industrial society. Much of the best Soviet literature, however, was only published in the West or by means of samizdat. Some writers, such as Aleksandr Solzhenitsyn and Joseph Brodsky, were deported; some, including Aleksandr Zinovev, Vladimir Voinovich, Georgii Vladimov, and Vasilii Aksenov, emigrated.

The thaw had decisively ended with the show trial of Daniel and Siniavskii in 1966, and it was reinforced in 1970 when Aleksandr Tvardovskii was forced to resign as editor of *Novyi Mir* when his entire editorial board was fired and replaced with conservatives. Aleksandr Solzhenitsyn was denied publication of his novels *Cancer Ward* and *The First Circle*. The characters in those novels expressed many points of view, ranging from Stalinism to Christianity; readers could easily have assumed that the Leninist, pro-Socialist reformers in his novels were speaking for the "real" Solzhenitsyn. However, when he realized that his work would not be published, Solzhenitsyn concluded that Stalinism was not an aberration, but an expression of the essence of Soviet Communism. He then began to collect information from former victims of political repression, and complied a history and sociology of the camps, *The Gulag Archipelago*. By the end of the decade, Solzhenitsyn had begun to release his work into samizdat and to publish it abroad. In 1971, he was awarded the Nobel Prize for literature, which he accepted. The Brezhnev regime could not imprison so famous a writer, and Solzhenitsyn was deported to the West in 1974.

A new willingness to speak freely without regard to the official party line, known as "dissidence," first became evident in 1965 when two hundred people demonstrated publicly in Moscow to protest the arrest of Siniavskii and Daniel. In 1966, when the trial of the two writers began, sixty-three members of the Moscow Writers Union signed a letter to the Supreme Soviet and the Communist Party Congress protesting the charge of "anti-Soviet behavior" to literary works. Simultaneously, Aleksandr Esenin-Volpin began a personal campaign to uphold socialist legality. He attended trials of dissidents with a law book in his hand, insisting that Soviet laws, including the right of the public to attend trials, be observed. On December 5 (Soviet Constitution Day) in 1965 Esenin-Volpin appeared in Red Square with a sign that said "Respect the Constitution." The first time he did so, he was arrested, but when the police realized that there could be nothing illegal about such an act, he was released. In 1968 there were a number of public protests against the Soviet invasion of Czechoslovakia.

Dissidents risked official disapproval and losing their jobs, but the days of prison camps and execution were over. Opposition to government policy now carried the same sort of penalty as attending church: It was out of bounds to anyone who wanted to advance in a profession, but free speech was available to those who were willing to work in menial jobs. Ordinary people who attended public demonstrations or were found with samizdat literature were usually only arrested, abused (verbally or physically), and released. Organizers of demonstrations or writers of critical literature were given prison terms. Some prominent dissidents were punished by being confined in mental institutions. This was a convenient way of subverting socialist legality, since a person could be committed to an institution on the recommendation of a psychiatrist without having to make a case in a public court. Overall, repression was haphazard and inconsistent, a stop-gap measure and not a system of terror, and the victims were in the tens or hundreds, not the thousands.

There was virtually no communist idealism left in Soviet society, just as there was apparently none among the aging leaders of the Communist party. There were essentially three schools of thought: Russian imperialism, liberal nationalism, and democratic socialism. Russian imperialism, sometimes called "national Bolshevism," celebrated the Russian imperial tradition and represented Lenin and Stalin not as social revolutionaries but as leaders who restored Russia's greatness after the defeat in World War I. This was not entirely official policy, since, even though Brezhnev acted in the tradition of a Russian imperialist, he did not abandon lip service to communism and Soviet patriotism. Nevertheless, some "national Bolsheviks" were allowed to publish their views.

The second school, liberal nationalism, was typified by Aleksandr Solzhenitsyn, who was too much of a patriot to adopt liberal western critiques of Marxism. Instead, he rejected

Marxism because it was a "western ideology." Reviving the Slavophile tradition, Solzhenit-syn denounced rationalism, materialism, electoral politics, and unregulated capitalism, and advocated a return to what he imagined were the political and religious traditions of Russia before Peter the Great. Solzhenitsyn was distinguished from the national Bolsheviks because he blamed both Lenin and Stalin for causing Russia's misfortune and because he was op-posed to empire. Solzhenitsyn thought that the eastern Slavs (Ukraine, Belarus, and Russia) should form a single nation and should allow the other republics of the Russian Empire/Soviet Union to be independent.

Many Russian dissidents, however, continued to admire the Western liberal tradition, and they were represented by the physicist Andrei Sakharov. As a young man in the 1950s, Sakharov had played a key role in the development of the hydrogen bomb, but he later re-gretted his contribution to the arms race, and in 1958 and 1961, Sakharov wrote letters to Khrushchev warning of the public health dangers of radiation and asking that the Soviet Union cease testing nuclear weapons in the atmosphere. In 1970, Sakharov, with two other intellectuals, wrote an open letter to Brezhnev that called for an end to political persecution, multiparty elections, a fully independent judicial system, and recognition of human rights, including freedom of speech and conscience. Sakharov did not denounce democratic social-ism, and he was neither arrested nor deported. His access to the press was cut off, and in 1980, he was exiled to the city of Gorky (formerly Nizhnii Novgorod) an industrial city closed to western travel.

ROLES AND STATUS OF WOMEN

By the 1970s, more than half of all adult Soviet women had graduated from high school, and half of all students in higher education were women. Women were also well represented in the professions: 75 percent of Soviet physicians, 33 percent of engineers, and 48 percent of managerial professionals were women. At the same time, women earned approximately two-thirds of men's salaries; medicine, a field in which women were overrepresented was one of the most poorly paid professions. Women were also prevented from rising to the highest (best paid) levels in industrial management, government bureaucracy, or the Com-munist party. While 61 percent of technical specialists in industry were women, less than 6 percent of top managers were. The Communist party was approximately one-quarter fe-male, but fewer than 4 percent of the Central Committee were women, and in the Brezhnev era all members of the Politburo were men.

The increased housing construction begun by Khrushchev continued, and single-family units replaced communal apartments. By 1980, the nuclear family with an apartment of its own had become the norm, but apartments were still in short supply. Newly married cou-ples typically were not able to get an apartment of their own until their first child was born. The number of day-care centers increased, and live-in grandmothers, who cared for young children while the mother worked, became less common. Soviet economic planners did not meet the demand for labor-saving household devices, such as vacuum cleaners and washing machines. Soviet retail sales were not organized efficiently; long lines at retail stores were the norm. The double shift continued: shopping, cooking, cleaning, and childcare remained women's work, and the average urban woman spent thirty hours per week taking care of domestic duties.

The age of marriage declined. In 1979, 60 percent of women between the ages of twenty and twenty-four, and 80 percent of women from twenty-five to twenty-nine, were married. There was also an increase in the number of divorces; approximately half of all marriages ended in divorce. Two-thirds of divorces were filed by women, and drunkenness and abuse on the part of the husband were the most frequently cited causes. Average family size in cities in the European republics decreased to slightly more than one child per couple (population growth in the East was much more rapid). This was achieved primarily by traditional means of birth control and by abortion, since Soviet planners did not provide contraceptives in sufficient quantity (or quality). Indeed, abortion was not an emergency procedure, as in the West, but was a standard method of birth control. The typical abortion patient was a married woman with one or more children who already had several abortions. Abortions were provided at no charge, but doctors typically made the experience as unpleasant (physically and emotionally) as possible, in line with government policy which favored a higher birth rate for Slavic women.

Life for farm women was perhaps even more difficult than for urban women. Women in the countryside had higher rates of school attendance than men, but they were consistently discriminated against in employment. In 1960, only 6 percent of managerial positions on collective farms were held by women, and this figure never improved. As a result, the best-educated women moved away to the cities in numbers disproportionate to men. Those who remained, however, imitated the patterns of city women. Family size decreased, and the divorce rate increased, although to a lesser extent than in the city. Only one-quarter of farm marriages ended in divorce and farm families had, on average, more than two children.

Women were especially active in typing and disseminating samizdat literature, but the dissident movement, led by men, ignored feminist issues. Even those who rejected the politics and economics of communism, still accepted the Marxist conception of social class as being the fundamental social reality; gender as a category of analysis did not occur to them. Furthermore, many Russian nationalist dissidents revived traditional ideas regarding women's roles, and shared the official Soviet opinion that sex roles were dictated by biology, with men being active providers and women passive nurturers. Aleksandr Solzhenitsyn, for example, faulted communism for paying men too little for them to support their families and therefore forcing their wives to enter the work force. When feminism did appear, it was, as usual, the work of women; in 1979, a samizdat journal, *Almanac: Woman and Russia* documented the difficulties faced by Soviet women. Its editors were harassed into emigrating to the West.

SOCIAL AND ECONOMIC TRENDS

By the end of the Brezhnev era, the Soviet Union was an urban, industrial society. Close to three quarters of the population lived in urban areas, and less than one quarter were engaged in agriculture. Moscow had a population of 8.2 million, Leningrad had 4.5 million, and ten other cities in the RSFSR boasted more than one million residents. The Soviet Union was an industrial as well as a military superpower: It led the world in the production of oil, natural gas, cast iron, steel, and tractors. It also made great progress in space exploration. The Soviet leaders, having lost the race to put a human being on the moon, decided to lead in the development of space stations in which cosmonauts could live for long periods. The first space station, Salyut 1, was put in orbit in 1971, and over the course of the decade, the Soviet Union developed more advanced models. Consumer goods production also grew impressively. Between 1965 and 1975, the annual output of televisions doubled, refrigerators tripled, and automobiles increased six-fold. By the end of the Brezhnev era, more than 90 percent of Soviet households had refrigerators and television sets, and more than 60 percent owned washing machines.

Nevertheless, the basic problems of the planned economy continued. Quality was extremely low: Many tractors came off the assembly line needing repair before they would run, and more than one-quarter of household appliances were defective in one way or another. In addition, there was no real correlation between what was produced and what was needed. For example, steel plants produced sheets of steel that were too thick for automobiles, and auto manufacturers had to grind them down to a thinner gauge, wasting both time and resources.

Such flaws were widely recognized, and some tinkering was done. Factory managers were given somewhat greater autonomy (they were allowed to use some of their profits to pay bonuses, to fund welfare facilities, and to reinvest), but the essential command structure remained the same. Prices were set and raw materials were allocated by central planners, and the basic ratio of heavy to light industry did not change. The system only worked through informal dealmaking among factories as managers compensated for the mistakes and oversights of the planners by trading materials they were oversupplied with for supplies they lacked. The government overlooked what was essentially illegal activity because otherwise little would have been produced.

What made it possible for the Soviet economy to survive, despite its inefficiency in both industry and agriculture, was the export of natural resources. The decision by OPEC to raise the price of oil provided a shot in the arm for the Soviet economy. Between 1973 and 1979, the prices of oil and of gold rose by 500 percent, and the Soviet Union was the world's biggest producer of both. It used its profits to subsidize its inefficient system.

The greatest failure of the Soviet economy was in agriculture. Soviet industrial output was 80 percent the size of U.S. industrial production, but the USSR produced only 15 percent as much agricultural output as the United States. In fact, the Soviet Union was not able to feed itself, and continued to import wheat from the United States, Canada, and Australia. This low productivity was not caused by lack of investment: between 20 and 25 percent of all capital investment went to agriculture in the 1960s and 1970s. Part of the difference between U.S. and Soviet productivity can be explained by climate and terrain: Russia is both drier and cooler than the United States. Another factor, however, is that the assembly-line model of specialization of tasks does not work in agriculture. On collective farms, where planning decisions were made by outside agencies and farmers were assigned jobs and paid by the hour, output was low. On their private plots, where they had complete control over decision making and care of the crop from sowing to harvesting, farmers were at their most productive. (In fact, produce from household plots of less than one acre each provided one quarter of the food consumed in the Soviet Union.) The regime knew this was a problem. Experiments were made with a system in which farmers were allowed to form work teams given responsibility for all the operations involved in growing and harvesting a crop. Where this system was used, productivity rose by as much as twenty times. The system was abandoned, however, for ideological and political reasons.

Despite the dismal performance of Soviet agriculture, living conditions for collective farmers improved because of massive agricultural subsidies. Prices paid for farm goods increased, collective farmers were guaranteed a minimum wage (only 10 percent less than the urban wage) and were provided retirement pensions. Soviet planners also increased the manufacture of rototillers, to help farmers tend their private plots. Beginning in 1974, farmers were automatically given passports without having to apply for them.

It is difficult to assess the living conditions and quality of life for Soviet citizens. Pay for factory workers was comparatively low, but they enjoyed lifetime job security. Workers were rarely fired, were never "laid off," and unemployment didn't exist. Women retired at fifty-five, and men retired at sixty, although pensions were low and old people with no savings generally lived in poverty. All Soviet citizens were provided with free education, free medical care (including drugs), low rent on housing, and low taxes. On the other hand, Soviet per capita consumption of food was less than three-quarters that of western industrial societies, and the Soviet diet emphasized bread and potatoes and limited consumption of meat, vegetables, and fruit. Soviet society faced other problems typical of advanced industrial societies: rates of violent crime, child abuse, divorce, and alcoholism rose in the Brezhnev era.

Despite the poor quality of consumer goods, demand outstripped supply. The waiting list to buy automobiles was so long it could take years for a Soviet citizen to buy a car. The Soviet Union did not have to develop a system of consumer debt or installment purchases, since the lack of goods to buy meant Soviet citizens had no choice but to build up savings accounts; Soviet citizens could pay cash even for the purchase of automobiles. Just as industry only worked through extra-legal barter, so consumers had to resort to an underground economy—the black market. This included foreign goods that were otherwise available only through special stores reserved for the elite, as well as Soviet goods that employees stole for resale. Because of chronic consumer goods shortages, enterprising Soviet citizens who happened to come upon a shelf full of rare goods would buy up the lot to sell or trade on the black market. (Selling was illegal, although bartering—since it could be represented as the exchange of "gifts"—was permitted by law.) Appliance and auto repair and apartment remodeling was also provided by moonlighting workers who used tools and materials from the factory or shop they worked in.

If life was less than optimal for ordinary people, however, the Communist party had never had it so good. The party had given up communist utopianism and concentrated on maintaining the stability of the system and the material privileges of the elite. The Communist leaders controlled its members not through fear of punishment but by promise of reward. In the Soviet system, money was irrelevant, since everyone had more than they could spend. What counted was the power to bypass waiting lists for automobiles and other goods, admission to luxury housing, and access to special resorts, homes, and hospitals. There were special stores stocked with the best Soviet goods and imported gourmet food and luxury items, and there was a special system of clinics and hospitals which provided the elite the best medical care.

At all levels, union, regional, and local, the party maintained a ranked list (known as *nomenklatura*) of Communist party members, government officials, and industrial managers that indicated who was next in line for promotion when positions became vacant. It was not necessary to be a member of the Communist party to be on the list, but one had to be nominated by a member of the party. Consequently, personal connections were as important as technical qualifications in gaining promotion to a more prestigious position or relocation to a more desirable city. This system was dominated by patron-client networks. When an individual was promoted to a higher position, he owed loyalty to the person who promoted him, and he was able, himself, to offer promotions to his own subordinates, who, in turn, were beholden to him. (The masculine pronoun is used since the system was dominated by men, although women, to the extent they rose in the party hierarchy necessarily played the roles of both patron and client.) These personal connections were important in solving the problems of the planned economy, but they also resulted in corruption. The same techniques that permitted industrial managers to divert resources from one enterprise to another, in violation of the economic plan, could also be used for personal enrichment.

The party gave preference to the military and to those with higher education. Top military officials were appointed to the Politburo, and Brezhnev was given the military rank of marshal and named commander-in-chief of the Soviet military. In the late 1970s, half of all male college graduates joined the party (only 15 percent of female graduates did so). In addition, there were quotas, which ensured that members of non-Russian national groups appeared at the highest levels of the party. This was for show, however; Party membership was dominated by Russians, and Party ideology was colored by Russian chauvinism.

PEOPLES OF THE USSR

Khrushchev had taken the Leninist position that as communism neared, nationality would disappear and the peoples of the USSR would fuse into a single (Russian-speaking) Soviet proletarian identity. The Brezhnev regime required Russian language instruction in the first three years of elementary school throughout the USSR, it required all Soviet teachers to study Russian language and literature, and it used Russian as the only language of instruction in the Red Army. Otherwise, however, Brezhnev seemed to lack commitment to the Leninist ideal. The Soviet Constitution of 1977 viewed the fusion of peoples as it viewed communism: a distant ideal. In the Brezhnev era, ethnic identity in the Soviet republics flourished.

In the republics, the first secretary of the Communist party was of the titular nationality of that republic (i.e., a Georgian led the Georgian Communist party, a Tajik led the Tajik Communist party, etc.) and usually served for life. The second secretary, usually a Russian, was frequently rotated, in order to prevent him or her from developing local ties. This did not, however, prevent the development of tightly knit republican patron-client relationships that defended republican interests. These national parties did not subvert Communist rule, as might have happened in the 1920s, but were content to promote their own wealth and power. They also promoted the language and culture of republic's titular nationality in education and the media. There was a tendency toward the assimilation of minority groups in the republics. Children of mixed marriages were able to choose either parental nationality to be entered in their passport. Where one parent was Russian, children tended to chose to be Russian, but where one parent was of the titular nationality and the other was non-Russian, children tended to choose the titular nationality.

Active and passionate defense of national culture against creeping Russification was strongest in Ukraine and the Baltic countries. The Ukrainian government not only promoted Ukrainian language and culture within its own territory, it attempted to defend the interests of Ukrainian communities in other republics. Ukrainian dissidents protested the economic exploitation of their republic. In 1974, a National Popular Front arose in Lithuania which called for the immediate use of Lithuanian as the primary language of the Republic, respect for human rights, and an end of economic exploitation. Many also hoped for national independence in the long run. Estonians organized an Estonian National Front on the Lithuanian model, and in 1980, public demonstrations against Russification erupted in Estonia.

Similar events occurred in the south. Georgians resented the increased use of Russian in schools and universities, and in 1978, there were demonstrations against a proposed clause in the constitution that would have made Russian equal with Georgian as the language of government. Crimean Tatars were one of the few peoples deported by Stalin during World War II who had not been allowed to return to their homeland. Their cause was taken up by the samizdat *Chronicle of Current Events*, and beginning in 1968, they periodically staged public demonstrations.

In Central Asia, nationalism was not well developed, but neither did Russification make much headway. Less than 20 percent of the native population of Turkmenistan, Tajikistan, and Kirgizstan spoke Russian, and in Uzbekistan fewer than 15 percent did. In addition,

Islam thrived, as Muslims found ways of accommodating to modern society. They developed ways of praying at work that did not draw attention, and they often reduced the length of the fast of Ramadan. In Central Asia, the indigenization of the republican Communist Parties was particularly developed, as national elites formed extensive patronage networks based on ethnicity.

With the failure of Jews to move to Birobidzhan in the Stalinist era, it had become evident that Jews, as a religious and cultural identity, had no future in the Soviet Union. In fact, most Jews assimilated into Soviet society, adopting Russian literary and artistic culture and Soviet ideals of internationalism and social welfare. Beginning in the late 1960s, however, a number of Jews began to demand the right to emigrate—some for greater religious freedom, many more to escape discrimination in professional advancement. In the 1970s, the Brezhnev regime began to accede to their wishes, and by 1979, 200,000 Jews had been allowed to leave the country. They had to declare the intention to emigrate to Israel, but many went to Europe and the United States, instead.

The Brezhnev era also saw the rise of a popular Russian nationalism. It had begun as a nostalgia for old Russia as expressed by the Village Prose writers, and it became a popular movement with political overtones at the beginning of the Brezhnev era. In response to a plan to dam the rivers of Siberia and to divert their water to the Caspian Sea (where the water level had been falling), a Society for the Preservation of Historical and Cultural Monuments arose in protest. Part of the movement was driven by resentment at "Russian" water going to help Central Asia, and part was opposition to the flooding of many river valleys, which would cover old Russian churches and other cultural artifacts. The Society won, and the Soviet regime abandoned the river diversion plan.

CONCLUSION: THE END OF DETENTE

A new stage in Soviet history began in the late 1970s, as economic decline in the Soviet Union coincided with the rise of independent but simultaneous anti-Communist movements in Eastern Europe and the West. Detente, which had been begun by U.S. President Nixon, in his search for a way out of the Vietnam quagmire, had produced few results. Despite its willingness to sign arms control treaties, the Soviet Union had continued to pursue an aggressive foreign policy. American politicians, smarting over their embarrassment in Vietnam and in Iran, wanted the United States to take a harder line against the USSR.

They found their opportunity in Afghanistan. After the leftist, secularist coup against the Daud regime in 1978, bands of mujahidin (Islamist guerrilla warriors) formed across the border in Pakistan. They began to mount raids against the pro-Soviet government in Kabul and organize resistance among tribal leaders in the countryside. In July 1979, U.S. President Jimmy Carter began secretly to supply aid and weapons to Islamic insurgents. In the meantime, Soviet leaders were increasingly alarmed at the possibility that Afghanistan would fall to the mujahidin and that an Islamist Afghanistan would spread Islamic extremism to the neighboring Muslim Soviet Republics of Central Asia. In late December 1979, the Soviet Army moved into Afghanistan to prop up the secular, socialist government. Detente was dead, and the Soviet Union was drawn into its own "Vietnam."

_____ TEXT DOCUMENTS _____

Brezhnev, Report on the Soviet Constitution of 1977

In 1977, the Brezhnev government prepared a new constitution for the USSR to address changes that had occurred in Soviet society since Stalin's era. A draft constitution was widely disseminated among the population. It was discussed at public meetings, and individuals were invited to send written suggestions of changes. It was reported that 400,000 comments were received and that 110 articles were changed and one new one added as a result. In this excerpt from Brezhnev's report, he discusses the suggestions that were not acted upon.

- What does this reveal about the nature of "developed socialism" in the Brezhnev Era?
- What future social and political problems might proceed from this?

Some proposals have clearly run ahead of our time, failing to take account of the fact that the new Constitution is the Fundamental Law of a state of developed socialism and not of communism. We live according to the socialist principle, "From each according to his abilities, to each according to his work." To bypass this principle at the present level of economic development and social consciousness is impossible. Hence it is not possible, for instance, to accept proposals for the introduction of equal wages and pensions for everyone, or for basing wages and pensions solely on seniority, without taking account of skill levels and the quality of workmanship.

There have also been proposals either to abolish or sharply limit subsidiary small-holdings. However, it is well known that this form of labor, which does not involve exploitation, has a useful role to play in our economy at the present stage. That is why, in our opinion, the comrades are right who propose that the Constitution should emphasize that the state and collective farms shall assist citizens in running their subsidiary small-holdings. Besides, those who oppose subsidiary small-holdings are clearly worried not so much by their existence as by their abuse for the purpose of profiteering, instances of which, regrettably, still exist. It is here that the state agencies concerned should firmly exercise the right of control given to them by the Constitution, see to it that the plots of land made available to citizens are used rationally, for the benefit of society, and that the incomes from subsidiary small-holdings and personal labor conform to the principles of socialism.

A new historical community—the Soviet people—has, as we know, taken shape in the USSR. Some comrades—it is true that they are not many—have drawn incorrect conclusions

Source: *On the Draft Constitution (Fundamental Law) of the Union of Soviet Socialist Republics and the Results of Its Nation-wide Discussion. Report by Leonid Brezhnev to the Session of the Supreme Soviet, October 4, 1977,* [and] *Constitution (Fundamental Law) of the Union of Soviet Socialist Republics.* [Moscow : All-Union Znaniye Society], 1977, 8–9.

from this. They propose introducing in the Constitution the concept of an integral Soviet *nation*, eliminating the Union and Autonomous Republics or drastically curtailing the sovereignty of the Union Republics, depriving them of the right to secede from the USSR and of the right to maintain external relations. The proposals to do away with the Soviet of Nationalities and to set up a unicameral Supreme Soviet are along the same lines. I think that the erroneousness of these proposals is quite clear. The Soviet people's socio-political unity does not al all imply the disappearance of national distinctions. Thanks to the consistent pursuance of the Leninist nationalities policy we have, simultaneously with the construction of socialism, successfully solved the nationalities question, for the first time in history. The friendship of the Soviet peoples is indissoluble, and in the process of building communism they are steadily drawing ever closer together and are being mutually enriched in their spiritual life. But we would be taking a dangerous path if we were artificially to step up this objective process of the coming together of nations. That is something Lenin persistently warned against, and we shall not depart from his precepts. . . .

The Constitutional Commission has also received letters proposing that state functions should be vested directly in Party bodies, that the Political Bureau of the CPSU Central Committee should be vested with legislative power, and so on. These proposals are profoundly erroneous because they introduce confusion into the understanding of the Party's role in our society and tend to obscure the importance and functions of the bodies of Soviet power.

When our Party became the ruling party, it firmly declared at its Eighth Congress, which was directed by Lenin, that it implemented its decisions "through the Soviet bodies, *within the framework of the Soviet Constitution*" . . . and that while guiding the Soviets it did not supersede them, that it drew a line between the functions of Party and state bodies. This Leninist principle is recorded in the CPSU Rules, and was re-emphasized in the decisions of the latest Party congresses. We also propose to have it reflected in the new Constitution.

Protests Against the Invasion of Czechoslovakia, 1968

The Chronicle of Current Events *was a samizdat publication that provided news and information not reported in the official press. The following report comes from issue number three of the* Chronicle.

- What does this reveal about social activism in the Soviet Union? About the attitudes of the KGB?
- How does the Brezhnev Era compare with the Stalin Era? How "modern" was Soviet society?

On August 24th, in Moscow's October Square, a certain citizen shouted out a slogan against the invasion of Czechoslovakia and was roughly beaten up by some strangers in plain clothes. Two of them hustled him into a car and drove off; the third remained beside a second car. Indignant onlookers began to demand that the police should detain this participant in the assault. But the police only examined his papers.

Many incidents are known of non-attendance on principle at meetings held with the aim of achieving unanimous approval for the sending of troops into Czechoslovakia. There have also been cases where people have found the courage either to refrain from voting or to vote against giving such approval. This happened at the Institute of the International Workers' Movement, at the Institute of the Russian Language, in one of the departments of Moscow State University, at the Institute of World Economics and International Affairs, at the Institute of Philosophy and at the Institute of Radio Technology and Electronics.

Pamphlets containing protests against the occupation of Czechoslovakia have come to circulate widely in Moscow. . . .

The most outspoken protest against the aggression in Czechoslovakia was the sit-down demonstration which took place at 12 o'clock on August 25th, 1968, in Red Square. A letter from one of the participants in the demonstration, Natalya Gorbanevskaya, gives detailed information about this event:

. . . To the chief editors of *Rude Pravo*, *L'Unita*, the *Morning Star*, *L'Humanité*, the *Times*, *Le Monde*, the *Washington Post*, *Neue Zarcher Zeitung*, the *New York Times*, and any other paper which will publish this letter.

August 28th, 1968 . . .

Dear Editor,

I ask you to print my letter about the demonstration in Red Square in Moscow on August 25th, 1968, since I am the sole participant of that demonstration still at liberty.

[She lists the people who took part.] At midday we sat . . . [in front of St Basil's Cathedral] and unrolled banners with the slogans "Long Live Free And Independent Czechoslovakia" (Written in Czech), "Shame on The Occupiers," "Hands Off Czechoslovakia," "For Your

Source: Peter Reddaway, Ed. *Uncensored Russia. Protest and Dissent in the Soviet Union. The Unofficial Moscow Journal, A Chronicle of Current Events.* (New York: American Heritage Press; a division of McGraw-Hill Book Company, 1972), 96–102. Reprinted by permission of Random House Group Limited.

Freedom And Ours." Almost immediately a whistle blew and plainclothes KGB men rushed at us from all corners of the square. They were on duty in Red Square, waiting for the Czechoslovak delegation's departure from the Kremlin. They ran up shouting "They're all Jews!" "Beat the anti-Sovietists!" We sat quietly and did not resist. They tore the banners from our hands. They beat Victor Fainberg in the face until he bled, and knocked his teeth out. They hit Pavel Litvinov about the face with a heavy bag, and they snatched away from me a Czechoslovak flag and smashed it. They shouted at us, "Disperse, you scum!" But we remained sitting. After a few minutes cars arrived, and all except me were bundled into them. I was with my three-month-old son, and therefore they did not seize me straight away. I sat at Execution Place for about another ten minutes. In the car they beat me. Several people from the crowd which had gathered, ones who had expressed their sympathy with us, were arrested along with us, and released only late in the evening. During the night searches were made of all those held, on the charge of "group activities flagrantly violating public order". . . . After the search I was released, probably because I had two children to look after. I am continually being summoned to give evidence. I refuse to give evidence on the organization and conduct of the demonstration, since it was a peaceful demonstration which did not disturb public order. But I did give evidence about the rough and illegal actions of the people who detained us: I am ready to testify to this before world public opinion. . . .

[signed] Natalya Gorbanevskaya

. . . Reports have come in of incidents in other towns of the country. In Leningrad and the Baltic Republics leaflets condemning the invasion of Czechoslovakia have come to circulate widely. . . .

The Estonian student who wrote CZECHS, WE ARE YOUR BROTHERS on a cinema wall in Tartu on the night of August 21st-22nd was savagely beaten up while in detention. His kidneys were damaged and he is still in hospital. . . . Now he has been removed from hospital by KGB men, and so far nothing is known about his fate.

Leningrad. On the night of August 21st-22nd, 1968, a 20-year-old Leningrader, Boguslavsky, wrote on the sculpture of three horses by Klodt: BREZHNEV GET OUT OF CZECHOSLOVAKIA. He was arrested immediately on Anichkov Bridge and two weeks later was sentenced under article 70 to five years in a strict-regime labor camp. In October the Russian Supreme Court, considering his appeal, reclassified his action under article 190-1, and consequently altered his sentence to three years in an ordinary-regime camp (the maximum penalty under this article). . . .

Novosibirsk. On the night of August 25th, 1968, slogans condemning the invasion of Czechoslovakia appeared on several public buildings in the Akademgorodok suburb of Novosibirsk. One of them read: BARBARIANS—GET OUT OF CZECHOSLOVAKIA. Dogs were used in the search for those who had written the slogans, but no one was found. From previous experience it was known that the slogans would not wash off easily and so they were covered with newspapers.

Editorial, "Freedom for the Kitchen?"

This essay by L. Libedinskaia appeared in the newspaper, Literaturnaia gazeta, *on February 22, 1967. It was a reply to an earlier editorial, by Eduard Shim, who argued that women should be freed from heavy labor responsibilities so they can care for their families.*

- How does this reflect official Soviet attitudes toward women?
- How does Libedinskaia make her argument?
- What does this reveal about trends and attitudes in Soviet society in the 1960s?

. . . Is it harmful to carry heavy weights around in production? Yes, it is harmful! But this is a matter for the labor safety code. Medicine and medicine alone must determine with complete precision just what work a woman can do and what she cannot do. (Thus women's soccer was duly forbidden.)

But who can forbid women to carry extremely heavy bags of potatoes, and bread, bottles of milk and other food from the stores and the markets? No one. This is how it has been for centuries: If you have a family you have to feed it, which means you have to carry. And no one will think it unnatural, no one will reflect that this is just as harmful as hauling heavy things about in a shop. In production however, a woman retires on pension at the age of fifty-five, while a house-wife has no pension age. . . .

"Women will still shoulder a double burden," Eduard Shim writes, "no matter how much we urge men to wash diapers, scrub floors and cook."

There is no need to force men to do such thankless tasks. Let them design new machines, build houses, paint pictures, and write books. But help women emancipate themselves from their stultifying daily cares!

During the war, in my student years, I had to dig ditches at Moscow's defense lines; gather firewood; serve at a hospital, working at the radio center for dispatching transport; climb power transmission line poles; and trudge along railroad tracks for many kilometers in freezing weather. But each of these jobs, and some were very hard, had meaning and purpose; this is probably why I remember them now without horror. But the kitchen sink endlessly filling with sticky cups and greasy plates makes my flesh crawl.

Is it really impossible to make machines for washing dishes? And they should be cheap, even if at first they are produced at a loss—surely our women have earned such a gift. . . .

Why not create another ministry in our country—a united ministry of everyday services? And a woman should be appointed Minister of it, one who once had to shoulder all the burdens of housework herself. Give her funds and broad powers. Allow her to display initiative without having each of her measures approved at several levels, and believe me, the new Minister will find hundreds of ways to take care of the everyday needs of her countrywomen.

Source: *The Current Digest of the Soviet Press,* Vol. 19, no 15 (May 3, 1967), 13–14. Translation copyright by *The Current Digest of the Soviet Press,* published weekly at Columbus, Ohio. Reprinted by permission of the *Digest.*

I have no doubts as to Eduard Shim's good intentions. Nonetheless, as I read his article I could not help recalling the old Oriental proverb: the ordinary woman has as much sense as a hen, and the extraordinary one, as a pair of hens." In his reasoning there is a latent desire to put woman in her place, the place allotted to her for centuries. . . .

A woman can do everything! But just what must she do?

"We must concede that one of woman's chief services is her work in bringing up children." But who knows how to rear children in general? How many discussions and arguments have centered around this question. The public organizations have shifted the main burden of upbringing to the school, the school has shifted it to the family, and in the family it is the woman who must assume this burden. Does this not mean to some extent that the man is relieved of responsibility for molding the child's personality? Many a woman knows what it means to raise children without a father. How difficult it is! Was it by chance that the people coined the bitter word "fatherlessness?" To watch over a child's spiritual growth painstakingly, unobtrusively, every day and every hour, to help and guide him is not only the woman's direct obligation but also the man's. After all, fatherlessness exists even when the fathers are alive.

Woman must, of course, be given more free time, but by no means for the purposes of shopping, doing the laundry and cooking. She needs it in order to be able to read unhampered, or simply to think, to be silent for awhile, or to wander about alone in the city or the woods. Eduard Shim asserts that woman's position will change for the better when every "head of the family," i.e., the man, can fully support the family and the woman will not have to work for the sake of the wages.

There are all different sorts of families. I have some friends—a man and wife who are both doctors of science, both professors. Both head large laboratories, read papers at international congresses and publish their scientific works; their salaries are identical. But in addition the wife must think of their daughter's upbringing, and see that there are always starched shirts in the dresser for her husband and that the table is set when guests arrive.

So who is the head of this family? And should this woman be freed from her work in the laboratory so that she can devote more time to housework?

Yes, the moral and material incentives are indivisible.

They are indivisible also because earning money on her own gives a woman independence.

One often hears women who have devoted themselves entirely to housework in families where the fathers can afford everything needed complain bitterly that their husbands reproach them for their inability to save money. Any woman who has any self-respect at all would not only dig ditches but do the dirtiest work, if only to avoid hearing humiliating reproaches and to have the right to spend the money she has earned as she sees fit.

How many wives would no longer have to put up with the perpetual female humiliations if each were materially independent and unafraid of the possibility of being left alone and losing the benefits of her husband's position! . . .

Eduard Shim is right—women should be freed from heavy physical labor. She should not be freed for the kitchen, however, but from the kitchen. This will show genuine concern for women.

The Meskhetians

The Meskhetians are Turkic language speakers who lived in southern Georgia. They were at first classified by the Soviet government as Turks, then in 1935, they were re-classified as Azerbaijanis. In 1944, during the Second World War, they were again de-fined as Turks, and they were deported to Central Asia. In 1956, after Khrushchev's secret speech, it was announced that all ethnic groups who had been unjustly deported would be allowed to return to their former homelands. Some were actually allowed to do so, but the Meskhetians were not.

- What does this reveal about Soviet nationality policies?
- What does it reveal about social protest, the rule of law in the USSR, and the methods of the KGB?

On November 18th, 1968, B. P. Yakovlev, an official of the Central Committee of the party, received [once again] a delegation of Meskhi representatives in Moscow—the twenty-fourth of its kind. During his talk with them, Yakovlev granted the Meskhi permission to settle in various regions of Georgia, and fifteen to thirty families were even allowed to settle in Meskhetia. Although this permission was not confirmed in writing, the Meskhi people de-cided at their meetings to trust this indefinite form of permission. However, those who were prepared to get up and go have met with persistent opposition: they are refused references from the places of work releasing them, they are not removed from the military service reg-ister, and no transport is provided for them.

Eight families from the kolkhoz "Ady-Gyun" in the Saatly District of Azerbaidzhan left for Georgia, abandoning their homes and belongings because they had been refused trans-port. They were given work at a state farm in the Makharadze District of Georgia, but were very soon dismissed, and deported back to Saatly District by the police. . . .

The Meskhi from the kolkhoz "21st Congress of the Party," also in the Saatly District, man-aged to procure seven vehicles for their journey, but they were stopped by the police and forced to escape into Georgia on foot, leaving behind their belongings as trophies for the Saatly District police. There are many similar stories. Georgian railway stations and termi-nuses have become crowded with homeless people, deprived of their belongings and their work, with no roof over their heads, systematically driven out of their homeland the moment they set foot in it. Whole families with small children, old men, and invalids are involved.

On April 19th, 1969, the President of the Temporary Organizing Committee for the Return of the Meskhi to their Homeland was arrested in Saatly. He is Enver Odabashev (Khozre-vanadze), an officer in the reserve, who took part in the Great Patriotic War. Odabashev was attending a teachers' conference, during which he was called outside. Waiting for him on the street was the district Procurator Kadirov, with two unknown men. The Procurator then lured Odabashev to the police station under false pretenses, and left him there. Odabashev

Source: Peter Reddaway, Ed. *Uncensored Russia. Protest and Dissent in the Soviet Union. The Unofficial Moscow Journal, A Chronicle of Current Events.* (New York: American Heritage Press; a division of McGraw-Hill Book Company, 1972), 276–279. Reprinted by permission of The Random House Group Ltd.

was held there until one o'clock in the morning, with no explanations and no food, and then summoned for interrogation by an investigator of the district Procuracy, Farzaliyev. The interrogation lasted until 3:30 in the morning, thus violating the statute of Soviet law which states that interrogations may not be held at night, except in urgent cases which cannot be delayed. Then Odabashev was put into an unheated room, where he soon caught a chill, dressed as he was in light clothing. In protest at his arrest by force and deception, and at the arbitrariness of the whole affair, Odabashev began a hunger-strike.

After Odabashev had been detained, a search was carried out in his house. Local police inspector Ummatov, Procuracy investigator Farzaliyev and others made the search, during which they took away from an archive copies of documents addressed to the party, the government, and the people.

When they found out about Odabashev's arrest, on the morning of April 21st, the Meskhi left their work and came from all the village settlements in the area to gather in Saatly at the district party committee building, where they demanded the immediate release of their teacher of the people. When they met with refusal, the hard-working Meskhi sent express telegrams to L. I. Brezhnev and V. Yu. Akhundov. The crowd did not disperse. Late in the evening of April 21st, the secretary of the district party committee, Babayev, who had been in Baku, returned in great haste, probably sent by the republican party organs. After lengthy deliberations with representatives of the Meskhi, the district committee secretary ordered Odabashev to be released.

Odabashev was brought in for interrogation, already prepared and photographed for deportation the next morning, and told: "Sign here, we're releasing you." The district police chief Mirzoyev, and the Procurator Kadirov, who had finally appeared, began shouting and threatening and demanding that Odabashev should not travel anywhere or participate in any meetings. That night, after his spell in a cold cell, and hungry from his strike, Odabashev signed a blank sheet of paper which the investigator, Farzaliyev, handed to him, as well as the record of his interrogation. No one can tell how this blank sheet will be used.

When the old teacher was let out into the street, he was met by the crowd of Meskhi, who had not dispersed although it was now late at night. They shouted: "Freedom! Equality! Homeland or death! Our teacher lives!"

Reports began to circulate to the effect that Odabashev's arrest was to have been the first of a series of arrests of other activists. For the moment, however, the people's reaction has put a stop to the unlawful actions of the authorities. Still, the threat of arrest has, as before, come to hang over active participants in the movement for a return to the homeland.

The Georgian government suggested earlier to the Meskhi that they settle in other areas of Georgia, in particular in Kolkhida [i.e. Colchis, in west Georgia]. By June 1969, 505 Meskhi families had arrived in Georgia. The Georgian population welcomed them as brothers, and helped them settle in. But on June 7th there was a round-up of Meskhi who had already arrived and found work, as a result of which they were sent off by train in various different directions. The fate of many of the victims of this round-up, or their whereabouts, are not known.

VISUAL DOCUMENTS

Figure 20-1 Portrait of L. I. Brezhnev

This is an official photographic portrait of Leonid Brezhnev (1906–1982).

- Compare this with the representations of previous leaders, and consider similarities and differences.
- What qualities is it intended to convey?

Source: Getty Images Inc.—Hulton Archive Photos

Figure 20-2 Constructing a Gas Pipeline

This photograph, taken in January 1975, shows the construction of a gas pipeline connecting natural gas deposits under the tundra of the Khanty-Manaiysky with the Ural industrial region.

- What does this reveal about the level of Soviet industrial development?
- What does it suggest about the challenges of economic development in North Central Asia?

Source: Keystone/Stringer.

Figure 20-3 Russian Farm Women
    This photograph of women working on a collective farm near Novgorod was taken in the middle of the 1970s.
- Compare this with previous depictions of women and agriculture.
- Consider the continuities and the changes. What light does this shed on the nature of Soviet society?
Source: National Geographic Society.

Figure 20-4 Old Man in Samarkand
    This photograph of a man in Samarkand (Uzbekistan) was taken in the 1970s.
- What does this suggest about Uzbek society?
- What does it reveal about the impact of Soviet policies in Central Asia?
Source: National Geographic Society.

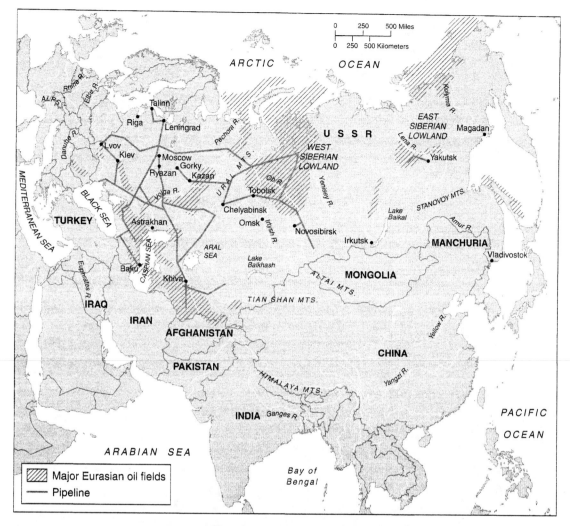

Figure 20-5 Eurasian Oil Fields and Soviet Oil Pipelines in the Brezhnev Era
- What does this reveal about the integration of the Soviet economy?
- What role did oil play in the Soviet economy?

_____ FOR FURTHER READING _____

(In addition to the books by Brown, Clements, Hosking, and Suny from the previous chapter.)

Alexeyeva, Ludmilla. *Soviet Dissent: Contemporary Movements for National, Religious, and Human Rights.* Middletown, CT: Wesleyan University Press, 1985.

Bialer, Seweryn. *The Soviet Paradox: External Expansion, Internal Decline.* New York: Knopf, 1986.

Breslauer, George W. *Khrushchev and Brezhnev as Leaders: Building Authority in Soviet Politics.* London: Allen & Unwin, 1982.

Dunlop, John B. *The Faces of Contemporary Russian Nationalism.* Princeton, NJ: Princeton University Press, 1983.

Hajda, Lubomyr and Mark Beissinger, Eds. *The Nationalities Factor in Soviet Politics and Society.* Boulder, CO: Westview Press, 1990.

Holloway, David. *The Soviet Union and the Arms Race.* New Haven, CT: Yale University Press, 1983.

Hough, Jerry. *The Soviet Prefects: The Local Party Organs in Industrial Decision-making.* Cambridge, MA: Harvard University Press, 1969.

_____. *How the Soviet Union is Governed* (Cambridge, MA: Harvard University Press, 1979).

Kerblay, Basile. *Modern Soviet Society.* New York: Pantheon Books, 1983.

CHAPTER TWENTY ONE

THE DISSOLUTION OF THE SOVIET UNION, 1979–1991

As the 1980s began, the Soviet Union appeared to be at the height of its power and influence. It was an economic superpower, contributing 20 percent of the total global industrial output, and producing eighty percent as much industrial output as the United States. It was a military superpower as well, matching its only rival, the United States, in nuclear missiles and military hardware in general, and exceeding it in troop strength. The Soviet Union was aggressively projecting its influence abroad; it had forced the Polish government to suppress an anti-communist trade-union movement, and it was applying the "Brezhnev Doctrine" to Afghanistan, defending the socialist government there from subversion by Islamist mujahidin. Nevertheless, there was a mood of malaise in Soviet society. The Brezhnev "Era of Stagnation" was bereft of any kind of idealism; the dissident generation of the sixties was middle-aged and tired of fighting the regime, and Party leaders had long since ceased to talk about building communism. Brezhnev died in 1982 and was succeeded by two communists of his own generation (Iurii Andropov, 1982 to 1984, and Konstantin Chernenko, 1984 to 1985) who allowed the stagnation to continue.

This ended in 1985 when the fifty-three-year-old Mikhail Gorbachev became General Secretary of the Communist party. Gorbachev was filled with enthusiasm for revitalizing the Soviet experiment by returning it to its Leninist roots. He promoted economic reform, called for democratization of Soviet society, and announced a new era of peace and cooperation with the capitalist world. In fact, Gorbachev brought the Cold War to an end. He withdrew missiles from eastern Europe, negotiated a major reduction in nuclear weapons with the United States, and ceased to aim nuclear missiles at targets in the United States. Gorbachev also renounced the Brezhnev Doctrine. He withdrew Soviet forces from Afghanistan, and he gave up control over the nations of eastern Europe. At home, Gorbachev made elections more democratic and permitted freedom of speech and artistic expression, he ended the Communist party's monopoly on power, and he began to restructure the economy on free-market principles.

However, Gorbachev's reforms released social and political forces that he could not control. As the press became freer and revealed problems and abuses in Soviet society, and as the economy began to deteriorate, the population became increasingly disillusioned with the Soviet system. As the Communist party relaxed its grip on political power, political actors—both inside and outside the Communist party—began to imagine alternatives to the Soviet system. In the context of this political transformation, an utterly unexpected development occurred: The Soviet Union was dissolved. The fundamental contradiction of Soviet nationality policies finally was resolved: The fifteen Soviet Socialist Republics acted on the Leninist principle of the right of nations to self-determination, and seceded from the Union. The Russian Empire, after seventy-four years in Soviet form, came to its (apparently) final end, leaving behind fifteen sovereign nation-states. Such an occurrence is without precedent in history: A rich and powerful empire, not facing economic collapse, popular uprisings, barbarian invasion, or war, peacefully voted itself out of existence.

EURASIAN CONTEXT

Western neo-liberals used the economic troubles of the 1970s to discredit demand-side economics and the welfare state and aggressively to promote the virtues of monetarism, free markets, and individual responsibility. Margaret Thatcher, the first western leader to espouse these values, became Prime Minister of Great Britain in 1979; she blamed inflation on excessive government spending and the economic recession on socialism and the labor movement. Once in office Thatcher practiced supply-side economics by cutting taxes for the wealthy and spending programs for the poor. She attacked the power of trade unions, and she privatized Britain's state-owned industries. By the mid-1980s, life for lower-income Britons deteriorated, but inflation ended, the economy grew, and the wealthy prospered. Helmut Kohl, who became Prime Minister of Germany in 1982, followed Thatcher's lead. He cut spending on welfare, froze wages of government employees, and cut taxes on corporations. Socialist leaders in France and Spain, did not pursue Thatcherite privatization, but they did tend to follow supply-side, monetarist policies.

In eastern Europe, too, there was a rising tide of dissatisfaction with socialism, though in the East the desire for freedom of speech and action was at least as important as the hope for greater prosperity. Poland led the way. Strikes by workers had occurred sporadically in the 1970s, but they had been suppressed. In 1978, the former archbishop of Krakow, Cardinal Wojtyla, was elected Pope (choosing the name John Paul II), and his visit to Poland the following year inspired a surge of Polish nationalism. Soon after, a major strike at the shipyard in Gdansk forced concessions from the Polish Communist party, and Lech Walesa emerged as the leader of Solidarity, a ten-million-member national trade union. The Brezhnev regime told Polish Communist leaders that if they could not restore order, the Red Army would do it for them. In the autumn of 1981, General Wojciech Jaruzelski became the leader of the party, imposed martial law, broke up Solidarity, and imprisoned its leaders.

After Gorbachev became General Secretary of the Communist party in 1985, his ideas about restructuring socialism had immediate consequences in eastern Europe. In the summer of 1986, the Communist parties of Poland and Yugoslavia reorganized and allowed a massive influx of younger members. A year later, when Gorbachev visited Czechoslovakia and Romania, he was given a chilly reception by Communist leaders but was cheered by crowds in the street. In March 1988, while on a visit to Hungary, Gorbachev announced that the Soviet Union would no longer interfere in eastern Europe. Two months later, Hungary removed the barbed wire fence separating it from Austria, and East Germans by the thousands traveled to Hungary on tourist visas, then crossed the border to Austria on their way to West Germany.

In August 1988, Lech Walesa was asked by the Polish government to mediate a miners' strike with the promise of future reform. The following April, Solidarity was legalized, and elections to the Sejm (parliament) allocated 35 percent of the seats to non-Communists. A popularly elected presidency was created, the judiciary was made independent, and Roman Catholicism was declared the official religion. By the end of the year, the cabinet was composed of seven members of Solidarity and only four Communists. General Jaruzelski won the first election as President and served through 1989, but the Sejm called for new elections in 1990, and this time Lech Walesa was elected President.

In October 1989, Gorbachev visited Berlin where he was greeted by thousands of cheering East Germans. After he left, having notified the East German government that the Red Army would not protect it, public demonstrations against Communist rule increased. Communist party leader Erich Honecker announced his retirement, and the entire Politburo and Council of Ministers resigned. On November 9, 1989, the Berlin Wall, the most famous symbol of the Cold War, was first opened and then dismantled by ecstatic crowds. In January 1990, East Germans elected a non-Communist government, and negotiations to unify East and West Germany began. Reunification was completed October 3, with East Germany losing its separate existence and accepting the flag, currency, constitution, and government of the Federal Republic of Germany.

Yugoslavia, Czechoslovakia, Hungary, Bulgaria, and Romania followed roughly the same timetable. By the spring of 1990, massive public demonstrations forced the Communist party in each nation to permit multiparty elections, and before the end of the year all but Bulgaria and Romania were governed by non-Communist administrations. In Bulgaria a coalition of communists and socialists governed, and in Romania vote fraud temporarily kept the regime of Nikolai Ceaucescu in power. By the autumn of 1991, however, a popular revolution in Romania (in which more than a thousand citizens were shot by the army before the army mutinied against the government) had brought down Ceaucescu, and a multiparty system had emerged in Bulgaria.

In the 1980s, Turkey became an associate member of the European Economic Community and it followed European economic patterns. The government declared its faith in the free market, removed state controls on the economy, and encouraged foreign trade. There was, however, a rising tide of opposition to the government's economic policies and European orientation manifested in the public practice of Islamic traditions. In the countryside, there was increasing segregation of the sexes, many women adopted traditional hair covering and even veils, and more parents sent their children to Islamic schools. An Islamist political organization, the Welfare Party emerged, but it won no seats in Parliament through the 1980s.

On April 1, 1979, Ayatollah Ruhollah Khomeini was elected President of Iran. He led the transformation of Iran into a theocracy; the government enforced Islamic law, secular parties and movements were suppressed, and candidates for public office needed the prior approval of a commission of Muslim clerics. Khomeini proposed Iran as a model for Islamic countries and promised aid to Islamist movements in the Middle East.

The Iranian model threatened all secular governments in the Middle East, none more than Iraq, which was ruled by the secular Arab nationalist Ba'ath party. In the fall of 1980, Saddam Hussein, who had become ruler in 1979, ordered an invasion of Iran. The pretext of the war was a boundary dispute, but Hussein's larger objectives were to annex Khuzistan, a province with large oil deposits and populated by an Arab majority, and to bring down Khomeini's government. Iraq was aided by its traditional ally, the Soviet Union, but also by the United States, which was equally opposed to the spread of Islamism in the Middle East. Even with aid from the two superpowers, however, Iraq's modern military was no match for the suicidal patriotism of the Iranian army. In fact, Iran quickly took the offensive and soon threatened Iraq. Increased support from the United States forced Iran to agree to a cease-fire in 1988.

In Afghanistan, however, the two superpowers opposed one another. In this case, the United States supported the Islamists, and joined Saudi-Arabia, Pakistan, and China in aiding the mujahidin insurgency against the secular government that had been installed and was being defended by the Soviet army. The Soviet Union attempted to compromise with the Islamists by allowing opposition parties and even by forming coalition governments, but the mujahidin would accept nothing but total victory. The tide turned in 1986 when U.S.-made "Stinger" missiles (shoulder-fired anti-aircraft missiles) were introduced and used by the insurgents to decimate the Soviet helicopter force. The futility of the struggle soon became evident to Mikhail Gorbachev, and he began a phased withdrawal that was completed in February 1989. Two years later, the mujahidin took Kabul.

China had begun economic restructuring in 1978, when Hua Guofeng, who had succeeded Mao as chair of the Communist party, announced an economic modernization plan. The plan gave managers greater decision-making powers and rewarded them for efficiency and profitability; it also provided for larger private plots for farmers. Hua's successor, Deng Xiaoping, went even further. He allowed agricultural communes to divide land, tools, and livestock among individual households, and he permitted a portion of the harvest to be sold on the free market. Productivity increased so much that China began to export grain, soybeans, and cotton. In industry, Deng gave sole responsibility for production to factory managers and allowed them to keep one-half of their profits. By 1987, the Chinese economy was largely regulated by the market, and the government planning bureaucracy was dismantled.

Deng also streamlined the bureaucracy, professionalized the civil service, and oriented the judiciary toward the rule of law. His goal, however, was efficiency, not democratization. The Communist party maintained a monopoly on power, enforced strict ideological conformity in education and the media, and suppressed popular dissent. In May 1989, one million Chinese students, inspired by the transformation of the Soviet Union and eastern Europe, gathered in Tiananmen Square in Beijing to demonstrate for democracy. The square was cleared by tanks and machine gun fire, killing perhaps three thousand demonstrators and wounding an additional ten thousand. Deng was no Gorbachev.

POLITICAL DEVELOPMENTS

Brezhnev suffered from poor health in the last years of his life, but he kept his party and state offices until the day he died in 1982. He was replaced by Iurii Andropov, head of the KGB since 1967. Andropov did not mount any innovative reforms, but he did try to make the system work more efficiently. He prosecuted corruption in the party, mounted publicity campaigns to reduce alcohol consumption, and attempted to reduce absenteeism by requiring the police to randomly stop people on the streets to see if they should have been at work.

Andropov had been grooming a young man from Stavropol, Mikhail Gorbachev, for party leadership. In 1978, Gorbachev had been brought into the Secretariat, and in 1980, he was made a full member of the Politburo. When Andropov became General Secretary of the party, he promoted a number of Gorbachev's clients to positions of influence. However, when Andropov suddenly died in 1984, the party passed over his protege, whom they considered to be too progressive, and made the seventy-three-year-old Konstantin Chernenko General Secretary. The old guard could not keep Gorbachev from the number-two position on the Politburo, and when Chernenko died after less than a year in office Gorbachev succeeded him.

Mikhail Gorbachev immediately announced his intention to revitalize the Soviet economy, called for upgrading old factories, and demanded an improvement in the quality and quantity of consumer goods. In the summer of 1985, Gorbachev shook up the Central Committee and the Politburo, removing some of the old guard and appointing his own associates. One of his appointees to the Central Committee was the Party's first secretary of the Sverdlovsk district, Boris Yeltsin, who was famous for his campaigns against inefficiency and corruption. In February 1986, Gorbachev introduced the concept of *perestroika* or "restructuring," declaring the need for the USSR to "radically transform all spheres of life." He specifically called for greater autonomy for producers. In March, Gorbachev appointed Yeltsin to the Politburo.

A major turning point occurred on April 26, 1986 when a reactor at a nuclear power station in Chernobyl, Ukraine, blew up, killing at least thirty people, injuring many more, and causing forty thousand to be evacuated from the area. Soviet newspapers at first reported nothing, while the West was publishing reports from observers in Scandinavia who had detected a cloud of radiation that could only have come from a major nuclear disaster. Finally Gorbachev decided to allow full newspaper coverage, and the era of *glasnost* or "openness" began. Gorbachev began to remove censorship from the news media and fired a number of conservative journal editors, replacing them with progressives. Through the news media, the people demanded more information about the dangers posed by the Chernobyl disaster, and this freedom rapidly expanded into criticism of other aspects of the Soviet system.

Gorbachev also began to end political repression and ideological uniformity. In December 1986, he permitted Andrei Sakharov to return to Moscow and public life, and in early 1987 he released 140 dissidents from prison and exile. He declared a complete end to censorship: full glasnost for the news media, and freedom of thought and artistic expression for Soviet society as a whole.

Later in 1987, however, conservative Communists began to call for a brake on perestroika, and in November Gorbachev made some concessions. While denouncing Stalin's "enormous" crimes, he praised his collectivization policy and his leadership in World War II. In addition, Gorbachev sacrificed one of his most outspoken supporters, Boris Yeltsin, who had been stridently criticizing the slowness of reform. Gorbachev allowed the conservatives to remove Yeltsin from positions of power, first from the Central Committee (November 1987) then from the post of first secretary of the Moscow party organization (February 1988).

Nevertheless, Gorbachev's program of reform continued. In the spring of 1988, he announced term limits for officials, called for multiple candidates in all elections and greater responsibility for elective bodies. Conservatives were able to prevent multiparty elections, but even so, political culture was changing. In June 1988, when the Nineteenth Communist Party Conference was held, it not only permitted free and open debate over policy issues, it televised them to a nationwide audience. Soviet citizens, who had long known that rural poverty was a problem and that education and health care were deteriorating, and had been shown by the media that these problems were part of fundamental flaws in the system. They now also discovered that the Communist party had traditionally concealed the real state of Soviet society.

In the fall of 1988, Gorbachev proposed changes that would increase the power of elected government over the party. He arranged for the elimination of the indirectly elected Supreme

Soviet and the creation of a directly elected Congress of People's Deputies. This Congress would be the highest legislative body, and would choose a Supreme Soviet to draft legislation and a President to serve as chief executive. The first Congress was elected in the spring of 1989, and it, in turn, elected Gorbachev President of the USSR.

Despite the fact that 85 percent of the seats were guaranteed to candidates approved by the Communist party, the Communist dictatorship was over. Many conservative communists who ran unopposed were not elected because more than 50 percent of the voters in their districts voted "no." Furthermore, Gorbachev released all party members from party discipline, and encouraged them to speak and vote according to their personal views. The 15 percent of non-Communist deputies (which included Andrei Sakharov and Boris Yeltsin) played a prominent role in the work of the Congress.

Over the course of 1990, the program of openness and democratization was completed. In March, the Supreme Soviet repealed Article Six of the Constitution, which stated that the Communist Party was "the leading and guiding force of the Soviet society." In June, the government formally ended censorship and declared freedom of expression and the right of access to information from foreign sources. In October, freedom of conscience was reaffirmed, parents were allowed to raise their children in the Church, and churches were allowed to open schools and disseminate literature. The Communist dictatorship was over.

FOREIGN AFFAIRS

Ending the Cold War had been a part of Gorbachev's program from the very beginning. In April 1985, he declared a one-year moratorium on the testing of nuclear weapons, calling on the United States to follow suit. He also halted the deployment of medium-range nuclear missiles in eastern Europe. One year later, Gorbachev announced a three-month extension of the moratorium, again asking the United States to join him, and he proposed the elimination of all nuclear and chemical weapons by the year 2000. In October 1986, at a meeting in Reykjavik, Iceland, Gorbachev and U.S. President Ronald Reagan came close to agreeing on arms reductions, but negotiations broke down over Reagan's refusal to give up plans for a missile defense system (known as "Star Wars"). The following month, however, Gorbachev committed the USSR to a non-nuclear future, and talks with the United States resumed. In 1987, Gorbachev and Reagan agreed to eliminate intermediate-range nuclear missiles completely. In April 1988, Gorbachev announced a ten-month timetable for withdrawing Soviet forces from Afghanistan, and in the summer, Gorbachev and Reagan discussed the possibility of reducing their nuclear arsenals by half. It was on this occasion that Ronald Reagan declared that the USSR was no longer an "evil empire." Negotiations for a Strategic Arms Reduction Treaty (START) were completed in July 1991, in the administration of U.S. President George H. W. Bush. Under the agreement, the Soviet Union would reduce its nuclear stockpile by 25 percent (from eleven thousand to eight thousand weapons) and the United States would reduce its stocks by 15 percent (from 12,000 to 10,000). Missiles, heavy bombers, and mobile missile launchers were also reduced.

Soviet hegemony over eastern Europe, and the question of Germany's future, had been central in the Cold War, and here, too, Gorbachev reversed Soviet policy. He both encouraged the leaders of eastern European Communist parties to begin democratization and informed them that the Red Army could no longer be depended on to keep them in power. In 1988, during a visit to France, Gorbachev referred to "our common European home," and he declared that it was "inadmissible to interfere in another country's internal affairs." He lived up to his word as the nations of eastern Europe brought communism to an end, and he accepted the reunification of East and West Germany. The Cold War was officially brought to an end in November 1990 with the Charter of Paris (signed by all the major participants in World War II), which announced the end of confrontation and the beginning of an era of democracy, peace, and unity. The Warsaw pact officially dissolved itself on April 1, 1991; NATO remained intact.

CULTURE AND RELIGION

Gorbachev's original goal was not to transform the Soviet Union into a liberal, free-enterprise system, but to reinvigorate socialist idealism and grass roots activism and to return to Lenin's vision of social democracy. One of his first attempts at this was a revival of the old communist campaigns for scientific atheism to counter the rise of religion during the Brezhnev era. This was Gorbachev's first failure. Not only was there little interest in aggressive atheism, but once freedom of speech was permitted, crude attacks on the superstition and irrationality of religion (which in the past could not be rebutted by the faithful) could now be publicly answered.

Gorbachev gradually realized that religion was a powerful social force that had to be accommodated, and he was therefore receptive to the Holy Synod in April 1988 when they requested a meeting with him to talk about the future of the Russian Orthodox Church. He agreed that the Church should be recognized as a public institution, and he allowed them to summon a Sobor to restructure the Church. The Sobor (the highest governing authority in the Russian Orthodox Church) met in June. It abolished Khrushchev's 1961 church regulations, created self-governing parishes independent of local government, and restored the traditional authority of the parish priest. It so happened that 1988 was the thousand-year anniversary of the adoption of Christianity as the state religion of Kiev Rus, and Gorbachev made the commemoration of the millennium an official, government-sponsored event. He transferred ownership of the Danilov Monastery, which had been confiscated by the state, back to Church ownership so it could be used for the celebrations.

There were no more atheist propaganda campaigns, and Gorbachev let it be known that his own mother was a Russian Orthodox believer and that he himself had been baptized in the faith. In 1989, the Church was allowed to own private property and to publish and disseminate religious literature, and in 1990, the Supreme Soviet passed a law recognizing religious freedom. Some Church leaders wanted Russian Orthodoxy to be granted special status by the state, while others opposed such a return to the past. The government continued to uphold the separation of church and state, and it did not privilege Russian Orthodoxy over other faiths. Religious freedom meant that Muslims were now allowed visas to make the pilgrimage to Mecca, and freedom of speech meant that all religions could publish literature and broadcast their message on radio and television. Numerous Christian sects, including Baptists, German Lutherans, Roman Catholics, Quakers, the Salvation Army, the Unification Church, and the Church of Scientology, attracted large followings. Buddhism also became popular, and many Jews began actively to practice their religion.

Support for education had not been a high priority in the Brezhnev era; not enough schools had been planned, and maintenance had been ignored. The economic downturn that resumed in the late-eighties meant that Gorbachev made little progress in this regard.

Schools were overcrowded and deteriorating. If the school system was not renovated physically, however, it was transformed intellectually by perestroika. Freedom of speech and thought applied to education as well as other aspects of culture. Courses in Marxism were no longer required, and the history curriculum was rewritten. In 1988, final exams in history in secondary schools were canceled because teachers had been revising the history of the twenties and World War II while textbook and standard exams still contained the Brezhnevite orthodoxy regarding Lenin's legacy and Stalin's leadership in the war.

Perestroika affected culture, as well. The Soviet public that had previously heard nothing but good news now regularly read about bad economic trends, drug addition, and rising crime. Seventy years of banned literature, art, and film were suddenly available. Pasternak's *Dr. Zhivago,* Zamiatin's *We,* and the works of Bulgakov, Nabokov, and Solzhenitsyn were all printed in the Soviet Union for the first time. Solzhenitsyn's *Gulag Archipelago* had a particularly profound impact, opening the eyes of Soviet citizens to the inhumanity of the Soviet prison camp system. Socialist Realism was abandoned, and writers experimented with new approaches including postmodernism. In addition, the Soviet public had access to western literature, television programs, films, news, and pornography.

Roles and Status of Women

Perestroika broke very little new ground as far as women's issues were concerned. Gorbachev continued to promote Lenin's idea that women needed more representation in government, and he said that the party should attempt to guarantee that women make up half the members elected to local soviets and one-third of those elected to the higher levels. He also insisted that executive boards should have the same proportion of women as the legislative body that chose them. At the same time, however, Gorbachev adhered to traditional Soviet biological determinism: He said he wanted to increase economic productivity so women could "return to their purely womanly mission." He also sponsored protective labor legislation for women and extended maternity leave to eighteen months at full pay with an additional eighteen months of unpaid leave.

Gorbachev did introduce some new elements in the Party's concern for women's issues. He was responsible for legislation that granted fourteen days of leave for parents to take care of sick children. These days could be taken by either parent, implying that men could be equally involved in child care. Gorbachev also declared that works by "ideologists of women's movement" should be published, and feminists gladly took advantage of the new freedom of speech. Feminists debunked biological determinism and argued that gender roles are socially constructed. They insisted that husbands should share housework equally with their wives, and that the liberation of women would also liberate men.

Women continued to be exploited economically. In the 1980s, 90 percent of women worked outside the home, and women made up 53 percent of the paid labor force. Women also continued to work the double shift. In 1989, it was estimated that women worked 76 hours a week (counting time spent at paid labor and housework), while men worked only 59. Women continued to be denied professional advancement. Women made up 75 percent of schoolteachers but 39 percent of principals, 60 percent of all engineers but only 6 percent of factory directors, 67 percent of all physicians but 90 percent of pediatricians and only 6 percent of surgeons. Thirty-three percent of the Communist party were women, but only 8 percent of the Central Committee were. In the entire history of the Soviet Union, only three women had ever served on the Politburo and only six on the Secretariat.

SOCIAL AND ECONOMIC TRENDS

Social trends of the post-war era continued through the 1980s. The population rose from 262 to 287 million between 1979 and 1989, and the percentage of the population living in cities rose from 63 to 66 percent. The proportion of those engaged in agriculture fell from 15 percent in 1979 to 12 percent in 1987. As the Soviet Union became more urbanized, families became smaller and divorce rates increased. In the late 1970s, more than 80 percent of urban families had two children or fewer, and in the RSFSR, the average family size decreased from 3.4 persons in 1970 to 3.1 in 1989. In the 1980s, the Soviet divorce rate was second in the world only to that of the United States; almost half of all marriages ended in divorce.

Perestroika allowed the public discussion and social acceptance of homosexuality for the first time since before the Stalin era. Article 121 of the Soviet Criminal Code, criminalizing sex between men (but not between women), had remained in effect since it was initiated in 1933. In the early 1980s, about one thousand men were sentenced every year under the law. In 1984, the first known organization to promote the rights of gay men was formed in Leningrad, but it was soon suppressed by the KGB. In 1989, however, the Moscow Gay and Lesbian Alliance was formed, and a newspaper devoted to gay and lesbian issues, *Tema,* began publication. In the summer of 1991, gays and lesbians held an international conference, sponsored a film festival, and organized public demonstrations for gay rights in Moscow and St. Petersburg.

Glasnost of the Gorbachev era revealed that the Soviet Union had acquired some of the negative features of modern industrial societies that had been previously concealed. Drug use was increasing, crime rates were going up, and HIV/AIDS had become an epidemic. The most serious public health problem, however, was alcohol abuse, which had been on the rise since the beginning of the Brezhnev era. By the mid-1980s approximately 15 percent of household disposable income was spent on alcohol. Vodka has long been the favored alcoholic drink among the Slavs, and the tradition of binge drinking had serious consequences for public health. Drunk driving and drinking at work was a major cause of accidents, and death from alcohol poisoning was unmatched anywhere in the world. Excessive consumption of alcohol was largely responsible for the decline in life expectancy for men from sixty-seven years in 1964 to sixty-two years in 1979.

The first of Gorbachev's reforms was to limit alcoholic abuse by raising prices and cutting production. Some vineyards were converted to other agricultural uses and a number of distilleries were closed; in 1985, the production of vodka was cut by one-third. This had an immediate beneficial effect on society: The overall death rate fell measurably, as did murder, suicide, and infant mortality. Deaths from alcohol-related accidents declined by one quarter. It had a detrimental effect on the state budget, since sale of vodka had been a significant source of revenue. Gorbachev's anti-alcohol campaign was also extremely unpopular. By the end of the 1980s, home-brew and illegally distilled vodka had begun to satisfy the pent-up demand.

In 1985, Gorbachev also initiated campaigns for greater labor discipline and for acceleration of productivity by attempting to reengage the enthusiasm of workers for building communism. Like his campaign against alcohol, these were briefly successful. In the first half of the 1980s, the Soviet economy had been growing at an average rate of only 2.5 percent a year; in Gorbachev's first two years as General Secretary, industrial production and labor productivity both increased by more than 5 percent. Nevertheless, serious problems in the economy remained. Agriculture continued to absorb a disproportionate amount of investment. Profits from oil exports, which had kept the Soviet economy afloat in the Brezhnev era, sharply declined as the world price of oil fell in the 1980s, and Gorbachev's only alternative was to promote greater productivity.

In 1986, Gorbachev had begun to talk about the need for market pricing and for using profit and loss to improve efficiency, and in 1987 he carried out a series of major reforms. A law on cooperatives permitted private ownership in service, manufacturing, and foreign-trade industries. A law on state enterprises allowed factories to set output based on demand. Factories were required to fill state orders, but could sell excess production as they wished. They were expected to be self-financing (meaning that they could go bankrupt), and they were permitted to cut wages. The law also provided for worker councils, with a role in planning and administration, to be elected in every factory. A law on foreign investment provided for partnerships in which the Soviet partner provided the factory and workforce while the foreign entrepreneur provided capital and technical expertise. Finally, Gorbachev tried to promote private entrepreneurship in agriculture. A new law allowed families to lease land, to sign contracts for delivery of crops, and to take charge of the agricultural process. On collective farms, restrictions were lifted on the size of private plots. The government did continue to regulate prices and to allocate investment in agriculture.

Nevertheless, economic growth declined. The combination of central allocation of resources and control of prices with the decentralization of decision making caused new kinds of bottlenecks and disjunctures. Growth continued to slow, while prices rose and shortages in consumer goods and even food appeared. Such shortages had already been evident in the Brezhnev era, but after 1990 there were even shortages in the supply of bread—Russia's staple food.

While Soviet leaders were searching for a solution to this economic decline, the Soviet Union dissolved. In the West, it became a widely accepted truism that the economic failure of Communism caused the collapse of the Soviet Union, but this was not the case. Soviet economic difficulties simply provided a context in which the politics of dissolution operated. The Soviet peoples could no longer be convinced that Communism could produce prosperity, but this did not mean that an economic alternative could not be built within the structure of the USSR. The dissolution of the Soviet Union issued from the desire of the leaders of the national republics, and especially of Russia, to assume the status of sovereign and independent nations. Paradoxically, the economic catastrophe that befell the peoples of the former Soviet Union was fully realized only after the union was dissolved and Communism abandoned.

THE PEOPLES OF THE UNION: THE DISSOLUTION OF THE SOVIET UNION

The Soviet Union was the last of the European colonial empires to come to an end. Great Britain had withdrawn from India in 1947 and from Ghana in 1956, France left Vietnam in 1956 and Algeria in 1962, and Portugal clung to Angola and Mozambique until 1975. The Soviet empire ended all at once in 1991.

The process by which the Soviet Union fell apart has much in common with the end of the European overseas empires. The colonizing powers drew boundaries that created countries where they had not existed before, encouraged the native population to think of themselves as a nation, and educated them in the Western principles of liberty, equality, and the right of nations to self-determination. Similarly, one of the effects of Soviet nationality policy was to foster the national identity of the peoples of the union, particularly of the Soviet Socialist Republics. Each of the SSRs had all the elements of a nation-state: flag, national anthem, official language, and each had been encouraged to celebrate its history and folk culture. The Soviet

Union went further than any of the other European colonial powers; its constitution actually recognized the right of the Republics to secede from the Union.

There are, of course, important differences between the Soviet Union and the western European colonial empires. First, the economic relationship between the core and the periphery was not as exploitative. One may actually question whether a core and periphery existed. Many Russian nationalists certainly did, observing that Russian oil, gas, and other natural resources were transferred to other republics at prices far below their real value. Furthermore, Soviet economic policies fostered remarkable progress in the periphery. In 1989 the average per capita GDP for the republics of Central Asia and the Caucasus, which had all been pre-modern in the 1920s, had reached $5,257 per year. This compares favorably with neighboring countries: in the same year Turkey's per capita GDP was $3,989, Iran's was $3,662, Pakistan's was $1,542, and Afghanistan's was $1,000.

Second, as a contiguous territorial space, the Soviet Union was much more tightly integrated than any overseas empire. The Soviet government built roads, railroads, airports, and telecommunications networks that integrated the entire union. It provided medical centers, schools, and universities to its whole population. Rates of literacy and life expectancy were far higher in the Soviet periphery than in any of Europe's overseas colonies.

Third, the Soviet government had fostered the notion of a common Soviet homeland and a common Soviet identity unlike any other empire. Although the Soviet government was dominated by officials of Russian ethnicity and although the Russian language was the common language of the union, Soviet identity was expressed in terms of universal human values (in the Marxist language of proletarian internationalism). This program was so successful that in the spring of 1991 when a referendum on the future of the Soviet Union was held, two-thirds of the population voted to preserve the union.

These three differences had one ultimate cause: What really held the Soviet Union together was the Communist party. While the USSR had the form of a federal association of fifteen technically independent states, real political power was exercised by a unitary, centralized Soviet Communist party. The various republics could not think of independence because their Communist rulers would not let them think of it. In retrospect, it was inevitable that Gorbachev's program of democratization would end in the dissolution of the Soviet Union. As soon as the Communist Party lost its privileged political position, there was nothing to prevent the Soviet republics from exercising their constitutional rights.

The first republics to demand independence were Estonia, Latvia, and Lithuania. Although they had been a part of the Russian Empire before 1917, they had been independent nations in the interwar period and had been incorporated into the Soviet Union against their will during World War II. Baltic nationalism was first publicly exhibited in August 1988, when tens of thousands of people remembered the forty-ninth anniversary of the Nazi-Soviet Peace Pact (in which Hitler had agreed to allow Stalin to annex the Baltic countries) by forming a human chain 400 miles long from the southern border of Lithuania to the northern shore of Estonia. In May 1989, the Lithuanian government declared Lithuania a sovereign nation, and the Lithuanian Communist Party affirmed the declaration in December, but Gorbachev announced that he would not permit secessions from the Soviet Union.

Nevertheless, Gorbachev's own program of democratization contributed to the further growth of nationalism. At the same time that he had arranged for a directly elected Congress of Deputies for the Soviet Union, he had also pushed the Union Republics to create similar bodies. In the spring of 1990 elections to these Republican legislatures took place, and nationalist parties did very well in Estonia, Latvia, and Ukraine, and they won significant majorities in Armenia and Lithuania. No sooner was the new Lithuanian parliament seated than it voted for independence again. This time, Gorbachev declared an oil embargo against

Lithuania and sent in Soviet troops. In May, the Lithuanian government announced that it was temporarily suspending its declaration of independence, but it asserted that its claim of sovereignty was not negotiable. In June, Gorbachev ended the oil embargo and promised Lithuania independence within two years.

While this was occurring, even more fateful events were transpiring in the Russian Republic. In the spring elections, Boris Yeltsin had begun to appeal to Russian national sentiment, representing Russia as an oppressed victim of the Soviet system. He pointed out that the Russian republic was unlike the other republics, which had their own Communist Parties, radio and TV programming, their own news media, their own Academies of Science, while Russia had none. (A hostile critic might have argued that the *Soviet* Communist party, the *Soviet* Academy of Sciences, etc., were dominated by Russians and were, in fact, agents of Russian imperialism.) Yeltsin, who had become nationally famous when he had been removed from the Central committee by the anti-perestroika conservatives, also had an economic reform program. He argued that reform at the union level was impossible, it could only occur at the republic level, and that Russia should take the lead. Yeltsin received 84 percent of the vote in his district, and he became chair of the Russian Supreme Soviet. On June 12, under Yeltsin's leadership, the Russian Supreme Soviet declared its sovereignty. The other East Slav republics quickly followed Russia's example. Ukraine declared its sovereignty on July 16, and Belarus on July 27. In November the Russian Supreme Soviet declared that Russian law had precedence over Soviet law.

This introduced an entirely new ingredient into the mix. If Lithuania or Armenia, for example, withdrew from the Soviet Union, the nature of the union would hardly be affected; the loss in population or resources would be insignificant. The withdrawal of the Slavic core, however, was an altogether different matter. Russia, Ukraine, and Belarus made up 70 percent of the Soviet Union's population and contributed 80 percent of its industrial output. Furthermore, the Slavic heartland tied the union together; without it there would be four non-contiguous regions, Central Asia, the Caucasus, Moldova, and the Baltic states. More importantly, the remaining republics would have no reason to continue an association. Many had not, after all, entered the Russian Empire (or the Soviet Union) of their own free will, and those which had joined by treaty in the early 1920s found their technical "independence" to be a fiction. Without Russia there would not have been, nor could there be, a Soviet Union.

At the beginning of 1991, the focus shifted again to the Baltic states, where Gorbachev seemed determined not to permit secession. In January, Soviet military forces entered the region to arrest draft dodgers and to enforce conscription. Huge demonstrations erupted in Vilnius and in Moscow against this intervention, and Boris Yeltsin condemned the invasions and supported the right of republics to secede from the union. On January 13, "Bloody Sunday," fifteen Lithuanians were killed by Soviet paratroopers as they suppressed demonstrations and seized government office buildings. The Lithuanian population responded defiantly; in a referendum in February, 90 percent of Lithuanian voters voted for secession from the Soviet Union.

Gorbachev, in the meantime, was attempting to find a new political arrangement that could salvage the Soviet Union. He began by holding a Union-wide referendum in March 1991. Across the USSR 80 percent of registered voters voted, and of these 76 percent voted to preserve the union. In the Russian Republic 71 percent voted in favor of the union. (Armenia, Estonia, Georgia, Latvia, and Lithuania refused to participate). Gorbachev then drew up a new union treaty which affirmed the USSR as a voluntary, democratic union of equal republics, each with the right to secede. Republics were expected to make financial contributions to the central government and to manufacture goods according to a central plan, but they would retain sovereign control over tax revenues and their contributions to the center would be voluntary. This treaty was approved by the Supreme Soviet in June and was to be officially signed by the Republics and go into effect on August 20, 1991.

The situation changed dramatically on August 19, the day before the new Union Treaty was to go into effect, when conservatives staged a coup d'etat against Gorbachev. A committee led by the Premier, the head of the KGB, and the ministers of Defense and the Interior, announced that Gorbachev was unable to continue to govern (he was placed under house arrest while on vacation in Crimea), and that they would restore law and order and continue democratic reforms. They also canceled the new union treaty.

Leaders of most of the Republics denounced the coup, and popular demonstrations took place in a number of cities, including 200,000 demonstrators in St. Petersburg and 150,000 in Moscow. Moreover, the Red Army proved unreliable. Many military units simply ignored orders to mobilize, and even those troops who did obey a directive from the Emergency Committee to surround White House (the Russian Parliament in Moscow) made it clear that they would not use violence against the crowds that assembled. Boris Yeltsin took advantage of this by going among the soldiers, standing on a tank, and calling for a general strike to force the return of Gorbachev. Citizens barricaded the streets around the Parliament and prepared to resist the army. Three defenders were killed. On August 21, the coup collapsed. Troops were withdrawn from Moscow and the Baltic, the coup leaders resigned, and the Supreme Soviet voided the decrees of the Emergency Committee.

This provided an opportunity for public expression of hostility to the Communist party. In many cities, statues of Communist leaders (including Lenin) were toppled and KGB buildings were defaced. The Russian parliament voted to adopt the imperial Russian white, blue, and red flag, Leningrad changed its name back to St. Petersburg, and many other cities across the USSR returned to their pre-Soviet names. In addition, more republics declared their independence, and by the end of August, Georgia, Armenia, Estonia, Latvia, Lithuania, Ukraine, Belarus, Moldova, Azerbaijan, Uzbekistan, and Kirgizstan had all declared or reaffirmed their independence. Gorbachev's new union treaty was never ratified.

There was no question that a future Soviet Union would be much smaller than the one that had existed before the coup. In fact, one of Gorbachev's first acts was to recognize the independence of Estonia, Latvia, and Lithuania. The real question was whether the USSR would exist at all. Boris Yeltsin, President of Russia, was determined that it would not, and that its role in Eurasian and world affairs would be taken over by the Russian Republic. In September, Yeltsin nationalized all oil, natural gas, and coal reserves and all hydroelectric and nuclear power facilities within the RSFSR. He also began to negotiate an economic treaty with other Soviet republics as if the central Soviet government did not exist. In October, he reduced Russia's direct financial contributions to the treasury of the USSR, and Gorbachev's administration began to run out of money.

Yeltsin's western economic advisers had been arguing that the transition from a planned to a market economy and from publicly to privately owned capital was too complex a process to permit gradual change. They convinced him that a single, all-encompassing change would minimize social costs, and that this process could not be accomplished by a parliament, but could only be imposed by a centralized authority with little or no debate, haggling, or compromise. In this spirit, at the end of October, Yeltsin announced his intention to pursue "shock therapy," that is, allowing prices to be set by the free market, and he asked for extraordinary authority to pursue other economic reforms. On November 1, Yeltsin was named Prime Minister of Russia, and he was given emergency powers to pass laws by personal decree. He then announced a plan to privatize industry, transfer land to farmers, and end wage and price controls.

Yeltsin then used his new power to continue his assault on the Soviet central government. He seized all financial agencies of the USSR that were on Russian soil, including the Repository for Precious Metals, the mint, and the Ministry of Finance. He cut off all remaining Russian financial contributions to the USSR, causing eighty ministries and other state agencies to shut down, and he instructed the IMF and the World Bank to deal with Russia and other republics instead of the USSR. In early December, Yeltsin nationalized the USSR's central bank, and asserted Russia's responsibility for all Soviet debts and its payroll, including the armed forces, and he announced a ninety percent pay raise for all military officers.

On December 8, the presidents of Russia, Ukraine, and Belarus, the three republics who had signed the 1922 treaty that created the USSR, voted to rescind the treaty and disband the union. They agreed to create a Commonwealth of Independent States (CIS) which would be a voluntary association of former republics administered by a council made up of the constituent heads of state. These "Minsk Accords" were ratified by the Supreme Soviets of the three republics a few days later, and the other republics of the USSR were invited to join.

Needless to say, from the point of view of the Soviet government, Yeltsin's actions were quite illegal and unconstitutional. (To draw a parallel with the United States, it would be as if the governor of Kentucky claimed to own the gold in Fort Knox, or if the governors of the thirteen original states decided to rescind the U.S. Constitution.) Gorbachev denounced the signing of the Minsk accords as a coup d'etat and called for another nationwide referendum on the Union. On December 10, Gorbachev called on the General Staff to support him, their constitutional commander-in-chief, and to endorse his plans to preserve the union. The next day, Yeltsin reminded the Soviet officer corps of the pay raise he had given them and asked for their support. The General Staff did nothing, thereby accepting Yeltsin's actions.

On December 16, the Russian Supreme Soviet declared itself the legal successor of the USSR Supreme Soviet. The next day, Gorbachev introduced a resolution into the USSR Supreme Soviet to suspend the Russian action, but Russian delegates to the USSR Supreme Soviet walked out, depriving it of a quorum. On December 18, Yeltsin decreed that Russia would assume control of the property and functions of the Soviet Ministry of Foreign Affairs, the KGB, and the MVD. Russia nationalized the Bolshoi Theater, Moscow State University, and the Hermitage museum. On December 21, eleven Soviet republics (Azerbaijan, Armenia, Belarus, Georgia, Kazakhstan, Kirgizstan, Moldova, Russia, Turkmenistan, Uzbekistan, and Ukraine) met in Almaty, Kazakhstan, and affirmed the creation of the CIS. The sovereignty of each republic was recognized, and they agreed that CIS activities would be coordinated by a council composed of heads of state. No decision was made regarding financing, borders, citizenship, or control over military forces and nuclear weapons.

On December 23, the European Community officially recognized Russia as the legal successor to the Soviet Union, and on December 25, the Russian Supreme Soviet changed the name of the country from RSFSR to Russian Federation. On the same day, Gorbachev resigned as President of the USSR, and the Soviet flag was lowered from above the Kremlin. On December 26, the Soviet Congress of People's Deputies acknowledged the dissolution of the Soviet Union and voted itself out of existence effective at midnight on December 31. On January 1, 1992, the Russian nation began a new era in its history.

Gorbachev Outlines Party's Changing Role

In November 1987, Gorbachev called a Communist Party conference to discuss the further implementation of perestroika. This excerpt comes from his closing remarks to the conference.

- How does Gorbachev characterize the nature of his reforms?
- What is the relation he sees between party and society?
- Are there contradictions in this that could have anticipated the failure of perestroika?

Restructuring means millions of new apartments and thousands of new schools, hospitals, theaters and sports complexes, it means improved food supply and better-quality goods, and it means the democratization of all public life. But this can be achieved only through intensive, highly productive work, good organization, discipline, responsibility, and cohesive and united actions. This means that restructuring will affect every collective and all of society. The basic responsibility for the success of the stage that is beginning and the basic work load in organizing the actual implementation of the new tasks rest with the CPSU, with the Party's cadres. . . .

The second stage of restructuring, the essence of which is that it is to involve millions of people in actual work, will not proceed as it should unless the Party develops the democratic process. Who will direct and stimulate all this? The Party. It is the Party that bears responsibility for the development of the process of democratization. But if it is to be capable of expressing the requirements of the new stage, it must itself undergo change. . . .

In these conditions, the Party should not so much take on the task of directly resolving questions as pose for itself another, more difficult task. That of directing, coordinating, uniting and giving impetus to the social activeness of the masses through Party organizations and cadres, through Party control, through the creation of a healthy, energy-charged atmosphere in cities, in districts and in collectives. . . .

So far, they have not been fulfilling their role completely. It is necessary that communists bring to each plenary session, to each meeting, people's thoughts and sentiments, everything that is worrying the people. Unfortunately, elected Party agencies have still not rid themselves of inertia, conservatism and overorganization. . . .

Unfortunately, one still encounters officials who do not know or do not understand the new tasks and are afraid of activeness on the part of the communists, of the working people. It is necessary that life be in full swing in every Party committee, that people consider this Party agency their home and go there with their joys and concerns. But the main link now is

Source: *Current Digest of the Soviet Press.* Vol. 39, no. 47 (1987): 10. Translation copyright by *The Current Digest of the Soviet Press,* published weekly at Columbus, Ohio. Reprinted by permission of the Digest

the primary Party organization. That is where we must now concentrate all our attention if we are to step up the communists' activity as much as possible. . . .

Cadres who are rich in promises but not in deeds, who operate in the old way, who adhere to a position of dependence and take a "leftovers" approach to social matters—people will not follow these leaders. The Party should keep all these questions under its supervision. And responsibility, comrades! Responsibility! Only then will people sense the Party's vanguard role in restructuring. . . .

Another thing. The collectives must be prepared for economic accountability. I think that there is a great underestimation of this question in the Party, in economic management and in the labor collectives. Some have taken a really serious attitude toward it and are doing solid work. But so far not everyone has understood the importance and complexity of the task. Some people think that everything will proceed easily—of its own accord, as it were. Or they say that the leadership can't do anything else, that they will once again be forced to pay for just any kind of work, for low-quality output. No, comrades, this is impermissible now, and it will not happen. . . .

It is necessary to bring economists' writings into the press. Take the "round-table" discussions, in which scholars and practical workers can exchange opinions. For some reason, they have become a rare phenomenon in the newspapers and on television. Let them be held. . . . Party work must be written about with a knowledge of what is happening. . . .

Generally speaking, the press has become more militant, but it must get its second wind, as must the entire Party and the entire country. We must move forward and not get stuck at the frontiers reached yesterday.

We must do more work with journalists. It used to be simpler things were prohibited, they were not authorized. No, every journalist and editor should be an active individual and bear civic responsibility for his activity. Party officials should have broader contacts with journalists through collective meetings and on an individual basis and they should visit editorial collectives. Furthermore, Secretaries of the Central Committee, Secretaries of territory and province Party committees and members of the government should meet and talk with journalists more often. . . . The press is a part of our cause, the cause of the entire Party and of all the people. That's how it must be treated. . . .

Everyone knows that, having firmly embarked on the path of expanding democracy, we have given up the prohibitions that were characteristic of the period of stagnation. We will continue to advance along the path of socialist democracy and the strengthening of socialist values and freedom of thought and creativity. The Soviet people are a people of the highest culture and education. They will always sort out what is good and what is bad. The affirmation of our moral values, the elevation of man, the rejection of everything that is alien to socialism, and freedom of creativity and creative diversity this is our path in culture. . . .

Uzbek Culture in the 1980s

This except comes from a report to the CPSU Congress, "The Tasks of The Republic's Party Organizations in Further Improving The Effectiveness of Ideological Work in Light of The Demands of The 27th CPSU Congress," by I. B. Usmankhodzhaev.

- What does this reveal about Uzbek culture, society, religion, and gender relations?
- What does it suggest about the success of the Soviet project, and what does it imply for the future?

. . . What are the principal negative phenomena?

First, in the past two decades an idealization of the historical past and a departure from class positions in assessing certain historical events and personalities have assumed an increasingly broader scope in the social sciences, literature, art and other spheres of spiritual life in the republic. . . .

Second, a process of the coalescence of the ordinary consciousness of many cadres with religious dogmas has actively taken place and is continuing to take place in the republic, which has led to a virtual spiritual compromise with religion. As a result, some people now show two faces, as it were: a public and political face, when they stand up for our ideals, and an everyday face, when they observe religious ceremonies. They skillfully use the first face on the job, and the other one in the family and at their place of residence.

Third, the absence in upbringing work of a clear-cut orientation toward the broad affirmation of the Soviet way of life and the principles of communist morality has led to the deformation of a number of national customs and traditions and to the appearance and taking root in the minds of part of the population of stereotypes that are at variance with the spirit of our society and are leading to the erosion of its moral foundations and assessments of situations and stances in life. . . .

Fourth and last, the flagrant violations that have been committed of the Leninist principles of the selection of personnel, including ideological personnel, have led to a situation in which our ideological staff continues to work in a one-sided fashion, is out of touch with concrete practical affairs, continues to frequently create an atmosphere of window dressing and the illusion of well-being, glosses over shortcomings, and doesn't always support the healthy critical voices of Communists and working people. . . .

Serious distortions can be encountered, such as, for example, those in the third edition of "The History of the Uzbek Republic" and in the Uzbek Soviet Encyclopedia. These works give a sketchy portrayal of the Party's activity in fusing the revolutionary struggle of the proletariat with the national-liberation movement in the period of preparation for the October Revolution and do not do enough to bring out the treacherous role of the national bourgeoisie and the counterrevolutionary essence of the Basmachi movement [of armed resistance to the Soviets in Central Asia 1918–1924—Trans.]

Source: *Current Digest of the Soviet Press*, vol 38, no. 40 (November 5, 1986): 10–11. Translation copyright by *The Current Digest of the Soviet Press*, published weekly at Columbus, Ohio. Reprinted by permission of the Digest.

... Idealization of the past and a nonclass and antihistorical approach have led to a situation in which a long line of feudal despots, such as Timur, continues to parade across theater stages, movie screens and the pages of books, despots who, at the unthinking hands of certain writers and contrary to historical truth, are presented as humanists and farsighted politicians. ...

Today religion is not simply a variety of the anti-scientific world view. It often serves as the ideological basis for the patriarchal way of life and has a negative effect on social processes ...

Charlatans of various sorts who, posing as ministers of religion, have ensconced themselves in virtually every community unobstructedly preach Islamic dogma, engage in quackery, and distribute literature, tape recordings and videofilms of religious content. As a rule, such persons engage in no socially useful labor and lead a parasitic way of life. The lavishness of family and domestic ceremonies, especially weddings and funerals, that is sanctioned by religious public opinion is one factor that impels people to seek unearned income and to steal ...

It is especially alarming that significant numbers of Communists, including Party officials, are susceptible to flirting with religion and to observing the ceremonies it dictates. ...

Sometimes intolerable conditions are created around those who dare to speak out against religion. Moreover, all this is done with the connivance of Party agencies. ...

Many of our executives, Party, Soviet and Young Communist League officials, propagandists and agitators stubbornly evade personal participation in atheistic work and steer clear of openly criticizing before the population the reactionary essence of the Muslim dogmas and customs that the sharia [Islamic law] dictates–furthermore, they frequently avoid using the word "Islam" altogether. ...

There is no need to talk about the successes in the emancipation of women; they are self-evident. Against this background, however, the ugliness of certain manifestations of a feudal-bey attitude toward women stands out all the more distinctly.

... [T]he secret buying and selling of young women in the form of bride money continues in a number of districts. There are a great many instances of the slighting of women in the family and of the degradation of their honor and dignity ...

... [S]ome people, often using unearned income, hold noisy weddings lasting several days and attended by many people, gatherings that go on late into the night and, furthermore, disturb the tranquillity of thousands and thousands of people. The participation of children in trade, and sometimes in speculation, is not decreasing. And how many tragic breakups of young families have occurred for the sole reason that they were created for love but contrary to the parents' wishes.

Single Young Women Workers in Moscow

This is an article from a popular magazine, Ogonek, *titled "Single Young Women Face Tough Life as Workers in Moscow."*

- What can you infer about the effectiveness of economic planning? Economic trends and patterns?
- What does this reveal about gender issues in the last years of the Soviet Union?

According to figures cited at the June 19, 1986, plenary session of the Moscow City Party Committee, in the past 15 years over 700,000 outside workers have been recruited to work in Moscow (at a cost of roughly 10 billion rubles). At the same time, factory modernization and the elimination of manual labor was proceeding slowly. Industrial managers were "corrupted" by this approach and slacked off in their efforts to accelerate scientific and technical progress. Labor discipline and public order grew lax, labor turnover increased. Approximately 50 percent of all those who had been enlisted to work in Moscow's economy left the enterprises that had hired them.

The Petr Alekseev Fine Fabric Mill is one of Moscow's oldest enterprises (next year it will mark its 150th anniversary). It operates around the clock, the equipment is dilapidated and the ventilation is poor. It's obvious why there's no way you could get some Muscovites to work there. Over 90 percent of the factory's 2,000 workers come from outside Moscow; most are young women. But they live a bit better than most such workers; the mill has just built a modern new dormitory with accommodations for 520. Child care is also provided.

Recently, however, the management decreed that husbands would no longer be permitted to live in the dormitories. When asked, "What are we supposed to do, get divorced?" the director merely replied that this was not management's concern and that women shouldn't get married until they have housing. And this response from an enterprise that supposedly looks after its workers! . . .

Provincial young people are lured by the bright lights of the big city; not all of them are keen to improve themselves culturally, get an education and become skilled specialists. The majority want a good salary and a separate apartment—that's the limit of their dreams. Well, they also want a good marriage, of course (with a Muscovite, even though the statistics show that this is unlikely).

Removed from familiar surroundings and left to their own devices in a huge, strange city, many of the newly arrived female workers are doomed to casual encounters that fail to bring them happiness. And no matter what—next morning they face the rumble of the machines and the arduous monotony of their labor. After work they return to the boredom, crowding and incessant noise of the dormitory. All this causes conflicts and mutual hostility among dormitory residents. Not long ago a young single mother died in a shared room, her baby in her arms. She was afraid to ask for help from her neighbors on the other side of the chintz curtain, who had come to hate her because of the baby's annoying cries.

Source: *Current Digest of the Soviet Press,* vol. 39, no. 52 (January 27,1988): 17–18. Translation copyright by *The Current Digest of the Soviet Press,* published weekly at Columbus, Ohio. Reprinted by permission of the Digest.

Many of the girls adapt poorly to the rhythm of Moscow life and suffer from nervous disorders. Doctors note that the young women who get pregnant usually have complications and more often than not suffer miscarriages or are compelled to seek abortions.

Those who succeed in getting a Moscow residence permit try to find a husband. But even if they do, where will the young family live? Usually the couples have only their beds in dormitories meant for single workers. Intentionally or not, enterprise managers keep people from starting families. From their viewpoint, marriage is followed by children, which means that the woman will leave her job for at least 18 months [at full pay]. And she'll also need accommodations in a family dormitory.

If women don't marry by age 30, some have babies anyway, "for themselves." They don't want to miss the joy of motherhood. On the other hand, there are those who view their children merely as a means of obtaining a separate apartment—but it proves to be of little help.

In one family dormitory, eight single mothers and their children live together in four small rooms. When one child comes down with an infectious disease, eight machines are idle. And the children we saw were very nervous and sickly. It's no wonder!

How long must young women live as "single girls" in these dormitories? An outside worker will normally obtain a permanent residence permit in five or six years, and she can put her name on the waiting list for housing after 10 years' residence in Moscow. This means that 20-year-old women can expect to get housing when they are nearly 40, provided that they are good workers. Until then they are supposed to live in a dormitory!

For over 50 years attempts have been made—in vain—to prohibit or at least limit the construction of new industrial enterprises within the Moscow city limits. The 1971 general plan envisaged the construction of 327 enterprises and organizations outside the capital, but only a small number have been built. Moreover, Moscow's plants are being modernized mainly by increasing the number of workplaces, because an enterprise's status and the salaries of its executives are determined by the size of the work force. This vicious circle only aggravates the problem of outside labor.

So what should we do? Abolish the system of hiring outside workers once and for all? V. V. Tuliakov, senior inspector of the Moscow City Soviet Executive Committee's labor administration, opposes approving any further recruitment of workers from other cities and also points with concern to the covert hiring of outside workers through the vocational-technical schools.

But Ie. G. Antosenkov, Director of the Research Institute of Labor, is against purely administrative solutions and argues that only efficient production and the improvement of the economy as a whole—and not just in Moscow—can effect a radical change in the situation. He sees encouraging signs, however. With enterprises everywhere now shifting to full economic accountability and reducing their work forces by 5 percent to 7 percent, the problem of recruiting labor for Moscow and other cities will eventually be replaced by a new concern—ensuring full employment.

Opposition to the 1991 Union Treaty

This essay, "Address to the People," appeared on the front page of the conservative, Soviet patriotic newspaper, Sovetskaia Rossiia, *on July 23, 1991. It was written in objection to the new Union Treaty, scheduled to go into effect on August 20, and it was signed by fifteen generals, political leaders, and writers, some of whom participated in the attempted coup of August 19.*

- What is implied by each of the appeals made here?
- What role is played by communist values? Soviet values? Russian tradition?
- Whom do the authors blame for the country's problems?
- What does this portend for the future?

Dear residents of the Russian Republic! Citizens of the USSR! Compatriots!

An enormous, unprecedented misfortune has befallen us. Our homeland country, a great state that was given into our care by history, nature and our glorious ancestors, is perishing, breaking up, and being plunged into darkness and nonexistence. . . . What happened to us, brothers? Why is that sly and pompous rulers, intelligent and clever apostates and greedy and rich moneygrubbers, mocking us, scoffing at our beliefs and taking advantage of our naivete, have seized power and are pilfering our wealth, taking homes, factories and land away from the people, carving the country up into separate parts, embroiling us with one another. . .? How did it happen that . . . we admitted to power people who do not love this country, who fawn on their overseas patrons and seek advice and blessing there, overseas? . . .

We summon the working people, whom the present-day Pharisees promised abundance and good pay but who are now being driven out of the factories and mines and doomed to hunger, no rights, and despondent standing in line for financial help, a hunk of bread, and the charity of the wealthy and the bosses.

We summon the industrious peasants, who have been worn out by the ignorant authorities and whose current fate is being decided by those who yesterday destroyed the villages and drew up utopian programs, imposing a one-sided exchange on grain growers and dooming plowland to desolation and the surviving farms that feed the country to destruction.

We call on engineers, whose hands, minds and talents have created a unique technical civilization and a mighty industry that has ensured the people's well-being and protection and enabled the homeland to fly into outer space. . . . We are a country of idled enterprises, silenced power engineering, vanished goods, and bewildered and impoverished engineers removed from creative activity.

We call on scientists, who have advanced the development of Soviet science in a worthy manner, amazed the world with the fruits of their labor, and accumulated in laboratories and institutes discoveries for the next spurt into the 21st century, where we hope to have a fitting place in human civilization. Instead of this, demagogues and malefactors are

Source: *Current Digest of the Soviet Press*, vol. 43, no. 20 (August 28, 1991): 8. Translation copyright by *The Current Digest of the Soviet Press*, published weekly at Columbus, Ohio. Reprinted by permission of the Digest.

destroying precious accumulated discoveries, scattering collectives of researchers, closing whole areas of science . . . and dooming the best minds to vegetation and to fleeing the homeland for prosperous countries, where their talent will nourish the development not of their own country but of foreign lands.

We turn our voice to the Army, which won mankind's respect for its selfless feat of saving Europe from the Hitlerite plague, to the Army that has inherited the best qualities of the Russian and Soviet Armies and resists aggressive forces. Our glorious defenders are living through difficult times. . . . We are convinced that the fighting men of the Army and the Navy, loyal to their sacred duty, will not allow a fratricidal war or the destruction of the fatherland and will act as a reliable guarantor of security and a mainstay of all the healthy forces of society.

We turn our voice to the artists and writers, who bit by bit created a culture on the ruins of the defeated classics, who came up with images of beauty and goodness for the people and expected a flourishing of the arts in the future but found destitution and a lowering of creativity to the level of a pitiful farce designed to amuse businessmen and the wealthy, in which the people, cut off from spirituality, deprived of an ideal and governed by immoral and sly people, are removed from history and turned into a cheap work force for foreign manufacturers.

We appeal to the Orthodox Church, which, having gone through Calvary, is slowly, after all the beatings, rising from the grave. The church, whose spiritual light shone in Russian history even during dark time, is today, while still gaining new strength, being torn by strife and wounded in the eparchies and parishes, and is not finding proper support from the temporal powers that be. May it hear the voice of the people calling for salvation.

We appeal to Muslims, Buddhists, Protestants and believers of all persuasions for whom faith is synonymous with goodness, beauty and truth; today they are being assaulted by cruelty, ugliness and lies that are destroying their living souls.

We appeal to parties, both large and small, to liberals and monarchists, to centralists and local-autonomy advocates, to bards of the national idea. We appeal to the Communist Party . . . Communists, whose leaders are destroying their own Party, giving up their Party cards, are rushing into the enemy camp one after another—playing the traitor, demanding the gallows for decent comrades—let the Communists hear our call!

Young people, our hope and flower, who are being corrupted, placed at the service of false idols, and doomed to idleness, lack of talent, drugs and crime.

Old people, our wisdom and pride, reliable toilers and our tireless breadwinners, whose lot has been penury and mockery of the lives they have lived and profanation in printed and televised slop by those who are striving to kill memories and to pit generations against one another. . . .

Women, who are denying themselves the highest natural right—to continue the family by bearing descendants—because of a fear of engendering poverty and filling the army of a civil war with soldiers, afraid of their own love and their own motherhood. . . .

Let us start out on the path of saving the state this very minute. Let us create a people's patriotic movement in which everyone, while having his own will and influence, will unite in the name of the supreme goal of saving the fatherland.

VISUAL DOCUMENTS

Figure 21-1 Gorbachev and Reagan in Red Square
   In this photograph, Gorbachev is welcoming U.S. President Ronald Reagan to Moscow.
- Compare this with previous representations of Soviet leaders.
- What messages are being sent?
Source: AP/Wide World Photos.

Figure 21-2 Anti-Gorbachev Demonstration

In the early spring of 1991, Gorbachev was struggling to keep the republics of the Soviet Union united, and one of his more serious opponents was Boris Yeltsin, at that time a deputy in the RSFSR Congress of Deputies and chair of its Supreme Soviet. Gorbachev tried to oust Yeltsin from his seat in the Congress, and on March 25, Gorbachev banned all demonstrations in Moscow. Three days later, 100,000 pro-Yeltsin demonstrators rallied on Manezh Square in Moscow. Gorbachev did not use force to enforce the ban. Some have seen this as a turning point in the dissolution of the Soviet Union.

- What does this photo reveal about trends in Soviet society and the success of perestroika?
- Compare M. S. Gorbachev and Deng Xiaoping of China. What is the significance of the differences?

Source: AP/Wide World Photos.

Figure 21-3 Moscow McDonald's
    The sign says that this McDonald's restaurant was opened on January 31, 1990.
• Consider the various meanings this building could have had for residents of
    Moscow.
Source: Stock Boston.

Figure 21-4 Yeltsin, August 20, 1991

An attempted coup to remove Gorbachev from power and end perestroika began on August 19, 1991. Boris Yeltsin, then President of Russia, went to the Russian White House, which was surrounded by the Soviet Army, and, as the photo here shows, got up on an armored vehicle and call on the soldiers not to support the coup leaders.

- How does this image compare with previous representations of Soviet or Russian leaders.
- How would this image serve Yeltsin's political interests?

Source: AP/World Wide Photos.

FOR FURTHER READING

(In addition to the books by Clements and Suny from the previous chapter.)

Brown, Archie. *The Gorbachev Factor:* Oxford: Oxford University Press, 1996.
Buckley, Mary. *Perestroika and Soviet Women.* Cambridge: Cambridge University Press, 1992.

Bunce, Valerie. *Subversive Institutions: The Design and the Destruction of Socialism and the State.* Cambridge: Cambridge University Press, 1999.

Dunlop, John B. *The Rise of Russia and the Fall of the Soviet Empire.* Princeton, NJ: Princeton University Press, 1993.

Goldman, Marshall I. *What Went Wrong with Perestroika.* New York: Norton, 1992

Holmes, Leslie. *The End of Communist Power: Anti-Corruption Campaigns and Legitimation Crisis.* New York: Oxford University Press, 1993.

Hough, Jerry F. *Democratization and Revolution in the USSR, 1985-1991.* Washington, D.C.: Brookings Institution Press, 1997.

Laqueur, Walter. *The Dream that Failed: Reflections on the Soviet Union.* New York: Oxford University Press, 1994.

Lewin, Moshe *The Gorbachev Phenomenon: A Historical Interpretation.* Expanded edition. Berkeley: University of California Press,1991.

Ries, Nancy. *Russian Talk : Culture and Conversation During Perestroika.* Ithaca, NY: Cornell University Press, 1997.

Solnick, Steven L. *Stealing the State: Control and Collapse in Soviet Institutions.* Cambridge, MA: Harvard University Press, 1999.

Suraska, Wisla. *How the Soviet Union Disappeared: An Essay on the Causes of Dissolution.* Durham, NC: Duke University Press, 1998.

CHAPTER TWENTY TWO

THE RUSSIAN FEDERATION: 1991–2004

Russia began the post-communist era of its history in dismal circumstances. Boris Yeltsin's radical and rapid transition from state-owned industry and central planning to private enterprise and the free market created hardships for the Russian people. By the end of the decade of the 1990s, Russia's gross national product had fallen to half its 1991 level, half the population lived in poverty, and the average life expectancy had declined by five years. The immediate economic benefit of privatization went mainly to former members of the old Soviet nomenklatura, and the majority of the population were worse off materially than they had been under communism.

The end of the Communist party's monopoly on power and the development of a justice system based on the rule of law were welcome developments, but great political problems remained. The nomenklatura hierarchy was dismantled and politics was opened to all, but the political system was nevertheless dominated by former Communist party members—of whom Boris Yeltsin was the most outstanding example. Yeltsin enacted a new constitution that established a presidency with far more extensive formal powers than any office in the old Soviet system. The new parliament was weak, and political parties ineffective—many of them existing only in the capital with virtually no national organization. Publishing and the news and entertainment media had become independent of the state, but Yeltsin was able to manipulate the media in his election campaigns. At the beginning of the new century, the Russian economy has begun to recover, but questions remain about the future of democracy under Yeltsin's successor Vladimir Putin.

THE EURASIAN CONTEXT

The collapse of the Soviet Union and Russia's program of radical privatization was interpreted by western neoliberals as the final proof of the superiority of private enterprise and market economics. The World Bank and the International Monetary Fund aggressively promoted privatization, monetarism, and supply-side policy to the developing nations of the world, including the nations of the former Communist bloc and the former Soviet Union. In 1995, the World Trade Organization was created to facilitate international free trade and reduce government intervention in the market.

The unification of western and central Europe into a single political and economic entity came closer to reality with the signing of the Maastricht Treaty in early 1992. This treaty transformed the European Economic Community into the European Union, a political as well as economic unit which took on many of the characteristics of a sovereign state. An elected European parliament was given authority to set union policies on education, public health, consumer protection, the environment, and economic integration. The EU established uniform fiscal and monetary policies including a common currency, the Euro, and began to plan common foreign and defense policies.

The Baltic nations and the nations of the former Warsaw pact have followed a similar path since the end of Communist rule. Free multiparty elections were held throughout the region in 1990-1992 and non-communist liberal-nationalist parties won parliamentary majorities, though communist parties (with new names) continued to attract a significant number of votes. Elections were generally considered to be free and fair by international observers. They all joined the IMF and the World Bank, and committed to privatization and the free market. Small- and medium-sized enterprises have been largely privatized throughout the region, but major industries still remain in government hands. Poland and the Czech Republic have privatized to the greatest extent; Romania and Bulgaria have privatized the least. All these nations are working toward joining the European Union; Poland, the Czech Republic, Hungary, and Slovakia officially joined the EU on May 1, 2004. Additionally, all Baltic and former Warsaw Pact nations have taken a western orientation as far as foreign relations and national defense are concerned. Poland, Hungary, and the Czech Republic joined NATO in March 1999, and the remaining seven joined NATO in May 2004. They are, in fact, closer to the USA diplomatically than to western Europe. In 2003, when the United States was unable to secure UN or NATO support for the invasion of Iraq because of the opposition of France, Germany, and Russia, President George W. Bush organized a coalition which included Bulgaria, Czech Republic, Estonia, Ethiopia, Hungary, Latvia, Lithuania , Poland, Romania, and Slovakia.

National separatism became an issue in only two of the former countries of the Communist bloc. In 1992 Czechoslovakia peacefully split into two new nations: Slovakia and the Czech Republic. In Yugoslavia, however, the aggressive pro-Serbian policies of Slobodan Milosevic in the late 1980s led to separatist movements by other Yugoslav nations. At the beginning of the new century, after a series of civil wars and a NATO bombing campaign against Serbia, Yugoslavia had disintegrated and was replaced by the nations of Slovenia, Croatia, Bosnia-Herzegovina, Serbia-Montenegro, and Macedonia.

The former Republics of the Soviet Union (except for the Baltic states and the Russian Federation) have followed quite a different political and economic path from that of eastern Europe. In eastern Europe, communism was brought down by massive public demonstrations, and non-communist parties quickly dominated the political process. In the Soviet Union, however, popular demonstrations were significant only in opposing the coup attempt of August 19, 1991. The dismantling of the Soviet Union and the creation of independent nations was undertaken by former Communists who used the process for their own political and economic gain. From Belarus to Tajikistan, a common pattern has emerged: the country is led by a former official in the Communist Party of that republic who was elected president in the early 1990s and continues to be reelected by large majorities in elections that do not meet international standards as fair, equal, and transparent. In all states, the government either owns or intimidates the media and interferes in politics. Civil liberties, including freedom of religion, are routinely violated, and Uzbekistan, Kirgizstan, and Turkmenistan have been accused of serious human rights abuses. Georgia may be an exception to this pattern: In December 2003 former Communist Eduard Shevardnadze was forced to step down as president as a result of massive public demonstrations protesting electoral fraud, reminiscent of the end of communism in eastern Europe.

The economic pattern in these former Soviet republics is also similar. Most of them have joined the World Bank and the IMF and are committed to eventual free-market policies, but little progress has been made. Some privatization of farmland and small- and medium-sized enterprises has occurred, but key sectors of the economy, including heavy industry, energy, and telecommunications, remain in government hands; governments continue to control prices to a greater or lesser extent. Uzbekistan, Kirgizstan, and Turkmenistan have made the least progress in this regard.

In Turkish politics, the government continued its struggle against Islamism in the 1990s. The Islamist Welfare Party, which had failed to elect any members of parliament in 1987, won one-fifth of the vote in 1995, becoming the largest single party in the parliament. Soon after, however, it was declared illegal and disbanded by the Turkish Constitutional Court for violating the principle of secularism. In November 2002, the Justice and Development Party, a party with strong Islamic values but which affirmed a commitment to secular government, captured thirty-four percent of the vote. To bring its economy more in line with European trends, Turkey signed agreements with the IMF to reform social security, public finance, and banking, and liberalized the telecommunication and energy markets. The Turkish privatization board began to privatize a number of state-owned industries including oil refining, tobacco production, the telephone company, and some state banks. Turkey has become a part of the European customs union, but has so far been turned down for admission into the EU because it continues to apply the death penalty and because it is charged with human rights violations. Turkey continues to align itself with NATO and to remain aloof from the Arab Middle East, but its traditional interest in Central Asia continues. It has joined the Economic Cooperation Organization with Iran, Afghanistan, Pakistan, and the former Soviet Central Asian nations Azerbaijan, Kazakhstan, Turkmenistan, Uzbekistan, Tajikistan, and Kirgizstan.

After Iraq's defeat by U.S.-led UN forces in 1991, the United Nations demanded an accounting of Iraq's weapons of mass destruction and the freedom to inspect Iraqi weapons facilities; it imposed a trade embargo until Iraq complied. Despite the harm caused to the civilian economy by the trade sanctions, Hussein continued to impede inspections and to deny possession of weapons of mass destruction. In 2003, the United States and Great Britain invaded Iraq, deposed the Ba'athist government, and installed a provisional government with the goal of building a representative democracy and privatizing the economy. The U.S.-led coalition soon discovered that Hussein in fact did not possess weapons of mass destruction, and, after a brief period of relief at the removal of a dictator, the Iraqi people became increasingly hostile to the occupying forces. By the spring of 2004, it was clear that the population saw the western powers as occupiers and not liberators and that the creation of a stable, democratic Iraq was very unlikely in the short term.

In the 1990s, Iran followed world trends in implementing some free-market reforms and encouraging private trade and service industries. It has not, however, privatized oil or heavy industries and continues some degree of central economic planning. Iran promotes Islamic government in the Middle East, and it opposes western influence in the region, although it did not officially oppose (and unofficially welcomed) the U.S.-led invasions of neighboring Afghanistan and Iraq. While Iran continues to be a theocratic state in which women are oppressed and freedom of speech is denied, there is evidence of a rising reform movement that adheres to liberal values. In 2004 it was unclear which trend would prove to be more powerful.

Even after the Soviet Union withdrew from Afghanistan in 1989, it continued to send military and economic assistance, and the secular government in Kabul held its own against the mujahidin. When the Soviet Union dissolved at the end of 1991, however, this aid came to an end, and in April 1992, Kabul finally fell. An interim coalition government of mujahidin factions was established, but it soon collapsed because of ethnic rivalries. Anarchy reigned in the countryside, and warlords produced opium and extorted money from merchants and international traders. In the fall of 1994, the Taliban ("students") Party formed, funded by Saudi Arabia and Pakistan and led by Mullah Mohammad Omar, a famous anti-Soviet resistance fighter. The Taliban's goal was to end corruption and warlordism and to create an Islamic theocracy; by 2001, it had gained control over more than ninety percent of the country. Iran refused to recognize the Taliban government because of its mistreatment of the Shi'a population, and the United Nations refused to recognize it because of human rights abuses including the mistreatment of women. The Taliban also gave asylum to Osama bin Laden, another anti-Soviet fighter who, after the end of the Soviet Union, began to direct terrorist attacks against the West. After the destruction of the World Trade Center on September 11, 2001, the United States led a NATO invasion of Afghanistan that removed the Taliban from power and installed a provisional government with a western, secular orientation. In 2004, however, like Iraq, Afghanistan was far from stable; regional warlords still controlled much of the country, and human rights abuses continued.

In China, after the suppression of pro-democracy demonstrators in 1989, conservatives were in the ascendant until 1992, when Deng Xiaoping again managed to promote economic liberalization. The government began large scale privatization of unprofitable state enterprises and continued to streamline the state bureaucracy. The Chinese Communist Party continues one-party rule and close ideological control over education and the press. There appears to be increasing respect for the rule of law, however, and in 2004 the constitution was amended to recognize the right to private property. The Chinese government is committed to a "socialist market economy," and encourages foreign investment and foreign trade. After two hundred years of weakness vis-a-vis the West, China is rapidly recovering its traditional role as hegemonic power in east Asia. The central government is tightening its political control over Xinjiang, Tibet, and Inner Mongolia, and is following aggressive policies of Sinification. China supported the U.S.-led invasion of Afghanistan, and opposes Islamism in Central Asia. In 2001, China organized the Shanghai Cooperation Organization with Russia, Kazakhstan, Kirgizstan, Tajikistan, and Uzbekistan to promote regional stability and combat terrorism, and in the same year China and Russia signed a Treaty of Friendship and Cooperation.

POLITICAL DEVELOPMENTS AND FOREIGN AFFAIRS

On New Year's Day 1992, Russia began its post-Soviet existence as an independent, sovereign state. On January 2, Russian President Boris Yeltsin began to implement his promised radical economic program. He removed price controls on everything but bread, vodka, public transportation, and energy, and he announced a program for privatizing the nation's industrial capital. Privatization was to proceed in two stages: first small- and medium-scale enterprises would be given away, then large-scale industry would be sold for cash. To accomplish the first objective, the government distributed vouchers with a face value of 10,000 rubles to every Russian citizen or permanent resident. Vouchers were intended to purchase shares in enterprises identified for privatization, but they could be also be sold or invested in voucher funds. By June 1994, the voucher privatization was completed, with 100,000 privately owned corporations.

In the meantime, however, the Russian economy had collapsed. On the first day that prices were freed, the inflation rate jumped to 250 percent, and by the end of the year it had reached 2,600 percent. The savings accounts of ordinary Russians were quickly emptied and retirement pensions lost all their value. Voucher privatization was a major disappointment as well. As many as twenty-four million Russians were swindled out of their vouchers, more than fifteen million when the MMM Invest corporation (an investment fund) went bankrupt. In addition, the end to central planning meant bankruptcy for many enterprises and unemployment for their workers, something that had never happened in the Soviet Union. Between 1992 and 1995, the gross national product fell by forty-five percent, industrial production fell by sixty-two percent, consumption fell by thirty-three percent, and average life expectancy fell from 63 to 58 years of age.

This led to a political crisis. Many members of the Supreme Soviet opposed Yeltsin's economic program and attempted to rescind the power to make law by decree that he had been granted in the fall of 1991. Yeltsin refused to be limited, arguing that the Supreme Soviet was inferior to the Presidency. He argued that he had been elected in a free nationwide vote in 1991, while the Congress of People's Deputies (which elected the Supreme Soviet) had been elected in 1990 when the Communist Party still dominated the electoral process. Yeltsin made much of the fact that eighty percent of the Russian Congress of People's Deputies were former Communists.

In December 1992 the Congress of People's Deputies reiterated the Supreme Soviet's demand that privatization and market pricing be ended, and it proposed a constitutional change to reduce the Presidency to a ceremonial post and to create a parliamentary government. A proposal to remove Yeltsin from office did not pass, nor did one to subordinate the Council of Ministers to the Supreme Soviet. However, Yeltsin's widely hated Prime Minister (who had masterminded the disastrous economic reforms) stepped down and was replaced by a moderate. Both Yeltsin and the Congress agreed to hold a nation-wide referendum on their key political and economic disagreements.

In March 1993, before the referendum took place, the Congress formally stripped Yeltsin of his power to issue decrees or to appoint ministers without the approval of the Supreme Soviet. It also prepared a law that would have placed television and the press under the control of the Congress. Yeltsin responded by signing a decree that introduced direct presidential rule, reaffirming his power to issue decrees with the force of law and his right to dissolve the Congress and call new elections. The Constitutional Court declared Yeltsin's actions unconstitutional, and a bill of impeachment was again submitted to the Congress and again failed narrowly.

The referendum was held in April, and Yeltsin was vindicated. Fifty-eight percent voted to keep him in office, fifty-three percent supported his social and economic policies, sixty-seven percent supported early elections to the Congress of People's Deputies, and only forty-nine percent wanted early elections for the Presidency. Yeltsin announced that elections for the new legislature would be held in September and that he was establishing a commission to write a new constitution. Yeltsin presented a draft constitution, drawn up by his own advisers, that gave the President extremely broad powers and reduced the influence of the legislature. He also announced that he would rule by decree until the new constitution was in place and a new representative assembly elected.

The political crisis deepened. On May 1, there was violence in Moscow when pro-parliament demonstrators attempted to diverge from the parade route that had been approved by the government, and the police used force to prevent them. In June, regional representatives to the Constitutional Commission demanded more autonomy from the central government than Yeltsin's draft provided. Later in the summer, the Congress drafted amendments to the current constitution that reduced the president to a ceremonial head of state and that established criminal penalties for government officials who refused to obey parliamentary laws. Yeltsin responded by issuing a presidential decree dissolving the Congress of People's Deputies and the Supreme Soviet. He also announced an election to be held in December, which would serve as a referendum on his proposed constitution and would elect the new legislature established by that constitution. Russia's Constitutional Court, however, ruled that only Congress could call for a referendum and that Yeltsin's decree violated the Russian Constitution. It also ruled that the Constitutional Commission had no foundation in law. As a result of these rulings, the Supreme Soviet removed Yeltsin from office and named Vice President Aleksandr Rutskoi Acting President.

Yeltsin then ordered the army to disperse the Supreme Soviet. Soldiers surrounded the Russian White House (Parliament Building) and turned off electricity, water, and the telephone system. The Russian army tried to remain neutral and avoid violence, and at first it only blockaded the White House to prevent supporters from taking food and supplies to the besieged legislators. However, after pro-parliament forces seized the state television station and attempted to take over the Moscow telephone center and to break into a military armory, the army decided to back President Yeltsin and to suppress the parliament with force. On October 4, the White House was bombarded with artillery fire until those inside the building surrendered and were taken into custody. The army also suppressed pro-parliamentary supporters in the worst street fighting in Moscow since 1917. According to the official count, 145 were killed and more than 800 were wounded.

A brief period of presidential dictatorship ensued, until the referendum on the constitution and election of the new legislature occurred on December 12. Yeltsin censored the media, closed opposition newspapers, and restructured regional and local government, creating new regional councils appointed by himself. He issued decrees on the economy that furthered privatization and liberalization of the market. Yeltsin used the state-controlled media to promote approval of his constitution, and after the vote, the government asserted that it had been approved by 54 percent of eligible voters. Some newspapers subsequently accused the government of vote fraud and claimed that fewer than 50 percent of registered voters had actually voted, making the referendum invalid. Nevertheless, there was no political or social movement to overturn Yeltsin's victory.

The Russian Constitution of 1993 created a strong presidential government. The President is head of state and commander in chief of the armed forces. The President appoints and dismisses the Prime Minister and the cabinet, ambassadors, the head of the State Bank, the Constitutional Court, the Supreme Court, the procuracy (state attorneys), the Security Council, and the Supreme Command of the armed forces. The President chairs meetings of the Security Council and the Supreme Command, conducts foreign policy, directs domestic policy, and can initiate legislation. The President is empowered to dissolve the Duma and call new elections, declare martial law and states of emergency, issue decrees with the force of law, and veto laws passed by the legislature.

The Federation Council, the upper house of the legislature, has 178 members, 2 from each of the 89 regions of the Russian Federation. It confirms presidential nominations of chief judges, draws territorial boundaries, confirms the dispatch of troops abroad, and can veto laws passed by the Duma. The State Duma, the lower house, has 450 members, half elected from local constituencies, half elected from a national slate with proportional representation. The Duma confirms presidential nominations of prime minister, and can vote no confidence in the cabinet. It writes laws and can veto presidential decrees. The Duma can override a veto by the Federation Council and both houses can override a Presidential veto by a two-thirds majority.

The new Duma was not as docile as Yeltsin had hoped. The Russian-chauvinist (misnamed) Liberal-Democratic Party of Vladimir Zhirinovskii won the greatest number of votes in the elections, and had the second largest number deputies in the Duma. Zhirinovsky had supported the suppression of the parliament in September, but he also denounced the corruption of Russian government and the privatization process. As a whole, the Duma was no more enthusiastic for radical economic reform than the old Congress and Supreme Soviet had been. In addition, it granted amnesty for all those who had been arrested in October. (Yeltsin had wanted to turn them over to a military tribunal and to seek the death penalty on the charge of conspiracy to murder.)

Despite the disproportion between their respective powers, President Yeltsin worked quite cooperatively with the new parliament. Nevertheless, he continued to present himself as above party politics and did not attempt to create a pro-government party. Instead, he built up a huge presidential bureaucracy, and used his influence over the media to promote his policies. In 1995, with inflation and unemployment still high and his approval ratings now almost negligible, Yeltsin faced the prospect of losing the elections scheduled for 1996. Yeltsin summoned Russia's wealthiest oligarchs (those who had used privatization to their advantage) and negotiated loans totaling 500 million rubles using as collateral shares amounting to 40 percent of Russia's state-owned petroleum and mining operations. Yeltsin used the money to pay government employees who had not been paid in months or even years, and to fund a massive advertising blitz that secured him reelection. The government subsequently defaulted on the "loans," and the shares in government enterprises that had been offered as security passed into the hands of the oligarchs.

For the rest of the decade, Russia's economic and political situation was abysmal. Members of the legislature, whose office carried immunity from prosecution, were notoriously corrupt, and organized crime leaders secured election simply to avoid arrest. Regional leaders gained power at the expense of the center. Yeltsin's health deteriorated, and he was unable to lead effectively or to turn the economy around. When Russia faced a serious financial crisis in 1998 caused by increasing bankruptcies and a shortfall in government revenue, Yeltsin resolved it by devaluing the currency and defaulting on foreign debt. His popularity again fell sharply.

On December 31, 1999, Yeltsin abruptly announced his resignation and appointed Vladimir Putin, his Prime Minister, to serve as Acting President, until the presidential election in March 2000. Putin was a former KGB officer who had been associated with the reform movement in Russia since 1990 and risen rapidly in Yeltsin's administration. He had served as Prime Minister since the summer of 1999 and had won popularity for his aggressive measures combating Chechen secessionism. Another factor in his popularity was his sober and reserved demeanor, which compared well with the erratic and intemperate Yeltsin. Putin prepared for the election by mobilizing support in the business community, taking advantage of his association with Unity (a new political party he had fostered while Prime Minister), and by using state television and newspapers to promote his campaign. He won with 53 percent of the vote in an election judged fair by international observers.

Putin's goals were to strengthen the state, restore law and order, and reinvigorate economic reform. His first action was to reestablish central control over Russia's regional units by subordinating them to seven new federal districts, each headed by an administrator appointed by himself. Putin also increased the central government's proportion of taxes at the expense of the regions. Next, Putin began to reduce the power of financial oligarchs, who (he said) exercised undue political influence. He arrested several media tycoons, charged them with embezzlement of state resources, and allowed them to emigrate, after they turned their media holdings over to the government. Putin improved government finances by levying a flat 13 percent tax on income, and by ordering deep cuts in nuclear and conventional military forces.

In foreign affairs, the most pressing concern for Russia has been its relations with the former republics of the Soviet Union. The Commonwealth of Independent States has not become a vital institution, and Russia's relations with its new neighbors are for the most part bilateral. Russia's greatest conflict has been with Ukraine. Russia had claimed possession of Crimea and some border regions in eastern Ukraine that are nearly 100 percent Russian and has opposed Ukraine's plan to join NATO and the EU. However, the two countries have an economic stake in cooperation; Ukraine is dependent on Russian oil and gas, and Russia uses Ukrainian pipelines to deliver oil and gas to western Europe. In a Friendship Treaty of 1997, Russia agreed not to seek border adjustments and both countries agreed to share the Black Sea Fleet and the port of Sevastopol. In December 2004, Russian influence in Ukraine suffered a setback when a presidential election was overturned due to electoral fraud. The candidate favored by Moscow lost a second election to Viktor Yushchenko, a politician supported by the U.S.A.

Belarus and Moldova have ceased pressing for membership in the EU, and instead are moving toward an EU-like relationship with Russia in which there would be common citizenship, a customs union, and coordination of laws and economic policies. Kazakhstan and Kirgizstan may soon join this customs union. Armenia, which feels threatened by Azerbaijan and Turkey, is virtually an ally of Russia. Russian relations are strained with Georgia, which Russia accuses of harboring Chechen terrorists. Relations with Uzbekistan, Tajikistan, Turkmenistan are uncertain, since they are developing political and economic ties with China and Turkey. Nevertheless, Russia provides support to the leaders of all five Central Asian republics in their struggle against political Islam, which Russia continues to perceive as a threat to its remaining Muslim territories.

Even before the end of the Soviet Union, Boris Yeltsin sought good relations with the United States and western Europe. He continued the START negotiations begun by Gorbachev, and in 1991 he reduced the Russian nuclear arsenal by 30 percent. In 1993, Russia and the United States agreed to deactivate two-thirds of their remaining nuclear force, and in 1994 Yeltsin and U.S. President Bill Clinton agreed to cease targeting the remaining missiles at one another.

Russia has strongly opposed the expansion of NATO to include the nations of the former Warsaw Pact and USSR, feeling itself surrounded by a U.S.-dominated military alliance, but it has been unable to do so. On the other hand, Russia itself agreed in 1995 to join the NATO Partnership for Peace which included all the former communist nations. The program was intended to develop cooperative military relations for peace-keeping and humanitarian operations, and to promote transparent defense planning and democratic control over the military. One of its goals was to remove all nuclear weapons from Kazakhstan and Ukraine, which was achieved by 1996.

Russian leaders supported the U.S.-led Gulf War in 1991, but they were upset at not being consulted prior to U.S. and British military attacks on Iraq in the summer of 1993 and again in 1997. The greatest strain in relations came over the NATO bombing campaign against Serbia in 1999, which Russia opposed. Through the nineties, the United States consistently objected to Russia's suppression of the Chechen secession movement, but after the terrorist attacks on America on September 11, 2001, each country had more sympathy for the other's commitment to war on terrorism. Russia fully supported the U.S. invasion of Afghanistan in 2001, and indicated that it would not oppose U.S. use of airfields in Central Asia.

Russia did oppose other U.S. policies in the Middle East, however. Russia considered Iran to be a key ally in the struggle against subversive Islamist movements in the Caucasus and Central Asia, and so it continued to sell arms and nuclear reactor technology to Iran despite U.S. opposition. In addition, Russia joined France and Germany in opposing the U.S.-British invasion of Iraq in 2003 and resisted U.S. requests to forgive Iraq's huge debts to Russia.

CULTURE AND RELIGION

The Russian Orthodox Church has continued to play a prominent role in the Russian state. In the last years of the Soviet period, there were tens of millions of admitted religious believers, and many more than this hung icons in their homes, put Orthodox crosses on graves, and celebrated Church holidays. By 1990, Orthodox services were being performed in cathedrals in the Kremlin and state television was broadcasting religious services. In his campaign for President of Russia in the spring of 1991, Yeltsin publicized his attendance at Easter services, and after his election he invited Patriarch Aleksei to play a role in his inauguration. Since then, the Church has thrived. In the 1990s, an estimated 60 percent of the population of the Russian Federation declared themselves to be Orthodox believers.

Putin, like Yeltsin, has been anxious to associate himself with the Church, but the Russian state is interested in Orthodoxy as a symbol of historical continuity, not as a state religion. In fact, the Russian Federation is a secular state and upholds the principle of separation of church and state and the freedom of conscience. In 1995, the Yeltsin administration formed a nine-member consultative body, Council for Cooperation with Religious Associations, which included two Russian Orthodox, two Roman Catholics, two Muslims, and a Buddhist, a Jew, a Baptist, a Pentecostal, and Seventh-Day Adventist.

The Patriarch of the Orthodox Church, too, supports the separation of church and state, but some secular politicians promote Orthodoxy because of their own nationalist agenda. The Duma passed a law in 1997 that denied "nontraditional" churches the right to publish tracts, set up schools, or minister in hospitals or prisons, and defined nontraditional as having existed in Russia for fewer than fourteen years. This law has had a minimal effect at the national level, since the Constitutional Court ruled that it could not be applied retroactively. Nevertheless, at the local level non-Orthodox religions are often denied the right to buy land or rent buildings to use for churches or schools. Mormons, Jehovah's Witnesses, and pentacostals have reported discrimination and harassment.

Muslims make up the second largest religious community in Russia, totaling about 20 percent of religious believers, and Islam is recognized as one of Russia's traditional religions. The government grants visas to Muslims who make the pilgrimage to Mecca, Muslim publishing houses are free to print and disseminate the Koran and other religious literature, and mosques have been built in cities with large Muslim populations. In 1995 Muslims in Tatarstan created a Union of Muslims of Russia to improve interethnic understanding and to combat the idea that Islam is an extremist religion. At the end of the 1990s, however, the government began to monitor and regulate visas for Russian Muslims to study at Islamic schools in the Middle East, fearing the spread of Islamism.

During perestroika Jews had been allowed to immigrate without restriction, and in 1990 alone 188,000 did so. The trend continued in Russia, and between 1992 and 1995, an average of 65,000 Jews emigrated every year. In 1996, however, the Russian government began to limit the activity of the Jewish Agency, which it believed was responsible for enticing and funding Jewish departure. In addition, some Jewish emigrants have returned to Russia, after discovering that their economic and social status was lower in Israel than in Russia and that Russia was a safer place to live.

Judaism has been making the same sort of resurgence as other religions after communism, as many Russian Jews seek to recover their religious and ethnic heritage. In 1996, a Russian translation of the Talmud was published for the first time since before the Revolution of 1917. According to official figures, Russia's Jewish population rose from 500,000 in 1992 to 700,000 in 1995. There is no official anti-Semitism and there are laws against hate speech, and for the most part Jews are not subjected to anti-Semitic discrimination or violence, although there are virulently anti-Semitic Russian chauvinist groups.

In the Soviet period, Russia led the world in the number of books sold per capita, and Russians were prolific readers of newspapers and journals. Russian reading has dropped sharply since the end of communism. Beginning in the tsarist period and continuing through the communist era, when news reporting was strictly censored, writers of literature were respected as "the conscience of the nation," and literature was avidly read "between the lines" for alternative views to official ideology. With complete freedom of speech, press, and political activity, literature no longer serves this purpose. Fewer books are bought, and a number of "thick journals" have gone bankrupt. It has not helped readership that literary writers have turned to postmodernist writing with little broad appeal. In the 1990s, the icons of the recent past, the dissidents and the thaw generation, have fallen out of fashion. In addition, traditional psychological novels about everyday life are no longer popular, perhaps because life has become so grim. In the 1990s, the detective novel emerged as the most popular genre even for literary writers. Themes of crime, murder, kidnaping, and the mafia fit with the times, and in novels the "good guys" can win. Pornography has also become a very popular genre.

ROLES AND STATUS OF WOMEN

The end of communism and the rise of Russian nationalism was devastating for the status, the social and political role, and the well-being of women. It seems that politically powerful men were as anxious to end the communist doctrine of equality for women as they were to preserve the Soviet belief in biological determinism. In 1989, about one-third of the Supreme Soviet were women, whereas in the Duma elections of 1995 only 45 out of 450 deputies were women, and only 1 of the 178 seats in the Federation Council was filled by a women. The trend worsened. By 1999, the percentage of women in the Duma had fallen to 7 percent, and only 1.3 percent of Russia's ministries, executive bodies, or state committees were headed by women.

As the economy collapsed, women were the first to be demoted or to lose their jobs. The trend began with the decline in the economy at the end of perestroika. Between 1889 and 1990, women's participation in the workforce fell from 51 to 48 percent. In the 1990s, women made up about 75 percent of the unemployed. Furthermore, women's wages, which had never been more than two-thirds that of men's under communism, declined to 40 percent in 1995. One cause was that women were fired from higher-paying jobs as engineers and technicians and rehired as unskilled service employees. Women were also discriminated against in employment in the higher-paying private sector, where only 25 percent of jobs were held by women.

Russia also experienced unprecedented poverty rates, and poverty was predominantly feminine. At the end of the 1990s, more than half of single-parent families, almost always led by women, lived below the poverty line. Single mothers were also particularly hurt by the decline in government services. Day care centers closed down or began to charge fees, and the stipends that the state paid for each child covered less than ten percent of the cost of bringing up a school-age child.

In the new Russia, women were increasingly commodified and abused. In the Communist era, the iconic woman was either a buttoned-up professional woman or a farm woman in a head scarf and formless gown. After the media was freed of government control, it began to glorify western-style sexualized femininity. Beauty contests presented women as sexual objects, and semi-nude female models were used in advertising. These new attitudes provided an environment in which sexual harassment became the norm. Employment advertisements for secretaries frequently included such phrases as "wanted: attractive girls, under twenty-five" or "wanted: women without complexes." It was not uncommon for employers to demand sexual favors as a condition of employment. According to surveys, one out of four women was a victim of physical sexual assault in the first five years after the end of communism. In 1994, thirteen thousand rapes were reported.

The one field in which women could find easy employment was prostitution, and female poverty, combined with the commodification of sex, made it a booming business. The media portrayed prostitution as a glamorous and legitimate way to earn a living, and a survey of high school students conducted in the mid-1990s discovered that 60 percent of young women leaving school thought that prostitution was the most attractive profession.

With near unanimity, Russian men and women continue to believe that marriage is essential to happiness and self-fulfillment. Modern contraception is still not a part of routine government health care; most contraceptives that are available are donated by international agencies. Less than 25 percent of women of childbearing age use contraceptives, and abortion continues to be the principal method of birth control. In 1995, there were 225 abortions for every 100 live births. Half of all babies born cannot be breast-fed because their mothers are too undernourished to produce sufficient milk. Women still perform 75 percent of housework, and in the first half of the 1990s, spouse abuse became a serious problem. In 1993, there were 200,000 reports of physical abuse of wives, and 14,000 women died as a result of domestic violence.

On the other hand, in important material ways, the market system has brought some benefits to women. Retail sales have been simplified and stores are well stocked, so women spend far less time standing in lines. In addition, women have much greater access to items such as pantyhose, sanitary supplies, and contraceptives than was the case in the Soviet era.

SOCIAL AND ECONOMIC TRENDS

Although the Soviet economy had begun to shrink in the last years of perestroika, the real collapse came after the transition to market policies and privatization. Russia's gross national product fell steadily from more than $550 billion in 1989 to slightly more than $300 billion in 1998, a 46 percent decline. Furthermore, privatization has done little to modernize Russian industry: Russian manufacturing is still inefficient and uncompetitive with the West. Foreign investment, which was expected to transform the economy, has been directed toward petroleum and mineral resources and not manufacturing. Russian income from foreign trade in the 1990s derived mainly from the export of raw materials: oil, gas, gold, and gems. Most of Russia's imports were consumer goods and machinery.

Nor has agriculture developed as expected. In December 1992, all collective farmers were given the right to an equal share of the land and were allowed to form joint stock companies, or cooperatives, or to separate into family farms. However, Russia's participation in the world economy has permitted the importation of cheap food, and Russian farmers have been unable to compete and have little incentive to innovate. Few family farms were created, and one-third of all collective farms remained in their Soviet form. From 1990 to 1999, meat, milk, and grain production suffered a 50 percent decline, while flax and wool output fell by two-thirds. The government continued to subsidize agriculture, but the farm economy has remained in depression and the tradition of rural poverty continues.

Yeltsin's economic advisers continued to believe that agricultural reform could not occur until farmland was turned into private property that could be bought, sold, and mortgaged. His efforts to accomplish this were relentlessly opposed by the Duma, which shared the traditional Russian view that farmland must be a community possession. Yeltsin's 1993 constitution guaranteed the right to own land and deeds of ownership were given to farmers, but the Duma refused to pass the laws necessary to permit the purchase or sale of land. In 1996, Yeltsin issued a presidential decree allowing farmers to buy and sell land, but the Duma again countered with a law that forbade sale of land by anyone but the state. Only in 2002 did the Duma finally approve a law giving saleable title of land to farmers, with the limitation that farmland could not be sold to foreigners.

Gauging the overall effect of privatization on the population is difficult. Employment and wage data are grim. Unemployment remained at around 12 percent for the decade of the 1990s, but more devastating still was the decline in wages; the average wage was cut in half. At the end of the decade, approximately 40 percent of the population (and almost 60 percent of children under six) lived in households with incomes below the poverty line. The minimum wage in 1998 was only 87 rubles ($4.00) a month. On the other hand, it should be recalled that there were very few goods available for purchase in the Soviet era, and wages therefore went into savings accounts. Wages may have fallen, but there are now actually goods on the shelves. The material standard of living might actually be improving.

Still, government support of medical and social services declined, and throughout the first decade of post-communism, infant mortality steadily rose and life expectancy steadily fell. Moreover, poverty, stress, and depression made alcohol abuse an even greater problem under capitalism than under communism. A 1995 Russian study found that as many as 60 percent of blue-collar workers and 20 percent of white-collar workers were regularly drunk. In 1991, thirty-six thousand Russians died of alcohol poisoning, while in 1994 the number had climbed to fifty-three thousand. Increased alcohol consumption by pregnant women has contributed to the rise in infant mortality, as well as birth defects and childhood disease. Increased use of alcohol by men has led to the dramatic rise in domestic violence and to murder in general. The Russian murder rate is now three times that of the United States, and second in the world to South Africa. The use of drugs has also increased. In 1995, about two million Russians used narcotics, more than twenty times the figure for the entire Soviet Union in 1985. It was estimated that the number of users was growing by 50 percent a year in the mid-1990s.

The breakdown of traditional social and economic values created an environment in which organized crime (called *mafiia* in Russian) thrived. In the middle of the 1990s, it was estimated that organized crime controlled half of the banks, four-fifths of foreign joint ventures, and two-fifths of the economy as a whole. There were approximately three thousand organized gangs with sixty thousand members. Mafiia groups terrorized or bribed the police and made little attempt to conceal their activities. Assassins actually advertised their services in newspapers, and in the middle of the decade, Russia averaged at least one gangland-style murder each month. Assassinations included Duma deputies, government officials, judges, mayors, bankers, business executives, sports figures, and investigative reporters. More than twenty reporters were killed in 1994 alone. Besides being involved in big business, mafiias also took control of ordinary crime: drugs, gambling, car theft, kidnaping for ransom, and "protection."

While privatization and the market system hurt the majority of the population, it was taken advantage of by a small group of insiders to enrich themselves. Official corruption, which had been endemic under Communism but kept under control, became the norm under capitalism. Industrial managers and economic planners knew which enterprises would be profitable and had an inside track to acquiring ownership. Additionally, the government, in an effort to keep production costs for industry low, set the wholesale prices of oil, gas, and steel at only a fraction of their market value. Enterprise managers acquired these resources ostensibly for industrial production, but instead of using them to manufacture goods for the Russian market, they sold them abroad for huge profits. The new free market economy provided opportunities for young western-educated MBAs to establish stock exchanges and a banking industry. Banks played the central role in the second phase of privatization, when the remaining large- and medium-scale enterprises were sold for cash.

As a result of these developments, Russian society has become increasingly stratified. In 1991, the poorest fifth of the population earned 12 percent of the national income while the richest fifth earned 31 percent. By 1997, however, the poorest fifth earned only 6 percent and the richest fifth earned 45 percent. At the end of the decade, a mere 1.5 percent of the population had gained possession of 65 percent of the national wealth, while 20 percent of the population earned less than minimum subsistence income.

The end of Communism has been very good for former Communists. In Yeltsin's central administration about 75 percent of all officials were former members of the nomenklatura, while at the regional level this figure was 80 percent. At regional and local levels, the first secretary of the Communist party normally took over as head of the local civil administration, often without even moving to a new office. Furthermore, former Communists have been the principal beneficiaries of privatization, and one might conclude that the end of communism was engineered by the Communist party elite in order to enrich themselves by looting the public wealth. Sixty percent of Russia's millionaires and 40 percent of all business-owners are former Communist party members. It must be kept in mind, of course, that these are all *ex*-Communists, who no longer are part of an entrenched political organization. The current Communist party is an ordinary party more committed to Russian nationalism than Marxism.

PEOPLES OF THE RUSSIAN FEDERATION

Russia did not become a unitary nation-state but remains a multiethnic federated republic. The Russian constitution guarantees the equality of all people without regard to religion or ethnicity. It also recognizes the rights of peoples to preserve their native culture, and the right of each person to use his or her native language for communication and education Of the eighty-nine territorial units into which Russia is divided, twenty-one are national republics [including Chuvashia, Kalmykia, Komi, Sakha (Yakutia), Tatarstan, Bashkortostan, Ingushetia, and Chechnya] and ten are autonomous national regions (including the Buryat, Chukchi, Evenk, and Koryak regions).

Russians nevertheless dominate Russia politically, economically, and culturally. Russians make up more than 85 percent of the population, are a significant part of the population of all the national republics, and constitute a majority in all but one of the autonomous regions. During the 1990s, governors of the regions exercised considerable local control and fought to preserve their ethnic identity and privileges, but Putin's reorganization of Russia into nine federal divisions has diminished regional political power. There have also been outright independence movements in Tatarstan, Bashkortostan, and Chechnya, but this, too, has been fought by the government.

Chechnya (officially known as the Chechen Republic) declared independence in 1991, and three years later, Yeltsin sent Russian forces to suppress the secession movement. The Russian army bombarded and occupied the capital, Grozny, in 1995, but relentless Chechen guerrilla warfare forced Russia to negotiate a cease-fire and withdraw from Chechnya entirely. In the summer of 1999, however a series of bombings of public buildings in Russian cities were blamed on Chechen terrorists, and Prime Minister Vladimir Putin decided to reassert Russian authority in Chechnya. In 2000, Russian troops again seized Grozny, and again Chechen independence fighters took to the hills and continued guerrilla attacks on Russian forces. At the end of 2004, there was still no resolution to the dispute.

CONCLUSION

At the beginning of the twenty-first century, Russia's economic condition has begun to improve. President Vladimir Putin has begun a campaign against corruption, he has raised taxes and improved tax collection, and he has asked the federal government to take more responsibility for social welfare. A new mood of stability and progress has arisen. Inflation and unemployment have been reduced, and economic growth has finally resumed. If current growth rates hold, Russia can hope to regain Soviet economic output levels by the year 2015.

It is also likely that the power of the Russian presidency will continue to grow. Putin's campaign against corruption may also serve to enhance his own power and to control the media. Control of the news media by governing parties appears to be a Eurasian, if not a world, trend. Finally, although Russia is no longer the superpower that is once was, and is far from hegemonic in Eurasia, it remains a key player in world affairs. It is the largest country in the world, and one of the richest in natural resources. Russia has one-third of the world's known reserves of natural gas, one-quarter of its oil reserves, one-fifth of its precious metals, and one-fifth of its timber reserves. The real test for Russian leaders will be whether they can transform their economy from an exporter of raw materials to an exporter of value-added products.

_____ TEXT DOCUMENTS _____

Patriarch Aleksii II at Yeltsin's Inauguration

In the summer of 1991, Boris Yeltsin was elected President of the RSFSR, the first time a Russian head of state had been elected by the direct vote of the people.

- What does Aleksii's appearance at this event signify?
- Does Patriarch Aleksii's address have a political message? A religious message?

[After Yeltsin took the oath as President of Russia,] the Russian anthem was played. The Russian state flag was raised over the republic President's residence in the Kremlin. Aleksii II, Patriarch of All Rus, was given the floor. . . .

[He said:] You have taken responsibility for a country that is gravely ill. The 70-year destruction of its spiritual system and internal unity was accompanied by the strengthening of heavy external hoops of forced statehood. Three generations of people have grown up under conditions that have removed their desire and ability to work. First people lost the habit of spiritual labor, they lost the habit of heroic prayer, and then they lost the habit of mental labor, of aspiring toward an independent search for the truth. Finally, whether this was desired or not, the way of life that our society is now trying to get out of in fact put people out of the habit of the most ordinary labor, of diligence, of initiative.

There is no point today in looking for some kind of bearers of evil incarnate in our country, supposing that everything will sort itself out if they are removed from the political arena. As a pastor, I know all too well that evil thoughts are lodged deep in people's hearts and that there is nothing more complicated and more important than healing the human heart. I tell you this, urging you to proceed unceasingly on the basis of anthropological realism, if you will, the Patriarch continued.

[Turning to the President of the RSFSR, he offered his wishes that tolerance and wisdom never leave him.] Forgive people; after all, people—I am talking not only about your political opponents or associates but about all people in the Russian Republic—cannot be remade overnight, or over 500 days. Our sick society and people who have endured so much need understanding, love and tolerance. Therefore, it is incumbent on us to more often remember the words of the apostle: "Bear ye one another's burdens, and so fulfill the law of Christ."

[The Patriarch noted that] one cannot restructure the life of Russia while having constantly before one's eyes only the fact that there is evil in our life. After all, the evil had seemed so omnipotent and omnipresent. But we all survived and preserved a good deal of faith, humanity, good and light. This means that there was and is good in our hearts and in our Russia. I am convinced that it is more important for us to learn to take note of this good and understand it than it is to focus on the evil.

Source: "Yeltsin Sworn in as Russia's President," *Current Digest of the Post-Soviet Press*, vol. 43, no. 38 (August 14, 1991):1, 3. Translation copyright by *The Current Digest of the Soviet Press*, published weekly at Columbus, Ohio. Reprinted by permission of the Digest.

The choice of the people has placed a heavy cross on you. You bear responsibility not only before the people but also before God. You have accepted not honor, not privileges, but responsibility. As far as the church or religious associations and their future are concerned, the Patriarch said, we hope that the new President of Russia will promote the return of the church, its age-old sacred places, its churches and cloisters, and that Russia's participation in their restoration and rehabilitation will be provided for.

Patriarch Aleksy II read out an address signed by the leaders or representatives of Christianity—Orthodox, Catholics, Baptists—and of Islam, Buddhism and Judaism, who were present in the hall.

"Election by the people and the will of God have entrusted supreme political power in Russia to you," the address says. "Russia is not simply a country; it is an entire continent, populated by people of different nationalities, different convictions and faiths. We all wish it a peaceful and propitious future, and we all pray for you and hope that you will serve our homeland's good and its swift healing from the severe wounds dealt to it in the past years of struggle against the spiritual foundations of human life. We congratulate you on your election to the high post of President of Russia and hope that the lofty service to which you have been called will not separate you from the people and that you will respond sensitively to their pain, anxieties and hopes. The ideals of equality, freedom and spiritual rebirth to which you promised loyalty in the days before the election will, we hope, be unfailing guideposts for you in all the years of your activity in the post of Russian Republic President. On this first day of your high service, please accept our sincere congratulations and good wishes."

The Patriarch made the sign of the cross over B. N. Yeltsin and handed him the address.

Constitution of the Russian Federation, 1993

This constitution was largely the work of Yeltsin's own advisers. It was not adopted by the Constitutional Commission but was put before the people in a referendum. Fifty-four percent of the voters approved it.

- Compare this with the Fundamental Law of 1906 and the Soviet Constitution of 1936.
- Which Soviet values carried over into post-Soviet Russia? Which did not?
- Which political principles are more similar to the Fundamental Law of 1906? Which provisions seem to be entirely new?

ARTICLE 3.

1. The multinational people of the Russian Federation shall be the vehicle of sovereignty and the only source of power in the Russian Federation. . . .

ARTICLE 4.

1. The sovereignty of the Russian Federation shall apply to its entire territory.
2. The Constitution of the Russian Federation and federal laws shall have supremacy throughout the entire territory of the Russian Federation.
3. The Russian Federation shall ensure the integrity and inviolability of its territory.

ARTICLE 13.

1. Ideological plurality shall be recognized in the Russian Federation.
2. No ideology may be instituted as a state-sponsored or mandatory ideology.

ARTICLE 14.

1. The Russian Federation shall be a secular state. No religion may be instituted as state-sponsored or mandatory religion.
2. Religious associations shall be separated from the state, and shall be equal before the law.

ARTICLE 19.

1. All people shall be equal before the law and in the court of law.

Source: http://www.russianet.ru/~oldrn/politics/constitution February 16, 2003.

2. The state shall guarantee the equality of rights and liberties regardless of sex, race, nationality, language, origin, property or employment status, residence, attitude to religion, convictions, membership of public associations or any other circumstance. Any restrictions of the rights of citizens on social, racial, national, linguistic or religious grounds shall be forbidden.
3. Man and woman shall have equal rights and liberties and equal opportunities for their pursuit.

ARTICLE 26.

1. Everyone shall have the right to determine and state his national identity. No one can be forced to determine and state his national identity. Everyone shall have the right to use his native language, freely choose the language of communication, education, training and creative work.

ARTICLE 29.

2. Propaganda or campaigning inciting social, racial, national or religious hatred and strife is impermissible. The propaganda of social, racial, national, religious or language superiority is forbidden. . . .
5. The freedom of the mass media shall be guaranteed. Censorship shall be prohibited.

ARTICLE 37.

3. Everyone shall have the right to work under conditions meeting the requirements of safety and hygiene, to remuneration for work without any discrimination whatsoever and not below the statutory minimum wage, and also the right to security against unemployment.
4. The right to individual and collective labor disputes with the use of means of resolution thereof established by federal law, including the right to strike, shall be recognized.
5. Everyone shall have the right to rest and leisure. A person having a work contract shall be guaranteed the statutory duration of the work time, days off and holidays, and paid annual vacation.

ARTICLE 38.

1. Motherhood and childhood, and the family shall be under state protection.
2. Care for children and their upbringing shall be the equal right and duty of the parents.
3. Employable children who have reached 18 years old shall care for their non-employable parents.

ARTICLE 39.

1. Everyone shall be guaranteed social security in old age, in case of disease, invalidity, loss of breadwinner, to bring up children and in other cases established by law. . . .

ARTICLE 40.

1. Everyone shall have the right to a home. . . .
3. Low-income citizens and other citizens, defined by the law, who are in need of housing shall be housed free of charge or for affordable pay from government, municipal and other housing funds in conformity with the norms stipulated by the law.

ARTICLE 41.

1. Everyone shall have the right to health care and medical assistance. Medical assistance shall be made available by state and municipal health care institutions to citizens free of charge, with the money from the relevant budget, insurance payments and other revenues. . . .

ARTICLE 43.

1. Everyone shall have the right to education.
2. The accessibility and gratuity of pre-school, general secondary and vocational secondary education in public and municipal educational institutions and enterprises shall be guaranteed.
3. Everyone shall have the right to receive, free of charge and on a competitive basis, higher education in a state or municipal educational institution or enterprise. . . .

ARTICLE 59.

1. Defense of the homeland shall be a duty and obligation of the citizen of the Russian Federation.

ARTICLE 80.

1. The President of the Russian Federation shall be the head of state.
2. The President shall be the guarantor of the Constitution of the Russian Federation, and of human and civil rights and freedoms. . . .
3. The President of the Russian Federation shall define the basic domestic and foreign policy guidelines of the state in accordance with the Constitution of the Russian Federation and federal laws.
4. The President of the Russian Federation as head of state shall represent the Russian Federation inside the country and in international relations.

ARTICLE 83.

The President of the Russian Federation shall: a) appoint Chairman of the Government of the Russian Federation subject to consent of the State Duma; b) have the right to preside over meetings of the Government of the Russian Federation; c) decide on resignation of the Government of the Russian Federation; . . . e) appoint and dismiss deputy chairmen of the Government of the Russian Federation and federal ministers as proposed by the Chairman of the Government of the Russian Federation; . . . g) form and head the Security Council of the Russian Federation, the status of which is determined by federal law; h) endorse the military doctrine of the Russian Federation; . . . k) appoint and dismiss the Supreme Command of the Armed Forces of the Russian Federation; l) appoint and recall, after consultations with the respective committees or commissions of the Federal Assembly, diplomatic representatives of the Russian Federation to foreign states and international organizations.

ARTICLE 84.

The President of the Russian Federation shall: a) call elections to the chambers of the State Duma in accordance with the Constitution of the Russian Federation and federal law; b) dissolve the State Duma in cases and under procedures envisaged by the Constitution of the

Russian Federation; c) call a referendum under procedures established by federal constitutional law; d) introduce draft laws in the State Duma; e) sign and publish federal laws; . . .

ARTICLE 86.

The President of the Russian Federation shall: a) supervise the conduct of the foreign policy of the Russian Federation; b) conduct negotiations and sign international treaties of the Russian Federation; c) sign instruments of ratification; d) accept credentials and instruments of recall of diplomatic representatives accredited with him.

ARTICLE 87.

1. The President of the Russian Federation shall be the Supreme Commander-in-Chief of the Armed Forces of the Russian Federation. . . .

ARTICLE 89.

The President of the Russian Federation shall: a) resolve issues of citizenship of the Russian Federation and of granting political asylum; b) award state decorations of the Russian Federation, confer honorary titles of the Russian Federation and top military ranks and top specialized titles; c) grant pardon.

ARTICLE 90.

1. The President of the Russian Federation shall issue decrees and executive orders.
2. The decrees and orders of the President of the Russian Federation shall be binding throughout the territory of the Russian Federation. . . .

ARTICLE 91.

The President of the Russian Federation shall possess immunity.

Proposal for the Regulation of Prostitution

Prostitution has become widespread in Russian cities. The following proposal was written by Aleksandr Lando, Human Rights Commissioner for Saratov Province, and published in Nezavisimaya gazeta *in December 2000.*

- What does this reveal about the nature of prostitution in Russia?
- Compare prostitution in post-Soviet Russia with prostitution in imperial Russia. What does this suggest about the transformation of Russian society?

In the city of Saratov, . . . the police have files on about 800 prostitutes. Roughly a third of them are streetwalkers, and there are about 60 "escort" services, whose addresses are also known to the police. . . .

Seventy percent of the prostitutes on file are infected with venereal diseases. The results of questionnaires filled out by women in the sex trade in Saratov Province . . . confirmed that there is a correlation between prostitution and drug use. Drugs are used by 35 percent of prostitutes in Saratov, 57 percent in Engels and 82 percent in Balakovo. Eighty-four percent of those who use drugs (which is 54 percent of all women in the sex trade) indicated that they use them on a regular basis (more than once a week). A somewhat smaller percentage of those who use drugs (79 percent, or 51 percent of all prostitutes) indicated that they use them intravenously. More than half of those who use drugs intravenously (or 27 percent of all women in the sex trade) at least occasionally share needles or syringes with other people. . . .

In order to resolve specific issues involving the legalization or prohibition of prostitution, it is necessary to clearly define the legal status of physical persons directly rendering commercial sexual services and the legal status of physical and juristic persons providing commercial sexual services. In my view, there are significant gaps and contradictions in existing legislation on this matter. . . .

Proceeding from existing legislation, it is difficult to define [the legal status of a juristic person providing commercial sexual services]. But this has to be done, because there is a direct link between the sex business and the antisocial and illegal behavior of persons involved in it.

Girls who render sexual services stress that firms providing such services recruit teenage girls as young as 14 (minors); that their "bosses" fleece them, leaving them with 30 percent to 35 percent of the fee per client; and that their whole "job" is made more burdensome by having to steal from clients and by the worst thing of all: In order to keep the girls totally dependent and make sure they don't give up prostitution, they are "helped" to develop a heroin habit. It is practically impossible for people in their line of work to find anyone to help them, since the "protectors" of 40 percent to 45 percent of sex firms are not crime bosses but police officers, who, furthermore, feel they have the right to summon girls at any time of the day or night for free sexual services. . . .

I believe that the activity of sex firms should be thought about from the standpoint of implementation of Art. 10 of the Russian Federation Civil Code, which sets limits on the exer-

---

Source: *Current Digest of the Post-Soviet Press,* vol. 53, no. 1 (January 31, 2001): 7. Translation copyright by *The Current Digest of the Soviet Press,* published weekly at Columbus, Ohio. Reprinted by permission of the *Digest.*

cise of civil rights; point 1 of this article states that any form of abuse of rights by citizens or juristic persons is impermissible. Abusing rights is precisely what sex firms are doing, using existing gaps in the law to conceal what they are doing and making incredible profits from their activity by exploiting prostitutes and not paying taxes on the income they make.

And that income is enormous!

According to some estimates, the "gross turnover" of prostitution in Moscow is about $200 million a year. Roughly 45 percent of this sum goes directly to the prostitutes, 20 percent each to the pimps and bodyguards, and 15 percent to the police "protectors." . . .

Against the backdrop of the prostitution problem, another facet of the general inequality between women and men becomes clearly visible. Under Russian law, a prostitute faces administrative liability, but . . . a man who provides sexual services for money . . . faces neither liability nor even condemnation. It's as if male prostitution didn't exist. . . . Yet in Saratov, for instance, there is an entire firm that specializes in male services, and it makes very good money. There's even a five-hour wait for services there.

In conclusion, I would like to stress that if legalizing prostitution is immoral, prohibiting it through legislation is even less acceptable. If anything is to be prohibited, what should be banned by legislation is not the rendering of commercial sexual services by physical persons, but the provision of those services for profit by pimps and sex firms.

The rendering of sexual services by physical persons in exchange for payment is an evil. . . . A moral evil. But changes in the realm of public morals will not occur until there are changes in society itself. Until then, prostitution as a phenomenon needs to be regulated and controlled by the state. . . .

Russian Federation Policy
toward Minority Languages

The following report on the language policy of the Russian Federation comes from an article in Izvestia *in November 2002.*

- What does this suggest about the role of nationalism in the Russian federation?
- What does this suggest about the relation between the central government and the minority peoples of the Federation?

The State Duma passed yesterday on second and, immediately thereafter, on third and final reading a bill stipulating that the alphabets of Russia's official state language and the languages of the republics must be based on the Cyrillic alphabet. After the document goes

Source: *Current Digest of the Post-Soviet Press,* vol. 54, no. 46 (December 11, 2002). Translation copyright by *The Current Digest of the Soviet Press,* published weekly at Columbus, Ohio. Reprinted by permission of the *Digest.*

into effect, Tatarstan will have to repeal its republic law switching the Tatar language from the Cyrillic to the Latin alphabet.

The bill was submitted by the Duma's committee on nationality affairs because "issues concerning the written form" of the state language of the Russian Federation and the languages of the republics "are still unregulated." . . . The document was signed by representatives of the ethnic republics–Kaadyr-ool Bicheldei (Tuva), Sergei Budazhapov (Buryatia), Khapisat Gamzatova (Dagestan) and others.

[However,] the deputies from Tatarstan tried to oppose the bill. The leader of the Regions of Russia group, Oleg Morozov, said that since the republics that belong to the Federation have two state languages—Russian and the language of the indigenous ethnic group—the claim that the use of a different alphabet for the latter language undermines the foundations of the state is untenable. Tatar Deputy Fandas Safiullin took an even harder line.

"Nationalities' writing systems cannot be standardized; there is no precedent for that anywhere in the world," Safiullin said.

He proposed several amendments to the bill that were impossible to take seriously. For instance, the bill says that it will go into effect "ten days after its official publication." Safiullin suggested a different wording: "ten days after the abolition of the principle of the equality and self-determination of peoples, guaranteed by the Constitution of the Russian Federation." One of his amendments recommended "submitting to the State Duma a bill whereby the Russian Federation renounces its commitments to protect human rights and the rights of ethnic groups and to protect regional languages and the languages of ethnic minorities."

The State Duma refused to discuss the deputy's amendments on the grounds that they were submitted after the deadline set by the responsible committee.

The bill as passed stipulates that, at both the central and the regional level, other writing systems can be established only by federal laws. The Duma rejected an amendment proposed by Deputy Andrei Vulf, under which republics could have changed their languages' writing systems through their own laws or decrees. The majority of the deputies think the only appropriate place to decide the alphabet issue is in Moscow, through a special law. The regions are directed to bring their own legislation into compliance with the new law within twelve months after it goes into force.

The number of votes cast in favor of the document–336 (the minimum needed for passage was 226)–indicates that the Duma has a unified position on the issue. . . .

Figure 22-1 Russian Federation Coin
- Compare this coin with previous Russian and Soviet coins. What *is* represented here, and what is *not?*
- What does this reveal about Russian society and politics?

Figure 22-2 Vladimir Putin and George W. Bush
This photo was taken at a Summit meeting in 2003.
- Compare this with previous representations of Soviet and Russian leaders.
- What meaning would this message convey to a Russian audience?

Source: Corbis/Bettman.

Figure 22-3 Cathedral of Christ the Savior

The first Cathedral of Christ the Savior had been demolished by the Stalin regime in 1933, and in 1990 the Orthodox Church began to make plans to rebuild it according to the original blueprints. After the end of the Soviet Union, the Church and the government cooperated in raising voluntary contributions and planning the reconstruction. The building was completed in 1997, the interior was decorated in 1999, and the cathedral was officially consecrated in 2000.

• What does this reveal about the connection of government, Church, and nation?
• What does it say about Russian architecture?

Source: Getty Images, Inc.-Photodisc.

Figure 22-4 The St. Petersburg Mosque

The St. Petersburg Mosque was built in 1913 to commemorate the tricentennial of the Romanov dynasty. In the Soviet period, the building was allowed to deteriorate, but during the 1990s, it was restored to prepare it for the celebration of the three-hundredth anniversary of the founding of St. Petersburg in 2003.

• Compare the messages sent by this and by the Cathedral of Christ the Savior.
• Taken together what themes and trends in Russian society do these buildings reflect?

Source: AGE Fotostock America, Inc.

Figure 22-5 Miss Russia/Miss Universe
   Miss Russia, Oksana Fedorova, was named Miss Universe in 2002 at the 51st Annual Miss Universe in Puerto Rico.
- Compare this with Soviet images of women.
- What does this reveal about trends in Russian society?
Source: Getty Images North America.

Figure 22-6 The Newly Independent States and the Autonomous Regions of the Russian Federation

- How does this map help to explain Russia's concern for influence in the "near abroad?"
- On what principles do the autonomous regions of Russia generally seem to be based?
- What does this suggest about the nature of the Russian state and future problems it may face? Why does Chechnya stand a better chance of national independence than Tatarstan or Bashkortostan?
- Compare this map with the map from Chapter 20 (Eurasian oil fields). How does this explain Russia's reluctance to allow Chechen independence? Western interest in good relations with the nations of Central Asia?

_____ FOR FURTHER READING _____

(In addition to the books by Clements and Suny from the previous chapter.)

Christensen, Paul T. *Russia's Workers in Transition: Labor, Management, and the State under Gorbachev and Yeltsin.* DeKalb, IL: Northern Illinois University Press, 1999.

Goscilo, Helena. *Dehexing Sex: Russian Womanhood During and after Glasnost.* Ann Arbor : University of Michigan Press, 1996.

Herspring, Dale R., Ed. *Putin's Russia: Past Imperfect, Future Uncertain.* Lanham, MD: Rowman & Littlefield, 2003.

Kay, Rebecca. *Russian Women and Their Organizations: Gender, Discrimination, and Grassroots Women's Organizations, 1991–1996*. New York: St. Martin's Press, 2000.

Mickiewicz, Ellen. *Changing Channels: Television and the Struggle for Power in Russia*. Durham, NC: Duke University Press, 1999.

Neidhart, Christoph. *Russia's Carnival: The Smells, Sights, and Sounds of Transition*. Lanham, MD: Rowman and Littlefield, 2003.

Nichols, Thomas M. *The Russian Presidency: Society and Politics in the Second Russian Republic*. New York: St. Martin's Press, 1999.

Reddaway, Peter and Dmitri Glinski. *The Tragedy of Russia's Reforms: Market Bolshevism Against Democracy*. Washington, D.C.: United States Institute of Peace Press, 2001.

Urban, Michael. Urban with Vyacheslav Irgunov and Sergei Mitrokhin. *The Rebirth of Politics in Russia*. Cambridge: Cambridge University Press, 1997.

Wegren, Stephen. *The Land Question in Ukraine and Russia*. Seattle: Henry M. Jackson School of International Studies, University of Washington, 2002.

White, Stephen. *Russia's New Politics: The Management of a Postcommunist Society*. Cambridge: Cambridge University Press, 2000.

APPENDIX A

TIMELINE

Russia/ Soviet Union	Eastern Europe	Western Europe/ USA	Central Asia	Middle East	East Asia
1855 death of Nicholas I; accession of Alexander II.	1863 Polish uprising is suppressed by the Russian army.	1837–1901 Victoria, Queen of England. 1852–1870 Napoleon III, Emperor of France.	1860s Jadidist reform movement founded. 1865–1868 Russia conquers Tashkent,	1839–1876 Tanzimat: Reform in the Ottoman Empire.	1850–1864 Taiping Rebellion in China. 1858 Treaty of Aigun with Russia.
1861 Emancipation of the serfs. 1863 Reform of local government.		1858–1870 Unification of Italy. 1862–1871 Unification of Germany.	Bukhara, and Samarkand.	1848–1896 Nasir al Din Shah of Iran.	1860 Second Opium War. 1862–1874 Tong Zhi Restoration in China.
1864 Judicial reforms.		1867 Russia sells Alaska to the U.S.			1868 Meiji Restoration in Japan.
1873–1874 Movement to the People.		1870–1914 Scramble for Africa; peak of European imperialism.		1876–1909 Reign of Sultan Abdülhamid II of Turkey.	1876 Japan forces Korea to open two ports to Japanese trade.
1875–1877 Russo-Turkish War. 1879 *Zemlia i Volia* splits into *Chernyi Peredel* and *Narodnaia Volia*. 1881 Leaders of *Naraodnaia Volia* assassinate Alexander II.	1878 Treaty of San Stefano. Turkey loses most of its control over the Balkans.				

Russia/ Soviet Union	Eastern Europe	Western Europe/ USA	Central Asia	Middle East	East Asia
1881–1894 Alexander III.

1894 Russia and France sign a mutual aid treaty.

1894–1917 Nicholas II. | | 1888–1918 Wilhelm II, Emperor of Germany. | 1880–1901 Abdul Rahman Khan, King of Afghanistan.

1881 Turkmen are conquered by Russia and incorporated into the empire. | 1889 Committee of Progress and Union (Young Turks) forms.

1890 Anti-western boycott of tobacco forces Shah of Iran to rescind British tobacco monopoly.

1896 Shah Nasir al Din of Iran assassinated by a nationalist cleric. | 1895 Sino-Japanese War.

1896 Sun Yat-sen forms a revolutionary organization to overthrow the Qing dynasty.

1897 Russia secures economic rights in Manchuria.

1900 Boxer Rebellion. |
| 1903 Second Congress of the RSDRP meets in Brussels and London. Bolshevik and Menshevik factions are formed. | | | 1890s Surge of immigration of Russian and Ukrainian peasants to Kazakhstan. | 1905–1907 Nationalist, republican unrest in Iran. Britain and Russia intervene. | |
| 1905 Revolution; Nicholas II grants a constitution and a consultative assembly.

1906 Peter Stolypin is appointed Prime Minister. | | 1908 Austria annexes Bosnia-Herzegovina. | | 1908 Turkish Revolution puts Young Turks in power. | 1904–1905 Japan fights Russia to a standstill in Russo-Japanese War.

1910 Japan annexes Korea. |
| 1911 Stolypin is assassinated.

1914 Russia enters World War II, loses initial battles with Germany.

1915 Nicholas II goes to front to rally the troops; Petrograd left in the hands of Grigorii Rasputin.

February 1917 Russian Revolution begins. | 1908 Austria annexes Bosnia-Herzegovina.

1912, 1913 First and Second Balkan Wars. | 1914–1918 World War I.

1919 Versailles Treaty. | 1916 Kazaks, Kyrgyz, Turkmen, and Uzbeks rebel against conscription and loss of land to immigrants.

1918 Bolsheviks create the Turkestan Autonomous Soviet Socialist Republic, including most of former Russian Central Asia. | 1914 Ottoman Empire enters World War I on the side of Germany and Austria-Hungary.

1914 Britain and Russia invade and occupy Iran.

1919 France and England occupy the Middle East.

1920 Britain and Russia withdraw from Iran. | 1911 Nationalists overthrow the Qing Dynasty. Yuan Shikai becomes first president of China.

1916 Yuan Shikai attempts to make himself emperor; China falls apart. Period of warlord rule begins.

1916 Japan enters World War I on the side of the Allies. |

Russia/Soviet Union	Eastern Europe	Western Europe/USA	Central Asia	Middle East	East Asia
					1919 May Fourth Movement in China.
March 2 (Julian Calendar) Tsar Nicholas II abdicates.					
March 1917 Provisional Government and Petrograd Soviet form.					
October 25, 1917 (Julian calendar) Bolsheviks seize power.					
March 1918 Brest-Litovsk Treaty.					
1921 Kronstadt revolt.	1919 Admiral Miklos Horthy overthrows the Communist government of Bela Kun in Hungary.	1922 Benito Mussolini takes power in Italy.	1919–1929 Amanullah, King of Afghanistan.	1921 Turkey declares its sovereignty. Party (CCP) form.	1921 Chinese Nationalist Party (GMD) and Chinese Communist
1921–1927. Era of the New Economic Policy (NEP).		1923 Catastrophic inflation in Germany.	1924 Turkmenistan and Uzbekistan are made Soviet Socialist Republics (SSRs).	1923 Mustafa Kemal is elected President of Turkey.	1925 Sun Yat-sen dies, Jiang Kai-shek assumes leadership of the GMD.
1924 Lenin dies.		1924 U.S. Dawes plan stabilizes the German economy.	1925 Kazakh and Kirgiz are made Autonomous SSRs.	1925 Reza Khan, Commander in Chief, deposes the Shah of Iran and names himself Reza Shah Pahlavi.	1925 Major earthquake in Tokyo.
1926 Stalin and Bukharin win power struggle with Trotsky, Zinoviev, and Kamenev.		1925 Locarno treaties normalize Germany's relations with other European powers.	1929 Tajikistan is made an SSR.		1927 Shanghai Massacre.
1928 Stalin breaks with Bukharin, begins collectivization and first five-year plan.		1929 Great Depression begins in the U.S.A., spreads to the world.			1928 Jiang and the GMD unify China.
1929 Bukharin is removed from Politburo.					
1932–1937 Second Five-Year Plan.		1935 Germany begins rearmament.	1929–1933 Muhammad Nadir Shah, king of Afghanistan.	1932 Britain prevents Reza Shah from nationalizing Iran's oil.	1931 Japan invades and occupies Manchuria.
1932–1934 Millions die in a famine in Ukraine and southern Soviet Union.		1936 Hitler remilitarizes the Rhineland.	1933–1973 Mohammad Zahir Shah, king of Afghanistan.	1938 Kemal Attaturk dies.	1934 GMD military campaigns force Communists to begin "the Long March."
		1936–1939 Spanish Civil War.			

Russia/ Soviet Union	Eastern Europe	Western Europe/ USA	Central Asia	Middle East	East Asia
1935–1938 "Great Purges." August 1939 German-Soviet pact. 1939 Soviet Union invades Poland and the Baltic States.	1938 Sudetenland crisis; appeasement at Munich. September 1939 Germany invades Poland; World War II in Europe begins.				1936 Japan abrogates the arms-reduction treaties of the 1920s and joins Italy and Germany in the peace "Anti-Comintern Pact." 1937 Japan mounts a full-scale invasion of China.
June 22, 1941 Germany invades the U.S.S.R. December 1942– January 1943 Battle of Stalingrad. 1943 Battle of Kursk.	Spring 1941 Germany invades Balkan Peninsula.	1940 Germany invades Norway and France; Battle of Britain. June 1944 Normandy Invasion. 1944 Bretton Woods conference convenes to plan the future world economy.		June 1941 Turkey signs non-aggression pact with Germany. 1941 British and Soviet forces invade Iran and force Reza Shah to abdicate in favor of his son, Mohammed Reza Pahlavi.	December 7, 1941 Japan attacks U.S. navy and air force base at Pearl Harbor, Hawaii. August 8, 1945 The U.S.S.R. declares war on Japan. 1942 Battle of Midway. August 6, 1945 U.S. drops nuclear bombs on Hiroshima, Nagasaki, Japan.
May 8, 1945 Germany surrenders to the Red Army. 1949 U.S.S.R. tests its first nuclear bomb.	1946–1948 Countries of Eastern Europe are Sovietized.	1947 Marshall Plan to rebuild Europe is begun. 1949 NATO and the Federal Republic of Germany are created.		February 1945 Turkey joins allies, declares war on Germany. 1948 State of Israel is declared.	September 2, 1945 Japan surrenders. 1945–1949 Civil War in China between GMD and CCP. October 1, 1949 People's Republic of China declares its existence.
1953 Stalin dies; Beria is arrested and executed by other Soviet leaders. 1953 Khrushchev becomes General Secretary of the Communist Party.	1956 Wladislaw Gomulka becomes head of Polish Communist Party. 1956 Popular uprising against Communism in Hungary is suppressed by the Red Army.	1955 West Germany joins NATO. 1957 European Economic Community is formed.		1951 Turkey joins NATO. 1956 Suez crisis. 1960 The U.S. installs nuclear missiles, aimed at the Soviet Union, in Turkey.	1950 Japanese automaker Toyota produces 1200 automobiles. 1950–1953 Korean War. 1958 Great Leap Forward in China.

Russia/ Soviet Union	Eastern Europe	Western Europe/ USA	Central Asia	Middle East	East Asia
1954, Ilia Erenburg's novel *The Thaw* is published.					
1956 Warsaw Pact is formed. 1956 Khrushchev delivers "Secret Speech" at the Twentieth Party Congress.					
1957 The Soviet Union launches "Sputnik," the first satellite.					
1961 Cuban Missile Crisis.					
1961 Aleksandr Solzhenitsyn's *One Day in the Life of Ivan Denisovich* is published.					
1964 Khrushchev is forced into retirement. Leonid Brezhnev becomes General Secretary of the Party.			1963 Muhammad Zahir Shah, King of Afghanistan, establishes a constitutional monarchy with an elective parliament.		1964–1968 Cultural Revolution in China.
1966 Trial of Daniel and Siniavskii.	1968 Led by the Soviet Union, Warsaw Pact troops invade Czechoslovakia.	1968 Paris uprising.		1967 Six-day war.	
1972 The first Strategic Arms Limitation Treaty (SALT I) is signed by the U.S.S.R. and the U.S.		1973 Great Britain, Ireland, and Denmark join the Common Market.	1973 Muhammad Daoud Khan, a former Prime Minister, forces the King to abdicate and declares Afghanistan a republic.	1973 Yom Kippur War. 1973 The Organization of Petroleum Exporting Countries (OPEC) imposes a temporary oil embargo. "Oil shock" felt around the world.	1971 China and U.S. exchange ambassadors. 1976 Zhou Enlai and Mao Zedong die.
1974 Aleksandr Solzhenitsyn is deported from the Soviet Union.		1979 Margaret Thatcher becomes Prime Minister of Great Britain.	1978 Leftist coup in Afghanistan. Mujahedin begin war of resistance. 1979 Soviet Union invades Afghanistan to support the leftist, secular government.	1978 Shah of Iran flees massive popular uprising.	1978 Deng Xiaoping begins the "Four Modernizations."

Russia/ Soviet Union	Eastern Europe	Western Europe/ USA	Central Asia	Middle East	East Asia
				1979 Ayatollah Ruhollah Khomeini is elected President of Iran.	
1982–1984 Iurii Adropov is General Secretary of the Communist Party.	1981 Polish trade union "Solidarity" organizes a series of strikes. 1982 Helmut Kohl becomes Prime Minister of West Germany.			1980–1988 Iran-Iraq War.	1980 Japan becomes the world's largest exporter of steel.
1984–1985 Konstantin Chernenko is General Secretary of the Communist Party.					
1985–1991 Mikhail Gorbachev is General Secretary of the Communist Party.					
1986 Gorbachev declares the need for the Soviet Union to "radically transform all spheres of life."			Beginning in 1986 Central Asian nationalism becomes increasingly evident.		1986 Nine percent of all cars bought in the world are made by Toyota.
1988 Russian Orthodox Church celebrates the 1000th anniversary of the conversion of the Rus.	1989 "Velvet Revolution" in East Europe; popular demonstrations cause Communist Parties to give up power.	1989 Berlin Wall is torn down.	1989 Gorbachev pulls Soviet troops out of Afghanistan.		1989 Tiananmen Square massacre.
1990 Supreme Soviet removes Article Six from the Constitution.	1990 Lech Walesa is elected president of Poland.	1990 East and West Germany reunify.	1990 Turkmenistan is the first Central Asian nation to declare its sovereignty	1990 Iraq invades and occupies Kuwait.	
Summer 1991 Boris Yeltsin elected President of Russia.					

Russia/ Soviet Union	Eastern Europe	Western Europe/ USA	Central Asia	Middle East	East Asia
				1991 U.S.-led UN forces drive Iraqi forces from Kuwait.	
August 19–21, 1991 Attempted coup by CP hardliners.					
December 8, 1991 Presidents of Ukraine, Russia, and Belarus declare USSR at an end and create Common-wealth of Inde-pendent States.					
December 26, 1991 The Soviet Congress of People's Depu-ties votes itself out of existence.					
Jan 1, 1992 Yeltsin begins "shock treat-ment" of Russia's economy.		1992 Maastricht Treaty transforms European Economic Community into the European Union (EU).	January 1, 1992. With the end of the Soviet Union, the nations of Central Asia (like all Soviet republics) become independent.		Mid-1990s Japanese economy goes into recession.
1993 Yeltsin disbands the Congress of People's Deputies.	1999 Poland, Hungary, and the Czech Republic join NATO.		April 1992 Kabul falls to the mujahedin rebels.		
1999 Yeltsin announces his resignation and appoints Vlad-imir Putin "Acting President."	2004 Bulgaria, Estonia, Latvia, Lithuania, Romania, and Slovakia join NATO.		2001 The Taliban Party controls more than 90 percent of Afghanistan.

2001 U.S.-led NATO forces invade Afghanistan and re-move the Taliban from power. | | Early 2000s the Chi-nese economy booms. |
| 2000 Putin is elected Presid-dent of Russia. | 2004 Poland, the Czech Republic, Hungary, and Slovakia officially join the EU. | | | 2003 U.S.-led coalition invade Iraq and remove Sadam Hussein and the Ba'ath Party from power. | |

Appendix B

Guide to Transliteration and Pronunciation of the Russian Alphabet

As explained in the Preface, all Russian names appear in the form given in the 26th edition of the *Library of Congress Subject Headings* (2003), and all geographical terms are spelled as they appear in primary entry of *The Columbia Gazetteer of the World* (1998). All other names and terms will be transliterated from Russian according to the following modification of the Library of Congress transliteration system.

Russian Alphabet	Library of Congress	Used in Exploring Russia's Past	Pronunciation
Аа	Aa	Aa	father
Бб	Bb	Bb	ball
Вв	Vv	Vv	very
Гг	Gg	Gg	good
Дд	Dd	Dd	dog
Ее	Ee	Ee	yet
Ёё	Ëë	Ee	yolk
Жж	Zh zh	Zh zh	azure
Зз	Zz	Zz	zone
Ии	Ii	Ii	even
й	i	i	even
Кк	Kk	Kk	kitten
Лл	Ll	Ll	long
Мм	Mm	Mm	man

Нн	Nn	Nn	<u>n</u>o
Оо	Oo	Oo	b<u>oa</u>rd
Пп	Pp	Pp	<u>p</u>in
Рр	Rr	Rr	trilled "r" as in Spanish
Сс	Ss	Ss	<u>s</u>ing
Тт	Tt	Tt	<u>t</u>op
Уу	Uu	Uu	f<u>oo</u>l
Фф	Ff	Ff	f<u>oo</u>l
Хх	Kh kh	Kh kh	as in German "bu<u>ch</u>"
Цц	TS ts	Ts ts	hi<u>ts</u>
Чч	Ch ch	Ch ch	<u>ch</u>eese
Шш	Sh sh	Sh sh	<u>sh</u>ot
Щщ	Shch shch	Shch shch	fre<u>sh ch</u>eese
ъ	"	(omitted)	no sound
ь	'	(omitted)	no sound
Ээ	Ée	Ee	g<u>e</u>t
Юю	I͡U i͡u	Iu iu	<u>you</u>
Яя	I͡A i͡a	Ia ia	<u>y</u>ard

APPENDIX C

THE ROMANOVS

Only individuals who ruled (or who were parents of later rulers) are presented here. The dates refer to their reigns.

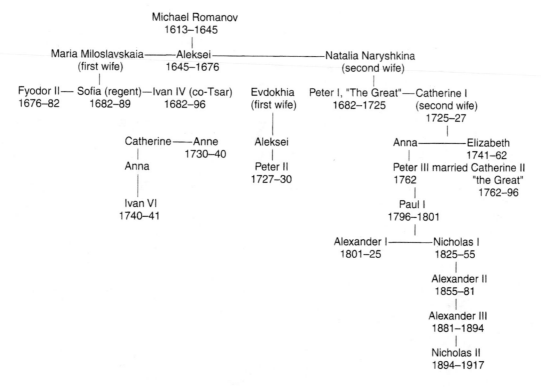

Michael Romanov
1613–1645

Maria Miloslavskaia———Aleksei———————————————Natalia Naryshkina
(first wife)   1645–1676   (second wife)

Fyodor II— Sofia (regent)—Ivan IV (co-Tsar)   Evdokhia   Peter I, "The Great"—Catherine I
1676–82   1682–89   1682–96   (first wife) 1682–1725   (second wife)
                                                                                 1725–27

           Catherine——Anne   Aleksei   Anna————————Elizabeth
                       1730–40   1741–62
           Anna   Peter II   Peter III married Catherine II
                                         1727–30   1762   "the Great"
                                                                          1762–96
           Ivan VI   Paul I
           1740–41   1796–1801

                                        Alexander I————Nicholas I
                                        1801–25   1825–55

                                                        Alexander II
                                                        1855–81

                                                        Alexander III
                                                        1881–1894

                                                        Nicholas II
                                                        1894–1917

GLOSSARY

Article Six of the Soviet Constitution   The constitutional justification of Communist one-party rule. It stated that the Communist Party was "the leading and guiding force of Soviet society." It was repealed by the Supreme Soviet in 1990 as a part Mikhail Gorbachev's democratization program.

Black clergy/white clergy   In the Russian Orthodox Church, parish priests, known as the "white clergy" must be married; they are not eligible for appointment to positions in the Church hierarchy. Monks, bishops, archbishops, and other church officials, known as the "black clergy" are celibate.

Black Hundreds/Union of the Russian People   Union of the Russian People, popularly known as the Black Hundreds, predominantly of lower-middle-class origin, was Russia's most xenophobic and nationalistc political party. Aided and abetted by the police, they attacked socialist demonstrations and carried out pogroms against Jews. Nicholas II accepted honorary membership in the Union of the Russian People for himself and his son.

Black Repartition   (See **Chernyi Peredel**.)

Bolsheviks   The faction of the Russian Social-Democratic Labor Party led by V. I. Lenin. It formed in 1903 and was distinguished by its activism (to be a member one had to be an active revolutionary, not merely a sympathizer) and its impatience for socialism (Bolsheviks believed that the "bourgeois-democratic" revolution could be transformed into socialist revolution without an intervening capitalist period). In 1918, the Bolshevik faction declared itself the only legitimate Marxist party and took the name "Communist party."

Chernyi Peredel   (Чёрный передел) When the Populist organization **Zemlia i Volia** split in 1879, those who chose to continue the Populist tradition of working among the people to stimulate popular revolution took the name *Chernyi Peredel*, "black repartition," for their revolutionary party. (Compare with **Narodnaia Volia**.)

Commune/mir (мир) The *mir*, also known as the commune, refers to the self-governing peasant village. Although the mir was typically stratified by wealth, the peasant community consistently presented a united front against the outside world of government officials and merchants. One of the remarkable features of the Russian mir was its practice of periodically redistributing land based on the number of able-bodied workers in each household.

Duma (дума) The name given to the Russian Parliament which was established as a result of the 1905 Revolution. There were four Duma elections between 1906 and 1917 when the Tsarist regime came to an end. "Duma" was also chosen as the name for the lower house of the legislature of the Russian Federation in the Constitution of 1993. (See **State Duma**.)

Federation Council The upper house of the legislature of the Russian Federation established by the 1993 Constitution. It has 178 members, 2 from each of the 89 regions of the Russian Federation. It confirms presidential nominations of chief judges, draws territorial boundaries, confirms the dispatch of troops abroad, and can veto laws passed by the Duma. (See **State Duma**.)

Glasnost (гласность) Glasnost, "openness," was one of the principal features of Mikhail Gorbachev's reform campaign. It meant that the government would begin to operate more transparently and that the media were free to report the news without government interference.

Gymnasium (plural, gymnasia), were secondary, college-preparatory schools, which emphasized Greek and Latin, and were the preserve of the nobility. (Compare with **realschule**.)

Indigenization (See **korenizatsiia**.)

Intelligentsia A segment of Russia's educated elite that thought independently and critically of the autocratic regime. The intelligentsia was typified by its idealism and selflessness, and its tendency to adopt the most progressive and radical trends in western Europe. The intelligentsia provided the members of Russia's revolutionary parties, from **Zemlia i Volia** to the Bolsheviks, but it also included educated people, especially writers and journalists, and professionals not employed by the government.

Kadets/Constitutional Democrats The Kadet party was formed during the 1905 Revolution by liberals and professionals. It was classically liberal, being committed to civil liberties, free enterprise, and an elected, sovereign parliament. It was the major opposition party in the Duma, continually demanding the right to initiate legislation and to hold the Tsar's ministers accountable.

Kolkhoz/Sovkhoz (колхоз/совхоз) The two most common forms of agricultural enterprise in the Soviet Union were the kolkhoz (collective farm) and sovkhoz (state farm). The *kolkhoz* was a cooperative organization in which the farmers collectively owned the land and implements and divided farm income among themselves. The *sovkhoz* was owned and operated by the state; sovkhoz farm workers were paid wages and received social benefits (similar to factory workers).

Korenizatsiia (коренизация) Korenizatsiia, indigenization, was a sort of Communist party "affirmative-action" nationality policy in which leadership positions in the party, administration, industry, and schools were filled by members of the titular nationality of each republic or region (i.e., Kazakhs in Kazakhstan, Azerbaijanis in Azerbaijan, etc.). The goal of *korenizatsiia* was to accommodate the nations of the Soviet Union to Soviet Communist rule, so they would see the union not as Russian imperialism but as a native and natural development.

Land Captain (See **zemskii nachalnik**)

Left Socialist-Revolutionaries (S-Rs) During the First World War, the Socialist-Revolutionary Party broke into Left and Right factions. The Rightists believed in defending their country against Germany and Austria; the Leftists hoped for defeat in the war because it would bring revolution. When the Bolsheviks took power in November 1917, the Left S-Rs supported them. (See **Socialist-Revolutionaries.**)

Mensheviks The faction of the Russian Social-Democratic Labor Party led by I. Martov and G. Plekhanov. It emerged out of the split in the party at the Second Party Congress in 1903. Mensheviks were not as disciplined as Bolsheviks, and they expected that the "bourgeois-democratic" stage of Russian history might last a significant time. After the Bolsheviks seized power, the Menshevik faction was suppressed. (Compare with **Bolsheviks.**)

Mir See **Commune/mir.**

Movement to the People Under the influence of the ideas of Populism (see **Narodnichestvo**), hundreds and perhaps thousands of young people spontaneously decided to travel to the countryside in the summers of 1873 and 1874 to inspire the peasantry to overturn the Tsarist system. The movement produced no results. The peasants were distrustful of the intelligentsia, whom they perceived as intrusive outsiders. In some cases peasants took advantage of the educational efforts of the populists, but they were not attracted to the populists' idea of socialism. Furthermore, mass arrests in the summers of 1873 and 1874 effectively brought the "Movement to the People" to an end.

Narodnichestvo (народничество) Narodnichestvo, or Russian Populism, refers to a movement among the Russian intelligentsia in the 1870s inspired by the idea that they should go out among the people and catalyze a mass movement against the tsarist regime. It was not an organized or unified movement. Some young people went among the people to teach literacy and primary education, some went to teach socialism, and some went to incite immediate insurrection. (See **Movement to the People** and **Zemlia i Volia.**)

Narodnaia Volia (Народная Воля) When the Populist organization Zemlia i Volia split in 1879, those who broke with the Populist tradition of work among the people and instead chose to use assassination to punish the government and frighten it into reform took the name of Narodnaia Volia, or "the People's Will." The executive committee of Narodnaia Volia began to plan the assassination of Alexander II, which they achieved in 1881. (Compare with **Chernyi Peredel.**)

New Economic Policy (NEP) In 1921, following the Civil War, the Soviet economy was in a shambles, and the Communist Party announced the beginning of a New Economic Policy. Under the NEP, the government would control the "commanding heights," including banking, foreign trade, heavy industry and mines, but the rest of the economy would be returned to private ownership and the market system. Ideological restraints were also relaxed; artists and writers were allowed creative freedom as long as they did not directly challenge the legitimacy of the Soviet regime.

Nomenklatura (номенклатура) Refers to the governing and managing elite of the Soviet Union. It involved a ranked list of Communist party members, government officials, and industrial managers that indicated who was next in line for promotion when positions became vacant.

Octobrists A moderate party that participated in the four Dumas between 1906 and 1917. Named after the "October Manifesto" in which the Tsar proposed a constitution and an elected parliament, Octobrists were committed to a constitutional monarchy for Russia.

Old Ritualists/Old Believers refers to that segment of the Russian Church that refused to accept the reforms of the Patriarch Nikon in the 1650s. Despite aggressive persecution and discrimination, Old Ritualist communities have survived in Russia until the present day.

The Church Sobor of 1971 invited the Old Believers back into the Church; it rescinded all the anathemas of the 17th century and recognized the validity of the old rites. It did not end the schism, however, since the Old Believers have not yet accepted the invitation.

Panslavs Adapted many of the ideas of the Slavophiles to the materialism and Realpolitik of the second half of the nineteenth century. They used the notion of Slavic racial unity to justify their demand that Russia should liberate the Southern Slavs from Ottoman rule. (See **Slavophiles.**) "

People's Will." (See **Narodnaia Volia.**)

Perestroika (перестройка) "restructuring," The term that came to stand for the reforms of the Gorbachev era. In 1986, Gorbachev used the word *perestroika* when he declared the need for the USSR to "radically transform all spheres of life."

Raznochintsy (разночинцы) Raznochintsy, people of various ranks, referred to people who didn't fit into the officially recognized categories of Russian society. In the reign of Peter I, it referred mostly to retired soldiers and lower-ranking officials who had not advanced far enough in the **Table of Ranks** to have earned noble status. After 1818, raznochintsy also referred to the children of those who had achieved personal noble status. By the middle of the century, it was used to refer to anyone who had gained an education and earned a living through mental labor but was not of noble blood.

Realschules High schools on the German model, which taught modern science, math, and technical subjects, and which were favored by the more practical non-noble classes. (Compare with **gymnasium**).

Russian Social-Democratic Labor Party (RSDRP) The Russian Marxist revolutionary organization. Local Marxist groups attempted to hold a national organizing conference in 1898, but it was broken up by the police. In 1903, a Second Congress of the RSDRP was held in Brussels and London; it adopted both a minimum program (a parliament, democratic elections, an eight-hour workday, and the transfer of all land to the peasantry) and a maximum program (socialist revolution and the dictatorship of the proletariat). Two factions emerged at the Congress, **Mensheviks** led by Iulii Martov, and the more militant and disciplined **Bolsheviks** led by Vladimir Ilich Lenin.

Russian Populism (See "**Narodnichestvo.**")

Samizdat (самиздат), "self-publication," refers to a method by which Soviet citizens circulated writings that the government would not allow to be published. Such forbidden literature was typed in multiple copies (using carbon paper) and given to people who would type more copies for further dissemination.

Serfs A serf was a peasant, bound to the land, and living under the jurisdiction of a gentry landowner. Although limitation of peasant movement had begun in the fifteenth century, the binding of peasants to the land was codified in 1649. Serfdom was ended by the Emancipation of 1861. Although serfs were not considered slaves (the property of landowners), there were no limits on the labor demands that the landowner could exact, and serfs lived under the landlord's legal jurisdiction.

Skhod (сход) The skhod, or village assembly, was composed of all heads of households in the peasant community. The skhod elected village elders and officials and appointed constables and clerks. It judged family and interfamily disputes, and punished immoral behavior and minor violations of the law. It also apportioned taxes, chose conscripts, supervised periodic redistribution of the land, and provided for social welfare.

Slavophiles Russian intellectuals in the first half of the nineteenth century who, under the influence of the European Romantic movement, attempted to discover true soul of the Russian nation. They found this in the Russian Orthodox Church and the culture of pre-Petrine Muscovy. Slavophiles opposed the secularism, individualism, and materialism of the West (and of Peter the Great), and celebrated the *sobornost* or "organic community" of Muscovite Russia where people had been united by faith and love, valued things of the spirit, and cooperated rather than competed with one another. (Compare with **Westernizers.**)

Sobor (собор) In the Russian Orthodox Church, a Sobor, an elected assembly representing the church hierarchy as well as local parishes, is the highest church authority. It elects the Patriarch, when the office becomes open, and it speaks with final authority on questions of faith.

Socialist-Revolutionary Party (SRs) Revolutionary Populism was reborn in 1900 when representatives of a number of populist groups announced the creation of the Socialist Revolutionary (SR) Party with the goal of mobilizing the peasantry to overthrow the old regime and to build socialism on the basis of the peasant commune. As in the past, the Socialist-Revolutionary Party contained two trends: one which wanted to foster a revolution by working among the people, another which wanted to bring down the government by assassinating public officials.

Soviet Intelligentsia Refers to the educated segment of the Soviet population that worked in intellectual professions including artists, journalists, academics, etc. It was similar to the Russian Intelligentsia of the nineteenth century because it embraced liberal values of intellectual freedom, skepticism, and cosmopolitanism, but it differed from the intelligentsia of the tsarist period because it was employed by the state and its economic well-being depended on conformity. Members of the Soviet Intelligentsia were not revolutionary, and their most subversive activity was to read and reproduce forbidden literature. (See **samizdat.**)

Sovkhoz (See **Kolkhoz/Sovkhoz.**)

State Duma The 1993 Constitution of the Russian Federation created a two-house legislature made up the Federation Council and the State Duma. The State Duma has 450 members, half elected from local constituencies, half elected from a national slate with proportional representation. The Duma confirms presidential nominations of prime minister, and can vote no confidence in the cabinet. It writes laws and can veto presidential decrees. The Duma can override a veto by the Federation Council and both houses can override a Presidential veto by a two-thirds majority. (See **Federation Council.**)

State Peasant After Russian peasants were bound to the land in 1649, those peasants who lived on land that was not owned by private landowners or the royal family were known as state peasants. Like serfs, they were bound to the land and could not move without permission, but unlike serfs, state peasants were self-governing and owed no obligations to private landlords. (Compare with **serf.**)

Stategic Arms Limitation Treaties (SALT) In the 1970s, the United States followed a policy of detente with the Soviet Union, which was aimed at accommodating and cooperating with the Soviet leadership. Detente was manifested in two Strategic Arms Limitation Treaties. SALT I was signed in 1972, SALT II in 1979.

Strategic Arms Reduction Treaty (START) Begun by Ronald Reagan and Mikhail Gorbachev and concluded in July 1991, in the administration of U.S. President George H. W. Bush. Under the agreement, the two countries reduced their nuclear stockpiles, missiles, heavy bombers, and mobile missile launchers.

Table of Ranks In 1722, in imitation of a recently enacted Prussian standardization of ranks, Peter issued a "Table of Ranks" to clarify the order of precedence among the wealthy elite. The Table of Ranks created three parallel hierarchies: civil administration, army, and navy. (For example, the highest level included, respectively, chancellor, general-field marshal, and general-admiral, while level fourteen, the entry level, included collegiate registrar, ensign, and midshipman.) At each level, the military ranks had precedence over the civilian.

Third Communist International (Comintern) The Second Communist International (which had coordinated the international Marxist movement in the nineteenth century) had dissolved during the First World War. The Comintern was created in 1919 by the Soviet Communist party, with its headquarters in Moscow, in order to replace the Second Communist International. Leftist Social-Democrats from around the world were invited to send delegates, and they were advised to model themselves on the Bolshevik pattern.

Warsaw Pact A defensive military alliance among the USSR and the communist nations of eastern Europe. In April 1949, the Allies had created the North Atlantic Treaty Organization (NATO), a military pact among the nations of western Europe and the USA intended to resist Soviet aggression. The Soviet Union initiated the Warsaw Pact in 1955 when a re-militarized West Germany joined NATO. The Warsaw Pact was dissolved on April 1, 1991.

Union of the Russian People See **Black Hundreds/Union of the Russian People.**

Westernizers A trend within the nineteenth century intelligentsia who approved of the reforms of Peter the Great and wanted Russia to continue the Enlightenment project of education, institutional reform, and constitutional government. (Compare with **Slavophiles.**).

White clergy See **Black clergy/white clergy.**

Zemlia i Volia (Земля и Воля) As a result of the failure of the Movement to the People in 1873 and 1874, a group of Russian Populists formed a centralized and organized underground political party, Zemlia iVolia, "Land and Freedom," to elude the police and to continue to incite revolution. Zemlia i Volia was no more successful than the Movement to the People had been, and it broke apart in 1879. (See **Chernyi Peredel** and **Narodnaia Volia.**)

Zemskii nachalnik (земский начальник) "Land captain," an office created in the reign of Alexander III to increase the power of the central government over elected zemstvos. Land Captains were appointed by the Minister of the Interior from among the local nobility. They were given the power to suspend local officials or prevent them from assuming office. The land captains also took over the duties of the justice of the peace (formerly elected) and were given the authority to arrest, fine, and imprison without trial.

Zemstsvo (земство) As a part of the Great Reforms of the 1860s, *zemstvos* were created to provide for limited local self-government. They were established at both the county and provincial level and were given the responsibility for general economic development and social welfare. Zemstvo boards maintained roads and bridges, built prisons, hospitals, and schools, and promoted industry, commerce, and agriculture.

Zhdanovshchina (ждановщина) The Zhdanov era, refers to the regimentation of culture after World War II under the direction of Andrei Zhdanov, head of the Leningrad party organization, member of the Central Committee, and close associate of Stalin. Socialist realism was reaffirmed and "art for art's sake" and imitation of foreign trends were forbidden. Zhdanov died in 1948, but his narrow minded, philistine, and xenophobic standards for art lasted for the remainder of the Stalin era.

Zhenotdel (женотдел) The Department for Work among Women was set up within the Communist Party to organize grassroots women's committees across the country to mobilize women in support the communist program. The Zhenotdel published a variety of women's magazines and hundreds of books and pamphlets teaching Soviet patriotism, providing Marxist analysis of current events, and attacking conservatism and religion in the countryside. In 1929, the Communist party shut down the Zhenotdel, deeming its mission accomplished.

INDEX